HUMAN DIMENSIONS CENTRE

INDIVIDUAL PSYCHOLOGY

We dedicate this book
to the memory of
Dr. Rudolf Dreikurs and his Adlerian family:
Sadie (Tee) Dreikurs and Dr. Eva Dreikurs Ferguson.

Individual
PSYCHOLOGY

THEORY
AND
PRACTICE

GUY J.
MANASTER
University of Texas, Austin

RAYMOND J.
CORSINI

Table of Contents

Preface

Although the literature on Adlerian Psychology, also known as Individual Psychology, consists of some estimated 10,000 items, incomprehensibly there are two major missing elements: (*a*) a general introductory text, and (*b*) full-scale presentations of case histories. We have attempted to provide both in this book and believe that we will meet the needs of the constantly increasing number of people who want a comprehensive introduction to what is one of the oldest and yet fastest growing of the personality theories.

Adlerian psychology is unique among the 80 or more personality theories in that it is openly and unabashedly moral in content: It not only contains a simple and comprehensive explanation of all human behavior—normal and abnormal—but it also contains (uniquely among these theories) a philosophy of life, and consequently it has the status of a religion, since it concentrates not only on what is, but on what should be.

Our system is humanistic—democratic, egalitarian—and yet it is based firmly on science, on experience, on logic. It does not employ complex terms or fanciful notions; and it is the essence of common sense. The reader is highly unlikely to discover anything new in Adlerian psychology but will be surprised to find substantiation of his or her everyday ideas of how and why people operate, and what is good and right and what is bad and wrong.

The authors happen to (*a*) have been indoctrinated in other systems of thought and practice prior to becoming Adlerians, and (*b*) received training from Dr. Rudolf Dreikurs, undoubtedly the second most important person, after Alfred Adler, in the history of Adlerian Psychology. We strongly believe that no one should accept a personality theory on faith, as one might take on a religion, but that one should examine and understand other points of view and then make a choice on the basis of full knowledge. Enthusiasm without full understanding is dangerous.

Our decision to co-author this book was based on the very evident fact that there just was not anything in the literature that fulfilled the requirements of a book that would be at the same time a complete exposition of the theory of and the practice of Individual Psychology. Our various students, associates, clients, and colleagues wondered why—and who—would do this. We were ourselves uncertain that we were qualified, and indeed we queried others to do this book, but were frequently told that we were among the most qualified. Accordingly, we began our preparations, starting with a rather complete analysis of what others had written, attempting to summarize not only Adler's original and fundamental writings, but also attempting to cover what others had written to supplement Adler's work. In doing this, we discovered something very interesting: almost nothing has been added in the literature that in any way contradicts anything that Adler said: Everything new appears to be additions to, supplements to, or further explications of basic thoughts of Adler. This is something unheard of, for example, in psychoanalysis, with all the varying and competing ideas that have followed the death of Sigmund Freud.

We attempted to systematically gather all major ideas so that there would be some discussion about everything important, since we wanted a comprehensive text; but then we emphasized various aspects of Adlerian theory and practice in terms of our own limitations and our own values.

The text of this book has been read in part or in its entirety by Adlerians and by several non-Adlerians, the kinds of people for whom this book was originally written. They were helpful in locating errors, inconsistencies, duplications, difficult passages, and so on. They include, and we wish to thank:

Carl J. Anderson
Mark H. Bickhard
Oscar Christensen
James Croake
Eleanor Funk
Diane Gerard
Amanda Harding
Timothy Hartshorne
R. John Huber
Douglas L. Keene
Roy Kern

Richard R. Kopp
Harold Kozuma
R. Mark Mays
Marian Morse
Arthur Nikelly
Walter O'Connell
Harry Olson
Sandra L. Pacheco
Frank C. Richardson
Alan Simpkins

The errors and inconsistencies, difficulties and problems that remain are our fault.

Lastly, we have tried to deal with the issue of nonsexist language by randomizing gender pronouns throughout the book. Our aims were fairness, equality and readability. We hope you will find us successful.

Chapter 1

Introduction

Throughout recorded history, there has been intense concern about the uniqueness of individuals: how personalities are formed, why people's behavior sometimes is so irrational, why individuals are so affected by the environment, why people behave in ways that range from socially valuable to useless, why some people change their life styles and their styles of life so radically, why some people's temperaments fluctuate up and down widely, how to deal best with people, and so on, and so on, and so on.

It is human nature to try to ask unanswerable questions: the answers are known variously as religion, philosophy, or theories. Some answers are codified and have logical relationships, forming *systems*. Thousands of systems refer to humans: religions, philosophies, and psychologies. Some are small and dying out, some are large and growing, some are simple, and some are complex. Be it the Roman Catholic religion or Zen Buddhism, be it spiritualism or existentialism, be it psychoanalysis or Transactional Analysis, intelligent, well-read, well-intentioned, and knowledgeable people hold onto the tenets of their beliefs, disregarding the claims and assertions of other competing views. A Baptist generally is neither interested in nor knowledgeable about Islam; a follower of Sartre is unconcerned with Scholasticism; and it would be hard to interest one who believes in the psychological theories of Arnold Lazarus into believing the theories of Arthur Lerner.

Adlerian Psychology contains the ideas about human nature, ethics, and other related issues of an Austrian-born psychiatrist named Alfred Adler. This system is also known as *Individual Psychology*. In this book, for the most part, we will, to save space, generally refer to this system as IP.

1

PURPOSE OF THIS CHAPTER

This introductory chapter provides a bird's-eye view of Adler's system. We begin with a paragraph found on the inside front cover of every issue of the *Journal of Individual Psychology,* as written by Dr. Heinz L. Ansbacher, its editor from 1957 to 1973.

> The *Journal of Individual Psychology* is devoted to a holistic, phenomenological, teleological, field-theoretical, and socially oriented approach to psychology and related fields. This approach is based on the assumption of the uniqueness, self-consistency, activity, and creativity of the human individual (style of life); an open dynamic system of motivation (striving for a subjectively conceived goal of success); and an innate potentiality for social life (social interest).

In this chapter we shall examine this statement in detail. We recommend that the reader reread this summary. We shall now expand on every important term of this statement in detail.

HOLISM

Is a human like a flower or like an automobile? Are we essentially unitary or are we made up of parts? Are we body/mind or are we body *and* mind? Are we an entity or an assemblage? Do we have a conscious mind and a separate unconscious mind, or do we have a mind with various aspects? Are we still ourselves when asleep or when drunk or when sick, or are we like Dr. Jekyll and Mr. Hyde?

Individual Psychology firmly takes the position that we are indivisible units. Like the flower which came from a single fertilized cell, we are a unity; we are not an assemblage of parts like a machine. Adlerians deny concepts such as those of Sigmund Freud that the human being can be divided into parts such as the ego, the id, and the superego. While such division can be done for heuristic (i.e., research, investigation) purposes, we deny that such thinking can ultimately be productive since the individual is a unity!

Now this may seem to be some abstract philosophical conception of little importance. Nothing could be further from the truth. In explaining human nature one always begins with basic hypotheses. Should the basic hypotheses be incorrect, further assumptions based on these hypotheses will also be incorrect, and a whole system of resulting beliefs will be essentially erroneous. For this reason it is important to begin with patently true assumptions. However, since IP, like all personality theories, is not a proven theory, it is important for the reader to think for him/herself on this as well as on every other issue. What do *you* think: Are humans *integrals* or *disjunctives?* Are you a unity, essentially a single individual, or are you composed of discrete parts in a clever assemblage? Do you have thoughts *and* feelings *and* desires *and* goals *and* memories, are you the sum of these or are they part of *you?*

The word *individual* in Individual Psychology does not mean the opposite of "social" or "group." Individual Psychology is not a psychology of individuals as opposed to groups of people. The term *individuell* in German has the connotation and denotation of a unity, an indivisible whole. It refers to the unique individuality of individuals.

Jan C. Smuts (1961) coined this word *holism* which we are discussing. Smuts said that personality was "fundamentally an organ of self-realization" (p. 290). According to Ansbacher (1961), Smuts himself was a self-realized or self-actualized man as described by Abraham Maslow (1954). Holism also relates to other concepts. One is the notion of Gestalt—the idea that the total is more than the sum of its parts. A simple example would be to take three equal straight lines. Line them up next to each other and you have one configuration; put them so that the end of each touches the end of another and you now have a different configuration. The first set is three parallel lines, but the second is a triangle! Surely the two configurations are not the same. The reflex-arc concept (Dewey, 1896) which introduced the concept of a nonelementaristic view of behavior is still another associated idea. Holism is also related to creativity. If anything happens only because something else caused it, then everything is determined. Then there would be no responsibility. No one would create anything. A poem would be caused, not created, as would any work of art.

Holism presents a challenge to the sciences of physics and chemistry based on Isaac Newton's laws of thermodynamics, specifically the first law, which reads, "Quantities of heat may be converted into mechanical work and conversely." This law represents a fundamental view of the conservation of energy: What goes into something cannot be more or less than what goes out. Smuts (1961) said, "Either the first law of thermodynamics must be given up, or life and mind are nullities" (p. 164). Physics and chemistry and biology are physical sciences. Newton's laws hold for the human body as a machine that uses calories of heat to operate, but this law of conservation does not apply to the mind.

According to Ansbacher (1961, p. 146), Adler appreciated the work of Smuts. Smuts reciprocated his feelings for Adler and stated that Individual Psychology was "in a way closer to common sense and kinder to human nature than was the science of the nineteenth century" (p. 285).

We can contrast some psychological theories in terms of holism: One view is that people are made up of divisible parts, such as Berne's (1961) Parent-Child-Adult, or Freud's (1964) Ego-Id-Superego. The other point of view is that people are unitary organisms. Biologically, the issue is clear enough: We start life when the sperm and egg fuse into a single cell, the zygote. As the zygote begins to expand and divide, subparts or organs begin to develop, and so the final entity, the human body, originates from a single egg. It is not put together piece by piece, as occurs with an airplane, an automobile, or a fountain pen.

PHENOMENOLOGY

Phenomenology essentially means "subjective, personal." It refers to a person's direct experience. That is, if you look at a picture by Paul Klee or Pablo Picasso or Margaret Keene, that picture is that picture—it *is* the reality. But *your* reality is your impression of it—what it means to you. You may find one picture exciting, another dull, another ugly. These are all personal views—and they are true for you. Reality, then is your impression, your view, your perception.

Adolf Hitler was idolized by millions and hated by millions. Every individual who had an opinion of Hitler had a personal, private view. This view for them was reality. If you come into a semidark room and you see a dog on the bed, this is your reality at that moment and you will react to what you see as though it were really a dog. Say that what you saw was a coat: the "real reality" was a coat, the "subjective reality" was a dog. Now if you are afraid of dogs, you will be scared by the coat because to you at that time the coat was a dog!

IP deals with this "subjective reality"—our impressions, views, perceptions, apperceptions, conclusions—and not with physical reality. If you believe you are God, *this is your reality.*

Phenomenology has important human consequences. Consider two children and say that one of them is much brighter than the other—actually has greater brain power. Now let us say that this "bright" child actually does poorly in school compared to the other. This difference in actual accomplishment may be due to phenomenology. The bright child may be discouraged, may have feelings of inferiority, may not like to study, may want to punish his parents by doing poorly, and so on. The reason for the academic differences may be due to the phenomenologies of the two children—one is ambitious, alert, and eager while the other is discouraged, resentful, and unwilling to learn.

This leads to one of the maxims of IP: *Adlerian Psychology is a psychology of use rather than of possession.* It is not what you have that counts, but rather what you do with what you have. Some people with advantages will fail while some people with disadvantages will succeed. Happiness, good grades, good children, and so on—the things that people want to attain—are a function more of phenomenology; that is, the person's view, and not only of "facts" such as high IQ, good environment, or favorable opportunities.

Let us now put in a caveat. Adlerian psychology is not 100 percent phenomenological. We recognize the importance of reality, of limits. A child born without legs has no chance of becoming a high jumper; a child with Down's syndrome will most probably never go to college. We recognize objective reality—conditions outside of and beyond the individual: physical, social, and economic factors set limits. For this reason, Individual Psychology takes an intermediate position relative to the determinism-indeterminism point of view. We neither say "You can become anything you want" (the pure indeterministic position) or "You are completely controlled by outside events" (the pure deterministic position) but, rather, we say, "Within the limits established by your biology and the environment, there is generally a lot you can do."

We Adlerians see this as the only proper logical position one can take: phenomenology (that is to say, the individual's total "mind") directs the person, who in turn is limited by biological/social/environmental conditions.

TELEOLOGY

Teleology means "purposive, moving toward goals." IP sees individuals constantly in the process of striving. We ask about a person when we don't understand him: "What is he after?" By this, we mean: "What is his goal?"

Now this may sound very obvious, but let us examine other points of view. Some systems of psychology, especially those that view the human as object, see the person as the result of the past, controlled by past experiences. They conceive of people as "learned," "trained," "conditioned"—and otherwise not free. The past determines the present. The individual is seen at any moment as the result of his or her past. This deterministic point of view is best found in the behavioristic psychologies.

A second viewpoint is the here-and-now position. This view says that any person at any time makes decisions in terms of how the immediate moment is perceived. So, the past and the future are not that important; the *now* is important.

The third point of view, the one that IP sponsors, is the teleological (from the Greek *telos*—goal), which says that the individual is best understood in terms of where he is going. Adler said, "Ask not whence but whither?"

There is truth to all three positions. In any human situation, the past, the present, and the future are involved. We make decisions based on *what has happened to us in the past, what the situation is now,* and *what we are after.* Say that you are in your room studying for an examination. The phone rings. You answer it and a friend asks if you want to see a movie. Now you have to make a decision. Many factors will enter into the decision: your *past* pleasure at seeing movies, your *present* state of physical comfort, your *future* intention to do well. There is a dynamic interaction among the past, the present, and the future. No one can deny the effects of the past, no one can deny the importance of the moment, and no one can deny the force of the future. But which of these three views of time is the most likely to lead to understanding ourselves and others?

IP states simply that we understand people and their behavior best in terms of their goals. If we know what a person wants, then we can best predict that person's behavior.

FIELD THEORY

This concept is rather difficult to explain. Let us try to make clear what it means to say that IP is a field theory by examining some basic concepts.

Dichotomies-Extension

Aristotle thought in terms of dichotomies. "Man is either an animal or he is not." "Things are either hard or they are soft." "People are either good or they are no good." Galileo, however, thought not in terms of dichotomies but in terms of degrees. "This man is a bit taller than that woman." "He is twice as hungry as he was an hour ago, but is one-half as hungry now as he will be in two hours."

Reductionism

Some people reduce things to their basic components. By dissecting, and otherwise analyzing, they reduce things to their elements. In our prior discussion on holism, the individual was seen as a totality who cannot be broken into parts: doing so prohibits a complete understanding of any person.

Interactionism

The Adlerian is concerned with verbs and not nouns: "In psychology, all nouns should be understood as verbs" (Rom, 1977, p. 27); that is what psychology is all about: wanting, desiring, moving, going, pushing, shoving, and things of that sort. All these terms represent action and imply interaction with the "environment." Some other psychological systems are static and directed to elements such as nouns—for example, the IQ, the Unconscious, Archetypes, and abilities.

IP is a relational psychology in which the individual is seen always in movement in a social field. Though one is a unique individual, he or she is not apart from others. We shy away from terms such as *schizophrenic* since it is a class designation, a category, and does not explain the richness of a striving person in a social field. Adler saw people in movement, directed toward personal goals, and these movements were always in a social field. In a field-theoretical point of view, all elements within the system affect each other Consequently IP represents a dynamic point of view.

SOCIAL ORIENTATION

This aspect is perhaps the most unique of Adler's contributions. Every other personality theory, as a matter of principle sticking to the rigid scientific viewpoint characterized by objective sciences, refuses to concern itself with such issues as goodness and badness. Some systems openly state that they do not contain any view whatever of morality. They are objective.

IP, in contrast, is subjective, taking a strong viewpoint relative to human happiness and success, and says that good comes from social integration and social concern. The central concept, which we shall now only touch on briefly, is *Gemeinschaftsgefühl.*

Adlerian Psychology says it is not enough to know what human nature is —how we develop, how we change, how we relate, what makes us human. All this is fine and good, and is part of science. Equally important is using knowledge for general human good, permitting people to grow and develop and advance and enhance themselves. Knowledge for the sake of knowledge is fine, but the use of knowledge is more important. Therefore, the student of human nature should not only tell the world *things* but should also give *messages,* should give *instructions.* The analogy might be in medicine: of what use is it to discover that smoking cigarettes develops cancer if this information is kept in professional journals and medical books? The information should be broadcast so that people will know enough to stop smoking if they want to avoid the risk of cancer.

The analogy is not perfect, no analogy is. Of all the major personality theories, only the Adlerian forthrightly states that to be happy and successful in life you have to be "good"—in a socially connected way. We have put the word "good" in quotation marks because as shall be discussed in Chapter 5, the concept of *Gemeinschaftsgefühl,* usually translated as "social interest," is quite complicated and has a considerable number of definitions.

The term *social orientation* contains still another concept. The individual is embedded in his/her society and cannot be studied in isolation. We have referred to this aspect already in considering field theory. We gain our standards from others; we do things because of others; our lives are fully related to others.

COMMON SENSE

Up to this point in commenting on the *Journal of Individual Psychology* statement we have finished analyzing the first sentence. Before we go on more, we would like to point out that the reader may have noticed something unusual. All we have written probably sounds familiar. You might even begin to wonder at this point what is new and different about IP. It all sounds so reasonable, so full of common sense. After all, people, you may say, *are* entities; they *are* unique individuals. After all, psychology involves one's unique perceptions and reactions to life. After all, you may think, a good way to understand people is to know what their goals are; and you may say that to point out that we are social creatures and need one another and find happiness by belonging and participating is nothing new. In short, you may dismiss what you have read as being simply common sense.

Adler was once criticized exactly for this: "But what you have said is nothing but common sense!" someone stated after one of his lectures. Adler is reputed to have said, "And, what's wrong with common sense?"

Can we at this point tell you a big secret about psychology? Many people think that psychology should be difficult to understand. If we present them with terms such as *abreaction, archetypal image, awareness context, cathexis, collective unconscious, contrasexual, cryptomnesia,* and so on, they will feel awed and impressed. But if we talk simple language, some people may feel cheated.

Well, we have to admit it. IP is simple in its theory and simple in its language. We can explain all human behavior, be it neurotic behavior, delinquent behavior, or crazy behavior, quite simply. What's more—we can readily prescribe behavior on the part of those who wish to change others. We treat maladjusted people as successfully as those who use more complicated terms. We have commonsense explanations. Let us give an example relating to the concept of the unconscious.

In the Freudian and Jungian conceptualizations, in an aspect of the individual called the *id* are found various horrible drives coming to the individual through the centuries, implanted in the genes of individuals. The child has a desire to kill its parents, or to have sexual relations with mother or father, has a built-in imprinted tendency to aggrandizement, and so on—all of these being biologically inherited. We Adlerians simply toss all these notions out as idle speculation; unproven fantastic theories with not the slightest evidence, *and* contrary to common sense.

As Adlerians we operate in terms of the simplest hypotheses, and reject anything cumbersome or mythological, which just does not seem sensible, especially if we can explain the phenomenon more simply. Certainly some people do have horrible thoughts. But they need not have inherited them. They could have invented them themselves. Sure, people do things without knowing why. Few of us have perfect insight into ourselves, but we need not posit an *un*conscious; we can simply say that memory, self-understanding, and so on, operate on a continuum and we may simply be unaware of some aspects of ourselves. Certainly what are known commonly as "Freudian slips" exist—but we need not posit any fanciful explanation to account for them. In short, it is possible to explain just about everything in psychology and do this simply. In a review of a book on psychodrama, J. L. Moreno complained that the author had made the complex simple. The author rebutted that Dr. Moreno had made the simple complex.

IP is a commonsense psychology, uses simple language, and yet can deal with the most complex problems.

UNIQUENESS

In the explanation of Individual Psychology, this word calls for some comment. We see each person as different from every other person, yet all people are alike! Harry Stack Sullivan said that people are more alike than different, and we would agree—but at the same time each of us is a unique human being. Now let us go into this subject a bit deeper.

Psychology is generally divided into three areas:

Cognition—thoughts, ideas, perceptions.
Affection—emotions, feelings.
Conation—willing, acting, behaving.

Each individual has a different personality. Adlerians call this one's "style of life"—one's unique way of operating. We each think, we feel, and we act differently. The unique combination of these three aspects of human behavior (we use the word behavior in two senses—a problem that plagues psychology: one sense is *observable action,* such as "I am right now typing this material, and so I am behaving"; but the other sense of the word has to do with *implicit behavior*—what goes on in my "mind"—my thoughts and feelings as I type) is what makes each of us a unique person.

Adlerians see the intellect—that is to say, cognition—as number one. *We are what we think.* Both feelings and actions are subservient to thoughts. To understand individuals we presume that in the beginning was the *thought;* after that came *feelings* and *actions.* Now let us attempt to give a general picture of how we come to have our unique styles of life.

As infants, most probably all we have is awareness of strong stimuli; and these stimuli most probably can be divided into three types: (*a*) neutral ones —these simply let us be and live and grow; (*b*) painful ones—these make us cry and scream and thrash about; and (*c*) pleasant ones—these make us gurgle and coo and be happy. So the child at 2:00 P.M. is fast asleep at peace with the world—condition (*a*); then at 2:15 P.M. the child is hungry and has stomach pains and cries—condition (*b*); and then while being fed, at 2:17 P.M., the child is happy—condition (*c*).

As the child goes through life, he wants to avoid condition (*b*)—pain—and he begins to generalize what to do to avoid being hungry, being yelled at, being spanked, being made fun of, and so on. These generalizations become precepts that he is not aware of—in short, they are in his "mind" but he has no awareness. This is what some of our psychoanalytic colleagues might call the *un*conscious. At least we can all agree that this material is not conscious. Nevertheless, each of us as we develop in life begins to assemble a series of conclusions about life—what is right and what is wrong, how to get what one wants, what people are like, what we are like, and so on. This collection of personal concepts is known in Adlerian terminology as "private logic" and represents our deepest views of self and others and life—in short, they represent our philosophy.

Given any situation, we then tend to react in terms of these *engrams,* if we want to think of them as physical impressions on our brain or in terms of these unconscious structures, if we wish to think in psychoanalytic terms. They make up our uniqueness. It is this combination of thoughts that makes up our uniqueness, and it is this combination that psychotherapists of the Adlerian persuasion go after to understand the unique human being and to help modify the person.

SELF-CONSISTENCY

By this time, some items in this introductory chapter will appear like old friends. Self-consistency should now be predictable. Adlerians view the human person as operating always in a consistent manner, operating to achieve certain goals. We do not believe in split selves or in internal conflicts or in anything, no matter how reasonable it may sound or how obvious it may appear, which in effect says that one part of the individual wants to go one way and one part wants to go another. The person, when viewed holistically, always operates in a consistent manner.

But—we can almost hear you shout this—*how about conflicts?* Say one has a real problem, such as duty versus love, or a real decision, such as whether to take another job or stay on the present job? What about this kind of situation?

Explaining this is no problem at all. Some people are consistent in the sense that they never have such problems. When a decision is to be made, they think over everything, and they just make a decision. Other people are consistent in that they never can make a decision and they agonize over everything. In short, the person who readily makes decisions is self-consistent in that respect; and the person who cannot make decisions is self-consistent in that respect.

But, you may persist, how about a person who has a really hard decision to make, and who is not a worrier, and who really does not know what to do?

We will agree that some decisions are difficult to make, such as whether to submit to an operation or not, whether to marry or not, whether to go along with another person's decision or not—but this still in no way indicates any lack of self-consistency.

Here is an example of such a situation. Jim is in love with two girls and he cannot decide whom to marry. One day it is Jill and the next day it is Jasmine. He feels torn, and worries about his decision. "How is it," he asks, "that one day I really love Jill and want to marry her, and the next day I am with Jasmine and now I want to marry her?" Some people might reply, "Hey, you are inconsistent, you can't make up your mind." Not Adlerians—we would say: "You are very consistent; you don't want to marry at all, and you are playing a game, and you probably play this 'on the one hand I want this and on the other hand I want that' type of game all the time."

People are extremely consistent but they may appear inconsistent, and they may be consistent in being inconsistent. The person who is alternately kind and then cruel has developed a pattern of kindness/cruelty; the person who is gentle and then rough has developed a pattern of gentility/roughness; the person who is understanding at times and unreasonable at times has also developed this pattern. These are complicated patterns that people develop. We see it, for example, in alcoholics. Some have a pattern of drinking heavily every day. This type of consistency is evident. Some will be sober for a year and then go on a bender for a week. And they will repeat this pattern consistently.

ACTIVITY

Two most important aspects of Individual Psychology applied to human behavior are (*a*) direction, derived from goal striving, and (*b*) activity. We see the human person as constantly moving toward goals. Consequently, activity —energy expended—is of great theoretical importance.

This concept does not necessarily relate to physical activity in the sense of someone being hyperactive but, rather, refers to rate of directed expended energy. Thus, one person will focus his or her energy to achieve a particular goal while another will scatter it in various directions. Another person will devote to a project only intermediate effort or partial effort.

The importance of activity relates to the major problem of psychotherapy: *encouragement.* Two people may have exactly the same goals, the same amount of energy, everything may appear identical, but one has courage and pursues goals actively, persistently, intelligently, and consistently, while another person will hesitate, fumble, and back away. For this reason, directed activity—going after one's goals in a sensible manner—is a prerequisite of a successful life and in psychotherapy is something that the therapist tries to get the client to achieve.

CREATIVITY

If you have taken courses in psychology or sociology, you may well have been told that human behavior results from two factors: heredity and environment. In some instances, you will be told, heredity is the more important component and in some instances environment is more important, but the two interact in practically everything—and they determine behavior. There just is nothing else! Anything else would be transpersonal—that is to say, mystical and speculative.

Adlerians do not agree. We see both heredity and environment as important, providing possibilities and limits. We posit something else: *creativity.*

We say, yes, we all do have hereditary limits and we do have environmental limits, but what the individual becomes within these limits is a function of the individual's self—*creativity.* In other words, we are self-made to some extent and we have to take credit for our personalities. Life is not simply determined by heredity and environment: the individual has choice, has freedom of will. We are not simply pawns in a complicated calculus of factors beyond ourselves. We are thinking units who, although caught in the web of influences of biology and society, nevertheless can extricate ourselves and move around freely and self-directed. We have the unique capacity among living creatures to determine our destiny to a considerable extent.

This view comes close to some religious and legal views. We are not afraid of being at times closer to the ideas of philosophy, theology, or jurisprudence than to academic psychology. There may be great wisdom in what "people believe," especially if these ideas are shared by many over a long time. It is just possible that folk wisdom, religious ideas, and other so-called superstitions may be correct and that so-called scientific knowledge may be incorrect. In any event, Adlerians believe in a creative self, in the ability of people to make decisions independently of direct influences of heredity and environment. We see people as responsible, not mechanically driven; as independent units with the ability to make free decisions; and we see a normal individual's behavior as being under his or her control.

FREEDOM OF CHOICE

From our point of view, the so-called scientific systems of psychology—reductionistic and materialistic—are essentially disrespectful of humans. Adlerians take the position that individuals are self-directed, creative, and able to make decisions. In a beautiful passage, Mosak (1979) writes:

> If my feeling derives from my observation and conviction that life and people are hostile and I am inferior, I may divorce myself from the direct solution of life's problems and strive for personal superiority through overcompensation,

through wearing a mask, through withdrawal, through attempting only safe tasks where the outcome promises to be successful, and through other devices for protecting my self-esteem. (p. 46)

We are not fooling ourselves when we think we have the ability to make decisions. Far from our being machines, the human condition includes choice, even though the choice may be "contaminated," as it were, by past experiences. People are able to rise above their surroundings and make surprising decisions.

OPEN MOTIVATION

What most people call psychology is what psychologists call motivation. We often say, "I wonder why he did what he did?" or "Why does she act as she does?" Both questions, in effect, ask about motives.

Many systems of psychology concentrate on "needs"—meaning tissue requirements, like water or food; or "drives"—meaning instinctlike pushes within the body such as sexual desires; or about social pressures—the demand that people conform to others. Adlerians agree to some degree; but since IP is a psychology of use rather than of possession, these social or biological forces are not seen as primary. Rather, the creative self directs the individual in terms of subjective goals using and fulfilling these needs, pressures, and so on, as appropriate for the individual in his movement toward his goals.

How can we make this vital point clearer? Throughout life we want. The child may want attention and direct his life to getting his parents' attention. He grows up and now still wants attention, and may try to get it through athletics. One person may try to get attention by being attractive, another by being witty, another by being clever, another by unusual mannerisms, and so forth and so on.

Adlerians view people as being on the go, in action, moving forward, constantly looking for short-term and long-term goals, mobilizing their biological and social resources, looking for their personal, unique, subjectively determined goals for success, goals which are their own inventions, the results of their creativity. To live means to make choices.

SOCIAL INTEREST

Adler felt strongly that mental health—personal success in life—was a function of an individual's social interest, which means "identification with humanity," a "feeling of community," or "belonging to life." Social interest is viewed as an innate aptitude, a potentiality that must be consciously developed. Possibly the best antonym for social interest might be "selfishness," although "anomie" also conveys an opposite of social interest. According to Adler all important life problems are social problems—*occupation* is a social issue since it relates to what one does, which in turn affects others; the *family* is a social institution, and how one operates within the family affects others; and *society* is a greater social unit, and certainly how one operates in society affects others.

Adler (1912), commenting on this topic, stated:

> It is such children [lacking in social interest] who become the criminals, problem children, neurotics and suicides. They are lacking in social interest and therefore in courage and self-confidence. (p. 341)

OTHER CONCEPTS

Striving for Perfection

Adler's theory has often been largely, and sometimes we think purposefully, misinterpreted by a large number of "authorities." For example, ask many otherwise well-informed people about Adler and you are likely to hear two concepts: "power" and "inferiority feelings." But when "power" is explained, the wrong interpretation will be given: namely, that Adler preached the importance of individuals becoming superior, attempting to subdue others, and ultimately taking over the world. As the reader knows by now, exactly the opposite is true. How could such a misinterpretation take place?

What Adler said in effect was that each person strove for self-improvement, having an innate desire to become better, to become superior, to move forward and onward. This is what is known generally as "growth force," and it is found in various guises in the writings of many personality theorists.

Adler stated that every person moved "from a perceived minus to a perceived plus"—as we have discussed in taking up the notion of activity and direction. Striving for perfection is movement directed at self-improvement and greater competency. This is different from striving for superiority over others, which clearly implies that the goal is to be above others, but certainly not "interested in their interests."

Fictional Finalism

This concept refers to the unconscious elements of the individual in establishing personal private goals, which are only partly in awareness. It is the goal that the individual created, and on which he acts. In short, we usually do not know what we are really after, but we behave consistently as if reality and our goals were not our own perceptions and our own fictions. This is one of the purposes of psychotherapy: to learn who we are and what we are about.

Life Style

The correct Adlerian term would be "style of life"—or one's unique personality. All the elements discussed so far add up to the dynamics of the life style. Essentially, what others see and what the individual knows about self is based on deeply established personal constructs, the so-called private logic. The beliefs that compose the music of one's behavior are together—the composition and the music—the individual's life style.

Inferiority Feelings

Behavior is usually affected by feelings of inferiority. Awareness of our deficiencies may generate feelings of distress and ideas of what we must be so as not to be inferior within our own self-perceptions. Feelings of inferiority are common, normal, and functional, in that they serve as motivators to movement, but the direction taken as a result of suffering from inferiority feelings determines whether the subsequent behavior is useful or useless.

SUMMARY

Now that we have cut up Individual Psychology into a lot of pieces, let us see if we can assemble everything into a meaningful whole. IP is essentially a philosophy of life and a theory of personality relatively simple in structure. IP has been accepted by many people as the best explanation for human nature, the best vehicle for dealing effectively with people socially, educationally, organizationally, therapeutically—the most useful guide for successful human behavior.

The Individual Psychologist sees people as unique, coordinated, logically related, intact, indivisible units—and not as assemblages of parts. People operate in terms of their phenomenology—perceptions, memories, ideas, concepts, values. Their outward behavior is a function of these elements, the so-called mind. The mind can be arbitrarily broken into cognition (thinking) and affection (feelings). Of the two, cognition is the master; affection (emotion) serves the purposes of the intellect. Our emotions are not simply the result of outside events but, rather, are due to our interpretations of these events. Every human being is goal-directed. Human behavior is the result of the tendency of individuals to move toward private goals, some not even known to the individuals. If a person is unsuccessful in life and wants better self-understanding, he/she may go for therapy. In Adlerian therapy, one of the main objectives is to understand a person's motives, which in turn are embedded in what is known as a person's private logic or personal constructs.

Individual Psychology gets its name from the basic notion of holism, that the person is an *Individuum*—that is to say, an indivisible unit. Yet Individual Psychology is really a social psychology in that it stresses strongly that the individual is meaningless except in social terms, and that the person operates in a social environment. Also, the normal, healthy, and successful individual belongs to life, sees himself/herself as part of the humanity—has social interest.

Moreover, while it is agreed that individuals are formed and directed to some extent by hereditary and environmental factors independent of the individual, nevertheless, people in the IP view are responsible and creative, and consequently responsible for themselves.

Putting this together in a different way, we see people as self-directed, unique, integrated, responsible, moving toward private goals (often without too much self-understanding) and basically always wanting to be part of humanity. If they are successful, they have social interest and therefore have courage. They feel they are part of humanity, not against it or outside of it.

Individual Psychology is an optimistic point of view. It sees the individual as central, intact, integrated, in control of self. It views life as an ongoing process, and sees people as striving for success, represented by their unique goals—fictions that they have developed.

This point of view is applicable and represented in all of life—in activities such as child guidance centers, parent training centers, schools, individual psychotherapy and group psychotherapy, mental institutional organizations, counseling of adolescents, of school children, of married people, dealing with psychosomatic problems, babies, diagnoses of personality disturbances, cultural conflicts, religion, business psychology, correctional psychology, social problems such as poverty and crime, substance abuse treatment, sexual problems, problems of old age, projective techniques, school systems, learning problems, mental retardation and its handling, and a host of other issues and problems.

Chapter 2

History and Current Status

PRECURSORS

It is important to know something of the person who develops a theory of personality in order to understand the theory fully. Adler (1956) summed up the reasons particularly well when he said:

> A psychological system has an inseparable connection with the life philosophy of its formulator. As soon as he offers his system to the world, it appeals to individuals, both laymen and scientists, with a similar trend of mind and provides them with a scientific foundation for an attitude towards life which they had achieved previously. (p. 197)

Both authors of this book have long attended annual meetings of the North American Society of Adlerian Psychology, the primary organization of Individual Psychologists on this continent. What kind of meeting would you expect this group of people to have? The meetings fit the requirements of a scientific gathering; that is, there are paper sessions and symposia on research, on theory and practice, innovations in therapy, counseling, and in the schools. *But,* the atmosphere and the interactions are like no other scientific meetings we have ever attended. It is as if social interest were the normative mode of operations for the community. People are friendly. There are no "big shots" or "little shots"; everyone is, and seems to feel, equal. Everyone is teaching and learning; everyone has value. It is hard to distinguish the formal meetings from the social functions from free time. There is laughter and seriousness in all settings. Interest in each other, interest in the task, and the living of the theory are as one. People who accept Adlerian theory exhibit the social, active, and optimistic tenets of the theory.

Another example of acceptance of a theory related to personal philosophy is an informal experiment that one of us carried out in class some years ago when B. F. Skinner's book, *Walden Two,* was popular. The book contained an account of Skinner's version of Utopia—how a controlled society would function in adherence to behavioristic principles. In order to run Skinner's Utopian society, some persons would set up reinforcement contingencies. The mass of people in the society would be controlled by the reinforcement schedules which the controllers devised. The assumption was that the mass of people would be idyllically happy in this society.

Students' reactions to Skinner's book were strong and split. In classes over some years, I asked those who liked this book to stand against one wall and those who disliked it to stand against the opposite wall. Next I asked all who had identified with the controllers to raise their hand, and all who had seen themselves as being controlled to kneel down. The effect was dramatic. Against one wall were all the people who liked the book with their hands in the air signifying that they were controllers. Against the other wall were the people who had not liked the book kneeling. This experiment illustrated how we accept theories which best fit our own ways of looking at the world and ourselves.

The reader should consider if the ideas in the book are personally acceptable. Do you, or do you not, accept this holistic, teleological, socially embedded view? Are our simple explanations and simple language compelling or repelling? If you are, or are thinking of becoming, a therapist or counselor, does this cognitively based approach attract you? If you already an Adlerian at heart, everything you read will make sense.

Psychological theories, like literature, art, and music, must stand the test of time. Lord Acton had a great deal to say about English society in the early part of this century. However, his insights were limited by his reference group, best indicated by his quip, "There are two kinds of people. Those who are good to their servants and those who are not." The age in which a theorist lives, to a greater or lesser degree, sets the intellectual tone of the theory and the group to whom it applies. We cannot here articulate the history of Western civilization as it affected the life and thought of Alfred Adler. Yet the reader should attempt to take a knowledge of intellectual history into account in trying to understand Adler and his theory, and in determining how much he was a man of his time, before his time, and a man for all time.

BEGINNINGS

Alfred Adler

The purpose of this biography is to give the reader a greater understanding of the essence of Alfred Adler, the times he lived through, the main events of his life, and to indicate some key themes of his theory and philosophy. In three short sentences, Manes Sperber (1974), in his highly interpretive description of Adler and his theory, introduces important themes: *birth order, social standing, health:*

> Alfred Adler, the second of six children, was born into a petty bourgeois Jewish family on February 7, 1870. The Adlers lived in Rudolfsheim on the outskirts of Vienna. Alfred was a sickly child. (p. 15)

Adler's ill health as a child and the death of his younger brother when Alfred was three profoundly affected him. His early recollections included memories of illness and pain, cemeteries, and death. He later found that such memories were quite prevalent among other doctors. Alfred Farau, an Adlerian psychologist and associate dean of the Alfred Adler Institute of New York, tells of a dialogue he had with Adler in 1927 when Adler noted that Farau seemed pensive. Farau said:

> "I thought about death, Dr. Adler."
>
> "You do it very often, don't you?"
>
> "That's true. This time it's worse. Something hit me."
>
> Adler smiled. "Did you make a discovery?"
>
> "Yes. I think death is a mistake."
>
> "You have to explain that."
>
> "Dr. Adler, do you believe that man has to die under any circumstances?"
>
> "If I had believed that, I never would have become a physician. I wanted to fight death, even to kill it, to be in control of it."
>
> "Dr. Adler, is the thought of personal death not a horrible thought?"
>
> "Not for me. I have reconciled myself to it a long time ago."
>
> "I get the feeling from time to time that life is an abyss. What can one do?"
>
> Adler was ready to get up. "Be on good terms with life. Stay in the abyss! That is all I can say; and live! If I could change the fact of death, I would do so. As I cannot help it, I neither make my days bitter thinking of possibilities I will not see, nor miserable by missing now what I can enjoy. . . ." (Manaster, Painter, Deutsch, & Overholt, 1977, pp. 68–69)

Adler's parents lived in a town on the outskirts of Vienna, eventually incorporated into Vienna. The area in which they lived was not predominantly Jewish, a relatively rare occurrence inasmuch as most Jewish people lived in "their own" neighborhoods in keeping with traditions and with laws that limited where Jews could live. Moreover, Vienna at that time was strongly anti-Semitic except in certain circles which were heavily Jewish. So Adler was raised on the outskirts of one of the intellectual capitals of his time in an area where, although quite assimilated, he and his family were minority group members.

The themes of illness or weakness and belonging by virtue of status and beliefs characterize much of Adler's theory as they do his early life.

Little is known about his grammar school years. He continued to battle his physical ailments to develop his own striving for perfection. Hertha Orgler (1973) notes that his early school adjustment was not good. He showed little confidence in his physical self and was fairly solitary. He did so poorly in mathematics that his teacher advised that he leave school and apprentice himself to a shoemaker. His father did not agree to this advice and Alfred got to work and in time became the best math student in the class. Adler said of that experience, "If my father had followed this advice and had let me become a cobbler, then I would probably have done a good job at that, but I would have believed all my life that there is such a thing as having no gift for mathematics" (p. 3).

He went on to study medicine at the University of Vienna, finishing in 1895 and although he had specialized in ophthalmology, he began to practice internal medicine.

During Adler's student years, German nationalism was the dominant political movement. However, Adler became active in the socialist movement. He attended some meetings but seemed not to have been drawn to the political aspects of the movement so much as to its Utopian notions. He seemed to have had a disdain for labeling people and discriminating people by group membership or identification. Two ideas very much in Adler's thinking which must have underlaid his involvement with the socialist movement were *(a)* equality of all people without regard to race, religion, or sex; and *(b)* the dialectic interplay of person and environment. In those days, compared to the other political movements, the socialist view appeared more compassionate and concerned for everyone.

He attended some of these meetings with a young Russian student, Raissa Timofeyewna Epstein, whom he married in 1897. She continued her active interest in socialist political affairs throughout their marriage. In 1898 Adler first published a pamphlet called *Medical Handbook for the Tailoring Trade.* As an illustration of the degree to which he was a man ahead of his time, he attempted in this book to show "the relationship between the economic conditions and the ailments of a specific trade and to point out the threats to the general health that spring from a low standard of living. Such an approach, which examines the person not as an isolated being but as a product of society, can no longer be ignored by the medical profession" (Sperber, 1974, p. 17).

In 1898 or 1900, Adler first heard Freud. In attempting to understand the relationship that developed between the two men and their dramatic break, it is important to realize that Adler already had a flourishing general medical practice. He had already developed fundamental views of the world from which his future theory would emerge. He was already working within the framework of illness stated in the Preface to *Study of Organ Inferiority and Its*

Psychical Compensation (1907/1917)—that illness results from inferior organs and exterior strain. Though he was 13 years younger than Freud, and considered Freud his teacher, Adler certainly was never one of his disciples, as is so often wrongly stated in other textbooks.

In 1902 Freud invited four men, including Adler, to his home to discuss problems of neurosis. The group became known as the Psychological Wednesday Society and later the Vienna Psychological Society. Over the years of their association, Freud and Adler could not have been said to be friendly. Adler pursued his own line of thought while contributing to the group.

A long treatise could be written on Adler's contribution to Freud's thinking, and Freud's to Adler's. The various biographies referenced in this chapter give some evidence of this. With Freud, whom he respected both for his seniority of age and his creativity, Adler used the "Freudian" language that the group employed. But his work never was "Freudian" in the pure sense. These two independent thinkers came together and worked side by side for a while, eventually splitting when the directions of their thinking and theories clearly became incompatible.

By 1910 Adler was nominated by Freud and elected the president of the Vienna Psychoanalytical Association and co-editor and co-founder of the journal of psychoanalysis, the *Zentralblatt für Psychoanalyse*. But the friction and bickering over divergent views presented by Adler in the meetings and in his articles in the journal continued.

> The final crisis came during the summer when the group was in recess. Freud wrote a letter to the publisher of the *Zentralblatt* announcing that he could no longer be editor together with Adler, so the publisher would have to choose between them. The publisher communicated the letter to Adler, who spared him the embarrassment of choice by resigning. As a logical consequence he also resigned from the presidency of the Vienna Society, and from membership in it. (Furtmuller, 1964, p. 344)

When Freud declared at the first meeting after the summer break that membership would not be permitted in Adler's group and in his, the break was final. About 10 members of the original group eventually became members of Adler's Society for Individual Psychology.

Alfred and Raissa Adler's children were Valentine, born in 1898; Alexandra, born in 1901; Kurt, in 1905; and Nellie, in 1909. In 1904 he, Valentine, and Alexandra were baptized as Protestants. In the years between the break with Freud and his entry in 1917 into the Austro-Hungarian army, Adler began to prosper. His involvement with his psychology grew greater and his attraction to politics diminished. His wife's political activities did not diminish and thus in part because of the natural affinity between much of his theory and socialist theory and his wife's interests and politically oriented friends, Adler continued to have in his circle people with strong socialist and Marxist orientation. His high social consciousness was raised even further by his duties during World War I as an army doctor. Ellenberger (1970) refers to a short note published in a Swiss journal in 1918:

> with the title: "A Psychiatrist on War Psychoses" and the signature of A.A., which almost certainly stood for Alfred Adler. "The author points out the paradox of the common people going to war with such a show of enthusiasm to endure so many sufferings for a cause that was not their own. The answer is that they acted in that way in order to escape the distressing feeling of their own helplessness." (p. 587)

Adler's broad feeling for all people—for the masses, for humanity—and his will to understand and improve their lot, even in the midst of his own difficult times in the war, comes through in this passage.

Phyllis Bottome (1957), a friend and biographer of Adler, quotes an "old friend" of his:

> Adler was never the same again after the war. He was much quieter and stronger, one soon became conscious that he was no longer ready to squander his good spirits on any subject that came up; it was as if he had concentrated all his powers into a single purpose. In a sense he was not graver; but he used his wits more earnestly. . . .
>
> "It seems to me," Adler said in answer to his questioner, but looking seriously from one to the other round the long table [at the cafe where he met and discussed with friends and students after hours and lectures almost every evening as was the Viennese custom] "that what the world chiefly wants today is Gemeinschaftsgefühl." (p. 120)

His greater seriousness and sense of purpose appear to some degree to be related to a need to round out his theory, to add to his perspective on the negatives, neurosis, psychosis, deviance, the positive movement toward others, a hope for individual mental health and the health and survival of humankind. From this point on Adler became even more an educator. He began to work within the school reform movement of the first Austrian Republic, establishing the first child guidance clinic in 1922, overseeing the proliferation of the clinics as well as an experimental school built on Adlerian principles, lecturing at adult education centers and at the Vienna teacher training college. His activity was ceaseless in an attempt to get his message, his theory and practice across to as many people as he could, and particularly those who would carry the message on to others, such as teachers, parents, and educators.

Adler made his first trip to the United States in 1926 and lectured in initially halting English, which he eventually learned quite well in his mid-50s, and was greeted with large, enthusiastic audiences. He lectured also in Belgium,

Czechoslovakia, Germany, France, Great Britain, Holland, Yugoslavia, Austria, Switzerland, and Scandinavia. In 1929 he was a visiting professor at Columbia University. In 1932 he, in effect, moved to America when he accepted the first Chair of Medical Psychology in the United States at Long Island Medical College. His pace and the pressure in these years must have been tremendous. Many of his "writings" were transcriptions of lectures written in hotel rooms.

When the Fascists came to power in 1936, the school reform was ended. The 32 Adlerian clinics in Austria as well as those in Germany were closed. His associates and followers in Central Europe were forced to scatter and flee for their lives. In 1935 Adler and his wife settled in America. His daughter Alexandra and son Kurt, now both psychiatrists, and daughter Nellie also came to the United States. However, his oldest daughter, Valentine, and her husband fled to Russia, their mother's homeland, a land in keeping with their political philosophy. Although it was later learned that they were caught in a purge and jailed for a long period during which they died, Adler was not to know of their whereabouts or well-being. He did not allow these upheavals and his grief to interfere with his work. Only through reports from his closest friends and family was his anguish over Valentine's loss known. In his last letter to daughter Alexandra, April 29, 1937, he wrote: "Vali causes me sleepless nights. I am surprised how I can endure it." (Manaster et al., 1977, p. 23).

His packed schedule continued. He took out the odd moment to sing and enjoy music, as he always had with friends, and he sought peace and diversion with films. But the call for his presence did not let up. Early in 1937 he again traveled to Europe on a lecture and demonstration tour. On May 28, while on a walk just before he was to give a lecture in Aberdeen, Scotland, he collapsed from heart failure and died.

Rudolf Dreikurs

When the Adler/Dreikurs Institute of Bowie State College in Maryland was opened, the addition of Dreikurs' name indicated the importance of this remarkable human being to Individual Psychology. There is no question that without his efforts, the progress of the Adlerian school of thought in America would have been delayed for many years.

Born in Vienna on February 8, 1897, where he obtained the M.D. degree in 1923, he left his beloved Austria as a consequence of Nazism and went to Brazil in 1937. From there he went to Chicago in 1939, where he began the lonely struggle to achieve recognition and acceptance of Adlerian Psychology (Terner & Pew, 1978).

Dreikurs was a combative person who was frequently embroiled in conflicts and controversies, but who stuck tenaciously to his guns; and while many other European Adlerians hid their loyalties in fear that they would not be accepted, he boldly announced his being an Adlerian and he trained followers, with great success. Practically single-handedly, he revived Individual Psychology. He started the *Individual Psychology News,* which later became the *Journal of Individual Psychology.* He started many family education centers and parent study groups. More than this, this indefatigable man wrote constantly, and his publications amount to several hundred stretching from 1925 through 1977. Our teacher died on May 25, 1972.

CURRENT STATUS

Publications

Alfred Adler withdrew from the Psychoanalytic Society of Vienna in 1911, and immediately thereafter he organized the Society for Free Psychoanalytic Research. In 1912, he changed the name of the organization to The Society for Individual Psychology. In 1914, Adler founded the *Journal of Individual Psychology (Zeitschrift für Individual Psychologie).* Carl Furtmuller was Adler's associate editor. World War I interfered with the publication of this journal, and from 1916 to 1923 no Adlerian journals were in existence. In 1923, Ladislaus Zilahi became the editor of the revived journal, which continued up to 1937, interrupted by World War II. The *International Zeitschrift für Individual Psychologie* was revived again in 1947 and lasted until 1951. Since then a number of regional journals have been published.

We now quote from "The History of the International Association of Individual Psychology," by Paul Rom (1977) (International Association of Individual Psychology, Directory, 1977–79):

> In 1940, when Europe was already at war, Dr. Rudolf Dreikurs, who had emigrated from Vienna to Chicago, brought out a small magazine named *The Individual Psychology News.* It served as an organ of communication between the Individual Psychology groups and workers. With its fourth year of publication it became a well-printed quarterly, called *Individual Psychology Bulletin.* After the founding of the American Society of Adlerian Psychology in 1952, it grew into the official scientific organ of the society under the new title of the *American Journal of Individual Psychology.* It now aimed to serve as a forum for Adlerians as well as to confront Individual Psychology with other schools, stressing identity yet helping to integrate Individual Psychology into the general development of psychology as a whole. In 1957 Heinz L. Ansbacher, Professor of Psychology at the University of Vermont, took over the editorship and renamed the periodical *The Journal of Individual Psychology*—much to the satisfaction of Adlerians outside the U.S.A. Under his editorship it maintained high academic standards. (p. 5)

Meanwhile, in the United States, a second publication was started—*The Individual Psychologist. The Journal of Individual Psychology* is mostly concerned with theory, practice and research, while the *Individual Psychologist* is chiefly concerned with counseling, materials, and other applications of Adlerian Psychology.

In Europe, a number of publications, including *The Individual Psychology Newsletter,* the *Zeitschrift für Individual Psychologie* (Austria, Germany, and Switzerland), *Bulletin de la Société Française de Psychologie Adlerienne* (France), *Revista di Psicologia Individuale* (Italy) are published by various national organizations.

Adlerian Organizations

The International Association of Individual Psychology holds a triannual meeting for delegates from all countries. A list of the meeting places may be of interest, as well as the dates, keeping in mind that Adler died in 1937, and that German fascism attempted a takeover of Austria in 1934 and finally succeeded in 1938. The war in Europe started in 1939 and ended in 1944.

Munich	1922	Vienna	1960
Berlin	1925	Paris	1963
Dusseldorf	1926	Salzburg	1966
Vienna	1928	New York	1970
Berlin	1930	Milan	1973
Zurich	1954	Munich	1976
Holland	1957	Zurich	1979

The member societies as of 1977 were in Austria, Denmark, France, Germany, Great Britain, Greece, Israel, Italy, the Netherlands, Switzerland, and the United States. In the United States, as in other countries, there are a number of smaller groups as well as a national group, and as of 1977, the following are the major constituent groups of the North American Society of Adlerian Psychology:

Alfred Adler Institute of Psychology of Chicago
Alfred Adler Institute of New York
Individual Psychology Association of New York, Inc.
Oregon Society of Individual Psychology
Western Institute for Research and Training in Humanics
San Francisco Bay Area Society for Adlerian Psychology

There are, in addition, in the United States, some dozen or so other state or regional associations not associated with the International Association. The

North American Society of Adlerian Psychology (NASAP) is divided into five regions. In Region 1, for example, the NASAP affiliated organizations are:

Adlerian Society of Human Relations, Bellingham, Washington
British Columbia Association of Adlerian Psychology
Laramie Institute of Family Education, Wyoming
Oregon Society of Individual Psychology
Puget Sound Adlerian Society, Mountlake Terrace, Washington

In addition, there are a number of unaffiliated local societies and groups, such as the Family Education Centers of Hawaii. The total membership of NASAP for 1981 is over 1,000 individuals, slightly larger than the German society.

Chapter 3

Dynamics of Personality

Everyone who has ever taken an Introductory Psychology course, or one in Sociology, has learned that "humans are social animals." Many other animals exhibit patterns of social behavior (Huber, 1978); however, only humans are totally social.

In addition to the extensity of their social behavior, humans can make rational judgments. We have the capacity for using and developing language. We speak, listen, write, and read. Although we think in codes, or symbols, the basis for higher order, rational thought, is language learned through socialization.

Humans are social within their world as they understand it—as they learn and perceive it; they are rational and communicative—but the rational and communicative is based on the social. The language one learns and the modes of thought one uses emanate from the society in which one lives. Individuals behave within their society and culture on the basis of what each has learned and understood.

Interdependence is the key word of human life. We make our decisions, choices, and carry out our actions in the interdependent, overlapping context of our social groups. Our actions, choices, decisions, and judgments are built on the attitudes and values and perceptions of our social groups as we come to understand them within the limits of our culture and its teachings—its rationality and language.

From an Adlerian perspective, all behavior is social because we use the language and thought system of our culture as well as the attitudes and values of our society. To be human is to be social. The classic story exemplifying the social nature of humankind is about a hermit. He lived on the side of a mountain overlooking a town. He had nothing to do with anyone in the town.

One day a volcano erupted and lava wiped out the town. So, the hermit moved to a place outside another town.

Even general patterns of behavior which appear to be "asocial" have social meanings—for or against others, in or out of coherence with the norms of society, within or without the bounds of common sense, useful or useless to humankind.

Two general rules of the dynamics of personality and the social context develop from the preceding paragraphs. First, through the individual's unique perceptions the world is understood. Therefore, through the sum of understandings, perceptions and consequent actions of individuals who comprise a group the norms and *common sense* of that group emerge.

Individuals may not see themselves and the world as most others in their group see them and the world. Group members may have a range of views about any individual, the world, society and its members. The interactions that individuals have with the people around them will cohere to the degree that their views agree with the greatest number of those around them. There usually are ways in which individuals are in agreement with some people around them. Individuals attribute attitudes to others and others do the same to the individuals.

In social living nothing is fixed, exemplifying what Adler said, "Everything could be different. . . ." Adlerians think, and prescribe, so to speak, on the basis of probabilities. A friendly person—one who greets people easily, converses readily with them, seems interested in others, seems to enjoy others' company —likely would have many friends. Although the above is *probably* generally true, there can be instances where such a person is not liked. Someone may dislike or distrust friendly people. So a friendly person will not receive 100 percent endorsement for such behavior, and the "antifriendly" person may find some people who like him and support his style of life.

Perhaps on the top of every page of this book we should have the statement:

PSYCHOLOGY IS A PROBABILITY SCIENCE

since practically everything we say has caveats and exceptions, special conditions, and so on and so forth. Adler made no claim that his system was perfect —only that he thought it had fewer errors than any other system.

Adlerians are eclectics. We accept from other personality systems and concepts and methodologies that make sense to us. Statements identified with a particular school of thought are not necessarily unacceptable. Historically, Adler and Freud exchanged ideas; and some ideas that are now "Adlerian" were probably suggested first by Freud, just as Adler's aggressive drive and his safeguarding sentiments were taken by Freud.

Individual Psychology is highly inclusive in terms of approaches. For example, we are behavior modifiers almost in the Watsonian-Skinnerian sense, with the exception that our modifiers should be elegant—that is to say, simple, natural, logical—and consequently we like natural and logical consequences, which are intrinsic rather than being extrinsic as are rewards and punishment. We like Albert Ellis' insistence on the primary importance of cognition, that it is not things as such that bother people but, rather, their interpretation, but we do not agree with his emphasis that self-gratification is the first of all laws. We like Carl Rogers' primary belief in the ability of people to find their own way, but we also believe in a counseling or therapy situation that teaching as well as learning is called for, and that a client need not thereby feel overwhelmed or dependent on the therapist.

We also believe that even though nomothetically there are definite laws, these are always probability laws: no matter how certain we can be that a blind person with palsy will not become an eye surgeon, lo! someone may call our statement and a blind and palsied person will perform cataract operations.

The important thing to remember is that nothing is certain. Not all first children are traditionalists. Not all only children are spoiled. Not all parents love their children. Not all children brought up by Adlerians will turn out okay. Nothing is absolutely certain when it comes to humans—it is always a question of probabilities. We believe Individual Psychology to be the broadest of all the systems, as well as the most nearly correct—the one with the fewest errors—the system with the highest probability of predicting human behavior, but still possibly incomplete and even in error in some ways.

BASIC DYNAMICS

Adlerians emphasize the distinction between useful and useless behavior. Some words about the difference are in order.

Each person is definitely a social being, a product of, a development of, and an example of society and culture. At the same time, each individual is his/her own creation. This means that an individual comes to unique conclusions, personal goals, lines of movement and direction which generally cohere with the interests and/or welfare of others.

According to Adler there are two basic human dynamics: (a) striving for significance *(Geltungestreben)*, and (b) social interest *(Gemeinschaftsgefühl)*. In meeting the three main tasks of life—*social relations, family relations, occupation*—all of us relate simultaneously to our concern for *who* we are and *what* we do—that is to say, our self-concept and our social behavior.

We can translate this into a dichotomy: *selfishness* versus *selflessness, personal ambition* versus *social concern, me* versus *you, ego* versus *cosmos.* The trick to successful living is to achieve both! If Jon is stealing, then he is operating to achieve significance in that now he is getting something that he wants. If Jon is studying, then he is operating to achieve significance in that he will become more capable. Both of these are attempts at significance. The difference, of course, is that one is useless and the other is useful behavior. So, too, in any behavior we can operate usefully or uselessly.

Fulfillment comes when one operates in both of these dynamics. For example, the child who studies to improve himself operates to achieve personal significance and also to make himself socially useful.

UNITY OF THE SELF

It is difficult to decide which is the single most important basic idea of Adler. Is it the notion that all people are in constant movement toward subjective goals in terms of their unconscious general desire to be perfect? Or is it the concept that full happiness and success in life means feeling part of the human race and participating with others? On this point Ansbacher (1978) states, "For Adler the unity of the individual is the most important basic assumption, from which all the others are derived" (p. 249a).

The concept of unity of the personality gains credence if we accept the notion of goal orientation. Imagine a group functioning together to achieve a single aim—say, climb a mountain. Each member of the group is a separate person, but the group as a whole functions as a unity due to the common goal. *Causa finalis* (final goal) is the governing principle of the individual and it acts in such a manner as to organize the individual into a unity. We are always moving forward in time, and during movement we direct ourselves toward this personal, not-too-well understood goal.

If we can understand a person's goal or predict another person's unknown-to-her goal, we then know her. But one may object—how about people who don't know what they want to do, or those who have conflicts? How about those people about whom others say, "They are so unpredictable"? How about contradictory personalities?

Even in these cases, there is a unity of the personality. To understand such an individual, one must understand his or her final goal. Let us take some puzzling examples.

Robert usually insults people when he first meets them, and then when they are hurt and turned off, he now institutes a policy of being nice to them, making up to them, and regaining their confidence. He once did this twice to a girl. The day after he first kissed her, he called her, and told her he loved another, thereby upsetting her terribly. He then laid a long campaign to undo the wrong, regained her confidence and, having done so, he then tried to force her sexually, prompting her to run away from him and go home alone. This kind of behavior has been his standard way of operating with people: after meeting them, he says or does something to hurt their feelings and then attempts to reestablish himself and, having done so, he again is likely to go after them to make up. This "crazy" pattern showed itself in many other ways. In school for example, he would study very hard and know his subject well, but he would "forget" to come to the final examination on time. He seemed to like contradictions, to develop confusing situations.

In therapy, the purpose of this contradictory behavior became clear: he was operating on the basis of several goals: (a) *attention*—getting people to notice him; (b) *power*—hurting people, showing them that he could affect them; and (c) *revenge*—hurting people and leaving them helpless to deal with him; and then he would go back to power and attention in his attempt to win them over again. His various shenanigans had a purpose: to manipulate people, make them notice him, make them realize that he was powerful. Just as the stock investor who buys and then sells stocks is operating in a purposeful manner, because his final goal is profits, so, too, apparently inconsistent people operate in a unitary, purposeful manner once we understand that person's goals.

All behavior of an individual fits together and expresses the individual's style of life. This is a central point in Adlerian thinking—everything one does, one's dreams, one's reactions are all related to the final goal of one's life, which differs in particulars but is always directed, overall, to concepts of perfection.

How does this relate to psychotics, alcoholics, and other miserable unfortunates who obviously are harming themselves by their paranoid ideas, by their self-aggrandizement, by their masochistic behavior, and so on?

We see such individuals as discouraged, and they turn their evident weaknesses into perceived strengths. The alcoholic seeks superiority through proving how low he can sink. "No one is more miserable than I!" he says, and now "proves" his superiority in a negative way by being the worst, since he cannot be the best. However, he is aiming always to be the "–st" whether it is "worst" or "best." The masochist proves how much he can suffer, what a saint or martyr he is, how superior he is to stand so much torture. According to Adler, the purpose of masochism often is to escape life's tasks, such as love and marriage. Through suffering masochistic saints can avoid facing life and they can maintain the precious feeling of moral superiority that they want so badly.

This notion of superiority was shown by the case history of a man in prison. At one time he was considered to be the "toughest" convict in the institution. At one time he got into a knife fight with another inmate and had an ear sliced off. Someone picked up his ear, gave it to him, and informed him that if he went to the hospital he might have it sewn back on. Billy contemptuously threw his ear away. This was one tough convict!

Some time later he was falsely accused of knowing of a planned escape attempt. He denied any knowledge. He was put in solitary for a week. On being taken out he was again asked about the attempt. Again, truthfully, he stated he had no knowledge of the plot. He was again put in solitary, for a month, taken out and requestioned, put back in solitary confinement for three months, and again on release stated he did not know. He was then put back into the regular prison population.

As a result of this experience, he decided to change strategies. From being the wor*st* in the prison, he was now going to be the be*st*, an example of the "–st," fir*st* or la*st* point of view. He took courses in typing and shorthand and other related subjects, and eventually became the warden's inmate secretary, gaining the most trusted position in the prison. From being the lowest of the low, he became the highest of the high. So while his tactics had changed, as did those of the investor who now buys and sells the same stock, his goal— to be *superior*—had not changed at all.

What this means, then, in terms of personality theory, is that we are united as individuals. There is no superego pulling one way and an id pulling us the other. Sure, there are forces affecting us, principally environmental forces, people in our past and in our present who try to make us do what they want us to do, but we react totally and in a unitary manner to them in terms of our final objective—which, we must add, often we do not ourselves understand.

When a person appears to be inconsistent, the very inconsistency may be consistent. We all try to achieve our goals and sometimes pursue an apparently crooked or zigzag way of operating, but if we can stand far enough away the behavior begins to make sense. This is one of the values of being a psychotherapist: one has an opportunity to help puzzle out the consistent meaning of apparent inconsistencies. People are consistent in their goals but may achieve them in apparently inconsistent ways. Any splitting of self, dividing of individuals into parts, is artificial, incorrect, and unnatural from an Individual Psychology viewpoint.

HEREDITY, ENVIRONMENT, CONATION

Adlerian Psychology can be explained in terms of these three terms. Heredity means the equipment with which a child comes into the world. The child at birth has a particular form, a certain number of fingers and toes, a particular skin tone, and hair coloring, and some built-in potentials which will be realized under normal circumstances, such as the attainment of a certain height, a certain weight, and certain visual and auditory acuity.

These biological-hereditary matters set practical limits on performance. An endomorph will probably never become a world-class sprinter. A child born with Down's syndrome (mongolism) will probably never become a professional mathematician. No child born totally blind will likely become a watchmaker. However, Adlerians are optimistic about the possibilities of people exceeding apparent biological limitations. In a book called *Born That Way*, the author, a spastic paralytic, tells how, despite the enormous handicaps of being unable to control his body movements, he earned the doctor of medicine degree —but we can be sure he did not specialize in surgery!

The *environment* also affects us profoundly. Our social system teaches us how to talk, what to think, what to value, what's important, what's not important. From earliest infancy, how we are treated by our parents and how others deal with us affects us enormously. We can probably be made courageous or fearful, optimistic or pessimistic to various degrees by how we are handled. If a set of identical twins were separated at birth, at 20 they may look identical, but if one was treated with consideration and deference, respectfully and in a friendly fashion and valued highly, that twin is likely to be quite different in his personality from the other twin who was treated in an inconsistent fashion, harsh at times, and pampered at other times.

Both environment and heredity have *some* influence on personality. Knowing both tells us something about the individual. Thus, if told that the next person we are going to meet is a young, black male, brought up in New York City's Harlem, who has been on welfare and lived in an apartment with his mother and seven siblings, we can make, in advance of meeting this young man, a fairly good general guess as to what his personality is likely to be. If the next person we are going to meet is a young, white man, brought up on a farm in Iowa by well-to-do parents, we can be fairly certain that we are going to meet a different personality.

But—a big *But—we could be mistaken.* This is because psychology is a probability science. Nevertheless, over time and with experience, we gain the ability to make fairly good predictions of personality on the basis of knowledge of people's heredity and environment before we even see them.

This is why Adlerians represent a psychology of *use* rather than of *possession.* This is our argument against William Sheldon (1970), who represented a constitutional deterministic psychology, and who said that structure represented function. The evidence against this position, it seems to us, is substantial. Patterson (1930) made a classic refutation of the position that there is a substantial relationship between physical and psychological characteristics. This is also our argument against the behaviorist position as exemplified by J. B. Watson's famous statement that given any normal child, he could make that child anything he wished. Adults can influence children only so far. Because the child has a mind of his own, what we label *conation,* he decides what to do with his life within the limits of heredity and environment.

We now have an explanation of why children from the same family may differ relative to their "personality" even though they all may look alike. One may become a criminal, another an honest businessperson, another may become more-or-less a bum, another a laborer, another a professor. Some may be well balanced and some not.

Dr. Rudolf Dreikurs told a story that illustrates this point quite well.

On the first day of school, every teacher examined the hair of all the children for lice. A half dozen children were discovered with lice in their hair. Two of them had the same last name. It turned out that they were brothers. Both looked as though they had been dressed from clothing cast away by the Salvation Army. Both were dirty as though they had not taken baths for weeks. Obviously they came from a filthy home environment.

A search of the school files showed that a sister was also enrolled in this school. The nurse called in this child. When the nurse saw this girl, her first reaction was that it was a mistake. The child was spotless, absolutely clean. There were no lice in her hair. The nurse visited the home of the children. She was appalled by the filthy condition of the home.

And yet in this horrible environment, this little girl of ten had managed to keep herself clean, to have attractive clothes, and to have conquered hereditary and environmental influences.

To summarize, Adlerian psychology, like all psychology, makes generalizations. Nothing is absolute. Thus, Adler, had he been presented with these two boys and if he had seen the home, might well have said, "No, it is not necessary that both of these two boys look like ragamuffins or that both of them have hair lice. Each of them could have independently decided to be personally clean despite the parents' influence and despite the home condition." And the appearance of the daughter could have borne him out.

Individual Psychology is a psychology of use—not possession. *What counts is how we use what we have.* Identical twins can have completely identical environments and yet one can go the useless route and the other the useful route. The difference can only be explained by the creativity of the individual.

Individual Psychology is a hopeful, positive psychology. It sees the possibility of all persons being useful and contributing members of society, content and happy in the process. If one is not useful, behaves only for oneself to the exclusion of others or in competition to others, the potential benefit for oneself and society diminishes.

It is within the capabilities of all people, regardless of their native endowment or environmental circumstances, to be useful and healthy members of the human group. The dynamics of personality, as described in the following chapters, is the story of how the biological capacities, social experiences, and environment, and individual creative abilities interact in the development and maintenance of the human personality.

Chapter 4

Biological Factors

Having just belabored the strong social and holistic nature of Individual Psychology theory, proceeding directly to a section on the biological component in personality may seem strange. Much theory in psychology relies heavily on biological determinants and it seems necessary to explain the Adlerian position in light of other positions. Adler and many of his principal descendants in American Adlerian Psychology—Rudolf Dreikurs, Alexandra Adler, Kurt Adler, Bernard Shulman, Ronald Pancner, W. L. Pew, Helene Papanek, Bina Rosenberg and others—had medical backgrounds. Adler came out of the scientific philosophical traditions of the early part of this century and passed through the Freudian camp. The effects of this on his early work are evident.

Over his lifetime Adler's view of the biological inputs and import on personality changed, but there was very little change in his view during the last 20 years of his life. Unfortunately for the general acceptance of his later view, some of his earlier positions were widely heralded, continued to be thought of as essential to Adler's position, and were juxtaposed to Freud's views as illustrations of the similarity or differences in their two views. Equally unfortunate, Adler did not clearly demarcate the point at which he no longer believed a certain view, or when he changed the meaning of a term. Only in later analyses of his work (for example, Adler, 1956, 1964a, 1978) can one see the changes clearly.

ADLER'S EARLY VIEWS

Organ Inferiority and Drives

At the time that Adler wrote most of his early papers, he was in transition from being a medical practitioner meeting regularly with the initial Freudian group (1907–11). As a practicing physician, he used a medical model. His first work which portends his eventual theory was *A Study of Organ Inferiority and Its Psychical Compensation* (1907). This book presented a psychological theory definitely biologically based. This underlying notion of inferiority continued through Adler's theory, but the biological base did not continue as strongly. In essence, the notion of organ inferiority refers to the ways in which individuals deal with an especially weak organ—the physical aspect of themselves. The basic notion is that the strength of all organs within an individual's body is not equal—some are stronger or weaker than others. The weaker organ may or may not be crucial in day-to-day functioning. However, it may seem to the individual that this organ weakness or deficit somehow tilts the balance against his/her potential for success in life. Without this notion coming necessarily to awareness, the individual either favors the weak organ and thereby strengthens others or makes efforts to strengthen the organ itself. In either event, the individual attempts to strengthen the weak organ. Sometimes these efforts are so strenuous or so prolonged that they make the weak organ or the related organs much stronger than normal.

Adler's discussion of this tendency to compensate was in terms of specific body organs. Rather quickly he moved from seeing the dynamics of this phenomenon only in purely body terms. It became clear to him that he had hit on a phenomenon which had much more far-reaching explanatory power than purely physical happenings.

In simple language, his idea went like this: When people note a physical "weakness," as when they conclude that they are not attractive, or that their hearing is not good, they make attempts to overcome that weakness. The unattractive person may use beauty aids or may concentrate on some other way of standing out, such as becoming exceptionally strong. From his medical work with circus performers, Adler noticed that daredevils in the circus were usually very short or had physical deficits or limitations. He began to generalize from the way in which other organs will take up the slack for the performance of a weak organ, to more global characteristics of the whole person's performance.

Many self-made wealthy men first had a bankruptcy or a business failure. Many world-famous geniuses somewhere along the line made serious conceptual errors; but these people did not let failure deter them: they used their failures not to make the same mistake, or else they corrected their mistaken assumptions. This is what a great mind and a great person is all about: and it may be what genius is in the long run.

Adler began to realize that although individuals may not notice a physical weakness consciously, they may have a sense that they do have such a weakness. The person who is not fast may become more cunning. A child, who probably is not aware that he is physically slow, begins to move toward the most advantageous spot for whatever he wants earlier than the others. By having a lead, he can still be the first out of the door. In essence, Adler generalized from the specific to the general, from the body to the personality.

Say that a child is left-handed, and that this bothers the child's parents and teachers, who try to "correct" this "deficiency." Because of the adults' attitude the child may see herself as having an inferior organ. Attention is directed to this "deficiency" and the child may do all sorts of things about it: accept this difference as a sign of one's general inferiority; attempt to improve the ability of the right hand, and perhaps become ambidextrous; or even attempt to be very good with her hands, perhaps becoming an artist, a sports player, a mechanic, and so on. So, the discouraged child may see left-handedness as a sign of personal inferiority while the courageous child compensates for this apparent disability.

Dreikurs (1953) makes this statement: "Examples of famous musicians whose hearing was impaired by constitutional organic inferiorities like Franz and Smetana; famous orators like Demosthenes ... famous painters with defective eyesight like Manet ... can be multiplied at will and clearly prove that frequently an organ inferiority provides the incentive for artistic achievements" (p. 31).

Both Adler and Dreikurs probably overstated the generalizability of the biologically based notion of organ inferiority. After all, out of the total population of artists, it may be that there are actually fewer visual disturbances than in the general population. Of the tens of thousands of musicians, we would guess that overall they have better hearing than the average. Picking on a few examples may not prove the rule, and we do not see these few examples as proof.

Adler came to believe that the process of regarding a defective organ operates rather in the reverse—first, a child starts off with a perfectly rational attitude of personal inferiority simply because he is inferior: after all, he can do less than his older siblings; he *is* much weaker and inferior to his parents. Having already established his inferiority, he may now become aware of and sensitive to any organic deficiency and this gives him evidence of personal inferiority.

Mike as a child felt inferior to other children who seemed brighter, stronger, faster, and more capable than he. (In reality, he was quite normal and perhaps even above average in most things; but since he was so ambitious, he was well below his level of aspiration.) Then, he found out via an eye examination that he needed glasses. This did it! This was the explanation for his inferiority. If only he had good vision! The knowledge of the vision problem *followed* the feeling of inferiority, but it became the explanation and the excuse.

It is at this point that Adler's notion about inferiority moved from being biologically based to socially based. The question is not whether there is actually a physical inferiority. The question is whether the person has the idea that there is something inferior about him. When a person has such an idea he acts to make up for this lack, in the same way that organs do compensate for their inferiority.

Adler's original conception of organ inferiority has some value in its own right but its greatest value is as an analogy for the behavior of the whole person, and as a springboard in Adler's thinking to a new understanding of drives, and a new concept—compensation and overcompensation.

Compensation

Adler looked at the way in which people used their body and inferred that a story was being told by the body. Variously referred to as body language or organ jargon, this was an indication that a particular aspect of the body was being stressed—an indication of compensation. A person who is particularly meek might be indicating that he feels weak and possibly this is his felt reaction to a feeling of weakness in one organ.

Overcompensation

Compensation implies balance, equity. When one organ makes up for another, or one aspect of personality makes up for another, the resulting compensation is an equitable functioning that evens things out. However, in personality functioning, the inferior aspect, or trait, as perceived by the person may be seen as needing more than an equitable compensation. The person may think that because he is weak he needs to be exceedingly strong, or because he feels not sufficiently smart he needs to be always active. This results in an overbalance. When an individual's efforts in one arena are excessive it may be that the person is trying to make up for a felt inferiority by standing out in another aspect of himself. We call this overcompensation.

Whereas in Adler's earliest writing the personality dynamics were the analogy for the more fundamental biological basics, the social and personality dynamics are now seen as fundamental and the biological dynamics as the analogue. The mechanisms of organ inferiority are simpler than the mechanisms of personality inferiority. Compensation in biology is simpler than compensation or overcompensation in personality.

Drives

Drives from the Adlerian perspective may be understood in one of two ways. We can run through the history of the conception in Adlerian psychology placing Adler's and Freud's notions in relation to each other, or we can state that the concept may be understood best by disregarding the causal views of drives. At one time Adler used drives in ways quite similar to Freud. It is necessary, therefore, to proceed through an account of Adler's use of the concept of drive to reach a contemporary understanding of drives by Individual Psychologists.

Probably, in the beginning of humanity, as with animals, there were mainly drives and instincts. Early humans probably survived primarily on the basis of instinctual urges and in the satisfaction of basic drives. He probably was indistinguishable from his ape cousins in most behaviors which demanded instant action or "no thought." However, he had begun to "think" in ways which allowed greater organization for himself and the community. When, in the process of evolution, concepts arose is not known. But over the centuries humans have come to rely, in daily cultural and social living, on ideas, notions, and ideologies. Much of the instinctual apparatus is still available for situations which demand their use, their unthinking call to action.

Still today, if one attempts to explain what really makes humans function, the tendency is to look for concrete basic urges—*drives.* This was the case at the turn of the century as psychodynamic psychology was developing. The basic physiological drives, like hunger, were already clearly acknowledged. And just as clearly, their explanatory power was insufficient. Yet the early psychological "scientists" needed "hard" concepts—tangible elements—to explain behavior. The times were not right for using "softer" concepts such as *values* or *ideas*—to explain behavior. Freud emphasized the sex drive, which had broad explanatory power and which was acknowledged as forceful and universal. Everybody had a sex drive, and they could feel that others did. Ingeniously, Freud expanded the powers of the sex drive to underlie all human behavior not distinctly allied with other basic physiological drives. In conceptualizing his expanded notion of the sex drive he began to envision the objects of the drives as important and in that manner came close to recognizing the cognitive and social natures of humans. However, in an attempt to remain close to a biological basis of behavior, in keeping with the temper of the times and the "scientism" of the day, he posited a mechanical, causal determination of the objects of the drives.

Aggression Drive. Adler had presented his idea of the aggression drive in 1908. It was seen by him as central to the person and superordinate to other drives. Adler took acts of direct physical or indirect symbolic aggression, which were understood as such in society, and expanded their meanings to all behaviors. Freud denied the usefulness of this concept although he later, in the early 1920s, "discovered" an aggressive instinct which he called Thanatos, a destructive instinct or death instinct.

The aggression drive had a direct link to what might be termed *basic* drives and urges. Self-preservation is to some degree dependent on aggression in a competitive world. This is certainly the case for lower animals. The history of humans is replete with examples of people turning to aggression such as wars when "higher order" faculties were not up to the task of resolving problems. Adler pointed out, however, the ways in which societies develop alternative modes for acting out the aggression drive, a prime example being sports.

Adlerians view aggression as part of the individual's movement to overcome difficulties in advancing toward the achievement of goals. If an individual's social interest is underdeveloped, then the individual's movement may show itself in hostile behavior. Depreciation of others is an example, since rivals are not seen as friendly competitors but as people to be put down. Such an individual does not operate in a friendly world, striving with others to achieve personal goals and ready to help others but, rather, is selfishly guarding his or her possessions, viewing others as enemies, and suffering if someone else makes an advance. Such individuals can become accusatory and suspicious.

In aggression there is always the element of being mistreated, of not getting one's rights or dues, of being endangered by someone encroaching on one's "territory." One can begin to develop ideas of persecution, and when the whole world is seen as the "enemy" we can then have a most persistent and difficult personality aberration—paranoia.

The individual can become self-aggressive. Now, the enemy is one's self! "I didn't do what I should have done!" the tortured neurotic says in self-accusation. "Shape up! Act right!" And so he accuses himself of misconduct, or of not working hard enough, or of a thousand other crimes. Guilt coming from self-accusations mixed with aggression can lead to a potentially dangerous individual who can only be treated with very great difficulty since if the therapist attempts to lower that person's standards the therapist is now viewed as an enemy.

Aggression is, therefore, not seen by Adlerians as a basic instinct, but rather as a kind of mistake made by people whose striving for perfection and achievement is not accompanied by social interest. No one is allowed to succeed except him and, consequently, the aggressive person moves toward his enemies with malice and hostility.

Need for Affection. About the same time—1908—Adler developed another notion, which may be included under the general rubric of drives and motives —the need for affection. When Adler originally presented this need, he saw it as a representation of "a strong drive life" (p. 50). He did not show how "basic" drives and this need were related though it was seen as an outgrowth of drives. As he explained it, one could see in children their wish to be held, fondled, touched, praised. To be touched and held could be stretched to be an illustration of drive fulfillment for a tactile need.

Development of the need for affection was the beginning of Adler's later development of social interest, a concept which includes the need for affection, belonging—potentiality which underlies the adequacy and healthfulness of human functioning.

Growth Drive. In his attempt to find a master motive, Adler went through all sorts of concepts. He talked of the need for *completion* at one time, in the same sense that the Gestalt theorist Bluma Zeigarnik used the term—the desire of individuals to be more complete and whole. He used the term *mastery* to refer to self-mastery and control, which has been usually confused as *power over others.* He referred to *perfection*—the desire to be the very best. And he finally settled on the concept of *superiority* as the master motive in the sense of an individual constantly seeking to move from the present situation, as observed and interpreted, to a better one, one that was superior to the present status.

Other personality theories have used a variety of terms for the same concept, thereby indicating a similar view of life, that people move toward goals. "Self-actualization" is the term used by Kurt Goldstein (1939) to indicate the organism's ultimate purpose. Carl Rogers (1951) had the same point of view when he said, "The organism has one basic tendency and striving—to actualize, maintain and enhance the experiencing organism" (p. 487). Karen Horney (1950) discussed the "need for perfection," and Robert White (1959) has centered on "competency" as the most basic intent of people.

All these personality theorists seem to agree: the organism is not static, not just seeking homeostasis but, rather, there is in all humans some movement in the direction of *becoming.* We label this the "growth drive"—thereby hopefully satisfying everyone who sees the individual dynamically moving upward, as an explanation for the difference between humans who are eternally *on the go toward perfection* and animals who *are content to be.*

Were it possible to reach back 10 centuries and bring back a cat and a human to life, the cat would have absolutely no trouble in adjusting herself, but the human would find a radically different world in most parts of the globe, although in some parts of the world, such as the rain forests of the Philippines, some ancestors of a thousand years ago would now find things just as they were then, but these would be the exceptions that prove the rule—that the human race is blessed—or cursed—with the drive toward growth and improvement, toward actualization and perfection.

Suffice it to say that in his transition from the biological to the social, Adler developed a social basis for human behavior which is today representative of the most modern and accepted views of motivation in psychology.

The degree to which the Adlerian view of motivation—or the reasons why humans behave—as well as the rest of Adlerian theory is central to contemporary psychology, is illustrated in a quote from an article by Robert C. Bolles (1978), entitled "Whatever Happened to Motivation?"

> Motivational ideas were introduced into psychology in order to correct certain deficiencies of the mechanistic, passive, structualistic view of the organism that once prevailed. The history of psychology suggests that as this once-dominant view of the organism gradually became replaced by a more cognitive, dynamic

and functional view, the need for motivational concepts gradually disappeared. Today, even nominally motivational theories of behavior do not seem to be very motivational. Now, we take for granted that the organism is active and is directing behavior toward certain goals. By applying cognitive principles to this view of an intrinsically active organism, it is possible to deal with all of the behavioral phenomena that have traditionally been regarded as motivational without invoking any motivational concepts. (p. 1)

Chapter 5

Social Aspects

The importance of the social aspect in Individual Psychology cannot be over-emphasized. Adler sometimes referred to his psychology as "comparative individual psychology" and, according to Sperber (1974), Adler at times insisted that this fuller name be used. *Comparative individual psychology* refers to the constant dynamic by which (*a*) individuals compare themselves to how they would like to be, and (*b*) compare how they see others and how they would like to be seen by others. As an introduction to this chapter, we can do another analysis of some of the terms used to describe Individual Psychology in Chapter 1, stressing the social aspects of the various concepts.

Holism refers to a perspective by which we view the entire pattern of the person behaving in the social environment; *phenomenology* refers to how the individual interprets experiences in comparison to the ways in which others understand the same type of experiences; *teleology* refers to the individual's goals, which are only meaningful in a social and comparative framework; and *field theory* indicates how the individual finds a place in a social field. Other assumptions descriptive of Individual Psychology, such as uniqueness, self-consistency, activity, and creativity also imply a social comparative approach. The *unique,* consistent self-created behavior of the individual is such, in comparison with other individuals; *consistency* is the constancy of social reactions to the individual and of the individual's stance vis-à-vis others; *creativity* is seen when different individuals react variously to similar situations; and *behavior* is inherently social—we always move or react in relation to others and social meanings. In the theory of Individual Psychology all behavior is social.

Individual Psychology sees the behavior of all individuals in a social context and social behavior in a broad, comparative framework—ethical and value laden, applicable within different cultural contexts. Cognitive, creative judg-

43

ments undergird individuals' consistent behavior and so Individual Psychology is able to understand the various behaviors of individuals as a function of their social world as they see it. In terms of the "common sense of social living," Individual Psychology evaluates the behavior of individuals and groups, with a social comparative view, to predict the healthfulness, satisfaction, and benefit of any particular behavior to the individuals, groups, society, and all humankind as well.

Most systems of psychology do not even attempt to consider the dialectical interaction of the individual and society. Of course, it is difficult to understand the dynamics of two forces interacting simultaneously, particularly if there are diverse internal dynamics operating on each force. Nevertheless, our task here is to try to explain the *common sense* of social living, while also explaining the dynamics of individuals interacting with society.

SOCIAL INTEREST

Possibly the single most unique and valuable concept in Adlerian Psychology is *Gemeinschaftsgefühl,* usually translated as "social interest." We shall now provide an extensive explication of this central and important term.

Social interest has grown in meaning, frequency of use, and centrality to Adler's theory over time. Ansbacher (1978b) explained how Adler attempted to "fit" this concept into later editions of earlier works. Prior to the end of World War I, Adler did not use the concept of social interest, probably because he was still under the influence of biological and drive theories of behavior. In 1918 he first used the term *social interest* "as an innate counterforce setting limits to the expansion tendency, aggression drive, lust for power, unless 'throttled' by outer or inner forces" (1918/1957), p. 145. By 1928, and for the last 10 years of his life, Adler saw social interest as a cognitive function: an innate aptitude which may be consciously developed.

Social interest thus became a potential or an aptitude that can be developed consciously through understanding and training by others or one's self, based on a social direction for individual growth striving. Social interest can be thought of as referring to various attitudes the individual has and how the abilities or traits of the individual are employed in dealing with the social world. It can also be viewed as a mode of operating with consequences both for the individual and for the social group. Beyond that it can be conceived of as a striving toward a better future for humankind, the world, the universe.

Adler (1929) stated: "Social interest is not inborn but it is an innate potentiality which has to be consciously developed" (p. 31). Much of what we will write about in this book about counseling and psychotherapy, child education and parent education has to do with consciously developing social interest.

Adler likened social interest to identification and empathy, and said that social interest is "to see with the eyes of another, to hear with the ears of another, to feel with the heart of another" (Adler, 1956, p. 135). "Social interest means . . . a struggle for a communal form" (Adler, 1964b, p. 275). From this one might infer that social interest is only a here-and-now concept that advocates conformity and belonging to a limited social group. Adler (1964a) attempted to eliminate this common misunderstanding by saying: "It is not a question of any present-day community or society, or of political or religious forms. On the contrary, the goal that is best suited for perfection must be a goal that stands for an ideal society amongst all mankind, the ultimate fulfillment of evolution" (p. 275). Adler (1956) also gave a more general, abstract explanation of social interest: "It means particularly the interest in, or feeling with, the community *sub specie aeternitas* (under the aspect of eternity). It means the striving for a community which must be thought of as everlasting, as we could think of it if mankind had reached the goal of perfection" (p. 142).

Views of Social Interest

Dreikurs (1953) acknowledged that the grander meaning of social interest was to look at behavior from the aspect of eternity, but he stressed the difficulty of people adapting to a changing, competitive, nondemocratic social situation fraught with inequality. He stated that social interest "does not mean . . . simply a feeling of belonging to a certain group or class of people, or benevolence toward the whole race" (Dreikurs, 1953, pp. 7–8). He asserted that a feeling of belonging was part of social interest. He wrote, "The ideal expression of social interest is the ability to play the game [of life] with existing demands for cooperation and to help the group to which one belongs in its evolution closer toward a perfect form of social living" (p. 8).

Hertha Orgler (1973), stressing another meaning for the concept "community feeling," points out that "Adler does not want human herds, an objection often made; he does not want blind subordination, but open-eyed coordination. His ideal is not self-sacrifice, but self-development of the individual's abilities for his own good and for the good of humanity" (p. 85).

Lewis Way (1962) interpreted social interest with both the immediate and ideal definitions in mind. Agreeing that cooperation was regarded by Adler as the greatest challenge of his psychology, he wrote that

Cooperation with life means above all relating ourself to the only standard we have so far found—the Community. (p. 197)
But, the usual English translation of the term *Gemeinschaftsgefühl* as "social feeling" is not fully adequate to convey Adler's meaning. The feeling for the *Gemeinschaft* is wider than the term "society" suggests. It embraces the sense of relatedness, not only to the human community, but to the whole of life, and

is therefore the highest expression of Adler's concept of Totality. It means the human being's sense of himself as a part of the unit of existence in contrast to the fear of standing in the cosmos as a single unrelated organism. (pp. 201–202)

Social feeling is the ideal Goal of Perfection, the goal at which all religions and moralities aim, since . . . the community is the fundamental concern of all. It is also the ideal norm of human behavior, which should serve us as a measure for every deviation. (p. 203)

Allen (1971) says that social interest

involves what might be termed an "extended self." A person whose sense of self extends beyond his ego is one who feels inextricable from the rest of mankind. He feels enriched by the accomplishments and joys of at least a number of others, and shares a measure of their sorrows and suffering. On the other hand, a lack of social interest may issue into an "extended ego." Such a person feels very much alone; he stands as a solitary warrior to protect his prestige from the multiform depredations which threaten on every hand. . . . Lacking "social interest," or what Tillich deemed "the courage to be as a part," he must remain ever on the alert and girded for battle.

All of us are determined to find a solution to this problem, the problem of place, the problem of belonging one way or another. (p. 17)

Heinz Ansbacher (1977) succinctly says, ". . . social interest actually means not only an interest in others but an *interest in the interests of others*" (p. 57, emphasis Ansbacher's). Kazan (1978) states that "Caring, as developed by Meyeroff (1971), expresses the range of meanings implicit and explicit in Adler's term" (pp. 9–10). "Caring is a process through which one helps another to grow and to actualize himself. In addition to caring for people, one may also care for many things, thereby helping them to grow. Caring gives meaning and order to life. When one's caring is comprehensive and inclusive, there is a basic stability in one's life and one is 'in place' in the world" (p. 8).

Bickhard and Ford (1976) raise a number of issues:

We know that social interest involves an innate potential for the development of the capacity for cooperative fellowship, but we do not know of what that potential, or that development, or that capacity consists. It was Adler's insight to recognize that social fellowship requires its own cognitive and motivational prerequisites; it remains for others to specify what those prerequisites are . . .

Another issue left unresolved is the relationship of social interest to morality. A human ethic must be grounded on the existence of choice and freedom within the framework of human nature. Adler's recognition of choice is explicit, and his discussions of social interest constitute a primary contribution to the understanding of human nature. . . .

The issue of the relationship of social interest to meaningfulness has also been raised by Adler. It would seem clear that human fellowship can manifest a powerful participation in an individual's construction of a meaningful life. . . . The structure of potential meaning must in some way be framed by the nature of being human. . . . (pp. 48–49)

A fundamental human desire is to belong. Whatever the evolutionary basis, such as necessity of mothering for a child to survive, all children want to belong, to "find their place" in the family, in the school, in the street—the three arenas in which they mainly develop. When they grow up, they want to find their place in their families, with their friends, and in their work. Human beings truly are social creatures.

The term *belonging* means about the same as *Gemeinschaftsgfühl* at the interpersonal level, but not at a more general transcendent level (Nystul, 1976). Belonging means feeling part of, being an integral element of, an essential piece of a society, whether it be a factory, a military unit, a school or one's family. If one is not inside the system, one is outside, looking in—and one is alone. This is a terrible feeling, a felt loneliness, not to belong.

We all want to belong, to find our place in society. Wise parents know this and help their children know they are loved and wanted. In a good school children will be supportive of each other. The problem in all groups is for each individual to develop as fully as possible without generating rancor and strife —so that each person will want everyone else to expand his or her potentialities to the maximum without envy or jealousy. This occurs when all persons feel they belong fully.

Many biological theorists, from Charles Darwin to Konrad Lorenz, agree that evolution is a synergistic process. Many biological theorists thus agree with Adler that something akin to social interest is part of humans' ancient evolutionary heritage. Essentially an Adlerian sentiment is stated by Allee (1931):

With the development of the nervous system, closer cooperation becomes possible and larger numbers are affected. There is much reason for thinking that many of the advances in evolution have come about through the selection of cooperating groups rather than through the selection of individuals. This implies that the two great natural principles of struggle for existence and of cooperation are not wholly in opposition, but that each may have reacted upon the other in determining the trend of animal evolution (p. 361). (Huber, Lomax, Robinson, & Huber, 1978, pp. 217–218)

Individual Psychology asserts that humans not only need other humans, but they also need to be needed, to have a feeling of belonging. Indeed, the absence of this feeling of belonging and of being wanted is probably the keenest and most devastating of all emotions, of being alone, being rejected, isolated.

The Practical Consequences of Social Interest

If, as some ethologists claim, people are fundamentally hostile and aggressive, we can expect that people will fight forever. There can only be temporary periods of peace since war is the natural state of humankind. But, if Adler is correct in his assumption of the social basis of human nature, we can make the following statement.

Wars (and other group conflicts) are a function of the desire of people to protect their group from danger of the aggression of other groups. Consequently, subjectively, most people at war are not offensive but, rather, defensive. They don't want to attack but only want to defend. War, paradoxically, is essentially an attempt at love, not hate! Love for family, for country, rather than hatred for the enemy, is the motivator! People who express hate are asking for revenge against wrongs (real or imagined) of others. The analogy to a dog who attacks an intruder is appropriate. A postman comes on the premises and the householder's dog attacks the postman. From the point of view of the postman, the dog is assaulting him, and is vicious. However, from the viewpoint of the dog, he is only defending his territory from an intruder, and *he* feels aggressed against. We have here an excellent example of multiple ignorance: the dog and the postman each see the other as the aggressor. Should the postman kick the dog, then the dog's hypothesis is confirmed, and should the dog bite the postman, the postman's hypothesis is confirmed: the other *is* dangerous, aggressive, and hostile.

It is possible for people to live in amity if, indeed, as Individual Psychologists assert, humans essentially have a need to belong. The answer seems to be to enlarge and increase our perception of the "human family," to include all of humanity.

Alienation and anomie are major problems in our society. Anomie refers to a society of individuals who do not share common values, common ideas, common ideals—each individual "doing his own thing"—separated from one another.

The same situation sometimes appears in families. Some families are loosely organized, made up of people just living in the same household. Naturally, some families approach the ideal of friendly warm relationships.

People can even become alienated from themselves. In essence they have a prejudice about themselves. People frequently come not to like themselves if they are constantly criticized. Parents with too high expectations tend to have children who become self-alienated. Groups of individuals who suffer social obloquy, such as southern blacks in pre-World War II days, are likely to have a common feeling of inferiority, each person feeling that he/she was not as good as they should be. This tends to generate feelings of inadequacy and isolation, leading to alienation from one's self. Alcoholics, homosexuals, drug addicts also often have self-alienation feelings.

Very distressing, of course, are youths who feel that they just are no good accepting their parents' criticisms as gospel. It is often healthier for these youths to form bonds with other youths to have some commonality. Often this becomes a kind of "underground" group since practically all adult-controlled forces—schools, churches, newspapers, radio, and television—boom the same message of youth being deficient.

It should be evident by now that alienation is the opposite side of social interest. A person who feels a part of society, who sees society as being accepting, has *Gemeinschaftsgefühl,* the antithesis of alienation.

Adlerian family counseling attempts to introduce behavior and concepts to make children feel wanted and belonging, not "good" or "bad"; Adlerian schools avoid dichotomizing children into "smart" and "stupid"; Adlerian therapy attempts to make people learn how to accept themselves with their frailties and weaknesses. These efforts are all directed toward generating social interest and away from alienation.

Individuals need some sense of belonging to an identifiable group. This may be a group with which they are constantly in contact or may be a group with which they feel affiliation by virtue of common ideology, but there must be such a group. In our experience, persons who profess social interest at the transcendent level to all of humanity, but who have no personal feelings of group belonging, are really expressing grandiose strivings for personal superiority. We have seen this phenomenon particularly with an occasional, isolated graduate student studying a foreign culture. It is as if he or she were saying, "When I know everything about this language and/or this culture, I will be accepted and then I will belong there."

Thomas Szasz (1961) considers "mental illness" to be a myth. Whether it is real or not is a matter of definition. From the Adlerian point of view, every individual is seen as engaged in the process of accommodating to life, adjusting to other people, finding a place in society, fulfilling potentials—in other words, attaining goals. Some individuals go into useless directions such as delinquency or insanity, which are mistaken ways of attaining feelings of superiority or of avoiding feelings of inferiority. Consequently, such maladjusted people are viewed by Adlerians as mistaken, not sick.

Conventional psychiatrists see the so-called schizophrenic as sick. Some Adlerians refuse to take this position. Perhaps the outstanding exponent of applying Adlerian thinking to schizophrenics is Joshua Bierer (1951, 1955; Bierer & Browne, 1960; Bierer & Buckman, 1961), who essentially takes the same position that Adlerians take toward treating normal children: *give them as much responsibility as possible: let them experience the natural and logical consequences of their behavior; and do as little to and for them as possible.*

The neurotic, the delinquent, and the psychotic are not different types of individuals; they differ from normals in that they have found useless methods of attempting to achieve the common goals of superiority. The schizophrenic is within his own self-created world and if he lives long enough he becomes God, needing to have no contact with anyone, secure in his knowledge of his personal superiority. The neurotic, through feelings of guilt and other evidence of heroic suffering, and the delinquent, with anger against the world, also have gone in socially wrong directions.

"Mentally ill" persons have mistaken goals as part of their life styles. Their behavior and thoughts are deviant, out of touch with the common sense of social living. They are people who do not operate on the basis of social interest. They are selfish—overconcerned with themselves—and so isolate themselves from others.

Adler (1956) wrote:

> In a neurosis we are always confronted with a highly placed goal of personal superiority. . . . That such a . . . goal of personal superiority betokens a lack of the proper measure of social interest . . . is understandable. The striving for personal superiority and the nondevelopment of social interest are both mistakes. However, they are not two mistakes which the individual has made; they are one and the same mistake. (pp. 240–241)
>
> All failures—neurotics, psychotics, criminals, drunkards, problem children, suicides, perverts, and prostitutes—are failures because they are lacking in social interest. (p. 156)

Adlerians generally equate social interest and mental health. Persons without social interest cannot be healthy, whereas persons with social interest may be healthy. Social interest is a partial definition of mental health.

> Social interest does not cause mental health. . . . Conversely, failures of social interest do not cause or explain failures of mental health; social interest is a [partial] explication of mental health, a definition. It describes what mental health is, not why it develops nor where it comes from. The theoretical function of explanation, causal or otherwise, must be served by other elements of the theory. For these functions we turn to such concepts as the inferiority [symptom] complex and the striving for personal superiority. (Bickhard & Ford, 1976, p. 49)

EQUALITY

A major philosophical aspect of Individual Psychology is equality. We see this force in all aspects of life. For example, revolutions are due generally to the desire of those who feel oppressed to have what others have. We see this tendency in groups generally held in obloquy—alcoholics, homosexuals, prisoners, drug addicts, gamblers, prostitutes—to form groups to ask for political and social equality. We see this mostly, of course, with adolescents who want to assert their power and want equality. And, naturally, whoever is "on top" —be it a dictator, or a "straight" person, or a parent—fights against the efforts of the underprivileged or underdogs to attain parity.

Adlerians take the notion that unequals are equal! This semantic trick causes some confusion. How can a child be equal to its parents? By "unequal" we mean objectively unequal, such as less powerful, less intelligent, less capable —as in the case of children, and by "equal" we mean at parity in the eyes of God and the law and society. Similarity does not mean equality and dissimilarity does not mean inequality (Corsini, 1981).

The Adlerian position on equality is best seen in the various Adlerian parenting books, such as Dreikurs and Soltz (1964), Beecher and Beecher (1966), Dinkmeyer and McKay (1973), and Corsini and Painter (1975).

Horizontal versus Vertical Views

Were one asked to explain the difference between the "normal" and the "abnormal" person one might simply move a hand from side to side horizontally and nod, and then run a hand up and down and shake one's head negatively. Horizontal—yes; vertical—no.

Adler's view of humanity is horizontal. All people are seen as equally worthy of respect and consideration, even though they are obviously unequal in some other respects. Neurotics, filled with feelings of inferiority, see people vertically. They see the world filled with people who are better or who are worse than they; and so they are in constant apprehension about their position in life. If they could take a horizontal view, then they would feel as good as anyone else, and would not be bothered by their status in life.

Allred (1974) discusses the horizontal view as leading to contentment and happiness, while the vertical view means one is "on a ladder" viewing others up and down. The vertical person is concerned with getting attention, bossing, counterhurting and disabling behavior (which are Dreikurs' four goals applied to adults). According to Allred, the horizontal plane relates to the concept of equality and responsibility of each to each. Horizontal-vertical contrasts are essentially religious-ethical views inherent in Adlerian thinking, and they reflect the concept of social interest related to mental health, of equality and democratic living in opposition to striving for personal superiority to be "above" others.

COOPERATION

Suppose that you were one of a dozen people shipwrecked on a deserted island. Assume that everyone on the island is about the same age, about the same physical condition. You are now in a world of your own. Let us now assume that to get the necessities of life (food, shelter, water, clothing) it is necessary for everyone to give 10 hours of hard work daily to the little community—and also that no single person could live on his/her own but would depend on others. Say only one person knew how to fish, and only one knew how to make a fire, and only one was able to climb to the top of a coconut tree, and only one was strong enough to kill deer and wild pigs, and only one was clever enough to make shelters. Now, let us say that one of the group simply did not want to do any work, be it gathering branches for firewood or drawing water. This person expects to eat, drink, and sleep.

What would happen in such a situation is not difficult to figure out. *Work —or die.* Individuals who deeply believe that the world owes them a living abound in our world. Some simply will not cooperate.

Where do such attitudes come from? Essentially such attitudes are derived from the environment. This means essentially the home environment, and usually the relationship with the mother. From the beginning there is a close interaction between mother and child. What happens when the child cries? Will mother drop everything and run to see why the child is crying? Will she pick him up, check if he is dry, try to feed him, and so on and so on? Or will she let him cry for a while and then make a cursory minimal investigation? Or will she let him cry and cry and cry? We are not at this point giving advice or making any comments about parenting. We want to show that mothers may react differently to their children's crying, and these different approaches are likely to have different effects on the developing attitudes of the children. Keeping in mind that our present concern is with cooperation, it becomes evident that in some cases a kind of agreement occurs between mothers and infants. Should the mother generally run at the first cry, this leads to an understanding. Should the mother make a cursory investigation, there also is an understanding. And if the mother comes only very reluctantly, there, too, is a different understanding.

The child learns to expect certain behavior from mother, especially if mother's behavior is predictable. The wise mother operates in such a way that the child learns to adjust to her schedule. He will learn the difference between wanting to eat at 4:00 A.M. and at 4:00 P.M. He will learn not to cry for no reason. He will learn that mother is not at his beck and call. He learns to adjust to the needs of others. He learns cooperation. This fundamental attitude is learned literally from the cradle. And so our mythical person who expects to eat without working on the deserted island may have gotten this pampered attitude early in life.

Humans and animals are at the same time cooperative and competitive. The question is which is the better way to live? This is a philosophical question which Adlerians answer simply: cooperation. We believe that mutual assistance, working harmoniously together, is the final answer because fundamentally we are social creatures, and only in a truly cooperative society can we find peace and fulfillment.

This does not mean that people should not try to achieve the best they can. A child who does his best in school, the youth who goes on to a professional career, the manufacturer who tries to become wealthy—each and everyone who works within the law is contributing to the commonweal. There is no conflict between a person amounting to as much as he can and cooperating with the world. Thus, should we, right now, working on this book, produce a volume that will be well received and sell well, we shall be at the same time enriching ourselves and the world. While we are, in a sense, competing with every book in psychology and more specifically with books in Adlerian psychology, at the same time we may be enhancing the sales of similar books. We would hope, for example, that the excellent edited books of the Ansbachers, from which we have drawn a good deal of our primary material, and the original works of Alfred Adler, from which we have searched for supporting concepts, will receive further attention as a result of the success of this book.

Cooperation and competition are interesting positions; and not always in conflict. Thus, in playing tennis each party is trying to win (competition) and yet each is cooperating (agreeing to play, agreeing on the rules, and so on). Even in fights there is a kind of cooperation. So when you see two children bickering, you may think that they are only competing, but actually if you think about it a bit more, often they are cooperating, each struggling within rules to achieve supremacy. Cooperation underlies all progress, and even useful competition.

USEFUL AND USELESS BEHAVIOR

Say a person is looking around for a rope. If he is going to lift something with it his behavior serves a good purpose; but if he intends to hang himself, this does not serve a good purpose.

This is an example of a value judgment, something that scientists avoid doing—eschewing "good" and "bad" and "right" and "wrong." A counselor generally attempts to avoid putting his/her values on someone else. Nevertheless, as human beings we have personal values, and we approve or disapprove of various actions of others to various extents, and we certainly do judge these behaviors, even though as counselors or therapists we may sometimes not express our opinions.

Adlerians use the terms *useful* and *useless* in a broader sense than "right" and "wrong" or "good" and "bad"—we ask ourselves whether any behavior will (*a*) succeed in achieving the intended objective, and (*b*) whether the objective itself is worthwhile.

Dr. Rudolf Dreikurs used to illustrate an example of (*a*) above by getting up from his chair and deliberately walking into the wall, then backing up and trying again. "See," he would say, "that is an example of useless behavior. I want to go out of the room, but I don't want to use the door. I therefore decide to go out through the wall. I don't succeed but I won't give up, and I will try again and again."

This kind of repetitive behavior is an example of useless behavior. An example illustrates a very common situation.

Example.   Mother has six children, ages 6 to 15. She estimates that she tells each one, on the average, about twice a day to clean their rooms. She has been doing it for every child since they were about age four. Simple arithmetic says that she does this kind of nagging behavior about 700 times per child annually, and at the present time, with six children, she is saying, "clean your room" or "make your bed" and the like about 4,000 times a year. For the oldest she has done this for 12 years, or has said this to him approximately 4,000 × 8, or 32,000 times. Overall, we estimated that she had made this kind of statement well over 150,000 times, and has about 150,000 times to go!

This is an example of useless behavior. Why would someone make more or less the same statement close to a quarter of a million times? The reason is evident: sometimes the children obey mother's request, and in this manner they more or less conditioned her. The mother, who wanted a neat house, did not know what else to do. She felt if she let things go, the house would be a jumble. On top of that she got confirmation of the rightness of her behavior since this was exactly what other mothers were doing.

From our point of view her behavior was useless, since it really did not accomplish what she really wanted: for her children to become self-sufficient and neat on their own.

The end of this story is that this mother was advised to (*a*) have an Adlerian family council (see Chapter 14), (*b*) ask the children whether they wanted to be solely responsible for their own rooms, (*c*) and if they said "yes" (they all did), for the mother (*d*) to agree *never again* to say anything about their rooms. The mother did just that—and eventually this system worked! The children began to take care of their own rooms. We now see two kinds of mother's behavior—repetitions of instructions and orders, which did not work; and the use of logical consequences (see Chapter 14), which did work. From the point of view of the mother, at both times she intended the same results, but one method was useless—it didn't work; and the other method was useful—it worked!

The terms *useful* and *useless* are used by Adlerians in another sense such as when the behavior is evidently directed to a useless goal, whether it be hurting oneself (as in the case of using narcotics) or of hurting others (as in the case of a child who is a bully). We can catalog literally thousands of useless common behaviors, such as nagging, overeating, smoking, being critical, aiming for impossible goals, committing criminal acts, doing reckless things, and so forth. Were we to examine any individual throughout the day, we would find that some people perform a fairly high percentage of useless acts while others perform relatively few.

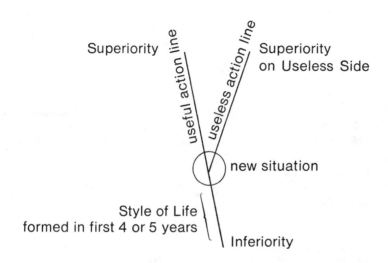

FIGURE 5–1. *Deviating to the useless side in face of a new situation.*
From Raymond J. Corsini, *Current Personality Theories,* Itasca, Il.:
F. E. Peacock Publishers, Inc., 1977, p. 60.

COURAGE

Life can be seen as two-dimensional movement: upward represents movement toward goals; and to the right or to the left represents movement toward useless or useful goals. How can we best describe the inner person in terms of concepts and feelings if they deviate to the right (useless) or to the left (useful)? Adler suggested the concept of *courage,* which essentially consists of two elements: *activity* (rate of movement toward goals) and *social interest.* Consequently, the highly active person who has interest in others is courageous—ready and willing to act to achieve in terms of his feeling of belonging to others.

Sophie Lazarsfeld's well-known statement, "Have the courage to be imperfect," has become a motto even found on T-shirts of Adlerians. The basic concept is that if one operates for the benefit of the group, it would be not trying rather than failing that would be the failure.

Courage is seen in many ways. One example has to do with marriage. A person could, subjectively, marry above him/herself (to obtain security, or to have a protector), or could, subjectively, marry below (to get a servant—one who could be kicked around). Either of these two kinds of marriage is imperfect and shows lack of courage. A good marriage would be between equals, people who neither look up nor down at the other. Any assumptions of one's superiority or inferiority over one's mate shows lack of courage, wanting to be inferior or superior. Even infidelity represents lack of courage—the incapacity of a person to totally trust another person. For this reason, Adler made the enigmatic statement, "Two is less than one."

Another example of lack of courage is found in criminals. The sneak thief is unable to face life on its own terms. The confirmed criminal—with his antisocial attitudes, who sees all police officers as bribe takers, all attorneys as being interested only in fattening their pockets, all judges as concerned only with their own fortunes—is a person who does not have the courage to belong to the world at large and who finds to his own satisfaction that others are really crooked like himself.

In psychotherapy, frequently the important aspect of the treatment is to get the person to become active in a constructive manner—to change his/her way of operating to achieve greater success, to give up self-defeating patterns. Essentially, this process helps the person to show greater courage.

RESPONSIBILITY

Individual Psychology sees individuals as responsible for their behavior. From the Individual Psychology view one is responsible for acting in the social interest and thus for behaving usefully. The natural consequences of social living make one chargeable for one's actions. The pain and suffering that come from useless behavior, from not facing one's responsibility and proceeding with courage, are natural consequences of a person's mistaken goals. If you do not hold up your end in life, it will fall on your foot.

PREJUDICE

Prejudice means prejudgment of an individual in terms of group membership. While it is entirely possible that people of certain reference groups may have some special qualities in common in contrast to other groups as a result of their common culture, some members of these groups will not have these qualities. To give an example, Oriental college students tend, as a rule, to be much more socially reserved and unlikely to ask questions in classes than are Caucasians. This is an experience one of the authors has had in teaching in Hawaii. However, there are some forward and aggressive Oriental students and some seclusive and quiet Caucasian students. Consequently, to acknowledge the fact that some groups do differ—as groups—from other groups in some behavioral respects is only to state what is true; but to prejudge any individual from any group as sticking to that group's norms is an example of prejudice. So, while Italians as a group are likely to show their feelings openly and in contrast Britons as a group are likely to be reserved, one cannot predict any single Italian or Briton no matter what his background is. To make assumptions about individuals in terms of group norms is an example of prejudice.

Prejudice generally tends to make another error. On a scale of favorability, the prejudiced person is likely to underestimate not only an individual but also the reference group in terms of particular clusters of traits. For example, as Clark (1965/1967) has shown, whites tend to denigrate blacks constantly, and thereby to harm them by actually "generating" the very traits that they assume blacks have. This is a kind of self-fulfilling prophecy.

What are the origins of prejudice? Why are all of us to some degree prejudiced—for and against various groups (since prejudice can be positive as well as negative)? The essential reason for prejudice comes out of feelings of inferiority. Prejudiced people are fearful, and they tend to establish stereotypes as scapegoats to enhance their self-image. This is an example of depreciation of others, which the neurotic does to safeguard his/her own image. When grouped, individuals who have the same sort of inferiority, whether it be social, economic, or whatever, seek for some common means of blaming their situation on some other classes of individuals. The sustaining factor is a feeling of inferiority.

Children, in their attempts to achieve acceptance—this most important of all social needs—will parrot their parents blindly, and accept their views and values unthinkingly. As the song in the musical *South Pacific* goes, "prejudice has got to be taught."

In the same way that there is an innate potentiality for the development of social interest, there is an innate potentiality for aggression. As people can learn to like, identify, and empathize with others, they can also learn to dislike them. It might appear that when someone identifies, empathizes, cares for the individual members of the group to which one belongs, he/she has social interest. This may be true. However, if the group membership gives the person the feeling that he is better than others and the purpose of the person's efforts to maintain a place in the group is to feel better than others who are not in the group, he cannot be said to have social interest.

Prejudice functions in this way: Undoubtedly there was for some a spirit of belonging to the group when the Brownshirts goose stepped through Nazi Berlin, or when Klansmen in sheets chased someone. They no doubt felt big and important and better, *and* a part of the group. But they had to feel part of the group in order to feel big and important, and they had to have someone, some other group, to be against and be better than. Their behavior was useless but, at least for the moment, their inferiority feelings were appeased. True social interest relates to all people at all times in all ways. Essentially, the message is: Love thy neighbor.

MALE-FEMALE RELATIONS

Why have women so often been seen as inferior to men? The greatest writers —Shakespeare, Hugo, Goethe, Dante; the greatest poets—Milton, Blake, Homer, Heine; the greatest composers—Beethoven, Brahms, Bach, Bizet; the greatest painters—Giotto, Rembrandt, daVinci, Corot; the greatest scientists —Copernicus, Galileo, Newton, Fermi—are men. And yet, in these fields— writing, music, painting, science—apparently women have as much chance as men to succeed.

How do we explain that three of the greatest women authors took on male names: George Eliot, George Sand, Isak Dinesen? How do we explain this in view of the fact that boys and girls overall do about the same on tests of intelligence and aptitude? How do we explain the fact that in private relation-ships between men and women, as in marriage, overall there is essential equality in common sense, in determination, in leadership, in control?

Why is it that men and women are essentially alike and yet differ so enor-mously in their productions and achievements? Why is it that out of a thou-sand names of eminent people, as might be found, for example, at the back of an unabridged dictionary, only 10 or 20 will be women?

One possible explanation, accepted by many, is that men are inherently superior in these areas, or are "naturally" (that is to say, biologically) superior in terms of creativity, drive, ambition, motivation, and the rest of the traits that lead to being outstanding in the arts, literature, science, and technology. This explanation is probably just as fallacious as the argument offered by some, principally Ashley Montagu (1954), that women are naturally superior.

The Adlerian point of view in this matter is relatively simple: all humans, regardless of sex, race, or other biological factors, are essentially equal in potential in terms of anything that has to do with creativity, productivity, inventiveness, and so forth, yet biological aspects can limit women, such as child bearing. However, the important and compelling reason for these differ-ences is that throughout the Western (and possibly also Eastern) culture the basic historical notions held by both men and women support the different roles that males and females should play. This is a very subtle prejudice and leads to subtle discrimination. We find it in such concepts that the man is the head of the family, using the word "man" to mean "human," using the pronoun "he" or "him" to mean he/she and him/her. For example, Orthodox Jewish men say a morning prayer in which they thank God for having made them men rather than women.

In a recent social gathering in which one of us participated, with all the men being Adlerians and all the women liberated, after dinner (prepared and set by the women), the women picked up and washed the dishes while the men sat around and discussed equality! No one realized the incongruousness between the convictions of the group—and their behaviors.

What this all means is that very insistent, insidious propaganda, found in the home, school, television, books, streets, and so on, act to limit women's movements. Subtle discrimination exists everywhere—and what is more, often the very people who don't like it (as in the example just given) participate in it unwittingly (or wittingly when it suits their purpose).

Alfred Adler was the first of the major psychologists to realize the harmfulness of male dominance and female submission. In a kind of unconscious retaliation, many women have become the critics and the arbiters of proper behavior, and they tend to take on the position of moral superiority. ". . . men continuously strive for superiority over women, while women are constantly dissatisfied with the male privileges" (Adler, 1927b, p. 97).

Male superiority is accepted as fact by many men and many women. God created man first, and then from a rib created woman, more or less as an afterthought, or as a companion or playmate for man, according to Bible mythology. In ancient Rome and among the ancient Jewish communities, the question of whether a woman had a soul was hotly debated. Even in Switzerland, a most advanced country, women did not have the vote until recently, and many of its laws are still grossly unfavorable to women. Among many religious groups, peculiar limitations are set on women. At the Wailing Wall of Jerusalem, the men and women are separated, with women getting a smaller portion of the wall. In Roman Catholic churches for many years the women were expected to cover their heads; and as recently as 1981 priests of the church must be males.

Derision and deprecation of women are common in our literature and mythology. Eve was the cause of man's downfall for eating of the apple of the tree of knowledge after listening to the serpent, and she induced Adam to sin also. In the heroic books of ancient literature, such as the *Odyssey*, the *Iliad*, the *Aeneid*, *Orlando Furioso*, the *Divine Comedy*, and *Paradise Lost*, the main heroic characters are always men, while women are depicted as frivolous, shrewish, fearful, and unreliable. In "La donna e mobile" (woman is fickle) a well-known aria, woman is referred to as "La piuma al vento" (a feather in the wind) and this is the general concept with which we have been imbued.

In contrast, and yet still in deprecation, is the veneration of the woman as mother, that is as the servant of man. The self-sacrificing woman as the mother in Victor Hugo's *Les Misérables* who sells her hair and then her teeth to buy food for her hungry child is seen as the epitome of female virtue. She becomes noble as she sacrifices herself, especially for a boy-child.

The low esteem for women is not only accepted by men. Tragically, it is accepted also by women, who have accepted the cultural stereotype as true in many cases. Of course, many women have defied and stood up against these limitations, such as Rosa Bonheur, Sally Stanford, Elinor Brown, Florence Nightingale, and George Sand. But historically they represented the exceptions that proved the rule.

Masculine Protest

Against the backdrop of the contemporary scene, to understand the formerly important concept of masculine protest, we have to look back to the early 1900s when it was almost universally assumed that men and women were psychologically different: men were seen as strong, brave, determined, aggressive, while women were weak, fearful, compromising, and gentle. In short it was "good" to be a man. Parents hoped that their first child would be a boy. Women did the cooking and the housework. Men went out into the world to struggle to earn a living. When there was serious talk, the men excused the women, who were expected to talk about embroidery and their gynecologists while the men discussed politics and business. In short, in the Western world, at least, both sexes generally accepted the fiction of male superiority.

As a consequence, since it was "good" to be male and not so good to be female, men wanted to be real men and women wanted to have male qualities and prerogatives. Men feared being dominated by women who would use their wiles to entrap them. To be ruled by a mere woman—why, that would be terrible. A man should be master of his own house—was he not the head of the family? Sexually, he did the pursuing and the seducing. A married woman submitted to the man. It was even improper for her to show interest in or to enjoy the sexual act.

In short, during Adler's productive years, masculinity was seen as superior to femininity. Because everyone wants to be superior, one wants to be masculine—more like a "real" man (the fiction of the real man as hard and powerful, determined and strong). Consequently, Adler used the term *masculine protest* to mean a desire to be superior, the desire for perfectionism. Historically, the same notion was said in many ways: the importance of aggression, the importance of being masculine, and the importance of perfection. In all cases, the drive was away from inferiority, a movement upward from weakness toward superiority.

The Women's Movement

A comparison may be made between Freud's term *penis envy* and Adler's term masculine protest. This comparison illustrates the differences between Freud and Adler and their systems of thought. Penis envy means simply that a girl wants a penis—that is, she would prefer to be a boy since he has something she does not have. This notion is supported by "castration fear," Freud's notion that boys are afraid their fathers may castrate them because of their Oedipus complex.

Adler completely disagreed with these ideas and saw individuals as concerned with power, achieving, attaining, or in White's (1959) view, with being competent. Consequently, that women would want men's privileges would be understandable, and indeed even to this day women protest the "superiority" that men generally have in employment and other social relationships.

In psychotherapy we frequently find that our clients who may be slightly built, or not very tall, who feel sexually below par or who otherwise feel that they are not "real" men in the swaggering tradition of movie heroes, are unhappy with their lot. The masculine protest is comprehensible as a social protest, of women against men's privileges and as a form of inferiority feeling of men not being as much of a "real man" as they think they should be.

In his book *What Life Should Mean to You* (1962), first published in 1931, Adler stated that "unless we truly have the feeling that men and women are equal . . . we shall have a very great obstacle to the success of marriage" (p. 275).

It is interesting to note, as Mosak and Schneider (1977) point out, that Adler did not refer to the "opposite sex" in referring to women but, rather, to the "other sex."

Frequently when individuals of an oppressed group begin to react against the dominant group, they make the same chauvinistic mistakes that had been made against them. Thus, we have concepts such as "black is beautiful," thereby implying that nonblacks are not beautiful, or "women are naturally superior" or "gay is good," and naturally from an Adlerian point of view, while such backlash concepts are understandable, they are equally erroneous.

The important thing to keep in mind is that value distinctions of male/-female, black/white, and others, are primarily *social* in nature rather than biological. While Freud and others in the psychoanalytic movement are essentially biologically biased, Adlerians see these stated differences as coming out of social attitudes, which in turn spring out of feelings of inferiority with attendant fears of being dominated. In short, men, afraid of the potential power of women, try to keep them down and in their place. And women, afraid of the power of men, try to overcome their social superiority.

Adler stated (1918/1957) that "The advantages of being a man, under such conditions [referring to society as it was], are very alluring. . . . It would seem that every woman wanted to be a man" (p. 108). This view is certainly not true today. Adler actually urged social reforms and legislative action to permit equality of men and women. Vytautas J. Bieliauskas (1974) reported three studies that examined projective test results of male and female college students which generally showed that there still was a preference for male roles in terms of stereotypes among males and females. Bieliauskas stated that "As long as the feminists are trying to show their *masculine* superiority they support the superiority of the masculine sex and thus accentuate the masculine protest" (p. 96). Jeanne Block (1973) makes the following related statement: "A redefinition of conventional sex roles and revamping of socialization practices are required if our society goal is to encourage individuation and personal maturity for our young" (p. 526).

Adler wrote, in 1927:

> We have no reason to oppose the present goals of the women's movement of freedom and equal rights. Rather, we must actively support them, because ultimately happiness and joy in the life of all humanity will depend on the creation of conditions that will enable women to become reconciled with their feminine role, and on how men will answer the problem of their relationship to women. (Adler, 1978, p. 24)

LIFE TASKS

Dreikurs, in his *Fundamentals of Adlerian Psychology* (1953), said:

> The human community sets three tasks for every individual. They are: work, which means contributing to the welfare of others; friendship, which embraces social relationships with comrades and relatives; and love, which is the most intimate union. (pp. 4–5)

In summing up the social aspects of the dynamics of personality, the Adlerian idea of life tasks is useful. In the quotation from Dreikurs, we can see that the life tasks which every individual has to face are viewed as being set by "the human community." These tasks are ours to meet by virtue of being members of the human community. When we think of the tasks—*work, friends,* and *love*—we realize how crucially important they are to the individual and to society, neither of which can achieve fulfillment without the successful resolution of these tasks. These tasks indicate the intertwining of the individual and society in Individual Psychology theory.

A fourth life task, "getting along with oneself" (Dreikurs & Mosak, 1967), and a fifth, the existential task, "the need to adjust to the problems beyond the mere existence on this earth and to find meaning to our lives, to realize the significance of human existence through transcendental and spiritual involvement" (Dreikurs & Mosak, 1966, p. 2), have been suggested. Although these additional tasks are not universally accepted among Adlerians, they do point to issues to be resolved.

The self life task and the existential life task are resolvable within the framework of the other three life tasks, as active, participating, equal members of society. One can only truly get along with oneself if one feels worthy, adequate, not inferior. One would have great difficulty finding meaning and significance in life if one is involved primarily in compensating for feelings of inferiority. In Individual Psychology the individual is seen, at least initially, as judging self-worth in relation to perceptions of others' worth. Without active interaction with others, one cannot come to a realistic sense of self-worth if one is not pursuing the challenges of the three life tasks.

Adler introduced the life tasks "for the sake of clarity." In their fullest sense they can be used to give great clarity to the human situation and are all encompassing. The notion of the life tasks is also useful in counseling and therapy, as will be discussed in Chapter 10. In this section, we emphasize the complete interrelating of the individual, his personality and behavior, and the social world, in its finite tasks and existential task—to the demand that to live the healthiest life, one needs social interest.

RELIGION

Most systems of psychology take a neutral position toward religion. In short, they have no position. Some schools of thought have a decidedly negative attitude, seeing religion as a relic of a superstitious past. Freud and Ellis are examples of theorists with strong negative attitudes toward religion.

Adlerians as individuals vary in their religious orientations, since some are atheists and some are ministers, priests, or rabbis. However, generally the most common Adlerian position toward religion is positive, viewing God as the concept of perfection. Whether one thinks that God created man or man created God, in either case God can be seen as a symbolization of superiority and perfection.

Adler, in trying to understand human nature, emphasized the importance of creativity. A person's creativity may be equated to God in the person. God is the creator. As a person creates his or her own personality, then in some manner that person, too, is a creator. If so, then the individual has responsibility of his or her own personality. Adlerians are against the mechanistic theories of the psychoanalysts on the one hand and of the behavior modifiers on the other. We posit the creative aspect of individuals which one might equate with a "soul" or with "Godliness." For Adler, religion was a manifestation of social interest (Jahn & Adler, 1933). Evil could be equated to error in life style (Ellenberger, 1970, p. 625).

Therefore, Adlerians need not be religious in the conventional sense—that is to say, they need not believe in a God as described in the Bible, for example, but they nevertheless believe that there is more to humanity than biological and cultural factors. This "extra," called creativity, might be equated to God. This "extra" is another unknown and probably unknowable factor. This same position could easily be taken by a priest and an atheist: both agree that there is something transpersonal in humans, beyond heredity and society, that must be taken into account. The priest might call this factor God or the Soul, while the atheist might call it Creativity or Uniqueness.

The Golden Rule

Religion may be seen as being a kind of organized "as if" conceptualization of cosmology, an attempt to establish a view of humanity that extends before birth and after death and which attempts to regulate human behavior—a total philosophy of life. Its origins are many, and psychologically may relate to fear of the unknown, such as what happens to a person's "spirit" or "soul" or "pneuma" after death. Also, the question of "luck" or "fortune" may be involved, such as "Why was my comrade killed in battle rather than me?" or "Why is it that last week I found food but this week I cannot find any?" In terms of regulating human behavior, the promise of reward after death, such as coming back to life as a higher organism or going to paradise, and the threat of punishment, such as going to hell after death if one has "sinned"—that is, if one has harmed others or violated God's commandments—are "intended" to keep people from misbehaving. Practically all religions have all sorts of injunctions, some apparently reasonable, such as "Thou shalt not kill," to some that appear unreasonable, such as "You must not eat in the presence of women."

In the last analysis, the essential component of most mature religions seems to be nothing else but the Golden Rule—*Do unto others as you would have others do unto you.* And in this sense, *Gemeinschaftsgefühl* is simply another variation of the Golden Rule, a restatement of the essence of religions.

Chapter 6

The Creative Self and Its Structure

Individual Psychology firmly holds that every normal individual is responsible for his or her behavior since we all have choices. Even though an individual's choice is limited to some degree by heredity and society, people generally create their own situations, make their own decisions, and so are ultimately responsible for their actions. In scientific terms, this concept is known as soft determinism—that is to say, human personality and behavior are only somewhat (softly) determined by forces outside the person.

This concept of soft determinism depends on what Adler called *schöpferische Kraft* (creative power). This means that the individual at any point in life has the ability to make judgments, to be inventive, and to make decisions. J. L. Moreno (1966) brought this concept to its ultimate development in his concept of spontaneity. He believed that normality and productivity depended on an individual developing creative potential to make good decisions so as to solve life's problems adequately.

All individuals are creative in the sense that from what they are given, their hereditary potentials and societal setting, they can "make something" of their lives. It is their decision which way to go: what occupation to follow, whether or not to marry, what subjects to study, which people to associate with and which to avoid. *It is not what you have that counts but, rather, what you do with it.*

Two individuals will interpret and act on the same situation differently. Faced with some obstacle, one will feel blocked and frustrated, but the other will find some way around or over or under the obstacle.

This creativity may be called "intelligence" in the sense that the person in any problematic situation decides how to react to the situation best, but different people will find solutions of varying quality. This kind of intelligence

65

is not equivalent to that measured by IQ tests, nor does it refer to any static concept such as attainment of information but is, rather, a fluid and dynamic aspect of the individual's ability to make good judgments and act appropriately. More specifically, this creativity is the crucial element that enables the individual to attain goals. Creativity and energy count. So, if one is smart enough to know the best way to get to a goal and if one will apply oneself properly, then satisfactory achievement is likely to result.

Adler referred to people as artists of their own personality—imperfect artists, after all, but nevertheless in charge of the one common artistic creation we all work on—ourselves.

Creative power underlies the notion of soft determinism in two ways. As artists we create our personality, our life style. In turn, our movement in life is directed by the goals we create. So we create our personality according to our own ideas and perceptions and then live our lives in fulfillment of our goals. In this way we decide and determine the general pattern of our life.

Within our self-created life style we live each instant, each act, each choice, and each decision. This means that if we understand a person's goals, we can understand the person. We can see a person always moving toward goals even by the smallest behavior, and certainly in major decisions. Many people limit their freedom of choice for action, decision, at any particular instant by their adherence to their previous decisions, not reacting spontaneously (that is, fully and intelligently) to the needs of the moment, being directed by past established behavior patterns and concepts. Theoretically they have freedom of choice in all situations. But personally they do not utilize this freedom because they act unthinkingly in accord with their feelings and preconceptions.

Consequently, individuals have the potential to behave in ways which allow them to be happy and successful, to choose satisfactory ways of life and situations and to make objectively positive choices. Individuals ofttimes create personalities which limit their happiness and contribution. We believe that all people can (with the proper knowledge and training) modify their own personalities, as well as those of others, to attain freedom of choice as well as happiness and success in life.

Why, then, if we create our own personalities and situations, do so many of us feel boxed in, feel that we have no choice, no freedom, and are not responsible for our lives? The dynamics of this paradox are the essence of this chapter.

INFERIORITY COMPLEX

Look at Figure 6–1, which we use to explain the inferiority complex. Each of the five lines represents a continuum. Mark it for yourself if you wish. The rating will be of yourself in comparison to others like yourself. For example,

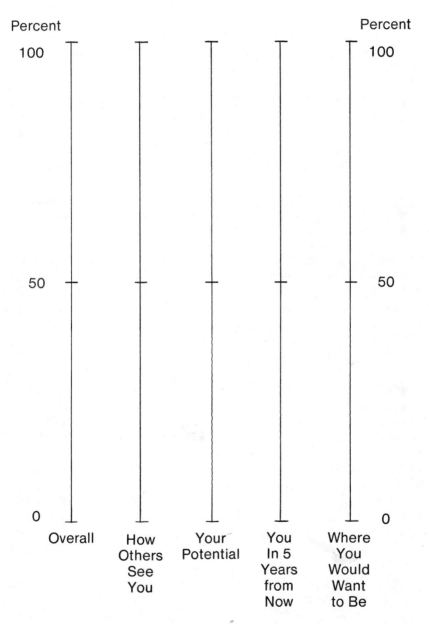

FIGURE 6–1. *Self-rating scale. Rate yourself overall as a total person relative to your satisfaction with your self and various estimates as explained in the manuscript.*

a 27-year-old white, married woman of moderate means might rate herself with her perception of other women of her color, age, and circumstances.

The scale is based on percentiles. Fifty is average. So, let us say that if we were rating this woman only for height, if her height were 5 feet 3 inches she might be exactly average in height. But the rating you are to make of yourself has to do with your satisfaction with yourself totally. If you think overall you are a successful, normal person to an average degree, you would rate yourself as 50; if less, then at 40 or 35, or 25, or lower. If you think of yourself as a failure, you might rate yourself as 5 or 10. If you have a good feeling overall about yourself, think you are okay, you may rate yourself at 75 or 85, or 95. The five ratings we suggest are:

1. Rate yourself overall as a total person in comparison with other people of your own group.
2. On the second line, rate yourself in terms of where you think others see you overall. Thus you may see yourself at 50, but you think that those who know you may rate you at 70.
3. Now, rate yourself in terms of what you think your absolute potential could be, if you had all the opportunities in life and all the means needed to achieve your goals.
4. Now rate yourself in terms of your future expectation, where you think you may be overall five years from now.
5. Finally, rate where you would want to be right now, what you think you should be at this time.

Draw five vertical lines on a sheet of paper (or if this is your book you can do it right in the book) and actually mark these five ratings. A bit later on we shall tell you how to determine if you tend toward an inferiority complex and try to explain what causes it. Please do the rating now, for it may tell you something about yourself.

OK, have you done it? It should only take a minute or even less. Put it down on paper. Doing it in your head is not enough.

Inferiority feelings as well as the inferiority complex are indicated by the extent of the difference between your rating of line number 1 "Overall—how you see yourself") and line number 5 ("where you want to be"). If, let us say, you rate yourself as 50 and would like to be a 60, then this "small difference" probably means you just feel a bit inferior; but if you rate yourself as 50 and would like to be 90; or if you rate yourself as 30 and would like to be 100, then you may have a strong feeling of personal inferiority.

What we have said is not really quite right in that there is a more subtle difference. Two people may each rate themselves, let us say, 30 percentage points below what they would want to be, and one person can accept the difference philosophically while another will think the difference is a catastrophe. The important point is this: it is not where one actually is, nor where one thinks one actually is, but rather one's reaction to the perceived difference that counts. For example, one of us had a client, a man in his early 30s, tall, attractive, a self-made millionaire, married to a beautiful and accomplished woman, well regarded in the community, who nevertheless felt he was a terribly inadequate person. He used his feelings of inferiority to his advantage in planning and successfully making a great deal of money to compensate for his feelings of inadequacy. But the more money he made, the less satisfied he was with himself. In the ratings of these five areas, he put himself at about 20 and stated that he only needed to be average—50. And yet he rated line 2, "what others thought of him," at 95.

Such serious distortions of self-perception may seem hard to believe. The example below represents a serious personal misperception and it has a comical element. One of us, working in a prison, had a conversation during individual therapy with an inmate. Below is part of the conversation.

Tim: One of my troubles is that I am so short.

Me: What's your height?

Tim: About 5 foot 10 1/2 inches.

Me: What's the height of the average man?

Tim: According to the books, about 5 foot 8 inches, but I don't believe that.

Me: Why not?

Tim: Everyone I meet is taller than me.

Me: How about me?

Tim: You are taller than me.

Me: I am 5 foot 8 1/2 inches, 2 inches shorter than you.

Tim: I don't believe it. You are over 6 feet.

Me: So, you think I am taller than you?

Tim: Sure.

Me: Well, we can settle that immediately. Let's measure ourselves.

We then went to a wall, and using a book, I measured him and he measured me, holding the book against the wall to form a right angle. Sure enough, his mark was about two inches above my mark.

Me: What do you think of that?

Tim: You cheated somehow.

Me: Well, let us get someone else to measure us. Would you go outside and get someone to do it?

Tim left and came back with another inmate.

Me: Will you tell him what you want?

Tim: We want to find out who's taller between us.

X: It is obvious that you are taller (to Tim). You are about an inch or two taller.

Tim: I don't believe it. Will you measure us?

X did what we had done before, and after the measurement:

X: Well, you are about two inches taller.

Tim: I still can't believe it.

But that is not the end of the story. Tim was in my therapy group and at the next session, I spoke as follows to the group. "I am giving each of you a 3 X 5 card and I would like you to write on it the first name of every person in the group. Please do so." (Each did that.) "Now, while we are sitting down, I would like you to put number 1 against the name of the person in this group (excluding me) whom you think is the tallest in the group, then put down 2 after the name of the person you think is the second tallest, and 3 for the next tallest, until finally put down 12 for the shortest person in the group."

They all followed these directions, and after the cards were collected, I proceeded to put the names and numbers on the board. I shall indicate what the findings looked like for two people.

	Ratees	
Rater	Tim	Pete
A	1	12
B	1	12
C	2	12
D	1	12
E	12	11
F	1	12
G	2	12
H	1	12
I	1	12
J	1	12
K	2	12
L	1	12

I then pointed out that Tim had been rated 1 (tallest) by eight people, second tallest (rating of 2) by three people, and 12 (shortest) by one person. I started a discussion of how this could be: how could someone in the group put him last on the list, meaning he was the shortest, when the majority had him as tallest. There were a number of theories to explain this phenomenon, including that whoever did it didn't understand the directions or perhaps was a "wise guy."

When I asked who had put Tim down as the shortest in the group, Tim put up his hand.

One of the group members, in shocked surprise, asked, "Are you trying to tell us that you believe that you are shorter than Pete?" Tim said that was just so—he thought that Pete was taller than he.

"You're crazy!" the other person retorted.

"Why don't you compare yourself with Pete? Stand up and see for yourself who's taller?" someone suggested. Tim got up and went to the center of the circle. He looked at Pete, who remained seated. "Why don't you get up?" "What for?" asked Pete. "To see who's taller, you or me." "You a wise guy?" Pete asked. "What do you mean?" Tim inquired, puzzled by Pete's attitude. "What it means is that you are trying to make fun of me. I don't take that from anyone," Pete continued. "Make fun of you?" Tim asked. "I am not making fun of you." "You mean to tell me," Pete continued, "that you really think I am taller than you?" "Sure, that's what I think." "You're crazy," Pete said, and got up, and he put his five-foot two-inch body next to Tim. Tim looked down at the top of Pete's head, stepped back, looked to make sure Pete's knees weren't bent. "You *are* shorter than me," he stated. "I just can't believe it."

This distortion of reality by a young intelligent man seems rather unusual, but so does the distortion of the millionaire who, despite being a self-made successful man, felt he was nothing. These distortions are a function of high ambition compensating for feelings of inferiority, of feeling incapable of meeting one's own high standards of achievement. It can become a paralyzing situation, and difficult to deal with since the afflicted person is so certain of his or her complete inadequacy that is hard to even communicate with such an individual on a commonsense basis.

INFERIORITY FEELINGS

We are born small and dumb, essentially helpless. It takes years of our efforts as well as help and attention of others to bring us to independence. There is a strong developmental rationale for our recognizing and retaining these notions of our smallness and our inadequacy through our lifetimes.

When Adler first understood that one kidney will work harder to make up for the deficiencies of a weak second kidney, he was setting the stage for almost 40 years of development of the basic notion that actual or perceived weakness, in anything from an organ to a total concept of self, is compensated for. As Adler investigated further, he again and again noticed that in one way or another, everyone has some feelings of inferiority, and that all people react in various ways to these perceptions of their inadequacies.

In some ways we all feel we are less than others and less than what we want to be. These feelings of inferiority may be well based in fact. If we feel in awe of the universe, less than its totality, there is a good reason for feeling this way. Mankind has spent forever coming up with myths, rituals, and other devices, for coming to grips with our essential inferiority—the existential task.

When we look at the mass of humanity, the totality of the earth, the present and all it entails, we are likely to feel insignificant. We might see that the world is the same in relative size for everyone and that we are equal to each if not equal to all. However, when we look outside of ourselves we are apt not to look at *each,* and we are most apt to look at *all.* We reinforce our belief of our "less than" stature.

We spend most of our life interacting with people in a circumscribed social arena. We look at individuals in our social world and perceive commonalities of strengths and weaknesses, values and attitudes normative to the group and everyone in it. In this everyday setting we also look to see where we fit in relation to them and whether we are more than, or less than, and we find— when young—we are *less than.* We are all, in our innermost feelings in child-hood, less than; we all have some basis for trying not to remain that way.

The dynamic of Adlerian Psychology is based on this premise: we all feel *less than* and want *not to.* The discrepancy between what *we think we are* and how *we think we should be or must be* leads to our feelings of inferiority. In our creating this felt discrepancy and our operations for not feeling inferior, much of our personality creativity lies. In the social and the personal meanings of our movements in life, the goals of our self-created life styles are exhibited, and the success or failure of our goals—our life styles—lie.

MOVEMENT

Adler (1930) stated that "we have constantly maintained the viewpoint that all is motion." Adler saw life as *process,* not as *content.* Psychology is a matter of verbs and adverbs, not of adjectives and nouns. Humans are always in action, going toward private and frequently unknown goals. The individual is always on the go in a complex calculus of goal-related activities. In evaluating people we usually not only concern ourselves with worthwhileness of the goal —whether the goal is useful or useless—but also with the degree of energy invested in the movement toward goals.

Adlerians see individuals as progressing in a direction and so are able to make predictions as to where the person was in the past, where he or she is now, and therefore where they will be in the future—and how fast they will get there. Imagine a checkerboard, and say that the individual is at the lower left-hand square at one point in time, and then is at the next diagonal square to the upper right at another point in time, and then say at the next diagonal to the upper right at still another point in time. We can then predict that this "law of movement" will continue and that he or she will later be in the next upper right square of the same color as the one originally started from and when, approximately. As the person continues in a chosen path, various difficulties will occur, but the person will tend to overcome them in terms of his or her personal life style. We can make an analogy of life to music. If we listen to a musical composition even for the first time, we are prepared, to some extent, for what is to come. The typical composer maintains a certain logic or integrity so that the piece from beginning to end has a particular structure to some predictable degree.

Adler (1932/1962, 1918/1957) stated that what is known as character is essentially the guiding line of a person's life style. We may almost compare it with a missile which has a compass, which regulates its flight, and a governor, which controls its speed. These attributes of direction and speed are formed early in life, in that each of us develops a kind of pace (referring to velocity) and also a constant direction (referring to goals) so that we can operate in life on a more or less predictable basis. When we know others' characters we are able to predict them in terms of these important dimensions—where they are going and how fast.

STRIVINGS

Adler moved through a number of concepts of movers, or motivators, of persons. Starting from the biological position with the aggression drive and the need for affection, he moved on to more social motivators. The first of these, which was short lived, was the *will to power*. This term proved, and continues to prove, to be unfortunate. It is often represented by textbook writers and others as a still applicable notion in Individual Psychology, when it is not. Adler's use of the term *power* has been, and continues to be, confused with Nietzsche's view of power, when, in fact, while they are theoretically similar, they are philosophically different.

"Power," as Adler used it, did not refer to power over others. It did not mean masterful, dominant, or dominating. "Power" referred, rather, to a sense of personal control over one's own life choices, as a compensation to cease the general feeling of inferiority and insecurity common to all people. It means independence, competence, capacity, self-control. Adler presented the *striving for power* concept prior to World War I, when he was still involved with a medical model with an interest in pathology. This was before his interests grew, or the applicability of his theory grew, to include normal people as well as abnormal people.

Striving for Superiority versus Striving for Perfection

Ansbacher (1978b), discussing the development of the concept of social interest, pointed out that Adler minimized the development and change in his theory over time as if the theory was complete and essentially unchanging from the beginning. This had the effect of creating misunderstandings and confusion which continues to this day. Ansbacher commented that Adler did not note changes and innovations in his theory and that Adler revised later editions of earlier works with new ideas inserted as if they had always been in the earlier editions; he continued to use terms that were no longer useful in his theory but with changed meanings; and he sometimes misattributed ideas to earlier times which were not introduced until later, or he did not admit that he had held an earlier, discarded notion. It seems probable that Adler did these things within his framework of a whole theory evolving from him—that is, with the feeling that all of his theory was as a whole and part of him—not to deceive and certainly not to confuse. Yet confusion has been the result in certain areas. Moreover, as the theory continued to evolve and grow during Adler's lifetime, we must assume that it would have continued to do so had Adler lived longer.

One of the areas where Adler might have made some modification in the presentation of his theory has to do with the nature of strivings and their direction. We will differentiate between "types" of striving in an effort to bring additional clarity to the nature of strivings and their directions.

The fundamental base for all human striving is the feeling of inferiority. These feelings, as we have discussed, emanate from awareness of the ways we are less than what we could be and from our creative notions of how we are less than what we could be or should be. We strive, therefore, to overcome this perception of being less than what we "should" in order to find what we perceive as our proper place within the human community. Although this striving sometimes is for a strange or useless place, nonetheless it is the place we perceive ourselves able to—or entitled to—reach.

Once the term *striving for power* was discarded, the two terms which Adler most frequently used were *striving for superiority* and *striving for perfection*. Over time, striving for perfection superceded striving for superiority as the basic human dynamic. However, the two terms were used by Adler and have continued to be used by others as essentially interchangeable.

In his most important paper on this subject, "On the Origins of the Striving for Superiority and of Social Interest," Adler (1933) "designated the basic human dynamics as a 'striving for perfection,' and wrote: 'Referring to the striving for perfection, or the striving for superiority, as which it manifests itself sometimes . . .' " (Ansbacher, 1978b, p. 142). This quotation illustrates the evolution these notions were taking in Adler's thinking. They may be explained in the following way.

All striving based on feelings of inferiority is an attempt to overcome these feelings. The striving itself is a movement representing a "growth force," an attempt to be more than, rather than less than, an effort to overcome feelings of inferiority. In the broadest sense, all striving is toward perfection—perfection in becoming "more than" in the eyes of the individual.

It is useful to make a distinction between these two kinds of striving. *Striving for perfection* means to move in the direction of social interest, in line with the common sense of communal living, toward greater competence (White, 1959), in a horizontal direction toward the useful side. *Striving for superiority* means to move in a vertical direction, toward personal superiority in relation to others for personal gain within one's own biased apperception not coherent with the interests of others and the common sense of social living.

Movement in striving for perfection and movement in striving for superiority are both efforts to overcome the individual's feelings of inferiority. To the degree that one strives for perfection we can expect positive mental health, a greater sense of well-being, sense of connectedness with others and humanity. To the degree that one is striving for superiority we can expect dis-ease, a sense of separateness.

GOALS

"Teleology—the fact or character attributed to nature or natural processes of being directed toward an end or shaped by a purpose" (*Webster's New Collegiate Dictionary*). Individual Psychology sees the "creative power of life," the uniqueness of the individual's movements, as being teleological, directed toward ends, purposes, and goals. The individual generally makes up goals unknowingly from the fabric of his or her own perceptions of what the world is all about.

> The most important question of the healthy and the diseased mental life is not whence? but, whither? Only when we know the effective direction-giving goal of a person may we try to understand his movements. . . . (Adler, 1956, p. 91)

Basic life goals, although generally unknown to the person, give direction to all behavior. To the degree that goals are in line with social interest, the direction of the person's life is useful, positive, and healthy. If goals are out of line with social interest and are an expression of striving for personal superiority, the direction of the person's life tends to be useless, negative, and unhealthy.

Goals of Children

Quite likely in the beginning of life children have few goals. We will use in illustration the four basic goals of children by which Rudolf Dreikurs (1947) classified children's goals into categories. They are a convenient method for understanding children's behavior—useful and useless.

Attention.   The first goal is attention. The most common reason for children's misbehavior is simply to get attention, to get parents to be busy with them. Essentially, they are saying: "Notice me! Watch me! Look at me! Pay attention to me!" All children want attention and if they do not receive it for competent and cooperative behavior, they will probably seek it by useless ways.

The discouraged child, who believes that he or she cannot amount to anything will employ useless means of getting attention—even if it means getting punished. Such a child would rather be punished than be ignored. We note here a most important point which makes us suspicious of primitive behavior modification theory. Paradoxically, punishment may be a reward. Children who have OK self-attitudes operate to get attention in positive ways; discouraged children aim to get attention through useless behavior.

Power.   The second of these four goals is power. The child is mainly concerned with proving his/her personhood. Getting one's way becomes the goal. The child who operates for power may be viewed as doing positive things—such as studying, and practicing, or if operating on the negative side will be viewed as stubborn, demanding, rebellious, wanting his/her own way. Using punishment does not work with a child whose goal is power since he/she will counteract the parents' power with his/her own means, gaining control and doing what he/she wants.

Revenge.   The third of these four goals, wholly negative and useless, is revenge. The child who has not succeeded in gaining attention, nor in doing what she/he wants, is now reduced to getting even, doing things to make parents angry.

Inadequacy.   The fourth goal of children who misbehave is the worst of all: inadequacy. This is a difficult goal for some people to understand. Such children in effect state through their behavior that they cannot succeed in life, that they are helpless. Their goal is to display inadequacy, not even bothering to try to operate in a useful way. Such a child gains whatever scraps of attention are granted to the inadequate. If you do not try, you cannot fail.

The first two goals can be positive or useful. Attention and power goals can lead to "good" behavior. Children operating on the basis of these goals may use them to social advantage. Thus, the child who learns card tricks and shows them can gain attention, or the child who works hard at school to gain good grades gets approval. The child who becomes a leader among children and becomes the school president is in a constructive and useful manner working for power. However, the two goals of revenge and of inadequacy are always negative.

This schema can be used in understanding adults. Some adults operate for attention, wanting to make good impressions, being recognized, being looked up to. We can see this in thousands of adult behaviors: people who dress attractively and even provocatively, people who use perfumes and makeup excessively, and those who want to be in the public eye. The desire to be noted favorably is very strong in most of us. Most adults obtain this attention constructively. Some, however, will behave in silly, dangerous and even illegal ways, whether it be trying to get into the *Guinness Book of Records* by swallowing live goldfish or by jumping over a fleet of trucks with a motorcycle. Their goal is attention for its own sake.

The desire to be powerful is seen in many ways. People who go to gymnasiums to learn to fight may be doing so. Those who study, or who plot to become rich, may be doing so. A common way to gain power is through getting others to do what you want.

When it comes to revenge, we usually find a paranoia-type attitude toward people, a lack of consideration of others, a flouting of the law. The Watergate scandal seems to be a clear example of people motivated mostly by the thought of getting even, seeing enemies all around them. The true professional criminal has this essentially hostile attitude toward the world. Those who are sour on the world, the cynics, the pessimists, and the killjoys, are all essentially operating on the basis of the third goal that Dreikurs described.

The ultimate of the fourth goal of helplessness leads finally to psychosis, especially deep depression and schizophrenia, where the individual just gives up. It is a kind of emotional suicide. "What's the use?" the person says, "I can't succeed out there."

PERSONALITY AS LIFE STYLE

Life style refers to a cognitive organization, a consistent pattern of thinking, and of behavior. Life style evolves from a biological being in a social context creating a sense of self in the world on which he acts.

Before going on it seems worthwhile to try to define life style in a concise manner. "For Adler, the term 'life style' denoted the fundamental premises upon which a person predicates his movement through the world. It is a set of ideas, schemata, and, not as in common parlance, habitual modes of behaving. Schematically the life style may be seen as a syllogism:

1. "I am ..."
2. "The world is ..."
3. "Therefore ..."

It is in terms of the proposition which follows the 'therefore' that the person thinks, feels, perceives, dreams, recollects, emotes, behaves, etc." (Allen, 1971, p. 5).

Life style has at least two levels of meaning. At the highest level, life style is the totality of the individual expressed "in all its parts," all behaviors, emotions, and thoughts moving in a unified direction. The unity of the individual's unique movement is the individual's life style. The observer does not, however, usually see the totality—cannot see the whole. Rather, one sees parts. We see how an individual behaves and what results and we infer that the individual is after what is gotten. The sum of an individual's behaviors is the person's life style. By an analysis of present and past behaviors, a sophisticated observer can then see the whole—the totality of the individual—and know one's life style.

The other meaning of life style is cognitive organization: what a person thinks. This determines the direction of movement toward his/her goals. Although life styles may contain conflicting views of self, world, and goals, the basic components are in the syllogism. The social influences, the manner of attaining basic convictions, are discussed at various places in this book. Suffice it here to repeat that what Adlerians refer to as the individual's *private logic* directs one's line of movement.

Let us give a simple example. A person might have a life style syllogism which goes:

1. I am small and weak,
2. The world is big and dangerous,
3. Therefore, I must be careful.

Such a simple set of ideas may direct all of one's behavior and can have ramifications in all areas of one's life. The development of such a life style occurs when we are children, becoming established at about four to six years of age. Certainly a child this age *is* smaller and weaker than most people around him, and if an only child, he is smaller and weaker than everyone around him. If the child sees "big" people as being dangerous, it makes good sense for a small person to be careful. If the child sees that greater care reduces hostility, his/her ideas are reinforced. With a few instances of this "truth," these ideas can become firmly fixed. When the child goes to school, if she/he does not do well on an assignment, she/he will take greater care next time. In everything children do they will prepare adequately, proceed with caution, attempt to find all pitfalls before moving on, and avoid all situations where they think they are "too small." This example is intended to illllustrate how an individual's private logic, a personal set of rules, can determine one's behavior.

How would one expect such a child to be as an adult? Probably careful, cautious; maybe highly organized and plodding, or compulsive; possibly fearful, reticent and retiring, or even isolated.

Basic Mistakes

In developing from a child to an adult, practically all people come to have mistaken ideas about life. If central to the life style, they are known as *basic mistakes.* One of us believes that if he were the Creator, he would rearrange development so that individuals did not come to the conclusions that make up the life style until they were at least 18 years old. This would mean that people would have a good deal of experience when they came to conclusions about themselves, the world, and how they should act. However, people come to these conclusions when they are young children.

We cannot expect a five-year-old to have an accurate self-definition, or view of parents and siblings, or an adequate picture of the world, or effective coping behaviors. When five-year-olds develop life styles they oversimplify, exaggerate, stress a particular part of life or themselves without knowing how it all fits.

Within our life styles we hold on to basic tenets, rules, and ideas. When these are out of line with reality we unknowingly fight to keep them. "Basic mistakes" may be seen as similar to Karen Horney's (1950) concept of "overdriven attitudes." According to Horney, the neurotic can be identified by irrational, insatiable, impossible, inappropriate attitudes. So too, basic mistaken life style ideas, when maintained to the point of irrationality, cause personal difficulties in life.

A therapist, in explaining an individual's life style, may include a listing of particular basic mistakes. The notion is simple and ofttimes is so clear to individuals in treatment that they can begin to act on different, less mistaken premises almost immediately.

Chapter 7

The Development of Personality

While Adler did not organize his thoughts about personality along developmental lines, nevertheless he was keenly interested in how people became the way they were. His ideas on personality growth can be put in a developmental framework, albeit not with the precision found in current developmental accounts.

For Adler the central issue for all people at the philosophical level was "how to belong, to fit in." The overriding day-by-day issue for each of us is "What is my place—where do I belong?" Subordinate to this issue are the questions "How should I behave?" "How do I find my place?" "How can I fit in as I think I should?" These simple questions are the basic existential and practical questions of humankind. The answers we give underlie the direction of our movement in life—our life style.

Humankind has not come up with the final answers to these questions, although many answers have been presented. Even within religious groups which purportedly accept a common answer, there are generally considerable differences of interpretation. We all answer these questions for ourselves in global and acknowledged ways, as well as in particular individualistic, unacknowledged ways. We each come to have some sort of answer even if we do not know that this has been done. These answers take place within the life experience of all individuals. Our perspective on the needs or pressures of self and others, the world, eternity, is interactive and, in a sense, circularly causal. The purpose of this chapter is to show how we come to develop our perspective of self, of others, and of the world, and how this process maintains itself.

FAMILY CONSTELLATION

The family is the primary social situation for the growing child. Family members are the first people the baby deals with, who affect the child during the important early period of life. The family is the primary socialization agent of the child. In the day-to-day life of the family, older family members socialize younger children, teaching them formally and informally how to behave. The efforts and expectations of the family are to make the child become cooperative. The child, with an innate potential for social interest, wants to belong to the family. The small young person has to figure out how to belong.

When you were young, small, not knowledgeable, in a complex world: what you knew best was your home, your family. Your family was where you "belonged." Older members of the family seemed to know what was happening in the world, what was needed to be done, how to get along. Older siblings seemed to fit into the family pattern easily. Older people had expectations for your behavior and the ways in which you should express yourself. You tried to figure out how to fit in, how to get approval. In this family setting you established ways for fitting and getting along.

The thinking-behavior-feeling pattern you established is your own creation, a personally developed life style based on your own perception of what you had to do to belong in the family. There are differences between your life style and that of other people as a result of each person's creativity.

Toman (1959) developed a theory of family constellation to predict success in marital relationships according to family constellation patterns. The general formula expresses the underlying notion of the continuing effect of family constellation throughout life.

> New (extra-familial, non-incestuous) interpersonal relationships will duplicate the earliest (intra-familial, incestuous) interpersonal relationships in degrees varying from complete duplication to none at all. What is more: the closer the new relationship comes in kind to old ones, to those already entertained, other things being equal, the better will the person be prepared for the new ones, and the greater their likelihood to last and to be happy and successful. (p. 6)

What Is a Family?

A family is composed of people who live together with structured interactions, formal and informal, with some degree of directionality, and some overall common goals. The family constellation is the structure of parental relationships to the children in general and the relationship of the children to the parents and to each other, as well as the codes by which the family lives.

The family constellation may be broken down into component parts. The following definitions may be useful in indicating the parts and the whole:

Birth order, order of birth, and ordinal position are ofttimes used synonymously and interchangeably; in other instances they have different and exact meanings which may be contradictory.

Family constellation, family configuration and sibship also suffer in usage with considerable overlap at times and distinct definitions at other times.

... The following definitions, or descriptions, of the key terms in the birth order field are recommended:

Ordinal position (order of birth)—"Ordinal, *adj.,* being of a specified order or rank [as sixth] in a numberable series." "Ordinal number, *n.,* a number designating the place (as first, second, third) occupied by an item in an ordered sequence." These definitions from Webster's (1976) clearly indicate the basis in mathematics of the term ordinal. Ordinal position and order of birth should be used when indicating the numerical place of an individual's birth in the order of birth in his or her family, as in first of two, or third of five.

Birth order most frequently implies the following definition of order: "A category, type, class or kind of thing of distinctive character or rank." Birth order terms (only, oldest, second, middle, and youngest) refer to categories or types of persons whose distinctive character may be known, described and, theoretically, empirically demonstrated. These birth order terms may also refer to rank in the numerical order sense, hence the confusion. However, they need not do so, as in the instance where two children in a family are spaced closely together, say two years apart, followed eight years later by two more siblings spaced closely. This sibship could be variously described as (1) oldest, second, middle, youngest; (2) oldest, two middles and youngest; or, and I think this is a preferable description of psychological birth order, (3) oldest, youngest, oldest, youngest. Obviously, using birth order as herein defined demands operational definitions by each researcher.

Sibship—"The quality or state of being a sib or a member of a sib," "a group of sibs." Investigations of all children in the family, which go beyond ordinal position or birth order as defined above, as when sex of siblings is also studied, may be said to be sibship research.

Family configuration should, perhaps, refer to analyses of the structure and identifiable social characteristics of the family, such as any or all of the above, intactness, parents' age, socioeconomic status, race, etc. This use is based on the definition of configuration as "relative disposition or arrangement of parts; interrelationships of constituent elements."

Family constellation—the relevant definitions of constellation include "a determining, differentiating, or individualizing pattern of groups," "a group of consciously related, especially emotionally significant ideas," "an assemblage or configuration of stimulus conditions or factors affecting behavior and personality development." Family constellation is the broadest, most inclusive term in this listing. It may denote aspects of all of the above-defined terms and may also refer to individualizing, emotionally significant stimulus factors, as it is used by Adlerians. When Adlerians use the term family constellation in its fullest sense, they include such factors as the personality of each parent; their cooperation; other significant relatives, like a grandmother living with the family; and the theme, or code, or motto of the family—the emotionally significant ideas individual to the family which may influence development within the family. (Manaster, 1977b, pp. 6–7)

BIRTH ORDER

Adlerian theory takes the commonsense position that brothers and sisters affect each other's personality. Within any family there are parental expectations for each child based on the child's sex and birth order. Every child within a family understands those expectations and his role in his own way. Thus, the oldest child often is delegated the parental surrogate for younger children. The youngest child may be pampered and spoiled by all others in the family.

Birth order refers, of course, to the sequential position of someone in the family but more important is the *psychological* position of the child.

In general ways, birth order affects characteristics of individuals if there are generalized expectations for holders of particular birth order positions in any particular culture. Adler found that such expectations generally existed and that in many cases, persons with particular birth order positions exhibited special patterns of behavior which were consistent life style configurations. It must be stressed, however, that psychological birth order assists only to a weak extent in determining the life style of the individual. No individual by virtue of birth order position *necessarily* exhibits any traits or patterns common to persons of that birth order position. As Shulman and Mosak (1977) state:

> Birth order assessment and research is often faulty because it fails to recognize that it is the psychological position of the child within the family which is crucial. This can only be understood for each subject idiographically and not through nomothetic laws or other statements of generalization. The criteria explicated "as characteristics of birth order positions and factors said to influence the effect of birth order position" provide helpful clues toward the understanding of the uniqueness rather than the typicality of the individuals. (p. 118)

We may think that it was inevitable that we would have become the same person we are now regardless of circumstances, no matter what family or what birth order we had. This notion is not accepted by Adlerians or by many other schools of personality theory. Adlerians see personality as being a complex function of one's (*a*) heredity, (*b*) social experiences, and (*c*) creative interpretations of (*a*) and (*b*). Since psychology is a probability science, predictions can never be near perfect; and indeed, they usually are of low predictive value. One of the "soft" determinants of personality is birth order position in the family constellation.

The first child for a period of time is the only child and obviously will remain so until there are other children. When another child is born, the only child becomes a *firstborn* with a *second-born sibling*. If they are close in age, there will probably be considerable competition between them for attention from the parents. However, if there is a large age gap, the firstborn may not see the second born as a competitor, and may continue to see him/herself as an only child, and not feel threatened by the sibling. But if they are close in age the first child may feel pushed and threatened. The firstborn will likely struggle to maintain supremacy as the second born tries to forge ahead while always feeling somewhat behind. Say that another child comes along. Now the second born is likely to feel squeezed—inferior to the first child and threatened by the third. The second child will then possibly take on the characteristics typical of the middle child. The last child in the family is likely to see his/her role as being that of the youngest, without any threat from anyone behind or the need to compete with those ahead. In large families, depending on age spacing between siblings, there may be a variety of configurations of family constellations with more than one oldest (oldest of separate subgroups of the sibship) and more than one youngest.

The important factor relative to birth order and personality development is the individual's perception of the role to be played and its demands and expectations. These perceptions may be influenced by age spacing, expectations by sex and the actual and self-perceived aspects the person attributes to self and others, but in the last analyses, they are the individual's creation and responsibility. With due caution about these generalizations (not universalizations!), general descriptions of various birth order positions follow.

Oldest Firstborn. When a second child is born soon after the first child, that is, within three years, the firstborn usually develops a wary and defensive stance toward the second. When there is a greater space between births, the second child seems to be more of a shock to the oldest child, and a greater threat seems to exist for the older child. Adler used the term *dethronement* to describe the situation and feeling of the oldest child, but he stated that later children, when displaced by a new child, may also experience this same feeling, although not as intensely.

It makes good common sense to comprehend how the oldest child might yearn for the good old days when he/she was an only child, and for him/her to attempt to regain the previous superior position. Oldest children are generally described as feeling entitled to an honored first position and striving to maintain that superiority, meanwhile holding a positive attitude toward the past, stressing tradition, and being conservative.

Second Born. The second child has the yardstick of the older sibling in measuring him/herself. This child tries to catch up to the older sibling. For this reason the second child tends to greater levels of activity in pursuit of catching up with the first. The interaction of abilities and areas of excellence between the first- and second born illustrates an important dynamic for understanding birth order. Looking ahead, trying to compete, the second child sees the strengths and weaknesses of the child in front of him/her.

Unless the family has a single criterion of adequacy, as in a family where nothing matters except obedience or brightness, the second child will usually make special efforts to excel in those areas where the oldest child is weak. Since the younger child wants to excel, there is a tendency to choose the area of behavior which has the greatest potential for succeeding by virtue of less competition from a sibling in that area. This behavior falls within what Dreikurs (1953) calls "the only fundamental law governing the development of the child's character: he trains those qualities by which he hopes to achieve significance or even a degree of power and superiority in the family constellation" (p. 41).

Middle Child. The middle child might perceive him/herself to be in an untenable position. The one in front has the privileges and power of greater age, while the one behind is not pressed to perform as responsibly or as well. The middle child thus may feel squeezed from both sides and feel particularly put upon and without a place, or may feel less pressured from role expectations and be able to excel on his/her own terms.

Youngest Child. The youngest child has nobody behind; all competitors are ahead. The other siblings may treat him/her as the baby and not a competitor. The youngest then has more possibility of being pampered and being faced with few demands. The child may come to expect that others will, and should, take care of him/her because, after all, he/she *is* the baby. With charm and a helpless manner the youngest may be able to have his/her expectations fulfilled. Adler delighted in noting that throughout history as well as in stories and fables, youngest children were portrayed as being exceptionally quick, bright, and ultimately surpassing their older siblings. It may be that in these cases the youngest views his/her position in the family psychologically as being last with the furthest to go, and then determines that he/she will go that little bit further, faster and better.

Only Child. The only child does not have the experiences integral to living with siblings. An only child need not attain unhealthy personality characteristics as a result of the lack of these experiences. However, the only child's environment may lead to conclusions with negative effects on future social living. The child may become spoiled and expect to be the center of attention, also may be reluctant to share attention or material things with others, having never had to do so. The only child may not therefore be as companionable as other children are. "Nonetheless, it should be noted that there is no evidence that supports the popular belief that only children are selfish, lonely, or maladjusted" (Falbo, 1977, p. 57).

Following Forer (1977), these are some of the generalities relative to birth order which can be found in the considerable research literature on this topic. By and large, these findings support Adlerian descriptions of birth order positions.

1. Firstborns achieve more than do later borns, especially in intellectual areas (Altus, 1966). Mothers relate differently to their firstborns than to later borns, and Forer speculates that this may explain the greater intellectual achievements of firstborns.
2. Firstborns show need for greater affiliation than do later borns, who are more independent (Adams, 1972).
3. Later borns tend to have more empathy with others than do firstborns (Stotland, Sherman, & Shaver, 1971).
4. Firstborns tend to generalize more than do later borns, who tend to be more specific (Harris, 1964).
5. Firstborns tend to be more fearful than are later borns. This may be because later borns are protected by the older children who have already had these experiences and need not fear them since they get reassurance from the firstborns (Collard, 1968).
6. Firstborns are more likely to be more influenced by authority and to be affected by public opinion. Firstborns tend to get more attention, positive and negative, from their parents than do later borns, and so firstborns are more likely to be more responsive to authorities and social pressure (Becker, Lerner, & Carroll, 1964).

Individual holders of these constellation positions may not see the demands and expectations in their families as they have been presented here. They may feel they did not compete in the manner expected. Their families may not have the competitive ethic so common in our society. In the final analysis, birth order holds a potential for influencing personality development but the parents, the individual, and a variety of other variables may negate this potential. To repeat, birth order family constellation personality attributes are generalizations—not universalizations!

POSITIONAL DETERMINISM

In considering birth order we run into the nomothetic-idiographic problem, as follows: after all, we can make generalizations about personality and birth order (nomothetic thinking), but there cannot be any strict determinism for any single child since the birth order position affects the child only in terms of how the child sees its position (idiographic thinking).

The concept of soft determinism means statistical probability. An older child is *likely* to be more responsible, a middle child is *likely* to be more competitive, a youngest child is *likely* to be more of a charmer. But, birth order does not determine these personality qualities. Birth order only makes these qualities more likely to occur in the particular birth order positions.

A may be the oldest; but *positionally* B may be the "first" child (if, let us say, A is retarded, and B takes over). What counts now is not mere chronological rank order but, rather, the child's interpretation of the meaning of his position in the family.

Shulman and Mosak (1977) list seven factors that influence ordinal position:

1. Age differences. If A and B are a year apart, this is not the same as if they were 10 years apart, in which case both may be "only children."

2. Large families. In large families one can have two sets of children. A, B, and C are born within 5 years of each other, and the parents do not have other children for 10 years, and now D and E are born. A is a firstborn, and so may be D.

3. Extra-family competitors. The family situation can be complicated by half brothers, brothers and sisters brought in by remarriages, adopted children, and in the case of extended families, by cousins or others who move into the family. In such cases, birth orders are meaningless and each case must be studied separately.

4. Gender differences. If A, B, and C are all boys and if in another family A and C are boys and B is a girl, the two situations are not psychologically alike.

5. Death and survivorship. If A was the first child, and lived, say, to age five, and then died, his or her effect on B may well continue not only in terms of the effect he/she has had on B, but also the memory of A in the minds of the parents may continue to affect B, who still has a competitor who is no longer present and beatable.

6. Special siblings. A "special" child can have various effects: a mentally retarded child, one in an institution, one with outstanding attributes, such as a child movie actor, can affect the other children disproportionately and in ways that cannot be anticipated.

7. Roles available. The socioeconomic situation or cultural-traditional-social views of the family may be such that girls are expected to stay home and help with the chores, while boys can run around; or the parents may prefer that girls and boys be treated with relative indifference, and so on.

Further positional possibilities complicate the situation. For example:

8. Social views. In black families, there may be values relative to the darkness of the skin of the children, and these may affect parental and sibling attitudes.

9. Parental prejudice. The parents may vary in terms of their desires about children. Thus, father may much prefer girls while mother may like boys.

10. Parents as models. Parents have their own personalities which may mix and merge in different ways to produce a unique family atmosphere.

Adlerians expect that the individual parents as well as the generalized family atmosphere are material which the child notices, or buys into, in developing his or her personality. In a noncausal system we do not say that parents' personalities and the family atmosphere cause the personality of the developing child but, rather, that they influence the development of the child's personality.

Clearly, a child learns, to some degree, possible ways to act through viewing the parents' behavior. The child can learn from other contacts, directly from neighbors and teachers as well as indirectly from the media. Parents are the most prominent models for the child's behavior and children tend to imitate their parents and other prestigious role models. When the family is composed solely of parents and one child, imitation and competition are most likely with and toward the parents. When there are other children in the family, more models are available.

What all this adds to is the following: Adler's concept that a child's position in the family has some general influence on the child's personality is probably true. However, the predictive power of knowing anything about a specific person is low if we know only the person's birth order, and this information is not too useful clinically. Psychotherapy is not nomothetic. It is highly idiographic. Low-order generalizations have little meaning in counseling or psychotherapy. What is important is how the subject viewed himself vis-à-vis others in the family. Consequently, while birth order researches are fine for heuristic information about human nature in general, they contribute very little (and, indeed, can even be harmful if used mechanically) in psychotherapy. However, the general theory of birth order and family constellations may be useful as a working guide in the individual case if sensitively applied with due caution.

SIBLING RIVALRY

Infants will die if not parented. Early life care in the form of shelter, feeding, handling, communicating, is generally known as "mothering." Possibly due to this vital need for "caring," after they no longer need physical help, children still want attention. While there is a limit to how much food can be taken in, or how much sleep or how much playing a child can do, the child's demand for attention can be practically limitless. A child can receive 10 hours or more of attention daily and still want more. This attention may have all sorts of meaning for a child, including proof of self-worth. Any child prefers positive attention, smiles, compliments, exclamations of delight, close attention, hugs and kisses, to negative attention, but many children will actually prefer negative attention (yells, slaps, criticisms) to being ignored. In a curious way, punishment becomes a reward for children who would rather be yelled at and punished than be ignored.

What is likely to happen if an "intruder" comes into the family, whether that intruder be a short-term visitor, such as a cousin who comes for a week's visit, or a long-term intruder such as an adopted child or even a new baby? Suddenly, the highly desired attention that one received from the parents is "stolen" from our little hero or heroine, who wants *all* possible attention. The circumstances are now ripe for what is known for sibling rivalry.

Now, something extremely important generally occurs which will influence their style of life. Each sibling, in an attempt to attain a greater portion of parental attention, searches to find ways to gain this noticing. Consider life for a child as a watch face. Say he can act in only 1 of 12 ways. Assume that 1 means "sweet," 2 means "smiling," 3 means "friendly," 4 means "shy," 5 means "active," 6 means "aggressive," and so forth.

Any child is likely to try one or more of these paths to see which works best in getting attention. Say that child A starts out on path 1, "sweet," smiling and simpering, and that this does not work. He may then try number 4 and will begin to act shy—maybe this will get attention! Say that mother and father, who want to stop the child from being too shy, give the attention the child is seeking. Since their attention rewards the child for being shy, he will act even more shy. The sibs, who are also competing for attention, will tend to establish rival ways of acting—and so brothers and sisters tend to develop different personalities. The greater the degree of sibling rivalry, the greater the resulting differences of personality of brothers and sisters. Given a family where the children have similar personalities, we can be fairly certain that they came from a relatively happy, homogeneous, well-balanced family; but if there are violent contrasts among the children, we can be fairly sure that in the family there was a good deal of rivalry.

Demand for attention is the first element that leads to sibling rivalry but, of course, there are other goals. The next demand, according to Dreikurs (1947), is power. Children become competitive relative to their ability to have personal power, to achieve and accomplish and to dominate the social environment. They get into power contests, tussles, arguments, screaming matches, and other "fights." These sibling conflicts frequently disturb parents. These conflicts are not only attempts at personal supremacy, but are also cooperative means to achieve attention! We have rather definite proof of the validity of this assertion. Children in a power contest have as their first goal victory over each other—that is to say, to get parents to side with them, or to get their way; but their second goal (and for some a primary one) is for both to get parental attention. Incredible as it may see, quarreling children are usually unconsciously cooperating for parental attention! The proof is that if parents are counseled to do nothing whatever about fights, no interference, no judging, no sending children out of the room, no refereeing, then the fights typically stop or are drastically curtailed.

Jim and Beth had two boys, ages 8 and 10, who were great fighters. Mother, a victim of polio, was in a wheelchair. When the father was out of the house, she had a great deal of trouble getting to the quarreling boys to separate them. She had a high-pitched voice and would use it to her maximum with wild yells that could be heard throughout the neighborhood in her attempts to stop them. Sometimes she would even throw herself on the floor from her chair to scare the boys into stopping their fighting.

We advised mother to (a) say absolutely nothing if the children fought, and (b) wheel herself as fast as she could as far away from any fighting, and under no circumstances to interfere.

Mother did not want to follow this advice since she had such an abhorrence of fighting. She was asked, as a way of convincing her, to keep a record for some weeks of the number of these "fights," and she was told to follow her usual routine. The first week she reported 47 interventions in fights, from a single loud "stop it" to tumbling from her wheelchair.

She then agreed to stop getting involved and to keep a record of fights. The record, week-for-week, went as follows, and this is typical: 47 (the original), 42, 28, 53, 12, 8, 31, 4, 2, 1, 0, 2, 1.

Note carefully the 53 and the 31, two "surges" commonly found when parents change their tactics. The evidence of this case and many others that we have worked on is that children get into these "power contests" in an unconscious cooperative effort to get parents' attention.

As children continue in their ways of operating to gain attention—the numbers on the clock face presented earlier—they continue to play these roles (unwittingly, of course) and thereby begin to slip into what can become a permanent life style.

We have found a most interesting phenomenon in doing Adlerian counseling: if parents deal with one child in a way to get that child to stop its nonsense, and if this so-called bad child no longer acts in a useless manner, almost inevitably the good child now starts to act up. It is as though the "good" child is saying, "What's the use of my being good? I am not getting any attention now, since my brother or sister is getting attention for being good. Let me try being bad." When the formerly "good" child becomes the "bad" child, this is the surest indication that real change has occurred. Goodness and badness in children are only two modes of attempting to gain attention.

Frequently, if parents do not interfere, formerly battling children will establish peaceful relationships—and some harmony will result. Smart parents find group projects for the children to work on, and will arrange for activities that call for cooperation. Mountain climbing, in which each person is attached to two others, is an ideal representation of what, in effect, a good family does. A camping expedition, with each child having assigned (or accepted) specific duties, is another example. The family playing some game according to established rules is another example. The family playing musical instruments is still another example: mother at the piano, father with a saxophone, big sister with a cello, big brother on the drums, little brother with a kazoo and little sister with bongo drums, and away they go in harmony.

Better yet would be a family that runs according to the egalitarian principles of Adlerian psychology, having a family council (Corsini & Rigney, 1970; Dreikurs, Gould, & Corsini, 1974), with the individuals relating in a democratic fashion. In such a family, while there would, of course, be sibling rivalries, they would tend to be few and far between.

In sum, sibling rivalry probably gets its original impetus from competition between children, fostered by parents in their attempts to diminish sibling conflicts. The children, in their intense competition for attention and power, find various ways, which are satisfactory to them, of getting attention, and these ways may harden eventually into their styles of life—their personalities.

FIXED LIFE STYLE BY AGE FIVE

No one personality theory has cornered the market on "truth." If Adlerian theory does not answer all our questions we must look elsewhere for supplemental information. We may gain further confidence in our theory if we take a close look at someone else's "truths." By investigating other theories we may find that the others' "truths" are similar to ours. Different theories may be saying the same things in different language, or may have discovered the same "facts" from slightly different viewpoints.

An Adlerian "fact" is that life style is fixed by the age of four to six. "By the time a child is five years old his attitude to his environment is usually so fixed and mechanized that it proceeds in more or less the same direction for the rest of his life. His apperception of the external world remains the same" (Adler, 1956, p. 189). Dreikurs (1953) taught that the child sees the world in general as paralleling his home environment and eventually the wider world on the basis of his initial apperceptions. "This explains why every individual by the time he is four to six years old has developed a definite character and why any fundamental change of character after the fourth to sixth year is almost impossible without outside aid through psychotherapy. Character is therefore simply the manifestation of a certain plan which the child has evolved and to which he will adhere throughout the rest of his life" (p. 43).

Confirmation of this comes from the extensive research work of Lois Murphy (1962) and her associates, who intensively observed large numbers of children over a period of time. "The first five years are the time when his [the child's] basic pattern of managing stimulation from the environment is established, during the emergence of fundamental ego functions, affects and drives" (p. 318). Murphy says that a characteristic style of reacting to the environment's stimulation is set by the age of six. The theoretical difference, whether the child is seen as active or reactive, is not as important for our purposes at the moment as is the confirmation of Adler's clinical observation by Murphy's experimental observation.

Jean Piaget, a theorist and empiricist, also confirms the "fact" in question. Intensive, systematic observation and controlled manipulation of children and their surroundings throughout their development is the essence of his method. The four- to six-year age period of cognitive development is referred to by Piaget as the "intuitive phase." "The intuitive phase is one of growing conceptualization. . . . At the close of the intuitive phase these operations (classes, relations, and numbers) become grouped into Gestaltlike structures which Piaget terms 'concrete operations' " (Hunt, 1961, pp. 198–199).

Around the age of five, children begin to classify and to "deal with logical classes and with logical relations" (Piaget, 1961). So, at the same age that Adlerians say the life style is fixed, Piaget says the ability to logically relate classifiable objects develops. Adler sees children's first conceptualizations occurring at this time also: the first categorizations on which the child builds his general framework of himself (weak or strong, good or bad) and the world and other people (good or evil, controllable or controlling).

Although Ernst Schachtel (1947) does not refer to exact ages, he seems to be saying about the same thing and relates it indirectly to another Adlerian subject:

> It is chiefly during the period of early childhood that the quality of the world around him changes for the growing child from a place where everything is new and to be explored . . . to a place where everything either has received a name and a label or is potentially capable of being "explained" by such a label, a process which will be pursued systematically in school. . . . The incompatibility of early childhood experience with the categories and the organization of adult memory is to a large extent due to what I call the conventionalization of the adult memory. Conventionalization is a particular form of what one might call schematization of memory. (p. 9)

In sum, personality theorists generally agree that life style is fixed at about age five—that the child has already established his own interpretation of himself and the world.

ADOLESCENCE

The term *adolescence* may refer to a particular age-group, like the teens, from 13 to 19; or it may refer to a biological state of sexual maturation, which may occur as early as 10 for girls and as late as the late teens for boys; or it may refer to the social independence of children, a transition stage between that of full dependence on parents to full independence as exemplified by leaving the parental home and getting married. So, we can speak of early adolescence or late adolescence, premature adolescence for the sexually mature young person who assumes adult responsibilities, such as a young girl whose father is a widower and who puts the burdens of a woman on his daughter, or late adolescence for someone, such as a boy in his 20s who is still in the home, living according to the parental rules.

> A unique individual comes into adolescence with certain conceptions of himself and the world, and how he must act in the world. He has had a notion of his body but changes occur in the body of this child as he goes through adolescence. These physical changes he has to cope with. For many children moving into adolescence, the ways in which they think about the world change. They move from concrete to formal operations. The child's ideas on what constitutes right and wrong and the inputs into decisions as to what is right and wrong also change in line with the moral development stages of Kohlberg.
>
> Basically it is these changes which take place within the child, within the developing adolescent. These changes are not purely physical and internal, however. As the child grows into adolescence, as he changes and begins to look like an adolescent and more like an adult, more is expected of him, new ways of behaving, new situations are open to him, and he is expected to act at least like an adolescent and maybe like an adult.
>
> We are brought, then, to the problem of the new adolescent attempting to maintain himself as a unique individual (that is, to hang onto the personality that he has developed as a child) in situations where it is not altogether appropriate still to be a child. At the same time we are expecting him still to be himself, to be the Joe, Tom, Sally, or Meg that he or she has always been and we are expecting; but he is trying to fit in, to belong, in these new groups with his new body and his new thoughts. . . .
>
> It is through a combination of personally, individually feeling that one belongs, with accurate perceptions that one does in fact belong, which is the thrust of adolescent development. And it would be remiss not to add the thrust of development throughout the remainder of the life cycle. (Manaster, 1977a, p. 128)

The true test of the effectiveness of parenting shows itself not in childhood but, rather, in adolescence. Many parents have been bewildered and shocked to find that their angel child upon achieving adolescence suddenly appears to change character and to become a monster. Children "play games," simulate, and try to please parents and thereby sometimes generate entirely false impressions. When these youth begin to change from being children to being young adults, and begin to perceive their newly acquired independence and strength, they may suddenly cast off the false mask they have been wearing and become themselves. The smile on the mask now becomes a frown—and as a matter of fact, it may even become a scowl, since children, in becoming young adults, may overreact. And so the "good" child suddenly becomes the "wild" youth.

Some change during adolescence is natural and desirable, and if the change is in a useful manner, with the youth taking on additional responsibility, this is a sign of good parenting; but if the child reacts with hostility or passivity in useless behavior, we can be sure that child has been mistreated psychologically, whether it be through neglect or through pampering—and who knows which of these is the worse? Perhaps worst of all is the child who does not change at all, who continues into adolescence as in childhood. Such children are scared to move toward adulthood and have no courage to assert themselves. Sometimes changes in adolescence are resisted by parents, and there can be violence.

Johnny was a big, slow, good-natured child, the younger of two. The mother was a soft, placating, long-suffering type. The daughter was the father's pet. Father was extremely strict with Johnny and used the whip often and severely. The father ruled the family with an iron hand and his temper tantrums were something terrible.

John did not do well in school, and eventually he was expelled. He had given the school a new home address, and so all school correspondence went to the home of his friend. He actually did not attend school for two years, leaving home early every morning, giving his parents the impression that he was going to school. Eventually, when graduation came, the father found out and went into a monumental temper tantrum. When Johnny came home that day, the father ran at him in a wild fury. Startled, Johnny punched his father in the belly. The father doubled up and lay on the floor, moaning.

From that moment on, the relationship in the family changed. The father no longer was the undisputed king of the family and he became second in command to Johnny. "Those who live by the sword, die by the sword."

We can expect that for children brought up along Adlerian lines—with respect, with parents using natural and logical consequences—adolescence will be a relatively painless and pleasant period for all concerned. As Adler (1932/1962) wrote:

> There are whole libraries of books on adolescence; and almost all of them deal with the subject as it if were a dangerous crisis at which the whole character of an individual could change. There are many dangers in adolescence but it is not true that it can change character. . . .
> For almost every child, adolescence means one thing above all else; he must prove that he is no longer a child. We might, perhaps, persuade him that he can take it for granted; and, if we could do it, a great deal of tension would be drawn from the situation. (p. 134)

At each new life stage, the adequacy of our established life style is tested. The "tests" in childhood, such as starting school or a new kid on the block, may, as many parents know, indicate that all is not as well with the child as the parents may have thought. The "tests" in adolescence, with the strong press for independence and assertions of maturity may, if they provoke prolonged strange or outrageous behavior, indicate a problem—that the adolescent's life style is not a good fit with social living. However, short bouts of upset can be expected and they are also natural for most adolescents, no matter how well adjusted.

DELINQUENCY

In the broad sense of the term, *delinquency* means "behavior disappointing to reasonable expectations" (Sheldon, Hartl, & McDermott, 1970). What makes a delinquent?

Adler, in 1908, when he still used the term, said "drives" explain the reasons for delinquency. Quoting from Adler (1956): "Every unsatisfied drive ultimately orients that organism toward aggression against the environment. The rough characters and the unbridled, incorrigible children can instruct us in the way the continuously unsatisfied drive for affection stimulates the path of aggression" (p. 42).

Adler is saying that a youth who is deprived of affection tends to be aggressive. Dreikurs put his four goals (1947) in this order: (1) attention-getting, (2) power, (3) revenge, and (4) assumed inadequacy. This order is not accidental. The child first seeks for attention and if he does not get it, he tries to demand it. There is a resulting battle between child and parent. Dreikurs (1968) says: "The battle between parents and children for power and domination may reach a point where the parents try every conceivable means to subjegate the culprits" (p. 29). He then goes on: "The mutual antagonism may become so strong that each party has only one desire: retaliation, to revenge his own feeling of being hurt. The child no longer hopes merely for attention or even power: feeling ostracized and disliked, he can see his place in the group only by his success in making himself hated" (p. 29).

We can tie Adler's early position that the child becomes aggressive due to "unsatisfied drives" and Dreikurs' contention that the child who does not get sufficient attention goes for power to make parents give attention and service and that not getting it, the aim now is to get vengeance. This young person now is uncooperative, unwilling to listen, does not like his/her parents, wants to get even, and begins to act in ways to discredit and harm them. The child becomes delinquent: won't do homework, won't do chores, talks back, is fresh, won't do favors, will "forget" what was promised, will dawdle, will upset the neighbors, will do things she/he is told not to do, and so on and so on. The motive of the child is revenge, and it may radiate from feelings against the parents to feelings against others—other children, the school, neighbors, and then everyone. A very clear example of this occurred in one of our counseling cases.

Oscar, a seven-year-old, was stealing. In the past several months the parents reported that he had started taking things from his parents' bedroom, such as toilet articles, perfume, war medals. After being warned and punished, he nevertheless continued, and had extended his stealing to his older brother's and older sister's possessions. When the stealing progressed to the neighbors, the parents went for professional help.

Interviewing the seven-year-old boy showed that he had very strong hostile feelings toward his mother: he wanted to be able to ride his bike with the other boys around the block. Mother had restricted him to the block they lived on, so that she could see him constantly. When she was advised to let him have the freedom to ride where he wanted, after some sharp discussion, she agreed to do what was advised—and the stealing stopped.

The answer to delinquency, of course, is prevention. But what forms of prevention? Again we come back to basics: the child must be treated with respect and given just due in the form of sufficient attention and consideration. Every child has a certain amount of need to be noticed, to belong, to feel part of the family, and if the amount given is not sufficient, the child then begins to start a power play, demanding attention and equality. The wise parent will include the child as much as possible in everything: work and play, making the child feel valued. This does *not,* and we want to emphasize the *not,* mean spoiling the child, catering to every wish. But, it does mean giving the child due regard and consideration, enough freedom to make choices, meanwhile using natural and logical consequences for disciplinary and training purposes.

Every delinquent starts in the home: children only attack others if they have been trained to attack in the family. Parents who are either brutal or neglectful or spoiling are equally liable to generate delinquents through their misguided methods of dealing with their young ones. For this reason we Adlerians, more than any other personality theory group, do family counseling in large groups, run parent training and parent study groups since we know that the origins of delinquency are almost always in the family. Better parenting is the major solution we recommend to counteract delinquency.

Chapter 8

Maintenance of Personality

While our personality generally maintains itself even if it should have faulty elements, drastic changes *can* occur through traumas and through psychotherapy. Thus, for example, a pampered daughter whose mother dies and who now becomes the little mother of younger children, may drastically modify her life style; or a person who has been quite unhappy and unsuccessful in life may go into psychotherapy and thereby change his/her life style considerably. But ordinarily, whether one has a good or bad life style—that is to say, a successful or unsuccessful way of life, one tends to keep it. But (*a*) why do we maintain our life style? and (*b*) How do we maintain it? *Why* and *how?*

WHY DO WE MAINTAIN OUR LIFE STYLE?

Our life style is a series of conclusions that we have about ourselves, about life, about the world, how to interact with others, what others are like, and what behavior will succeed. In other words, the life style is the blueprint we have about everything. It is *us.* It is therefore *our* philosophy of life, *our* plan of action, *our* tendency, *our* set. It represents the essence of us: *what we are.*

Consequently, life style is a most central part of us since it tells us what is right and what is wrong for us, what works and what doesn't, what should and should not be done. Since it is difficult for us to really observe ourselves vis-à-vis others, we tend to think that our ideas are absolutely right. Blaise Pascal once wrote that while we want more of life in almost every respect— to be more beautiful, to be stronger, to be smarter, and so on—one thing that everyone was satisfied with was our own common sense. We all think we have

97

good common sense, no matter how stupidly we act or how silly or how unsuccessful we are. Even if we have an unsuccessful life, we tend to cling to our sense of self as though to a life preserver when on the ocean—it is our means of survival.

Life style is a series of working hypotheses about life. Some people have terribly inefficient life styles—they are not successful at work or in the home or socially. We say of such people, "He's got a terrible personality," meaning that he has an incorrect life style. Or we may say, "She has a terrific personality," and in Adlerian terms we are saying that her life style is appropriate and successful. A life style enables us to organize ourselves, to evaluate new situations, to simplify life, to make predictions and in general to cope with life.

For all these reasons we maintain our life style, since even if it is not a good one, that is all we have. We can easily see that some other people have inadequate life styles. Mike is not successful socially because he constantly complains. June has a reputation as a liar. Herbert makes enemies through cheating. We see errors others make. And we can well ask: *Why don't they change? Why don't they use their common sense and stop their self-defeating behavior?*

People will not change their life style because they ordinarily (*a*) do not recognize the errors in their thinking and behavior, (*b*) even if these are pointed out to them, they do not know what to do instead, or (*c*) they do not have the courage to overthrow old patterns for new, unknown outcomes.

HOW DO WE MAINTAIN OUR LIFE STYLE?

Since people establish their life styles early and tend to maintain them even if the life styles are inefficient and ineffective, it certainly seems to be an anomaly that if all people are forward oriented and want to be happier and more successful, they will hold onto their incorrect concepts even though it is evident that their ways of thinking and acting are unsuccessful. So we have an interesting problem: how *do* people maintain a life style—whether it be "good" or "bad"?

We do this in three ways: (*a*) through adaptation, (*b*) through self-reinforcement, and (*c*) through success. Let us examine these three maintainers of life style .

Adaptation

Over time we learn to adjust to situations, and through constant practice we tend to "stamp in" our behavior patterns and ways of seeing life. We begin to fit into our life style, our uniqueness, the way we get to fit into a pair of shoes.

Self-Reinforcement

We tend to "inoculate" ourselves through our biased observations, by self-evaluation and self-justification. We are constantly planning to attain our ends. Even in our dreams we are making plans. We also employ our emotions to achieve our goals.

Success

That people succeed with ineffective life styles may seem to be contradictory, but we have to understand what is meant by "success." There is evident and obvious success, such as when a person gets a job or is given a diploma. But there is also a kind of success when a person interprets an event as a success even though it seems to be a failure to everyone else. A person may fail an examination and yet may see it as a success by such mental maneuvering as the following: "Had I studied, I would have passed—and I chose not to," or "Only fools study—I am above that." This kind of crooked thinking maintains a poor life style—the person is a success by avoiding recognizing failure.

Some people with inadequate life styles do succeed at some times in some places and with some people. A good example would be the "hippies" of the 1960s, who gravitated into their own orbits and reinforced each other in terms of their thinking. No one, after all, fails all the time. Experiments with pigeons show that if the bird has a success, say, every 100 times, this is enough to keep that bird working away at a task. People are not different in this respect: given an occasional success, they will persist. This explains gambling: even when the gambler knows that the gambling house has the odds in its favor and that he will lose everything if he persists gambling, he will continue.

People learn to behave in the manners which are judged appropriate by their society and social group at each step in the life cycle. The steps in this process are socialization, identification, modeling, and so on. People learn by virtue of the results of their behavior as members of their society. They learn by seeing what others do and by noting the effects of others' behavior as well as by trying out behaviors they think are appropriate for the outcomes they desire. What constitutes appropriate behavior differs by situation, status, social group, and age. So persons who want to belong to a certain group will act as they think someone of that age-group should act in each situation. We learn to "act our age." Human behavior becomes more involved and intricate as people get older, have more experience and knowledge, and have been socialized in a wider variety of groups. Through the process of development, people choose how they will fit into society. In this way they maintain their life style while becoming members of the human community.

Persons become part of society and its subgroups and act in such a manner that it serves their goals and allows affiliation. As people learn more, become more involved in intricate ways of living in a greater number of groups with a greater number of socially acceptable models, they also learn new ways of living their life style. They are developing strategies for reaching their goals and justifying their actions. People become amazingly expert and sophisticated at thinking about themselves in self-justifying ways. If they spend great amounts of time on such rationalizations, they are probably out of line with common sense and they thereby approach failure.

So in answer to the question of how people maintain their life style: the answer is that with experience and age, people learn to be themselves and to continue to fit into social arenas. By selecting where they want to fit and what they want to do, they increase the probability of reaching their goals. They also learn more complex ways of justifying their behavior within the framework of their continuing life style. Some of these ways of justification are known as defense mechanisms or, in Adler's term, safeguarding tendencies.

In terms of the triumvirate of thinking, feeling, and acting, Adlerians believe that thinking comes first. *First*, we think, *then* we act, and *then* we feel. Other theorists put the sequence differently: first we feel, then we act, then we think; or first we act, then we think, then we feel. In the treatment of maladjusted individuals, some therapists "attack" first the feelings, some the actions, some the thoughts.

It is a misconception, however, to think that Adlerians relegate feelings as a minor part of life. We consider such emotions as joy, happiness, warmth, love, satisfaction with self, acceptance of self, feelings of belonging as most important, but we see them as being the result of—*and not the cause of*—proper thinking and proper behavior. Adlerians say that we feel good if we act right and we act right if we think correctly.

To illustrate: A mother reports that she is upset because her child is not doing well in school. When she is questioned, we find that (in our judgment) she gets overinvolved with the child's school work and the child is rebelling against mother's pressure. So, working backward, we conclude about the mother that (*a*) she is unhappy, (*b*) her overinvolved behavior is causing the child to do poorly in school, and (*c*) her concepts about school and her child are incorrect. We now inform her that (*a*) her behavior should change, (*b*) things then most probably will improve, and (*c*) she will eventually feel better. She follows our advice about changing her behavior and things work out better. The sequence now is (*a*) *cognition*—mother has a new understanding of her child and her relationship with him, (*b*) *action* changes—she relates to her son in different ways, which leads her son into changing his ways, and (*c*) *emotional* changes—mother is satisfied since conflict is reduced. Her "mistake" may have been a complex of thoughts such as: "I am responsible for my child's education," "If my child does not do well academically, I am a poor mother," "If I nag my child maybe he will do better," "A good mother should supervise her child's education," and so on.

Let us assume that the child began to do better in school. If all this happens, we have the sequence *thoughts → action → feelings.* So, the steps in Adlerian counseling go: (*a*) first a change occurs in thinking, then (*b*) in action, and then (*c*) in feelings. In our Family Counseling Centers: (*a*) sometimes we might tell our clients to change their behavior simply because we tell them to do so, and then they act differently even though they do not understand why, but since they are desperate, they will follow any advice given them; then (*b*) upon changing their behavior, they note that things improve, and so at this point they begin to understand our theory and the mistakes in their thinking; and (*c*) they now feel better.

Or, the sequence might be: (*a*) the client does what is told without understanding or believing in it; (*b*) feels better because conflicts are reduced; and (*c*) comes to understand the logic and theory of our procedures and develops a mental attitude different from the beginning.

Let us move now to a much more subtle and more important set of misconceptions—those about ourselves.

BASIC MISTAKES

Each human being develops, over time, a series of concepts about self, about others, and about life which form that person's essential philosophy on which his/her life style is based. Adlerians call these concepts private logic. Conclusions resulting from one's private logic often do not fit what Adler called "the common sense of social living." We refer to these general mistaken conclusions as basic mistakes. Mosak (1979, p. 67) divides basic mistakes into five categories:

1. Overgeneralizations. Usually, such words as "all," "never," and "always," are implicit in this class of basic mistakes: "All people should admire me," "No one cares for me," or "I never get a fair break."

2. False or impossible goals of "security." The individual sees the world as a hostile place and believes that one is never free from anxiety, such as "Everyone is my enemy," "Everyone is on the take," or "I'll never make it."

3. Misperceptions of life and life's demands. These call for excesses: "Life is so hard," "All I can expect is suffering," or "People want too much from me."

4. Minimization or denial of one's worth. Expressions of personal defeat, such as "I am unlovable," or "I'll never succeed."

5. Faulty values. This usually has to do with concepts of behavior, such as: "You can't beat others unless you are unfair," The way to succeed is to lie and never tell the truth," or "Everyone is your enemy."

In the simplest sense, psychotherapy may be seen as a process of first finding basic mistakes and then correcting them. This may be the heart of psychotherapy, but to get to the heart may take a lot of time. Wouldn't it be interesting if it were possible for people to simply give data such as called for in a Life Style Analysis (p. 178), then everything would be coded and out would come a list of the person's basic mistakes! The patient would accept these as his/her basic mistakes, change his/her thinking, and would assume a new and better life style!

Unfortunately, people have so many defenses, to get them to see their mistakes and to correct them calls for the whole mystique of psychotherapy. Also, unfortunately, many people with serious basic mistakes have no way of ever knowing that there is a way of uncovering them.

From our files we have selected some patterns of basic mistakes to show some incorrect views of life.

A man who married four times unsuccessfully
1. He does not trust women.
2. He feels alone in life.
3. He is unsure of his success, but won't admit it; he is a smiling pessimist.

A young man chronically dissatisfied with life
1. He is overambitious; wants instant success.
2. He is too hard on himself; expects too much too soon.
3. He unnecessarily feels guilty as though he is letting everyone down.
4. He seeks overapproval from others.

An alcoholic nurse
1. She feels she does not belong to the human race.
2. She rejects people but thinks they reject her.
3. She trusts things more than she does people.

A rather complicated artist with a minor drinking problem; married unsuccessfully three times
1. Is overfearful and sees the world as filled with dangers.
2. Is innately distrustful of others' good intentions.
3. Constantly expects the worst to happen.

These basic mistakes are mostly of the "social" type. They relate to perceptions of other people and even, as in the last one, when they appear to be intra- rather than interpersonal, can be interpreted socially—the "worst" usually refers to lack of success with other people. A person with these incorrect basic concepts is usually completely unaware of having them.

Jim has been working on his master's degree for 11 years, and has accumulated several dozen completed master's theses, but he will not hand in any of them, since he feels that none are good enough. Also, he wants to quit his job as an elementary school teacher and go for a doctor's degree, but since he hasn't his master's, how can he go? Also, at age 33, he is still a bachelor. He has two girl friends and when he is with one of them he wants to marry *her,* but then when he visits the other he wants to marry *her*—and so he can't make up his mind. On top of that, even though he has a very high level of academic intelligence as revealed by tests, his grades are very spotty, with very few Bs and Cs, but a lot of Ds and As. He went for therapy; and after several months, he handed in a thesis, got his degree, gave up both of the women, quit his job, and registered for a doctoral program.

What had made the difference? It was the resolution of some of his mistaken ideas. When he admitted having them and saw how foolish they were, he changed his behavior. They were:

I cannot succeed.

My brother is superior to me.

No one can really love me.

I must always avoid taking chances.

Anyone familiar with Albert Ellis' Rational-Emotive Therapy or Eric Berne's Transactional Analysis will see their similarity to Adler's views.

This man thought he could not succeed, that no one could love him, and so on—*but he did not know this!* He was completely unaware of his private logic—and indeed when it was uncovered through life style analysis, at first he strongly disagreed with his therapist. He argued that he believed that he could succeed—after all, didn't he continue to try? If he felt he would fail, why would he keep trying? He felt he was lovable and offered as evidence the names of a series of women who had loved him.

His therapy was centered on determining the correctness of his basic mistakes. Finally, he "saw" life differently. He had a new conception of himself and of others. As a result, he began to operate differently in relation to others. He became a new person, basically because he recognized that he had these misconceptions, and he began to operate differently in terms of his new conceptions.

Every one of us has basic mistakes. It is almost impossible for us to come to maturity without at least one mistake. Usually there are more than one. They are central, usually not known to the person, but they are dearly held and highly resistant to change. They form the central psychological unity of the person. In their oversimplification, overgeneralization, gross impossibility, misperception or absolutism, basic mistakes generally refer to the syllogism "I am ... " "The world is ... " or "Therefore. ... "

A person may have a single major basic mistake. For example, a woman's life style syllogism may go: "I am not good. The world accepts only the good;

therefore, I must be good." The critical mistake in this life style is the demand on herself that she "must be good." She is also in error that she is not good and that the world is unswervingly good, but the critical mistake is believing that she must always, in every situation, be absolutely "good." The universality of this basic mistake is what gets her into trouble. A single basic mistake can be completely debilitating. An individual may never do anything she/he wants to do, or even think that one is entitled to do what one wants, because she/he is always doing "good" deeds, what others want, trying to be "good." And when a person is not actively "good," one probably spends time going over what has been done to see where one was not "good," feeling guilty about those times, and planning future "good" deeds.

Most often people who come for psychological help have more than one basic mistake. For illustration, let us consider someone whose basic mistake is "I am a little stinker; the world is rewarding of the big and good; therefore, I have to be big and good." The person is saying, "I must always be big, successful, number one and I must always without exception be good." Being good all the time to everyone may not allow one to contradict others, achieve more than others, or do anything that others may think badly of the person for doing. Even if one were virtuous, moral, and ethical to an exemplary degree, one's success would be received with some resentment, some disagreement, some dissatisfaction perhaps from a colleague or friend, boss or underling, spouse or relative. Moreover, there might be times when it would be difficult to do what had to be done for success, while still being completely "good." In effect, the two mistakes—the two goals to be *first* and to be *good*—are conflicting. Such is the nature of exaggerated goals. Such is the nature of basic mistakes.

EMOTIONS

The word emotion has the same root as the word "motivation." This is a clue to the purpose of the emotions: to move us, to serve as a goad to action. According to English and English's *Dictionary of Psychological and Psychoanalytic Terms* (1958), "Emotion is virtually impossible to define," but we can make some differentiations.

We regard emotions as being part of the person's life style. Two identical events occurring to two similar people can lead to quite different emotions. A good example would be any kind of failure, such as being defeated in some game. One person will show discouragement while another might react with the intention of doing better. Emotions are not in the event, whether pleasant or unpleasant but, rather, in the interpretation. Emotions function in conjunction with the person's goal of life. The perception of the event that leads to the emotion, whatever it may be, is directed by the person's intention.

Emotions are motivators. They "push" or "accelerate" or "enhance" the person's goal. We "manufacture" our emotions to enable us to achieve our goal. A good example is what happens to a person in a fight. He has been thrown down, and he gets angry, and this emotion has the effect of making him stronger. Had he been thrown down in a friendly wrestling match, for example, he would not be as powerful as he is when he is angry.

The Adlerian position is that "emotions are at the service of the intellect," which means that our emotions are controlled by our goals, by our ideas, by our intentions. According to Adler (1931), emotions can be described as conjunctive (happy, socially oriented) or disjunctive (unhappy, socially aggressive). Essentially, conjunctive emotions such as joy and love bring people together, while disjunctive ones such as hatred and fear separate people.

Recently one of us was part of a study to determine whether people readily understand the idea of emotions functioning according to disjunctive or conjunctive social movement, whether they understand emotions as movement toward, away, or against others (Horney, 1950). We asked 150 college students to rate a list of words describing emotions as to whether each moved the person closer to, the same distance from, or away from others. The emotions that the students saw as most moving one toward others were *love, friendly, caring,* while the emotions seen moving one away from others were *hate, used,* and *humiliated*—very much the conjunctive and disjunctive modes as described by Adler. Listed as keeping one equidistant from others were emotions such as *torn, frustrated,* and *temperamental.* Clearly, people see emotions as functioning as Adler explained:

> It may well be that the more complex and obtuse interpretations of the meanings of emotion are essentially a "cover-up," and a mechanism whereby we make ourselves seem more complicated and superior. As it can be shown that our emotions function to keep us the same distance from others or move us closer to or further from them, it may be possible to understand quite easily what we are feeling and doing. If we were to assume that the outcome was equivalent to the purpose, we could understand why we felt and did what we did. (Manaster, Cleland, & Brooks, 1978, pp. 252–253)

In contrast to theories that viewed emotions as disruptive, Adler saw them as helpful, facilitating movement in line with the person's goals. In the Adlerian position, that cognition precedes affection; to have an emotion there must be some thought beforehand. We think and then feel; emotions are directed by goals except, perhaps, in violent situations such as a sudden explosion when thought and feeling may occur practically simultaneously.

For this reason, in discussing abnormal behavior, Adlerians do not think or talk about emotional diseases but, rather, of intellectual mistakes. We do not excuse misbehavior due to emotions, since we believe that no one gets so angry that one doesn't know what he or she was doing. A person is seen as responsible, and if it does happen that one goes amok and does something violent due to anger, we believe that the anger only facilitates the underlying goal. Thus, one who murders someone first thinks, "I want to kill" and then in anger hurls herself at the other, but the thought occurred before the anger.

Since all behavior is seen as being purposive (moving one toward one's goal), and being on purpose (the responsibility of the behaver), emotions, too, are seen as being purposive. Emotions are part of the life style and are the energizers, activators and, in that sense, are the motivators of behavior.

Intrapersonal Conflict

According to Jacob Arlow (1979), psychoanalysis is a psychology of conflicts, and the most important conflicts are intrapersonal. The id and the superego are in conflict according to Freudian theory—the struggle between innate desires and social demands. Other personality theories put stress on internal conflict. For Albert Ellis (1962), conflict is somewhat like the Freudians: the desire to please others versus the desire to please oneself. For Otto Rank (1936), the conflict was between security and safety. Carl Rogers (1951) sees the conflict in people between living their lives as nature intended and their desire to please people. Similarly, George Kelly (1955) saw a conflict in people relative to their construing of reality: should they depend on themselves or should they accept the views of others? The work of Solomon Asch (1955) relative to social pressure essentially refers to this same kind of conflict between trusting one's own perception or depending on the perceptions of others.

Mosak and Lefevre (1976) discuss the Adlerian view of "intrapersonal conflict"—a situation in which people see themselves as victims of a conflict situation, having the impression (contrary to Adlerian views) that they are "powerless." In such situations they feel "torn apart"—being two individuals, such as the "good me" who wants to do the right thing and the "bad me" who wants to do what is wrong. The individual is supposed to use "will power" in such situations.

In Roman Catholic traditional thinking, the situation was personified by a "good angel" giving good advice sitting on one's right shoulder and by a "bad angel" on the left side giving bad advice, with the soul listening to both and making decisions which then would be acted upon by the body.

A person in conflict does not experience the situation as being one of simple choice but sees himself as the victim of life pulled in two directions—helpless. Feelings of helplessness lead to feelings of depression.

Now the person in such a situation will usually come to a resolution. Eventually, in some way or another, a decision will be made. However, at the time of the apparent conflict one cannot see any way out. One simply feels pulled in two directions. If someone were to say to you, "I really don't know what to do: on the one hand I love Jack and want to be faithful to him and keep my family; but on the other hand Bill needs me, and when I am with him I am rapturously happy," or "I know I have security with this job, and I can see myself getting a gold watch in 20 years and a good pension; but on the other hand if I break off and go into business for myself, I have a chance of making a lot of money and having my own business and being my own boss"—and so on—then you, as the outside adviser, might be able to say something like "Well, let's add up the advantages and disadvantages and see if we can come to a sensible conclusion and then make up your mind what is the best thing to do."

However, the other person might inform you that things are not that simple; that she is blocked and cannot move one way or another. Adlerians take the position that when an individual maintains an impasse for a long time, the person *intends* not to make a decision: it is her *purpose* not to decide! As a therapist, if your client tells you, "I simply cannot make up my mind: on the one hand I want . . . and on the other hand I want . . . and this has been going on a long time. I want to settle the issue, but I just can't," you would know that the person can decide, but will not.

Unwilling to take responsibility, remaining indecisive, means shirking one's obligations. The person expects that something will occur to settle the issue; then the person also can feel "good" that he did not make a bad decision or that he heroically struggled with such an enormous problem in view of his good intentions. In other words, everything is for "show" and not "for real." This is what Adler called the "yes, but . . . " syndrome.

Adlerians view this "yes, but . . . " situation, or intrapersonal conflicts, as attempts by individuals to avoid responsibility and still look good in their own eyes and in the eyes of others—suffering like mighty heroes, unable to make decisions. It is a kind of "game," using Berne's terminology, that the person plays. But to the struggling person it seems to be a very real problem. And it is real to the person in such a conflict: only to the outside observer is the conflict seen as an attempt to avoid responsibility. It is the Adlerian therapist's task to help the person in such a quandary to be able to see it for what it really is, and to help that person come to some resolution.

We may add one final point—something difficult to understand for those not in such situations. Even though the person with the so-called intrapersonal conflict may strongly say that a resolution is wanted, often this is just not so: *the person may want to suffer!* There can be a perverse pleasure in the discomfort that results when one has an intrapersonal conflict. What can this be? Going back to first principles, we can find this "payment." Remember that one of the most important aspects of human phenomenology is a feeling of self-esteem. By the tricky safeguarding manipulations of the individual, this weakness of not being able to make a decision, this immaturity showing itself in an incapacity to come to clear-cut and sensible judgment, becomes a kind of heroic struggle, so that the person can develop a feeling of moral superiority, saying to him/herself: "Look how bravely I suffer! What a hero I am!" And, consequently, the decision is delayed.

Anxiety

A student awaiting an examination is likely to feel anxious. A mother in a hospital waiting to hear from the doctors as to what damage has occurred to her child is likely to be anxious. Anxiety usually is a result of not knowing what is going to happen and what to do, a fear of the future. Such cases are understandable—whether one is waiting to find out what the size of the bill is for repairing a car, or waiting for the safe arrival of a child who is out much later than usual, or waiting to find out what the dentist's X ray shows—these are, so to speak, "real" fears, based on real situations. Indeed, it would be abnormal not to have anxiety under situations when the outcome is unknown and you don't know what, if anything, you can do or what will happen.

But how about a constant general feeling of anxiety? Suppose that someone is always fearful, always worrying, constantly on edge? What does this mean? And what can be done about it?

A state of constant anxiety is called an anxiety neurosis. According to Adler, anxiety of this type is likely to be a means of trying to control others. Another reason may be to escape from doing something that one feels one should do. In this way one is not tested and found wanting. Anxiety can be a way of avoiding demands or of not getting defeated. Essentially, it is based, as so many of the neuroses are, on a feeling of personal inferiority—not being good enough —which in turn leads to exaggerated aims of personal superiority, wanting to be more than one is.

Let us examine what has been said from a historical point of view of one man with high standards. If this person's actual behavior does not meet his standards, anxiety occurs because he does not want the "world" (including self) to know he was below standard. Anxiety now is the fear of becoming exposed as inferior or weak or stupid or "bad." He is now like Damocles who, according to a fable, sat at a banquet under a dangling sword, constantly aware that the sword was held by a single hair, unable to relax, always awaiting the sword's fall.

As unpleasant as anxieties are, they can serve a useful function, depending on their degree. Anxiety is a reaction to the discrepancy between a person's perception of *what is* and *what should be.*

If *What is=What should be* . . . **Contentment.**
If *What is>What should be* . . . **Satisfaction.**
If *What is<What should be* . . . **Anxiety.**

If there is a minus discrepancy between how the person sees herself and how she thinks she ought to be, anxiety results. Since no one wants to suffer, the anxiety feeling becomes a motivator and the individual searches for relief, whether it be useful or useless.

Useful relief means doing something to correct the felt discrepancy in some positive manner, such as stopping wrongdoing, getting more education, going for therapy, or making restitution for some wrong. Useless methods of escape are alcoholism, drug addiction, bizarre behavior, and even suicide. In any case, the action relieves the anxiety.

Adler discussed four ways that neurotics escape from these uncomfortable feelings: (*a*) *moving backward,* such as suicide, fainting, and hysterical paralysis; (*b*) *standing still,* a kind of general impotence, as though the person can do nothing but suffer; (*c*) *back-and-forth movement,* a kind of useless repetition, found in such nonsensical behavior as writing a paper, then tearing it up, rewriting it and retearing it up, over and over again, always being late, and never starting; and (*d*) *construction of obstacles,* that is, generating some means of not succeeding in actually solving the problem by generating some new problems. For example, to avoid taking an examination, one may get oneself expelled from school for breaking a rule, or may develop psychosomatic symptoms such as a migraine headache, which now incapacitates him/her.

Robert, a law student expelled for poor grades, fought for readmission and was eventually reaccepted. Now having "proved" his inferiority through having been kicked out of school, he went to the head of the class in grades. In this way, once he failed, he no longer needed anxiety and could do well.

One purpose of anxiety neurosis is to escape from facing possible failure, avoiding real or imagined major challenges. People can become so concerned with their fear that they can do little that is positive in meeting problems head on. Some people may escape into work, some into play, but if they do not face the essential problem—handling the difference between the *What is* and the *What should be*—such escapes are only temporary. Actively coping with the discrepancy means the anxiety will be relieved and will not return as readily.

Frustration. Feelings of frustration are somewhat different from what common sense tells us. Adlerians believe that feelings of frustration are often self-generated and that they are not necessarily implicit in the situation. In short, one does not have to feel frustrated by anything; if we are frustrated, it is simply because we permit this feeling to occur in us.

Let us examine the dynamics of frustration. You want something. But something in the environment prevents you from attaining your goal. You are stopped. These are the facts. Now come the feelings. They can vary from practically zero—"Well, that's the way it is"—to extreme—"I could kill someone!" These feelings are an accompaniment of our attitudes, our point of view. If we take a relaxed, easygoing, so-what attitude, we just don't feel frustrated when we get blocked. If, however, we expect that everything should go just as we want, then if we are blocked, we feel frustrated.

Don't confuse blocking, being stopped, or not getting your way, with feeling frustrated. Frustration is only a feeling and is in the service of our thoughts, and is not necessarily a result of not getting our way. If we feel frustrated by something, we should remember that it was our decision to feel this way; we didn't have to have these feelings.

Ellis (1962), with the same underlying rationale as Adlerians, sees frustration feelings as clearly being similar to anger. Both emotions are dependent on one's personal views—the things we say to ourselves. When things do not go the way we would like them to go, we may say "Well, this happens sometimes" and not feel bad at all and just go on about our business. However, if we demand that the situation or the other person be as we wish, if we say to ourselves, "This *should* not happen" or "She *should* do that," we will be angry. Feelings of anger and frustration are produced by our view of the situation—the "shoulds."

Guilt

Common thinking about guilt goes as follows: each of us has a sense of justice, rightness, correctness—what Immanuel Kant called the "categorical imperative"—a sense of morality—a conscience. If a person does something he knows to be wrong, feelings of guilt result. This seems quite logical. However, the Adlerian view expands considerably on this position.

Beecher (1950) sees guilt as being essentially an expression of one's striving for superiority! "Look how much I suffer because of my transgressions! How morally superior I am!" In this way, the inadequate individual sustains her impressions of superiority by this foolish maneuver, and interestingly enough, by showing the world (in some cases) and herself what a moral person she is, she is now impelled to repeat the performance of "sin" so she can further castigate herself. The purpose of all such neurotic feelings is to safeguard one's self-esteem, to make one feel OK. Thus the neurotic says, in effect, "I am a real hero in that I suffer so much because of my evil behavior." "I am a very good person really—look how I suffer guilt!" Thereby, an individual gets such satisfaction from suffering that one continues in this useless feeling and useless behavior and does not have to face the challenge of reforming. The classic example is the repentant drunkard, who takes a pledge to abstain from liquor when finally sober, feels terribly guilty, but then repeats the drinking again—and again—and again—each time feeling terribly guilty.

Such destructive behavior would seem to be completely useless but if we see the guilt as positive evidence to the individual of one's goodness and worth-whileness, we now can understand why the person continues her transgressions over and over again. It is to maintain—in this useless, painful way—feelings of self-esteem, to prove superiority.

A banker took a bribe—a small amount of money—to approve a loan. He then felt terribly guilty and went to a church, where he confessed his sin to a priest. The priest gave him absolution and as penance gave him the order to say some prayers. But this was not enough for our hero. He went to another priest and confessed to him. The same penance was given. But this still did not meet our hero's needs and he went to a priest with a reputation for being very strict. This priest also did not meet his needs, and he searched out still another priest, the chaplain of a prison, expecting to be excoriated, but this priest also gave more or less the same penance. Finally, the banker developed a series of physiological symptoms and he started going to physicians, who could find nothing wrong with him. Eventually he came into therapy.

An analysis of his life style showed two trends: an extremely high moral standard (for example, he would not allow his wife to use birth control methods because contraception was contrary to his religion) and yet an extremely low personal behavior standard (for example, he used vulgarity regularly). The contrast between the two standards led to guilt at all levels. When he finally understood the purpose of his need to feel guilty as a sign of his superiority, he gave up his "bad" behavior, realizing that this was just plain useless acting out.

As Bruck (1950) points out, a paradoxical aspect of guilt is that the person who feels guilty is more likely to continue the misbehavior than is one who does not: the person who criticizes the misbehaving individual thereby paradoxically enhances the possibility that the "sin" or "crime" will continue.

Conscience.   Where do children learn right from wrong? Are such aspects of people as fairness, honesty, justice, truthfulness, and goodness built in, part of, the human's biological equipment? Are they given to us by God as part of divine providence? Or are these learned attitudes? These metaphysical questions cannot be answered. However, the evidence provided by cultural anthropologists strongly suggests that if such attitudes are not socially learned, they are certainly socially reinforced. It so happens that within the mores of all major societies more or less the same values obtain. For example, all societies prefer a predictable person, whose words and actions coincide.

Should a person violate incorporated rules, he tends to feel guilty. Some people have an overactive conscience, sometimes to the point of absurdity, feeling guilty about any little thing. We call such people overscrupulous. Others have a very weak conscience and excuse themselves for everything. Such people are castigated with the designation of sociopathic or psychopathic.

Parental influences are probably the usual way of developing a conscience. "Johnny, that is not a nice word. People will not like you if you keep using it." The child picks up from his environment what is right and what is wrong fairly readily. We must tell a joke about this kind of thing.

> Teacher (to mother): Your son uses such bad language in school.
> Mother: I wonder where the hell he learns it.

Frequently in counseling we suggest that someone who has violated some canon of behavior not be punished or even reprimanded. Thus, let us say that Jim frequently drinks too much, and when he does, his wife criticizes him. The counselor may suggest that the next time he comes home drunk she say nothing at all, or even, perhaps, show solicitude. The intent, then, is for the husband to deal with his own conscience.

There is a subtle difference between conscience and guilt feelings. The former is a kind of cognitive understanding of right and wrong which can serve to correct behavior; the latter is a neurotic device of self-blaming with the frequent result of continuing misbehavior.

Insecurity

"Insecurity" can be understood as an awareness that one does not know where one belongs. People who are watchful, shy, timid, suspicious, and very careful are not sure who they are, who others are, and they tend to see the world filled with dangers or unknowns. They don't have a feeling of social belonging. Naturally, feelings of insecurity range from mild to severe. Thus, a normal person about to do something with some degree of risk—say, give a speech—may well feel insecure, especially if not well prepared or if in front of a hostile audience. At the far end of insecurity is the person who is afraid to do anything, positive that nothing whatever will work out, that no one will ever like him/her.

Insecurity may be "normal and natural" when there is a really solid objective reason for feeling uncertain, such as when awaiting a prospective employer's decision as to whether you will get a job for which you have been interviewed. This "normal" insecurity serves the purpose of making people aware that they have to buoy themselves up, get ready for what they feel insecure about. But neurotic insecurity has to do with the total individual. Let us attempt to explain its basic mechanisms.

Essentially, the reason for insecurity is a discrepancy between what a person wants or desires or thinks is right, and how he sees the actual situation. Thus, if one were to do some sort of performance in a strange group, one may feel insecure because of a fear that one may not perform as well as one should. One's expectations and desires do not coincide. The complete neurotic is always anxious and insecure, because he always knows that failure is likely. Such a person sees the world as a hostile place, and believes that one can only be accepted and secure if one is superior. To be accepted, one cannot be just oneself: one must be better than others.

This pervasive feeling is uncomfortable and, consequently it becomes a stimulus to action. The emotion of insecurity is a motivator. It affects us in such a manner to act to get rid of the feeling. So it is quite a complicated matter —and let's examine it a bit carefully.

1. A man has a certain aspiration about himself—what he should be.
2. He wants to be accepted.
3. He has a certain evaluation of himself.
4. There is a discrepancy between his self-image and his self-aspiration.
5. The self-image (what I am) is always below the self-aspiration (what I should be).
6. The person now makes the following assumption (without awareness): "Since I am not what I should be, I cannot accept myself; since I cannot accept myself, neither can others accept me" (Papageorgis, 1965).
7. As a consequence, in a social situation the person feels uncomfortable, insecure, and expects and reacts to all kinds of slights.

We can again see the purposive nature of the emotions—the feeling of insecurity motivates the person to move upward and onward in an effort to achieve greater superiority—to achieve a feeling of belongingness. All this may be put under the general heading of "guarding self-esteem," the perception of oneself as inferior, and the reaction of horror of this depreciation. In a perfect world, we would all be like lilies on a pond—perfectly level with one another, each equal to the other, even though each of us is different. Dreikurs (1971) called equality the challenge of our times. However, the general picture of the insecure person is something like that of acrobats who form a triangle, with a group at the bottom, holding up another group on their shoulders, and they holding a smaller group on their shoulders and then on top of them is one person. Who is really the most insecure? Surely the one on top; but the neurotic, if he were one of the anchormen at the bottom, would feel uncomfortable since he would want to be the top dog, as Fritz Perls (1969) would say.

However, if that person gets on top—whatever that may mean—the true neurotic is still insecure. This person can perform further mental gymnastics. "They only like me because I am successful." "They don't like me, just my looks." Or even "They are jealous of me." Or "Now that I am on top, I can fall."

Consequently the insecure person cannot ever be secure through having money or position simply because that person is always looking up and down —that is to say, is a vertical individual rather than a horizontal individual, living along a horizontal plane of equality (Allred, 1974). The only solution is to give up the goal of personal superiority over others, and to accept philosophically that we belong to life—because we are humans.

The neurotic will fight this concept, because it cannot possibly be believed that one can be accepted for oneself rather than for one's accomplishments. The person must be better looking, more talented, more capable—otherwise he or she is nothing. And the task of psychotherapy, of course, is to change this belief. However, the neurotic person clings to the belief of the need for improvement since she is likely to believe that were she to relax and just accept the fact that she is acceptable, she would no longer struggle for advancement and improvement, when exactly the opposite is true. Freed from neurotic beliefs of the need to be superior over others, she now not only feels comfortable and relaxed with people, but is able to accomplish more. This is a paradoxical situation. The analogy comes from an animal experiment.

A monkey is taught to open a simple lock that has several operations that must follow in sequence. This lock opens a door in which there is food. Whenever the monkey opens the box, he finds a banana.

If the monkey is well fed, he may open the box in 15 seconds, opening it purely for his own amusement, or some other reason unknowable to us. If the monkey sees food put in the box and he is moderately hungry, it may now take him 10 seconds to open the lock—since he is motivated. But if he is starving, the monkey will take much longer to open the lock because he is "over-motivated"—that is to say, is anxious. It is the same with people: insecurity may actually paralyze one—reduce one to a mass of quivering uncertainty.

Adler points out an analogy in this respect. Were a person alone in a jungle, he would really have a good reason to be insecure, since he is weak and unable to deal with wild animals. But in a group, he would feel secure since everyone would struggle to help if he were attacked by a wild beast. But if the person wants to be the best in the group, he now develops a feeling of insecurity since he develops the concept that only if he were better than others would he be acceptable. Basically, having social interest is the solution for resolving such unpleasant feelings as inadequacy, unacceptability, inferiority, and insecurity.

Sensitivity

Two individuals faced with the same unpleasant situation may vary considerably in their hurt due to their different degrees of sensitivity. As an analogy, two people can be pinched with the same degree of force. One can stand it with a shrug, while the other cries out.

The essence of the neurotic could almost be defined by degree of sensitivity. Suppose that two young men are going with two young girls. They are all of the same ages, and so on. But when the girls say "no" to the young men, one may laugh and persist in his attempt to get her to say "yes," while the other one will get hurt, leave the girl, sulk, and refuse to see her any more, since he has been hurt so easily.

Our colleague, Dr. Albert Ellis (1962) has seized on this aspect of human behavior through his A-B-C theory, and says, in effect, that it is not A, the Activating Event, that generates C, the Consequence, but, rather, B, the person's Belief System. We say the same thing, but we use somewhat different language and put this in a somewhat different perspective. B, the belief system, is, of course, cognition, but the belief system itself is tied up with sensitivity, the emotional aspect of the individual, which may be used to exaggerate or heighten the person's behavior subsequent to A—the activating event. So what Ellis calls B, the Belief System, is affected by S, Sensitivity, the emotional/cognitive component.

Oversensitivity is related to feelings of inferiority, and inferiority is a function of the distance between expectation and aspiration. The self-secure person tends not to be oversensitive. The confident person tends to use activity and thought to move toward useful goals. But one who sees a discrepancy between present status and what it should be is vulnerable to upsets due to sensitivity, using emotions rather than coping usefully to make up the difference between what one is and what one thinks one ought to be.

As Adler indicated, some people run after "slaps on the face," courting hurts, as it were. Such masochists appear to want to be hurt, to receive pain and rejection. In part this is explained as part of one's life style to be unappreciated and hurt, and consequently to keep to one's expectations of being mistreated. In a wide variety of ways, the oversensitive person—one who overuses emotion—tests life and others, provokes negative reactions and mistreatment. Such individuals pursue mistreatment with great intensity, searching for rejection and humiliation, getting a wry neurotic satisfaction when they do arrive, and saying, as it were, to the world, "See how I am mistreated!" How clever such people can be to upset others, to find strategies to be rejected, to be hurt. One does it by careless behavior, another by poor dressing, another by antagonistic words—but all to the same purpose to supersensitivity.

The explanation always lies in one's fictive goals: the goal of superiority through suffering. The oversensitive neurotic in effect says to the world: "Look how much I suffer! Look how involved I am with the way I feel!" Rather than having to cope with social living the neurotic copes with the way one feels, and the ways that others feel about the way one feels, and the way this person feels about the way they feel about the way he or she feels, and on and on. In a difficult world many people turn to their feelings as the only "real" thing they have.

DEFENSE MECHANISMS

"Defense mechanism," a psychoanalytic term, refers essentially to certain mental operations to prevent the psyche from becoming aware of a variety of anxiety-provoking situations. According to Peter Giovacchini (1977), the list, in order of importance, is generally as follows:

1. Rationalization
2. Repression
3. Displacement
4. Identification
5. Conversion
6. Isolation (intellectualization)
7. Reaction formation (overcompensation)
8. Undoing
9. Introjection
10. Projection
11. Denial

Adler accepted the basic notion that the person attempts (with little knowledge of "why") to safeguard feelings and may, consequently, engage in rather peculiar behavior. According to Adler, all neurotic behavior is "defensive," is "safeguarding" self-esteem. Such behavior, when covert, is known as *safeguarding behavior*, and when overt, is known as *excuses*. Both have the same purpose: preventing the person from honestly facing mistakes, disabilities, inferiorities, and thereby protecting self-esteem.

A difference between Freud's "defense mechanisms" and Adler's "safeguarding tendencies" is this: Freud saw the ego as being threatened by the id's demands but Adler saw the individual as being threatened by her perception of her inferiorities to meet the challenges of life in terms of her fictional goals. *I want to achieve something, but I don't. What shall I do?* One way to deal with this failure is to say that *I must not be equal to the task.* Another way is to think or say that *I didn't try hard enough, The task was not that important,* or *I was interfered with,* and so on. This "safeguarding" or "excuse" (depending on whether I think it or say it) helps me to feel good. What it amounts to is nothing more or less than a lie. It is a rationalization.

Compensation can be seen as a healthy way of dealing with feelings of inferiority. Compensatory behavior means one tries to do something constructive about life when threatened. Say that I am in a group and everyone talks about art. I feel inferior, since I know very little about the subject. If I say or think "Art is not that important" or if I keep away from these people, then these methods of safeguarding of my feelings may be considered inferior to my compensating by going to a library, reading up on art, and becoming knowledgeable about the subject. So we can see two kinds of safeguarding: positive/useful techniques, such as a weakling who has been threatened by a bully taking lessons in boxing (compensation); or negative/useless techniques, such as daydreaming about beating up the bully or depreciating him for his boorishness (safeguarding).

In everyday language, if we feel inadequate, we can either do something positive about it, such as improving in the weak area, or we can sulk and make excuses. The normal person copes adequately in life, evaluates the situation and attempts to compensate for the inadequacy in one way or another; the maladjusted person may become aggressive or may retreat or may go into a complex sort of thinking of trying to prove that black is white and that good is bad.

We had a client once who expressed the concept of positive behavior quite well.

> When my father died, I went to live with an uncle who had two daughters about my age. Both were extremely pretty, and had many beaux. Next to them I was awkward and huge. I had a choice to make: either I would sit in a corner and play the role of wallflower, or else I would try to become charming and interesting in my conversation and behavior. I took the latter route and despite my obvious physical shortcomings I had more than my share of admirers and even got a man for a husband that one of my cousins wanted!

One may wonder about the neurotic safeguarding tendencies, such as agoraphobia systems or any of the complex phobias: Why does the person have them if they are so unpleasant? The reason is simple: It is much better to have the symptom than to face the truth.

We have a client who is relatively impotent. Whenever he tries to have sexual relations with his wife, he finds it hard to achieve an erection; when he achieves the erection, he has difficulty keeping it; and if he manages to effect intercourse, he has difficulty in ejaculation. But instead of trying to cut down on his sexual activity, he constantly is annoying his wife with sexual attentions, thus attempting to generate an impression on her (and himself) that he is a potent man in pursuit of sexual activity, when in reality he is practically impotent! Were the wife to suddenly confront him with this fact, most probably he would be terribly hurt and would find another way of safeguarding his feelings. He might inform her that he could be very potent with another woman, but that she no longer interests him. Or he might deny the reality, and claim that he is potent, but that she minimizes his capacity. In any event, this neurotic individual gets enmeshed in his excuses and rationalizations and evasions and consequently in his inability to simply say "I am impotent" he establishes a considerable defense structure, none of which will do him any good in the long run, simply because the defense is to protect his feelings and view of himself.

The degree of self-awareness of these neurotic safeguarding devices varies. Even though this "barricade" is self-erected, and is the responsibility of the individual, the individual often stubbornly refuses to take this responsibility, will deny reality or, if pushed, may become quite nasty.

We had a client recently who was destroying his family through his extravagant habits. That he could not control money and that he was a spendthrift could not be denied. However, when his therapist stated quite innocently, "Maybe you will have to learn to handle your money better," instead of agreeing, the client shouted, "Don't you pick on me too, just like my wife."

Not only is there a useful and a useless way of dealing with perceptions about inferiorities; there is also a passive and an active way. A useful passive way might be to accept something and not deny it, as in the case of the impotent husband. A useless passive way might be to reject the truth, and begin to develop all kinds of safeguarding thoughts such as that he wouldn't be so impotent if his wife were more attractive. A useful active method of dealing with this uncomfortable perception of one's inferiority would be to do something active in compensation, such as studying a subject, exercises, and reducing. But there are useless active ways of safeguarding our feelings.

Depreciation of others, criticisms of friends and family, insults, practical jokes, prejudicial remarks, accusations, blaming, disparagement, cruel comments, and the like are active useless methods of pushing down others to make ourselves feel better.

Were we all perfect human beings, we would be open, honest, clear thinking, strong, reasonable, and see ourselves just as we are or, as Robert Burns put it:

> O wad the Guids the giftie gie us
> To see oursels as ithers see us.

But since few of us have been given this gift, whenever we are threatened by awareness of our deficiencies, we set up barriers to this awareness, generally known as "defense mechanisms." These barriers to common sense become our neurotic symptoms, and since they require energy to be maintained, energy we need to live normally and successfully is lessened. Naturally, one of the purposes of psychotherapy is to change the person's inadequate life style, which means that the person must become aware of reality and be more willing to admit deficiencies and more willing to give up neurotic safeguards.

SEX—THE ADLERIAN VIEW

Professor Ray Lowe once said, "For Freud, sex has man; but for Adler, man has sex." This more or less sums up the Adlerian position. Among the various appetites we have, biologically determined but affected by society, is the desire for and the pleasure of stroking and touching, with the kinds of touching that culminates with sexual orgasm being among the most powerfully pleasurable. This degree of pleasure is indicated by a timeworn joke.

A priest and a rabbi who were friends decided to share confidences while they were sharing a drink.

"Tell me, Jacob," the priest asked, "did you ever eat ham?"
"In confidence," the rabbi replied, "I have."
The priest nodded with satisfaction.
"Tell me, Patrick," the rabbi asked, "have you ever slept with a woman?"
"In confidence," the priest answered, "I have."
"Sure beats eating ham, doesn't it?" the rabbi commented.

Sex is one of the most powerful forces and for this reason every religion and every society attempts to regulate it. Freud was probably correct—but in our judgment for the wrong reasons—that if sexuality is denied or thwarted, maladjustment likely occurs. Living during Victorian times, he saw many examples of serious maladjustments as a function of sexual denial. And so he and his students concentrated on the supposed effects of sexual deprivation. One of his students, Karen Horney, was trained to look for sexual reasons for maladjustment. Upon coming to the United States and practicing here during the Depression, she found that maladjustments could be attributed mostly to economic and not sexual reasons. Were Freud starting his work in the 1970s rather than the early 1900s, in view of the contraceptive pill and the new morality that it has engendered, he might certainly not have viewed sex as the basic cause for maladjustment.

Adlerians see sex as one of many forces within the individual, such as the need for food and the need for sleep, but sleep and food are real "needs"—that is to say, they are biological requirements. Sex is quite different. There are many people who voluntarily deny themselves sexual expression and who are not in any way harmed by this suppression. Other "demands" or other "forces" can override sexual "needs," and individuals who deprive themselves of this pleasurable behavior can and do function quite well. So we do not see sex as a *need* but, rather, as a *desire.* We do not think that people who deprive themselves of sexual satisfaction for ethical, cultural, or religious reasons are necessarily harmed thereby. In short, we deny the pansexuality of the psychoanalytic camp.

The purposes of sex are many. From the viewpoint of the individual it may be attainment of a kind of ecstasy achieved by the pleasurable touching and stroking that occurs in various forms of sexual manipulation and subsequent climaxing. Climaxing is not necessary, either for men or for women, for complete sexual satisfaction. For some, the main purpose of sex is reproduction. However, in a sense humans have foiled nature's design for unlimited reproduction through methods of contraception and consequently they can have sexual pleasure without the natural consequence of having children. Undoubtedly, this freedom to have sexual relations without the natural consequences affects human relationships.

Sexual behavior has other purposes in addition to pure pleasure and reproduction. For example, a man and a woman, living together but not in harmony, may find that as a result of having sex, being cooperative in that respect, they will become relaxed and at ease with each other. A wife in therapy, talking about her husband, said "The only time he is nice to me is when he has an erection," thereby emphasizing the point we are making. Sexual participation with another calls for cooperative behavior. This sharing of intimacies tends to generate feelings of belonging and consequently relates directly to feelings of social interest because lovers are concerned not only with their own pleasure, as might occur with prostitutes, but also with the pleasure of others. It is a kind of deep intimate sharing that can have all sorts of other favorable consequences—affirmation of one's worthwhileness, consolation when one is depressed, and feelings of belonging.

Naturally, as with all potentials, such as the desire for food, excitement, or pleasure, the sexual appetite can be damaged or it can be used uselessly or harmfully. Rape, the violation of another person, is a prime example. Promiscuous behavior—flitting from lover to lover without ever making personal contact but simply coupling—is frequently an indicator of gross feelings of inferiority, as in the so-called Don Juan phenomenon where the individual attempts to find acceptance by quantity rather than quality. On this point Adler made the sage remark that "one is more than two," meaning that if a person has a lover this is better and more meaningful than if one has two—or more—lovers. Just as Mies van de Rohe said that "less is more" about architecture, we can say about sexual partners that "more is less."

If humans have sex rather than sex having humans, this precious gift can be used properly or it can be misused. What determines how sex is used ultimately comes to social interest. The person with a high degree of social interest will use sex wisely; the one without will use it improperly. Like all behaviors, sex is a question not of possession but of use. It is not what we have as sexual potentials (which will differ), but what we do with what we have that counts.

Abuses of Sex

In marriage, sex can be used for mutual enjoyment and for enhancement of the feeling of belonging, or it can be used as a weapon for blackmail or to depreciate the other person. The myriad ways that people can hurt each other in bed need not be recounted, but the situation is plain in many cases. Husbands and wives get at each other in negative ways through such "crazy" behaviors as withholding having climaxes purposely ("You can't make me come since I don't love you enough"), refusing to have sex ("I don't find you attractive"), or, of course, having sex with others ("I prefer someone else to you").

Sexual desires are much affected by personal attitudes. A person's interest in sex is affected by self-concept, and one of the earliest symptoms of maladjustment may be loss of sexual interest. This can be seen chiefly in men, for while women can simulate sexual interest, a man who is impotent cannot. A healthy individual, mentally and physically, ordinarily has a good, strong sex interest and capacity which can continue past the biblical three score and ten years.

In both men and women, what is known as "masculine protest" can affect sexual pleasure. This term simply means that the individual feels dissatisfied with herself. The woman may want to have the so-called privileges of men and may feel dissatisfied in being only a woman, and the man may feel that he is not a real man. Thus, the so-called masculine protest is only another, earlier name for feelings of inferiority but it is attached to the concept of perfect "maleness." Hopefully, this historical nonsense is being decreased by greater awareness that men and women fundamentally only differ in their plumbing, and hopefully the women's consciousness and liberation movements will contribute to the elimination of this totally foolish notion.

Frigidity or impotence are about the same, showing themselves differently due to biological differences, but both can be signs of lack of cooperation, lack of social interest, and a disinclination to face life in the three tasks of family, society, and occupation. Premature ejaculations also frequently are signs of immaturity and are related psychologically to bedwetting and other examples of lack of physical control. These disorders represent symptoms reflecting a deep lack of belief in one's self, a lack of self-confidence. The cooperative person who has respect for others and who is a responsible individual shows this by being able to be a real partner sexually, enjoying herself and helping the other also to achieve a high degree of pleasure from this so-important and valuable possession we all have—our sexual capacity.

It is evident that all roads lead to Rome. No matter what the deviation we deal with, no matter what the symptom, whether it be vaginismus, frigidity, impotence, premature ejaculation, satyriasis, nymphomania, or other sexual dysfunctions, they are due to the same reasons as practically all other deviations: lack of social interest, disinclination to cooperate with life, and feelings of personal inferiority.

Thus, if I have feelings of inferiority, my real problem may show itself in timidity or bullying, in avoiding work or becoming a workaholic, in sexual abstinence of profligacy, or in a myriad of other ways. The symptom is only a mask for what is underneath. Sweep away the mask (or symptom), whatever it may be, and behind that mask is always fear—fear of inadequacy, fear of inability, fear of unacceptability. This basic fear often has guilt related to it, or tension, or anxiety, and these emotions are themselves a kind of mask hiding a basic concept which is a cognitive basis for everything: *I am not good enough.* This is what we call the inferiority feelings, and when they are developed well enough they become the inferiority complex. Without exception, all psychologically based symptoms, sexual or otherwise, are based on fear, which in turn is based on poor self-evaluation.

Impotence

The lack of capacity of males to get an erection or to maintain it is generally known as impotence. A great many men suffer from temporary impotence. A little incident illustrates this. One of us was a co-leader in a therapy group with Dr. Dreikurs. This particular group was composed of men only. At one of the sessions one of the men complained of impotence. To listen to him, no other person had ever had this problem. When all were asked to raise hands who had suffered impotence at any time, every single man's hand raised. The sight of all these raised hands had the effect of "universalization" (Corsini & Rosenberg, 1955), and as a result this man was much relieved.

Most impotence is psychological and temporary. According to the anonymous authors of *Human Sexuality*, prepared by the American Medical Association Committee on Human Sexuality (1972), "Even prolonged impotence is psychological 90 percent of the time" (p. 109). The work of Masters and Johnson (1970) confirms this view.

Surveys about the reasons for this temporary loss of sexual ability in the male show that generally the reasons given by the males are family pressures, adverse incorporated messages generally from the mother, homosexual experiences, distasteful sexual experiences, fear, and the like. We may call these "behavioristic," or "conditioning," or "external" causes. For example, one of our clients, while in college, in bed with a prostitute for the first time, just about to commence intercourse, heard a nearby police siren and jumped out of the bed, certain that a raid was in progress. He was not only unable to complete that particular sexual coupling, but he became impotent and remained impotent even after marriage. Finally, after five years of impotence during marriage, he received counseling and was soon cured of his disability. In another case, recited in a group, to the amusement of the other members, a young man went to bed for the first time with a woman and got very excited, but she wouldn't have intercourse unless there was "protection." He got dressed, went out to a drugstore and came back with a condom. Again in bed, and again he had an erection. But this protection was not enough for her. She now wanted him to get some vaginal jelly also. He got dressed again, went down to a drugstore and got the required jelly. He brought it to her, she disappeared in her bathroom and eventually came out, ready to go. But now he was totally impotent! This, the narrator continued, was the only time in a long lifetime of sex that this happened to him.

So, impotence can happen to all men and for a variety of reasons, such as in the two incidents reported here. But, from the point of view of Adlerian psychology, which generally assumes an inward, phenomenological view, these two incidents can be explained differently—in terms of the male's view of sexuality. If he sees the sexual encounter as a kind of contest in which he must do well, then he does not have a relaxed attitude but, rather, he sees sexual coupling as a means of proving his masculinity. So, in the first case, where the individual was "conditioned" by the experience, it was not really the police siren that conditioned him, but his interpretation of the meaning of the siren. Supporting this notion was the reason why this man had originally come to therapy—it was not because of his impotence. Rather, it was due to a strange obsession. He had a good job and did well financially. However, he was not sure of himself and sought reassurance by applying for jobs that he had no intention of taking. After he was accepted for the job, he would then find reasons not to take it. Quite clearly this individual was unsure of himself and showed it by this strange compulsion to find if he was acceptable by employers as well as by his inability to function sexually. The major purely Adlerian source on impotence is by Rudolf Dreikurs (1933), *Seelische Impotenz (Psychic Impotence)*. Essentially, Dreikurs' main theme is that if a man confused his masculinity with his sexuality, he was likely to become impotent. The person who felt that he had to perform well sexually to be a real man was the man who was prone to sexual impotence. Mosak (1979) gives an amusing anecdote.

> Another patient, fearing sexual impotence, concurred with the therapist's observation that he had never seen an impotent dog. The patient advanced an explanation, "The dog just does what he is supposed to do without worrying about whether he'll be able to perform." The therapist suggested that at his next attempt at sexual intercourse, before he made any advances, he should smile and say inwardly, "bow-wow." The following week he informed the members of his group, "I bow-wowed." (p. 72)

Impotence is the analog of such situations as inability to take a test, inability to speak in public, and so on. The person wants to be best, wants to make a good impression and, fearing not doing well, or fearing not being accepted as outstanding, falls down on the job and does poorly. For example, should a man be criticized by his wife for premature ejaculation, he may now start to worry about his capacity and become unable to have an erection. Fear of failure leads to failure. However, a person with a healthy attitude, who can shrug off an occasional failure as "one of those things," and who takes an attitude of the importance of the total relationship rather than the partial aspect of a single failure sexually, is highly likely not to be bothered too much about such an experience. However, an insecure person, one who aspires to perfection, is likely to be crushed by even a single misfunction.

Vaginismus

According to Adler, vaginismus, pain in the vagina, can be the body saying "no," and as such, it is an example of translating into a physical feeling the woman's disdain for sexual relations, or dislikes of her being a woman, depreciation of men, or other psychological attitudes toward herself as a woman or against men. Naturally, there can also be purely physical reasons for such painful sensations.

Disinterest in sex, "frigidity," and inability to climax, often are expressions of attitudes of resentment toward life, dislike of a particular man or of men in general, unwillingness to go along with reality, or a retreat from normal sexuality. Often these symptoms or reactions are hostile in nature, intended to hurt or upset the sexual partner.

We have known of women with vaginismus of long-standing duration who suddenly no longer have the problem when they get a divorce and find a new sexual partner. In one situation known to us, the husband for many years had practically no sexual relationship with his wife for the reason that she was in great pain if they attempted intercourse. Following their divorce, she took on a lover bigger physically than her ex-husband, and the painful experiences were all gone. Often the purpose of these pains and other symptoms is simply to make the offending person go away—the person cannot bring herself to say this openly, and so it is done covertly.

Sex as A Weapon

In marriage, the partners are highly likely to differ with respect to their interest in sex, to have different levels of desire at different times, and to have different ideas about ideal frequencies. This situation is highly likely to be exploited by one or both of the marriage partners if the relationship between the two is flawed. Many married people just do not have sex with each other as part of the conditions of their unspoken agreement not to get along. Frequently, to compound the harmfulness of this situation, the two will give every appearance to the world outside of being a devoted and loving couple—when in fact they do not couple at all!

What one person may be saying to the other is simply this: "I dislike you so much that I don't want to have sexual relations with you." One, if really being mean adds, "And since my sense of ethics forbids me to have sex with anyone else, then I'll just do without." This punitive attitude is exactly the same as the dynamics of suicide when done for the purpose of hurting someone. One harms oneself to punish another. What are some of the dynamics leading to this horrible situation?

Mischief. It may be that the denier dislikes the mate and wants her to feel that the denier is giving up something just because he does not find her attractive. The intention is to upset the one denied, making that person feel less worthwhile.

Domination. This ploy is used by someone who wants to see the other on his knees, sometimes literally. It is usually a woman who plays this role, since women's sexual drives are not as insistent (even though just as strong) as men's. Therefore, Harry begs Matilda, his wife, for sex, while she disdains to deal with him. In this way she makes him her abject slave.

Superiority. As part of the dominance aspect, one may feel superior. After all, if Matilda has to ask Harry for sex, Harry can feel superior presenting of this largesse.

Suffering. Sex can be used as a weapon in a variety of ways to show suffering. "Oh, how painful intercourse is, how I suffer," one may say, thus taking a good deal of pleasure away from the other, who feels like a rapist. The psychological nature of this behavior is seen when the sufferer has an illicit affair, and suddenly the difficulty or pain is gone.

Sign of Failure. Diminished sexual interest may be related to the person's sense of self-worth. Thus, the impotent man or the frigid woman may tie in their masculinity or femininity with their sexuality, and if they do not do well in the world outside, they may show this by inability to function well sexually. Also, this, in a subtle way, is a form of blaming, saying, "See what you have done to me (here and everywhere)?"

Proof of Worth. Sex may be used as a proof of worth. Frequently, in our experience, it is the woman who most likely will use sex as a weapon to prove her worth, since that husband of hers, so successful in other ways, is inferior to her in bed. Again, this can be done in several ways, such as making demands on the other that cannot be met, or by withholding sex to make the mate beg for it.

When sex is used as a weapon, it eventually tends to lose its potency in various ways. That is, the weapon becomes useless, since after a while the injured person will counterattack in some way, or will retreat. Sex may become mechanical and no longer pleasant, and the relationship between the two partners will steadily deteriorate.

To couples who are using sex as a weapon, we make several suggestions.

1. Don't argue in bed. Much better to get up and argue somewhere else. Don't contaminate the "playpen" with fights. Bed should be for reading, sleeping, sexual play, and other pleasant activities.
2. If you have sex, do not have it except for personal pleasure. Even if you have to "forget" your partner, do it for full and maximum personal enjoyment.
3. Good sex relaxes both, makes both feel closer and more loving. Your mate may be playing some sort of sexual role out of fear of inadequacy. Be sure if you enjoy sex to let your partner know.

4. Using sex as a weapon hurts everyone, including yourself, and is one
    of the surest ways of making your partner seek elsewhere for a suitable
    partner.

The pervasiveness and purposiveness of the life style—personality—is reflected in all of one's behavior, thought, and feeling. The "how" and the "why"
of personality maintenance have been illustrated with many examples. They
are overwhelmed, however, in the holistic view, by the obvious efforts that
everyone makes to be one's self, to be whole and unique—to maintain, know-
ingly and unknowingly, one's personality.

Chapter 9

Personality Types

NORMALITY-ABNORMALITY

The word *normal* has at least two denotations. The first represents a statistical concept. So we say it is "normal" for boys to be taller than girls. Or we say that men "normally" earn more than women. The word *normal* in this usage does not imply values. It just tells us what things are like. The other denotation of the work represents values. Normal now means good or healthy or desirable. "It is normal for children to have a good appetite," one hears. Or one may hear the question: "Is he normal?"

This second meaning of the word concerns us here. *What is "normal?"* Since this is a philosophic question, we cannot give an absolute answer. Consider, for example, the issue of intelligence. If we took all 10-year-old children in the United States, we could, in theory, line them up in terms of their intelligence, with children at one end who are no more than living vegetables, and at the other end 10-year-old children who have the mental potential and academic knowledge of college students. Where would one separate the "normals" from the "abnormals?" Would abnormality be only at the low end? This would occur in the second meaning of the term: children considered to be mentally retarded would be placed in the "abnormal" group. Statistically, in the first meaning, the middle group would be called the "normals," with the abnormals at either end, so that we'd have abnormally bright as well as abnormally dull children.

In intelligence, appearance, or personality, or whatever, where to draw the lines between what is normal or abnormal is a subjective, not an objective, judgment. It depends on who is judging.

To understand the Adlerian view of normality in the subjective sense, a visual picture may be of value (see Figure 9–1). Imagine that the vertical line represents age. The horizontal dimension represents the continuum of Useful to Useless behavior. The horizontal dimension is a value judgment and represents a sensible person's view of four other people. A somewhat similar figure, originally drawn by Alfred Adler, was reproduced by Ansbacher (1977, p. 60). Adler's own terminology of Useful and Useless is also employed here.

Person A is in his 20s. He has gone more or less in a straight line along the useless path. He may now be in a prison or a mental hospital. The general lifeline of his history indicates that he will continue going from bad to worse.

Person B started off going in a useful direction but at age 20 he shifted and went toward the useless side and now in his 50s is well along a path of deterioration, perhaps is now an alcoholic. Person C, in the late teens, is moving well along the useful line and may be a successful student (work), a success at home (family), and a success with friends (society). Person D, now about 40, started out in life going in a useless direction, and about age 30 apparently had some sort of conversion experience and changed considerably. This might have occurred as a result of a marriage, a change of environment, or from successful psychotherapy. In any case, there was a strong and abrupt change, and in the space of relatively few years this individual has moved quickly from a most useless to a most useful position. And, finally, we have person E, who has been in the middle of the road throughout life.

For individuals A, C, and E, the direction they started in early childhood they maintained in later life. This is the usual situation and it explains why Adlerians are so concerned with early life education, and why we say that even if the parents of children are themselves in the useless direction they can help their children live useful lives by proper parenting. Cases such as B, who start well in life and then change from a useful direction to a useless one, are common enough. Ordinarily such individuals may attribute their downfall to drugs or some traumatic event, but from our point of view, they carried the seeds of their own destruction within them, as they pursued their self-created goals, and so their useful behavior may have only been apparent and not real. The same can be said of person D, who started out in life going in a useless direction and then made an abrupt change. Such individuals, while they are unusual, are nevertheless found at all levels of society—people who "wise up" and make abrupt personality changes of some magnitude.

Generally a bad start leads to a bad ending, but not always. Even if a child should start life poorly, moving uselessly as a function of parental mismanagement, by being pampered, for example, it is still possible to conquer parental mistakes through common sense, as well as by observation and conclusions from other sources: from books or movies, as well as from relatives, friends, neighbors, and teachers.

The abnormal person may start off with early life concepts of the importance of personal superiority or the notion that life owes him a living, but may swing

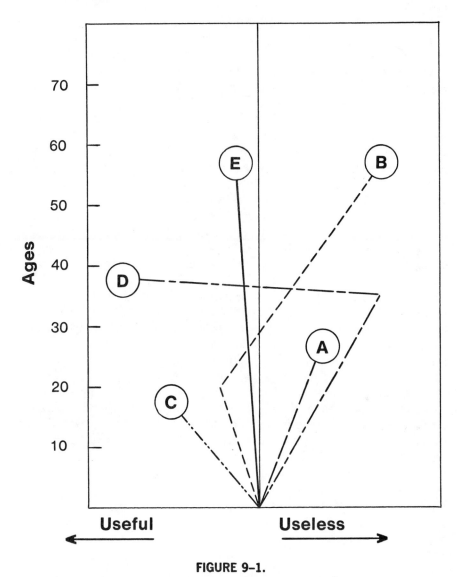

FIGURE 9–1.

back toward the useful side; or he may continue these misconceptions. However, if one goes off too far to the useless side we can begin to label the behavior "maladjustment," and if the movement is even more extreme, we can label the behavior "abnormal."

Abnormalities can show themselves in various ways: *(a)* by avoidance, by not meeting people, not participating in life; *(b)* by aggression, by being a bully, by hurting others or by stealing and other criminal acts; *(c)* by misconstruing life, seeing others as enemies, and so forth. The degree of maladjustment determines whether an individual is or is not considered abnormal, and the estimating of the degree is a personal judgment, until it is so extreme that it becomes a consensual, societal judgment.

How is it possible to become abnormal? It should be obvious to the deviating person that she is going in the wrong direction. But this is not so! The misguided individual can believe that her method of operating is toward a positive goal of superiority due to the self-deluding process called *private logic.* People manage excuses and so delude themselves by distorting reality. The criminal contract murderer argues: "If I don't do it, then someone else will." The ne'er-do-well makes excuses by saying: "The rich born don't have to work. Why should I? Where will work get me?" The suicidee says: "My suffering will be over and my wife will be punished for not loving me"; the schizophrenic thinks: "Withdrawal will be my solution. I will be in a better world of my own."

The abnormal person justifies his or her thinking and actions as the only way to achieve perfection. All personality deviations, without exception, depend basically on misconceptions of how to achieve personal superiority. These misconceptions, practically without exception, arise early in one's life.

Adler (1930b) said, "Social maladjustments are caused by the social consequences of the sense of inferiority and the striving for superiority" (p. 215). He went on to ask: Since all people have this sense and striving why don't all individuals develop abnormally? The reason he gave for people being adjusted "is that their sense of inferiority and superiority is harnessed by a psychological mechanism into socially useful channels. The springs of this mechanism are social-mindedness, or the logic of common sense" (pp. 215–126).

PSYCHOPATHOLOGY

Wolfe (1932) stated that:

> There is no human being who does not have this or that neurotic trait. We are all neurotics, for normality does not exist except as an ideal limit of human behavior. The reader is urged not to label himself a neurotic because he finds one neurotic mechanism in his life. It is not the function of mental hygiene to make angels, but to prevent flesh-and-blood human beings from crippling their activities and plunging themselves into wholly unnecessary unhappiness. (p. 294)

> The line between normal and pathological is very indistinct (Dreikurs, 1967, p. 8).

Within the theory of Individual Psychology the healthy, nonpathological person moves, psychologically and behaviorally, with courage and common sense in the social interest; yet even the healthy person has deviant private logic, areas of discouragement, and a sense of inferiority for which he compensates in ways out of the common sense. No one is perfect—superior—without fault and failures. This portrays the human condition and fits common sense. Everyone agrees with the statement, "Nobody's perfect." However, most people will have, at some dimly envisaged level, a reservation which says, "except me; I have to be perfectly good," "except I have to be perfectly successful."

Individual Psychology posits the responsibility of each individual in the creation on one's own personality. It logically follows that each individual uniquely varies in kind and degree from an unattainable, ideal healthy personality. Therefore, there is an infinity of life styles, symptoms, and possible pathological patterns.

Heuristically, it is not useful to only dwell on the uniqueness of each person —it prohibits general understanding. To understand people we must look for commonalities; to understand an individual we must look at the individual. We will understand more about any single person as we understand him within the context of the generalities and commonalities we understand about people in general.

Practically, scientists cannot deal with deviance from norms without generalizing and categorizing. Case studies are informative, and we have sprinkled this book with portions of cases. However, generalities are didactically more efficient.

Recognizing that we must always emphasize the uniqueness of the individual, nevertheless, for practical, teaching, and understanding reasons we lump people together on the basis of their common aspects. We do this in explaining pathology, understanding symptoms, and classifying personality types. The remainder of this section deals with generalities.

Neurosis

The traditional taxonomy of personality types is to divide people into five large groups: *(a)* normals, *(b)* the aments (retarded), *(c)* psychotics, *(d)* psychopaths, and *(e)* psychoneurotics. However, this classification, while it has a certain charm and logic, really doesn't help much since people are much too complex to neatly fit in this classification. Thus, we have all kinds of problems relative to the reliability of classification and also with respect to the meaningfulness of classifying individuals in these categories.

An interesting discussion once ensued in a prison setting. Dr. X argued that he had never yet seen a real psychopath. "How about Jerry Smith?" one of the group challenged him, mentioning a well-known convict. Dr. X thought a bit, and then finally said, "Well, yes, if there is anyone I know of who fits the classical description it is Jerry." All the others nodded. "But he is one in a million," Dr. X argued.

At this point someone got Jerry's chart—and lo! the examining psychiatrist had diagnosed Jerry officially: *Psychoneurotic.*

What *is* a neurotic? On a descriptive basis a neurotic is anyone who unnecessarily makes trouble for self and/or others by reacting to life illogically. One who unnecessarily feels guilty, or inferior, or suspicious or angry, or tense, is a neurotic. Thus, Charlie, chronically unable to make up his mind; Peter, always feeling guilty; Margaret, wrongfully believing she is stupid and unattractive—all are neurotics.

Adler first considered the genesis of neuroses as systematic maladjustment patterns stemming from various organic inferiorities. Later, he tended to view neurotic feelings as a conflict between two aspects of the individual: *(a)* the great desire for power, acceptance, superiority; and *(b)* strong feelings of inferiority. The statement "I want to be important but I feel I am a nothing" exactly expresses this conflict.

Still later, Adler saw neurosis as a movement away from social interest, with the person having a direction toward self-importance and consequently away from the good of the group.

As Dreikurs (1967) put it, the dynamics underlying pathology are the individual's private goals and life style versus social demands and social interest. Adler saw pathology as a conflict between the Private Sense and the Common Sense. "The neurotic person meets the conflict by hiding his Private Sense from his own consciousness, by not admitting his own tendencies when they conflict with his conscience, his Common Sense. He looks for alibis to excuse his social shortcomings. . . . If sickness or symptoms of diseases are used as alibis, the diagnosis of a neurosis is justified" (Dreikurs, 1967, p. 8).

A neurotic distances himself from others. This occurs in children who have been psychologically mishandled. Four fundamental ways of mishandling children are *(a) to neglect them, (b) to reject them, (c) to spoil them,* and *(d) to feel sorry for them.*

Perhaps the most central core aspect of a neurosis is discouragement. The million different ways that a person can show discouragement are a tribute to human ingenuity. In therapy, given enough time, neurotic problems almost always come down to the belief that one is not good enough, that one is unacceptable, that one cannot succeed, that one cannot belong. This pessimistic aspect may not appear for a long time due to people being clever in hiding their discouragement, but given enough time and with the therapist being patient enough, inevitably the most fundamental historical and concurrent element is neurosis is a deep discouragement: *no one can really love me; no one can really want me; I cannot really succeed.* From the point of view of an Adlerian therapist, any movement toward courage means progress. Here is an example:

Harold was fired from his management position for political reasons. He went into a depression, refused to go look for work, and eventually took a low-paying job in a grocery. Meanwhile, he brooded on the injustice of losing his job, moved from his neighborhood, and became a constant complaining nuisance to his wife and their two children. Eventually he went into therapy. One day, after several months of therapy, he mentioned to his therapist that he had changed jobs to one that paid slightly more. The therapist was quite pleased, and told his patient that this optimistic move presaged further developments. Soon thereafter, this man got the courage to look up his former employer, and was immediately rehired at a salary increase.

Harold's depression was a neurotic reaction, a refusal to participate with the realities of life. His complaining, refusing to do anything, represented his deep discouragement, a kind of "what's the use?" attitude. However, when he had enough common sense to seek a slightly better job, this showed that he had some beginning courage which would later enable him to do what was necessary to reinstate himself.

When Harold felt discouraged, he reacted in a useless manner—depression —and even after getting the job in the grocery complained of how life had mistreated him. When he began to have courage, he sought to improve his economic situation even though by a small amount.

Generally a neurotic rationalizes his cowardly behavior by establishing high ideals and by attributing low ones to others. By depreciation the person who is discouraged can look down on others. We see this fairly frequently with people with "superiority" feelings: they look down on others with such remarks as:

"I am honest and truthful, not like . . ."
"I will not cheat on anyone, unlike . . ."
"At least I do not drink heavily . . ."

This is what Adler called a "depreciation tendency." Such people find some compensatory way of telling themselves how "good" or "superior" or "long suffering" they are in reaction against feelings of worthlessness, the so-called feeling of inferiority, and they depreciate others.

Psychosis

The term *psychosis* does not have a clear referent. In describing abnormal individuals in a clinical situation, practitioners endlessly contradict each other in deciding what general category in which to put someone—neurotic, retarded, psychotic, psychopath, normal—and further, within each of these categories, there will be even more disagreement. For these reasons many people in psychology do not like the nosological systems imposed on them by courts, insurance companies, medical plans, and other agencies.

Nonetheless, it is evident that some people are just plain "crazy"—someone who walks about talking out loud to no one and making gestures; someone who drinks to the point of drunkenness and then attempts something very dangerous; someone who believes that the CIA and KGB are bugging his or her phone, someone who keeps making suicidal gestures or attempts. Certainly were you to encounter a man, as we did once in a mental hospital, who was curled up like a baby, whimpered if touched, would not eat, and who might suddenly explode into a violent frenzy, you would have to think, "This person is certainly abnormal."

The Adlerian position on psychosis is simple enough and should by now be predictable. The psychotic is a person *without* social interest and courage, one who has given up, and who has found some way of avoiding life's stresses and strains, through the "clever" way of being sick. Such individuals do not have psychological tolerance, and a "nervous breakdown" may be the result. Such individuals generally did not have social interest—they were loners, outsiders, bystanders, rather than participants in life. In practically every case of senseless mass murders, such as the famous *Unruh* case, the murderers are described as mild-mannered, quiet, self-contained—and we can read these terms as meaning "lack of social interest." Such people have incorrect views of life, of other people, of their family obligations, of social participation, and they misperceive themselves in relation to the obligations and challenges of life. The amount of psychological tolerance a person has is in part related to strength of relationships with others. The person who is psychologically alone faces away from a world seen as hostile.

From this we can see the importance of a good early family life, of solid relationships with others, the need that children and young adults have for encouragement by their parents and other relatives, so that psychological tolerance can be strengthened to meet the buffets of life with courage and determination. Those who cannot do so find escape methods. The neurotic finds escape in an attempt to avoid loss of self-esteem. The psychotic has given up and retreats from a reality too painful to bear. Why one person will be a "manic-depressive" and another a "schizophrenic" is not clear at the present time, but we can hypothesize that even the nature of the "mental breakdown" is related to the person's life style as well as possibly being due to some extent to intrinsic biological factors.

Whereas neurotics maintain or enhance self-esteem by escaping or avoiding particular life tasks, psychotics, more completely discouraged and lacking social interest, avoid the life tasks completely and substitute their own "tasks" which they fearfully deal with in their own, nonconsensual, way. The psychotics' "tasks" and goals are so out of line with common sense that when everyone views them as total failures, they may still be seeing themselves as being far superior to others because, from their view, only the psychotics are working on the *real* problems, only they know the score. Speaking of the psychotic, Dreikurs (1967) says: "Through delusions or hallucinations, he can impress himself with an assumed reality, which then conforms with his Private Sense. He lives in a world of his own, in which his personal goals find complete justification. He no longer adheres to the logic of life; he has his own logic shared by none" (p. 9).

Psychopathology has to do with the individual's personal law of movement and social interest. The neurotic moves painfully along a movement line less, rather than more, in keeping with common sense and social interest. The psychotic moves along a line that does not relate to common sense, the tasks of life, with deep discouragement, which greatly diminishes the possibility of acting on any social interest.

Psychopaths

The psychopathic personality is seen more as a social maladjustment than a personality maladjustment by most authorities (cf. Dana, 1965). That is a difficult distinction for an Adlerian to make. As all behavior and problems are social problems, then all personality maladjustments are social, and vice versa.

The psychopath never develops adequate social interest, has no real feel for common sense. The psychopath moves within consensual reality, appearing to accept the logic of social living but in fact only accepting the facade and procedures of social living for his or her own personal goals and private sense. Psychopaths do not accept the logic of social living, its rules and obligations, as having anything to do with themselves. Since they do not have or subscribe to common sense they do not feel "sick." However, when their behavior is in conflict with social custom or rules, they do feel put upon or put down by society. In this sense the psychopaths' maladjustments feel like suffering at the hands of society.

TYPES

Adler stated:

> We do not consider human beings as types, because every person has an individual style of life. If we speak of types, therefore, it is only as a conceptual device to make more understandable the similarities of individuals. (Adler, 1929/1969, p. 102)
>
> It is for teaching purposes only—to illuminate the broad field—that I designate ... types, in order ... to classify the attitude and behavior of individuals toward outside problems. (Adler, 1935a, p. 6)

Consequently, to make the common dynamics of individuals more under-standable, Adler and his followers developed descriptions of types of people. Although we usually think of these types as including only adult personality types, some types for children have also been developed. We will refer first to the childhood types both because they might make understanding the adult types easier, and because they are, generally speaking, the forerunners of the adult types.

Childhood Types

Emphasizing again the caution Adler so frequently made that everything can be different, the first of the childhood types has to do with children who suffer from diseases or imperfect organs. What may happen with such children? We know from our previous discussions of organ inferiorities that children may compensate for real or perceived weakness. They may become particularly strong in other areas unrelated to their infirmity, or they may battle especially hard to become strong in some area in which they have been sick or weak. But some will not develop themselves and their social interest. They consider that they have gotten the dirty end of the stick and feel humiliated and inadequate the rest of their lives. Today, children who are sick or handicapped have a much greater chance to receive training in useful skills and getting on with others than was the case in Adler's time. Nonetheless discouragement persists in children who have an evident weakness or physical inferiority.

The type of child who may not develop social interest is generally the pampered child. The mother, especially, may spoil a child who then comes to expect that others should do the child's bidding, satisfy all wants. The child will come to expect special treatment; expect to be served; will not understand responsibility for self and for others. Feelings of belonging, of cooperation, of social interest just are not found in such individuals. They become demanders, self-centered, bossy.

Over time, such a child grows, fixes a life style, comes to expect more, demand more, and become less likable even to those who have been in the past willing to serve him or her. The child may attempt to get others in his or her service by using charm, but usually, if others give service, the child expects still more. The pampered child tries to make others subservient in subtle ways and when they are indentured becomes the tyrant. When this child becomes an adult he or she still does not cooperate, and either charms others into service or revolts against others because they are not giving the child his or her due. "Every pampered child becomes a hated child" (Adler, 1956, p. 170). The neglected child does not come to know friendship, love, and cooperation. Looking ahead to life without feeling for and attachment to others, the ne-glected child will feel inadequate to meet life's problems. This child will distance him/herself ever more from others with no hope of winning them over.

> These three situations—imperfect organs, pampering, and neglect—are a great challenge to give a mistaken meaning to life; and children from these situations will almost always need help in revising their approach to problems. They must be helped to a better meaning. (Adler, 1932/1962, p. 20)

The above paragraph shows the dilemma of the childhood types. On the one hand there are situations which increase the probability of children coming to the kind of useless and mistaken notions listed as typical outcomes of those situations. On the other hand, they are descriptions of the types as outcomes. In either case it is the child who makes the decision, creates a life style in light of his or her knowledge and understanding of the world.

Adult Types

Adler at one time did separate people into types, purely for heuristic (research) purposes. His classification schema is very similar to the ancient typology of the Greek physician Hippocrates (Adler, 1956). Also it is somewhat similar to Dreikurs' typology of children's mistaken goals and this is in turn similar to one developed by Nira Kefir (Kefir & Corsini, 1974) in her conceptualization of the priorities of people.

After many years of research in personality types Hans Eysenck essentially rediscovered Hippocrates' four-type system. Using Adler's terminology, what are these four major types?

The first type listed may be considered the normal person—successful—who solves his problems well. Adler referred to such people as *Useful,* a common-sense designation. The second type, the *Ruling* person, is a dominator, a boss, one who wants his own way. The third type, the *Avoiders,* run away from problems, are escapers. And the fourth type, the *Getters,* are people who lean on others, who are dependent.

Although these four types do not perfectly fit a fourfold typology, they were

Hippocrates	Adler	Dreikurs	Kefir
Sanguine	Useful	Attention	Pleasing
Choleric	Ruling	Power	Superiority
Melancholy	Avoiding	Defeat	Comfort
Phlegmatic	Getting	Revenge	Control

FIGURE 9–2. *Typologies. Names of various types as suggested by four authors. Dreikurs' types are in terms of goals of children.*

developed by Adler according to two dimensions which explain the nature, or type, of movement of an individual. "The principles which guide me when grouping individuals into these four types are (1) the degree of their approach to social integration, and (2) the form of movement which they develop (with greater or lesser activity) to maintain that degree of approach in a manner which they regard as most likely to achieve success (in their own interpretation)" (Adler, 1956, p. 168).

Each of these types has greater or lesser degrees of movement and direction toward social interest. Any person can be plotted on a chart on the axes of activity and social interest. Employing a verbal description is valuable in conveying the essence of a person's personality to a student of the theory as well as to a client.

Many specific personality "types" have been described. No one is a "pure" type but probably a labeling of any person as a particular type could be useful.

Type labels such as "the victim," or "the baby" (Mosak, 1971) describe, to a greater or lesser extent, the life style of the individual. A type may represent a life style essence as in someone who sees himself as a bit less and others as bigger, being labeled "the little giant" and so on. A personality type may be synonymous with a basic mistake, as with a "morally superior" person who decides that only by being right can one securely establish a place in life. There is nothing wrong in *wanting* to be right. The mistake is in *needing* to be right. The exaggeration is the mistake—the absolute self-demand to be always right allows us to label a person as a "morally superior" type.

Frequently people have two goals which they variously seek. One of us used to counsel such a person. His problem was in the vain resolution of two conflicting goals. He was a bisexual who "needed" at the same time to be good and to have excitement. Please stop reading for a moment after this sentence and try to figure out how a bisexual male who needs to be "good" and is an excitement seeker might operate in life.

In thinking about the interaction of these two goals in one person you should be able to see the heuristic and practical value of types. Although your conclusions might not be completely appropriate for any one client, you probably formulated hypotheses about the person's dynamics. He could be "good" and find excitement at the same time by being used by individuals of all sexual persuasions, never knowing what he is going to do sexually (thus getting excitement) but always knowing he will be compliant to their wishes (thus being "good" to them).

The way this client construed the world, being "good" meant being a loving spouse. Excitement meant doing things with a tinge of mischief. When he was involved with a woman he was as available and pleasant as he could be. *But* this became dull. So he would, "for no good reason," just run off for a day, or even a week. "Innocently" he would stop off for a drink on the way home from work, drink too much, and find himself in a "gay" bar, or wake up in bed with a strange man. He would then feel guilty for the "bad" he had done, as well as turned on by the excitement.

Although insufficient work has been done on types in relation to pathologies, occupations, and so on, research in these areas would be highly useful. One of the authors works very closely with graduate-level students preparing to work in counseling psychology. Over the years, through teaching courses in Adlerian theory and diagnostics, many Life Style protocols have been collected and analyzed. Many of these students seem to have an exaggerated need to be good. This illustrates how people of particular life styles are drawn to particular occupations, as well as a general verification of the notion that counselors tend to be "good" people.

A real value of types is their communicability. If the therapist says to a patient, "It seems to me you are a _____ type; the kind of person who . . ." and if the therapist is correct, the patient can easily grasp the point and remember and use it. One of the techniques of Adlerian therapy is to develop the appropriate type and description thereof for each client. One time, speaking to a young woman who was terribly afraid of the dangers of life, we said, "You are like an ostrich with antennae. You stick your head in the sand trying to find safety but have to keep your antennae up to test whether your strategy is working." This strange picture made sense to her. There may be few others who are "ostrich with antennae" types. But the strategy of using types as dynamic descriptions can be helpful. Following are a number of common "types."

The Sorcerer's Apprentice. For this individual, life is just too much. There are too many demands. No matter how much one does, it is not enough. Obligations keep multiplying. No matter how one copes, tomorrow new and more onerous tasks will appear. One can never keep up.

Dolce far Niente. This individual avoids everything, and lies out in the sun, impervious to all cries and demands. "It is sweet to do nothing" is this person's theme song.

St. Sebastian. Saint Sebastian is traditionally portrayed as being martyred by having arrows buried into his body. The person who plays this role is a victim, constantly assaulted by others, is destined to suffer, to be a slave, to be hurt by others. This person sees him/herself becoming a saint for all the punishment taken.

Dr. Doolittle. This fictional character preferred animals to humans, and avoided contact with members of the human race, finding nonhumans to be essentially nicer and more understanding than men and women.

Charlie Walshes. This type of character, more than many others, has a propensity for exaggeration. This individual fantasizes all sorts of gloomy things and then acts as though the fantasy were real. This is a serious but nonpsychotic form of behavior. The individual could also be called a *Gloomy Gus,* except that a Charlie Walsh is more fanciful in his/her thinking.

Gloomy Gus. This person is the ideal pessimist. Nothing will work out. All will work to the worst advantage. No one will come on time. The movie will be rotten. The marriage will fail.

Mack the Knife. Mack is always looking for enemies and is ready to destroy them by force. Everyone is watching and waiting to get him/her; the world is a hostile place, and the only solution is get them first . This personality type is the prototype of paranoid thinking.

Little Orphan Annie. This person is alone in a hostile world, has no one to live for, no one to love him/her. The individual will never be able to become attached to anyone since no one can ever care for him/her. Such people find themselves constantly in a world of strangers, but go bravely and heroically, if naïvely, on.

Phil the Fiddler. These individuals are always looking for the main chance. Others get the breaks but not they, but someday their turn will come. Neither work nor industry counts; it is having a friend, someone to help, some magical event from heaven. It will happen if one waits long enough, and one must not do anything to make it come; it will come of its own accord.

Savonarolas. These individuals look down on others. They represent absolute moral superiority. Individuals who violate their rules and regulations need to be punished, and the Savonarolas will do the punishing, of course.

The Braggart. These individuals know everything and everyone, have done everything, and must let everyone know how good they are, how perfect, how much they have suffered, how hard they work.

We could go on with these characterizations for quite a while and list a long series of personality types, most of which would be familiar to the reader. Once in a while a rare type comes along, and for those who are collectors of personality types, it is a pleasure to see them—the Virgin, the Genius, the Misunderstood One, the Boy Wonder, the I Don't Care type, and so on; and even less frequent are the really involuted and convoluted types who fall into the category: No-one-can-figure-me-out-type, known also as Sui Generis.

PRIORITIES

In 1972 at an International Adlerian convention in Jerusalem, Nira Kefir introduced the concept of Priorities. Two publications discuss the concept in some detail (Brown, 1976; Kefir & Corsini, 1974). The basic notion is that life styles can be divided into four major categories: people are either *controllers, avoiders, superiors,* or *pleasers.* Kefir believes that long ago for any individual of one of these types a traumatic event generated an impasse, something to be avoided at all costs, a traumatized condition that will last throughout one's life. So that while apparently people are moving toward particular goals, such as pleasing others, in reality they are escaping impasses, such as being hurt by others. As she sees it, we are not really going toward a desired goal as much as we are escaping a threatening situation.

This is a kind of imprinting view: namely, that some event occurred long before our earliest memory which has scarred us to such a degree that it is permanently fixed in our psyches and essentially determines our personality.

In Jacqueline F. Brown's (1976) manual, discovery of priorities is part of a counseling program that has seven steps—four main parts and three subsets:

1. Body language. This first step gives clues to the person's priorities. For example, a body movement exhibiting hesitating, jerky movements says, "I'm not sure about you"—and this is a sign of a person likely to be a *controller.* On the other hand, a smiling person who keeps eye contact is likely to be a *pleaser*.

2. Verbal language.   The next diagnostic step is to listen to the words used by the person. One who has a lot of value judgments with words such as "ought to" and "should" is likely to be a superior, while one with problematic words such as "too much," "strain," and so on is likely to be a comfortee.

3. Gut responses.   Just as in attempting to figure out children's goals, one method is to determine parents' gut reactions; for example, if a parent feels annoyed by a child, most likely the child is an attention-getter. So, too, the counselor's gut reactions can give an idea of what personality type the counselee is. Consequently, if the counselor feels challenged, then most likely the counselee is a controller; should the counselor feel inadequate, possibly the counselee is a superior.

4. Presentation and recognition reflex.   Now, the counselor works with the counselee to attempt to come to a mutual understanding of the person's priorities. This stage has three parts:

A.   Lead discussion (of theory).
B.   Acting through (role playing).
C.   Guesses on the part of both (of final decision re: priority type).

SYMPTOMS

Most dictionaries define *symptom* in two ways: as a noun in general usage and as a noun referring to pathology in medical usage.

A simple example from the *American College Dictionary* shows: "*symptom, n.* 1. any phenomenon or circumstance accompanying something and serving as evidence of it; a sign or indication of something. 2. Pathol. a phenomenon which arises from and accompanies a particular disease or disorder and serves as an indication of it."

Neurotic symptoms are expressions of the neurotic's private logic which are different from the commonsensical behaviors which he still maintains (Nikelly, 1971). While the general thrust of the neurotic's behavior says, "I *won't* because my self-esteem might get hurt," the neurotic symptom says "I *can't* because I'm sick" (Krausz, 1959, p. 112).

Always in keeping with the individual's life style, the purpose of symptoms is either to safeguard the individual's self-esteem or to make excuses. One can protect self-esteem offensively or defensively—through aggression or by distancing oneself. The Adlerian psychologist attempts to determine the purpose of the symptom; that is, against whom or what it is directed, from whom or from what is the distancing movement.

In the "hero-martyr-saint" stratagem, the individual creates symptoms as intrapersonal struggles which can be fought, suffered, or overcome to demonstrate heroic or moral superiority. The "attention-service-love" stratagem includes those symptoms whose purpose is to get attention-service- and/or love from others. The "power" stratagem aims at manipulation of others and is most clearly exemplified by the temper tantrum of the child. "Revenge and retribution" may be the purpose of symptoms as in the case which one of us saw in which a teenage girl acted like a nymphomaniac, leaving evidences of her indiscretions for, and demanding monies for abortions from, her "goody-goody" parents.

Schizophrenia

According to Adler, schizophrenics, early in their lives, manifested a fear of life, thinking themselves incapable of meeting the three life tasks of family, society, and occupation. They therefore retreat from reality and create a world of their own in which they feel safe. In a sense, schizophrenia is similar in terms of mechanisms to daydreaming. The boy who cannot compete in athletic events, if he does not find satisfaction in some other activities such as academic work or mechanical work, may build an imaginary (but temporary) world in which he stars as an athlete, while the schizophrenic retreats into his own dark cave and shuts out the threatening outside world more or less completely.

Kurt Adler (1979) views schizophrenia as a function of self-centeredness. He states that, "As dependency increases, the development of trust in his own capabilities will lag far behind and he will more and more ask and expect help from others for everything." We then have the impossible combination of high self-expectations *and* the attitude of dependency in a person who does not have courage and who retreats from life through creation of that bizarre condition known as schizophrenia—a protective device to escape from facing reality.

Depression

Possibly the most common of all inward feelings and outward behavior of the neurotic variety is depression. Adlerians see these negative feelings that add up to depression: guilt, self-reproach, feelings of gross inadequacy, and feelings of hopelessness, as safeguarding behavior. The intent of these feelings is to sustain the fiction of personal superiority.

Now surely this view must seem absurd, especially to those who wish to find biological, hormonal, or dietary explanations, or to those who explain depression and similar symptoms in terms of situations such as a death in the family, lack of work, a business failure, and the like. This explanation also will not satisfy those who equate depression with fatigue, lowering of resistance, weather conditions, or the political climate.

Depression, from the Adlerian point of view, always has two purposes: *(a)* protecting the person's sense of self-esteem, and *(b)* deprecating the environment. Essentially the depressed person says: "I'm OK, you are not OK." Depression, when it is psychological—and we do not deny the possibility that in some cases there is a biological cause—is an attack on the environment, usually some person in the family, but sometimes on the entire world.

The earliest attempts at depression are seen in a child's wish to die or to be hurt so that someone will be sorry for what they did to the child. It is seen when a child wraps herself in a blanket and stares into space and refuses to answer a worried mother's call. It is a temper tantrum turned inward, to hurt someone else by hurting one's self. There can be a sweet element of revenge in depression: to make someone else worry and be uncomfortable and to make them feel guilty.

True to our basic premise about human nature, depression has a purpose: to make one feel good and others feel bad. "But this is nonsense!" someone in a depression will answer, "I feel rotten!" True enough, but let us remember that masochists suffer pain gladly. And depression is a masochistic attempt to salve one's ego through suffering, meanwhile also attacking others.

Depression is ordinarily found in "good" people who feel "helpless" and who can now "attack" others with impunity through their suffering. It is therefore a means of proving to one's self how good one is ("Look how much

I am suffering bravely") and a means of attacking others ("Don't you realize that my condition is your fault?"). Depression is aggression. Naturally, the depressed person sees such an explanation as nonsense at first because it is inconsistent with the image the person thinks he or she presents to the world.

Repression

Freud had a basic notion that people unconsciously "repressed" certain information, and that consequently they were not aware of the meaning or purpose of some of their behavior. A good example is forgetting someone's name: the real reason according to Freud was that a person "unconsciously" didn't want to know. However, Adler was of a different opinion. The person *consciously* did not want to know something and consequently he suppressed that information. It is almost as though a person had deliberately before-the-act told himself: "forget about it!"

What is the truth of the matter? Is such forgetting deliberate as Adler believed or is it not deliberate as Freud said? There is no direct way of knowing the truth, and one must decide the value of such disputed points by indirect ways: thus, if practically everything else about Adler's thinking makes sense, then we can accept the validity of this item on general faith even though we may have no proof; or, if we find that Adlerian practice works well, then we may go along with propositions whose specific validity is unknown. We don't know which is right: we merely report two views of the dynamics of repression. We prefer Adler's views because in comparison to Freud's, they put more responsibility on the individual and we don't have to posit a mystical conception such as "the unconscious."

Indecision

One of the most commonly stated problems presented to the therapist is the inability to make up one's mind, to come to a decision. Some people often seem to be on a fence, unable to make up their minds.

Adler referred to such people as "yes—but," and declared that they had a hesitating attitude toward life. They are on a fence, unable to make a decision; or they are seated on two chairs, as when one has a spouse and a lover at the same time. What they lack is *courage.*

Courage is the ability to make a decision, to take a risk. All of life consists of risks, but many people are avoiders, hesitators, and consequently they just will not take chances. Those who look backward in time and say, "If only . . ." and reminisce about what they could have done, those who say, "Now, I am too old . . ." are also hesitators, avoiders.

In doing therapy one of the questions we generally ask, and the follow-up, goes something like this:

> "You say you are not sure whether you will invite your mother-in-law to visit you?"
>
> "Yes."
>
> "What do you guess you will do?"
>
> "I just don't know."
>
> "Well, say anything, like '50-50 or '60-40'—some guess."
>
> "Oh, maybe there's a 51 percent chance I'll ask her."
>
> "No. I don't think so. I think there is a 100 percent chance you will ask her."
>
> "I guess you are right. I want to ask her, but I don't want to, but I think I will."
>
> "I am fairly certain you will. The question is now whether you want to enjoy her."

Hesitating neuroses, according to Adler, depend on the person attempting to solve problems in terms of personal ambition versus common welfare. It is, in a sense, the analogy of the line on the blackboard which Adler used to describe life. Going up is the growth drive, pulled by goals and pushed by fear, and going to the right is the "useless" way. The person is in the middle and can go to the right in terms of personal goals and gains or to the left in terms of social interest.

This now makes clearer the "yes-but" situation. The person faced with a problem says "yes" (social interest) but then finds an excuse to prevent himself from doing whatever it is and says "but"—and so remains frozen, unable to move. In older terminology such individuals were seen as having a failure of volition, an inability to make decisions, and they were termed *abuliacs*—but from the dynamic Adlerian viewpoint, we do not see this as a disease even though it occurs frequently in some people but, rather, the problem is of a person who cannot make up his/her mind whether to move in the useless, self-aggrandizing or self-pampering direction or in the useful social interest direction.

Those on a fence frequently do not want to make any decision. "What do you want from me?" they say, "I cannot make up my mind." This is a kind of immaturity, a hesitating attitude. Such individuals will develop a variety of subjective feelings to support their basic intellectual decision not to decide. One of these is anxiety. "Don't ask me to do anything" such a person says, "because I am too nervous." This is a clear case of emotions supporting an intellectual decision. To face the problem directly would call for a decision. To safeguard self-esteem people must develop some subjective feeling so that they will feel that it was not their fault that they couldn't face life; and so are "nervous," "tired," "exhausted," "tense," "fatigued," "pooped," "anxious." To be afraid of defeat is normal enough; but to refuse to fight so that one cannot either win or lose in the game of life is a prime example of being an escaper, having a neurotic attitude toward life.

The doubter attempts to preserve the status quo—to avoid a confrontation. "I don't know" this person says to life, "don't bother me now." Meantime, life marches on. As Alice in Wonderland learned, if you stand still life passes you by. Hesitators lose many chances; and before they know it, they think that what they want to do is too late now.

Forgetting

"I forgot" says a youth in reference to undone chores or homework. Undoubtedly the child did forget and undoubtedly if he had remembered he would have done whatever it was that was his obligation. But such "forgetting" is very suspicious: we can hardly doubt that the child "wanted" to forget and didn't realize this. Such forgetting really means that the person did not want to remember.

The mind is such a flexible and marvelous instrument that we can wipe out of our minds what is unwanted or inconvenient, and so "forgetting" at the same time is honest (the person subjectively feels he really did forget) and dishonest in that it tells us that the person really didn't want to remember. The Adlerian view of the unconscious is that awareness is on a continuum and is a function of what is known as the "set"—or the attitude—we have. So a child rarely forgets fun activities and often forgets unpleasant tasks. Forgetting is therefore in the service of the intellect, just as is true of the emotions. But Adlerians don't see the unconscious as a separate aspect of personality, merely as an area of lower awareness, on a continuum from extreme awareness to complete forgetfulness.

Chapter 10

Theory of Therapy and Counseling

BASIC CONCEPTS

The distinction between counseling and psychotherapy is variously seen by Adlerians. Corsini (1968) views the differences as quantitative, not qualitative. Thus, he hypothesizes that in counseling the counselor listens perhaps 20 percent of the time, while in psychotherapy the therapist listens perhaps 40 percent of the time; the counselor informs about 20 percent of the time, while the therapist informs about 1 percent of the time, and so on. Dreikurs (1967) sees counseling as being concerned with acute situations of immediate concern—generally a short-term process—while psychotherapy concerns itself with changing the person's life style, changing thinking about self and others—the "complete reorganization of the individual's life" (p. 258).

Historically, psychotherapy and counseling have different roots. Psychotherapy, a form of "talking therapy," has origins back to the Greeks and modern-day practice evolves from treatments used and developed in institutions for the mentally ill. Counseling in contemporary form emanates from vocational guidance, giving direction and information about education and work. The difference between therapy and counseling may be relatively unimportant theoretically but it does have practical significance.

Adlerians generally differentiate between the two by evaluating the client's difficulties. If a client is having problems in only one life task and this problem does not generalize to the other life tasks, it can be seen as a counseling problem that demands information and guidance—since the client is misconstruing a single life task area. If the problem generalizes to the other life tasks, then it demands psychotherapy; that is changing the client's life style. The mistakes, then, are within the client, within the client's perceptions, and cannot be sufficiently treated with information and guidance alone.

Regardless of whether the therapist/counselor is doing therapy or counseling, the same interpersonal dynamics and therapeutic strategies are operative. A good helping professional should be able to do counseling *and* psychotherapy. In the following pages we will use the terms *therapy* and *counseling* interchangeably.

Adlerians do not have a monolithic view about counseling and psychotherapy. The authors of this book have worked in various settings with other Adlerians, and we have found considerable differences in thinking and approaches, even though all accept the same theory. One Adlerian may be quite directive, while another is more nondirective. One likes to tell of personal incidents while another never discloses anything of a personal nature. Another likes to tell stories about other, unidentified, patients while still another may never mention anyone else—and so on. Even basic concepts such as determing life style or dealing with social interest are handled differently. Thus, Adlerians trained by Adler might ask for one early recollection, while Adlerians trained by Dreikurs will routinely ask for as many as 10 early recollections as part of the life style interview. Some Adlerians will concentrate their therapy around social interest while others may not even mention the term and take it up only indirectly. In contrast to other systems, such as Freud's Psychoanalysis, Rogers' Person-Centered Therapy or Ellis' Rational-Emotive Therapy, each of which is more or less fixed in how the therapist should operate, Adlerians are much less dogmatic. In the case of Freud's analysis, the "fundamental rule" has a patient talking without interruption; in the case of Rogers, the therapist attempts to listen empathically and reply nondirectively; and in the case of Ellis, the therapist locates and then disputes the patient's incorrect assumptions.

Indeed, an Adlerian therapist might operate exactly as a psychoanalyst, a client-centered therapist, and a rational-emotive therapist on the same day with three different clients. Thus, with client A, the therapist may simply listen and let the client spew forth whatever is on her mind; with client B, the therapist may forcefully dispute the client's misconceptions. And that same day the therapist might do role playing, use hypnosis, or other techniques. We Adlerians are not limited in any way in our operations: everything depends on the therapist's judgment; while our theory is solid, our methods vary. In short there is no "Adlerian way" of doing psychotherapy or counseling which excludes techniques, as long as the technique "fits" the theory and the client or patient. Indeed, Adlerians are liberal with regard to therapeutic interventions. For example, below is a list of Adlerians and their preferred therapeutic methods as listed in the *Handbook of Innovative Psychotherapies* (Corsini, 1981).

George M. Gazda	*Multiple Impact Training*
Nira Kefir	*Impasse/Priorities Therapy*
Lew Loconsy	*Encouragement Therapy*
Walter E. O'Connell	*Natural High Therapy*
Harry A. Olson	*Stress Movement*
Genevieve Painter	*Primary Relationship Therapy*

Undoubtedly, many other Adlerians have developed their own preferred procedures within the rubric of Adlerian philosophy and theory.

Adlerians are found in all settings: in private offices, in community centers, in schools, in mental hospitals, and in prisons. Adlerians work on a one-to-one basis, in groups, as teachers of parents. They do marriage counseling, personal psychotherapy, parent training, and school counseling. They are involved in social outreach programs to a much greater degree than are members of other psychotherapeutic groups. Adlerians generally don't see their work as the curing of the "sick" but, rather, of teaching the ignorant, guiding the lost and encouraging the discouraged.

WHAT IS PSYCHOTHERAPY?

Psychotherapy has all of the following elements: It is:

1. A formal relationship between two or more people.
2. Based on an agreement for full, free communication under conditions of safety.
3. Based on an internally consistent theory of personality.
4. Applied in a manner consonant with the theory.
5. For the triple purpose of improving the client's thinking, feeling, and behaving.

A lot of things that are "therapeutic," such as pills, social groups, making love, getting a job, reading a book, doing exercises, and changing one's diet, are not "psychotherapy" unless these activities meet the five criteria of (*a*) a relationship, (*b*) good communication formally established, (*c*) based on theory, (*d*) operates in accordance with the theory, and (*e*) aiming at total improvement of the total person. However, many things, including those referred to above, can be "therapeutic"—and to make things more complicated, psychotherapy may not be therapeutic! If X goes to Dr. Y for treatment, that person is in psychotherapy. If the treatment does him no good, the treatment was not therapeutic!

But people can get "help," improvement, personal gains in a wide variety of ways. Formal psychotherapy is expected to be one of the better ways—but it is not the only way—and not even the best way for some people. Thus, if Mr. A comes to a therapist, this may be a regressive step: it might have been better if he had not gone. A true and minor example is the following.

On the first day of teaching a course a student seated himself immediately in front of one of the authors, and started to read a magazine. The instructor decided not to pay attention, even though this same behavior went on week after week. At the sixth week all students took a test based on the textbook. Sure enough this student got the lowest mark in the class. The student was called in and the conversation went as follows:

Instructor: I called you in because I set the passing mark on the test at 70 percent and you scored below that. You were the only one to fail the test.

Student: I know that.

Instructor: To what do you attribute your poor grade?

Student: I have never read the text.

Instructor: Also, I don't think you have ever listened to my lectures.

Student: I try not to, but sometimes I hear some of it.

Instructor: At this rate you will probably fail the course.

Student: Well, that is what I want.

Instructor: Why would you want to fail?

Student: Well, my father wants me to go to this school, while I want to write the great American play.

Instructor: So, if you fail this course, this will prove to your father that you can't make it here? Are you aware you may get kicked out of the school entirely?

Student: As a matter of fact I was expelled last year.

Instructor: How did you get back in?

Student: Two reasons. First, my father is on the Board of Governors of this school, and second, I am a genius. I have an IQ in the 200 range.

Instructor: What can I do for you?

Student: Nothing.

Instructor: Well, I'll try to be of help by giving honest examinations and giving you an honest grade.

Student: What do you think of psychotherapy for me?

Instructor: What for?

Student: My father suggests it to straighten out my thinking.

Instructor: I am not sure if it would be of help.

Two weeks later, while leaving class, this same student came by and started a conversation:

Student: I'd like to have a conference with you.

Instructor: What about?

Student: What we were talking about two weeks ago.

Instructor: No, I am sorry. I am too busy, and cannot give you more time.

Student: Can I talk with you?

Instructor: OK, I am going to my car, and if you want to you can talk until I get to the parking lot.

Student: I have decided to go into psychoanalysis.

Instructor: That so? Why?

Student: To straighten out my head.

Instructor: Is that why you want to go?

Student: Yes, I am going wrong.

Instructor: And so you think you need psychotherapy?

Student: What do you think of my going into psychotherapy?

Instructor: I think I can do psychotherapy for you right now—before we get to the parking lot. (We were a minute away.)

Student: What do you mean?

Instructor: (Silence.)

Student: I don't understand.

Instructor: (Silence.)

Student: We're here. What do you mean?

Instructor: Grow up, you stupid son of a bitch!

As shocking as this may seem, it is a success story. At the midterm this student got a good grade. At the end of the term he got straight As in all his courses. He did not go to psychotherapy.

If he had gone into formal psychotherapy, he might have played the same game he was playing in school—wasting his father's money and his own time. The final remark to him was "therapeutic," but he was not in psychotherapy! And, it probably was the right remark by the right person at the right time! Incidentally, this young man kept in touch for several years, telling about his improvement generally and giving thanks for the statement with immediate therapeutic effect.

So, let us keep in mind that psychotherapy is not necessarily therapeutic and that therapeutic events are not necessarily psychotherapy. Therapeutic should refer to results and psychotherapy to procedures. Formal psychotherapy should have at least the five conditions expressed at the beginning of this section, and means a free, desired interaction at the verbal/symbolic level under safe conditions based on some consistent personality theory and some procedures consonant with the theory with the intention of amelioration of some symptoms to help the total person improve cognitively, emotionally, and behaviorally.

THERAPEUTIC STRATEGY

The Adlerian therapist according to Dreikurs (1967) has four goals:

1. Establishing a "good relationship."
2. Discovering the patient's private logic and hidden goals.
3. Helping the patient see the above, leading to better understanding.
4. Reorienting the patient, helping him to find better goals.

From the above it is evident that Adlerian therapy is an educational process calling for cooperation and trust, a willingness to be examined and explored, cooperating in finding new ways, and finally deciding to move in new directions. Consequently, it is not really a "doctor-patient" relationship of the usual type in which the doctor treats the patient but is, rather, a cooperative learning venture on the part of both.

Therapists do not save patients from destruction but work with them to help them discover better ways. For example, a patient is likely to talk about "good and bad" but the therapist will talk about "useful and useless." The Adlerian therapist attempts to generate an attitude of friendly equality, rather than looking down on the patient as an inferior. This attitude will puzzle and even upset some patients. Essentially, the therapist takes the attitude that the client is self-reliant, self-sufficient, responsible, the instant cause of his own misery, and that his problems are based entirely on mistaken goals, wrong perceptions, incorrect interpretations. The therapist will act as a friendly guide—willing to see the truth—to point out mistakes and to suggest better ways. Therapy from the Adlerian point of view is always based on cooperation.

The therapist wants to help the patient to get courage. There are many ways this can be done. The simplest is to pay close attention to what the patient is saying. The patient appreciates someone closely listening to what he or she is saying. The intention of the therapist is to really know the patient and, more than that, to show the patient that the therapist cares to hear what is said. In short, the therapist is serious about the client. The therapist tries to generate hope in the patient, to create the impression that even though up to now things have not worked out well in the patient's life from now on things can be better —it is a question of work, time, and patience.

To achieve the desirable state of cooperation leading to encouragement and a feeling of safety, the therapist and the patient come to an agreement, which need not be spelled out in words. This agreement has to do with their relationship. This is a role-expectation relationship in which the therapist and the patient operate as co-equals even though one is the teacher and the other is the student. This attitude of trusting-equals is crucial. It can even permit therapeutic relations and effects with colleagues, with friends, and even with members of one's family. Therapy is not a series of confessions but, rather, an attempt to clarify hidden goals and attitudes and to move in new and better directions.

Values

One of the most difficult aspects of psychotherapy has to do with values. Suppose, for example, that a client believes in a religion that the therapist feels is wrong in concept; or that the client believes in some unscientific subject, such as tarot card reading or astrology. Suppose, to make the situation more complex, that the therapist believes that these beliefs actually interfere with the patient's potential for development, growth, and change. Any attempt by the therapist to discuss these matters may make the patient resist and withdraw. In such cases, the therapist had better forthrightly state his or her position, and let it go at that. But frequently touching on these matters can be disastrous. Clever patients can introduce such items to the unwary therapist in their attempt to sabotage their own therapy.

Sabotaging

Why sabotage your own therapy through *resistance?* There is a strong basic desire on the part of people to remain themselves, not to change. This dynamic which can be so positively functional, giving people their consistency and sense of themselves, guiding their behavior, can also be negative—standing in the way of change. Even when present conditions are so bad that one will go to the trouble and the expense of psychotherapy, the person may come to therapy suspicious of the therapist, fearful of the process, unwilling to participate fully, looking for an opportunity to escape, to frustrate the therapist, to sabotage the therapy. The basic reason for this resistance is resentment at being in a situation where the implicit—and sometimes explicit—demand is always to change.

This common, mistaken, generally unconscious attitude is often dealt with by putting the therapist up, by setting high fees, having an expensive looking office and long waiting periods, and other such incidentals in conjunction with the therapist's superior position. Adlerians ordinarily do not play this game, but they try to generate candidness, equality, cooperation. It often takes patients a long while to accept this attitude. Some of them will have none of it. To them this attitude is patently a fraud, and the therapeutic encounter is off on a bad start. It is a kind of common benevolent paranoia.

A therapist in a situation of this kind must play his or her role straight, kindly cooperating for the person's self-understanding while paying no attention to the various signs of resistance, hoping that the client will see the mistaken game being played and will eventually discuss it. When discussed, no great feeling is to be generated, except perhaps information that all clients play such games, and the particular way and purpose of this client's game; it is part of the therapeutic process.

Should the therapist get involved emotionally with clients? Essentially, the proper attitude of the therapist is one of conviction that things will get better, a desire that the client will improve, with the responsibility for therapeutic outcome being up to the patient. "I'll do my best, and the rest is up to you" is the proper attitude. Win some, lose some.

The client wants to believe that the therapist cares. And every therapist does care, even if it is not really for the person but for the process. That is, if you as a therapist are dealing with a patient with, say, a compulsion to count windows, you should care to cure that problem, regardless of how you may feel about the person with the problem. So, we may not get emotionally involved with the person, but will get involved with the person's problem as part of helping the whole person.

Therapist as a Person

No one really knows what kind, if there is a kind, of person makes a good therapist. One can only speculate. The reason for our hesitancy is that we know many people who function as therapists, in and out of the Adlerian field, and there seems to be little that encompasses them all. Keeping to our trichotomy of Emotions—Cognition—Behavior, we would say something as follows about the ideal Adlerian therapist:

Emotionally—Strong, warm, friendly, caring, courageous, good-humored, positive.
Cognitively—Knowledgeable, intuitive, clear-thinking, keen.
Behaviorally—Quick, alert, paces properly, competent.

But these traits would probably be true of a therapist of any orientation. In selecting a therapist, it often makes good sense to "shop around" a bit before making a final selection. The reason is that regardless of orientation, it is the person, not the theory and not the methodology, that mostly counts. Therapy is a person-to-person matter. In the end *who* the therapist is equals in importance *what* theory is employed.

However, there is likely to be some sort of relationship between the kind of person one is and the kind of therapy one practices. After all, the kinds of people who are attracted to a deeply intellectual explorative therapy such as Analytical Psychology are highly likely to be quite different from people who go into a strongly behavioral therapy such as Psychodrama or from those who go into a contemplative system such as Person-Centered therapy.

Adlerian Psychology has been likened to William James' tender-minded temperament (Adler, 1956). Individual Psychology is rationalistic, intellectu-alistic, idealistic, optimistic, monistic in the sense of being holistic and unify-ing, religious in the sense of recognizing the value of values, feeling; and free-willist in believing in individual choice, decision, and responsibility. The Adlerian therapist, therefore, in all probability will be of tender-minded tem-perament. Obviously this is our bias, but we would ask the reader to consider the qualities or characteristics he or she would want in a therapist.

The qualities a therapist illustrates in therapy should be natural to the therapist. We suggest that the qualities in the above list constitute a highly useful mode to happy, contributing living. One of the authors had this pointed out to him forcefully in a discussion with a hardheaded philosopher about a book. The author felt that the philosopher praised him with the closing blast, "You damned optimistic, positive constructionist."

Therapist as Observer

Therapists of all orientations should be good observers and good interpreters. The basic notion of the unity of individuals leads Adlerians to the theoretical position that almost everything a patient does can be meaningful. *Does she come into a room timorously? Does he wait to be asked to sit down? Does she hold her purse in her hands or put it down? Will he try to light a cigarette without asking for permission? Will she start to talk or wait to be asked?* The therapist watches the patient carefully right from the beginning, and in a sense begins to "diagnose" the patient in terms of such terms as "fearful—apologetic—angry—puzzled—friendly" and so forth.

The therapist knows that every patient—we repeat here, every patient—is likely to play games, to sabotage the therapy, to show in the most unlikely ways strategies to resist therapy. And so the therapist is alert from the beginning of the contact that the patient is fundamentally on the surface concerned with improvement, but deep down is fundamentally afraid of any changes and may resist change. Any other view shows the therapist as naive. The mature thera-pist is aware that patients will play games. The therapist's first strategy is not to discover the game or to counteract it, but simply to refuse to play the game. This comes from the very fundamental notion that there are three directions of behavior on the part of therapists: to cooperate with the patient, to fight the patient, and to refuse to participate. The last tactic—ignoring the games patients play, except perhaps to bring them to the patient's attention—is usually about all that is necessary.

Cognitive Aspects of Therapy

While emotional procedures or behavioral procedures or cognitive procedures may be used to achieve therapy, from the point of view of a therapist operating as an Adlerian, the battlefield is cognition: *understanding, knowledge.* Therapy is actually a form of learning even though what is to be learned is often what one already knows in one way or another. Some call this kind of learning "emotional learning," meaning that one knows now what one knew before but knows it with great depth and intensity. "I knew I had feelings of inferiority, but I never realized how devastating they were, how they just drove me away from people," is the kind of statement often heard. How does Adlerian psycho-therapy achieve this greater knowledge and what is achieved?

Self-Realization.   One process involves the therapist doing little more than listening intently. Active, intense listening to what the patient says generates in the patient a heightened awareness of his own remarks. As it were, the client too listens to what he is saying! As a result, in a kind of feedback process, the patient begins to understand, to comprehend his own meanings. The essence of this process is identical to "free association" as practiced by the psychoanalysts or "empathic listening" used by the Rogerians. The client is the therapist, and the formal therapist becomes a kind of catalyst by doing practically nothing except listening intently.

Interpretation.   A second process is direct interpretation. The therapist listens until absolutely certain that she understands the patient's point of view, and then confronts the patient with the therapist's understandings. "Now, when you told him that it was not right for the two of you to be seen together, and he left, you felt that he didn't care for you . . . Is that not correct?" Then after the patient gives assent, the therapist may continue. "I don't think that is necessarily the only interpretation of his behavior. Maybe he felt that what you said meant that he was not a person you wanted to be seen with, and took your remarks as a rejection. I think that is an equally reasonable view."

Leading.   A common procedure for an Adlerian (and other therapists as well, of course) is to ask leading questions. "Why do you think he called you that night?" "Could you make a different interpretation of what your mother told you?" "What other ways do you think you could have handled the problem?" These questions are intended to lead the person to think in ways that the therapist believes would be more productive.

Goals. The therapist is interested in learning the client's goals. To change these, the basic mechanism is intellectual modification of concepts. The patient can be seen as having a built-in compass: East is self-defeating, negative, useless goals, and West is self-enhancing, positive, useful goals. We want to help the patient re-orient in a positive direction and operate toward positive goals. This occurs first in the mind, in the determination of the individual, and then will occur in behavior. Insight must be changed to constructive behavior.

Insight. Insight alone is not enough. Some patients play the insight or "aha" game, and use insights as a means of defeating the therapist and sabotaging the therapy. The "yes-but" type of person delights in gaining insight and then proving to the therapist that the new insight is useless. A correct kind of insight occurs when the patient realizes that the game being played with the therapist is the same means of defeating self and others in therapy as well as outside of therapy. For this reason, the therapist often must "attack," confront the patient with how he or she is trying to manipulate.

Confrontation. A powerful process in psychotherapy represents a kind of Socratic questioning, leading to confrontation. Essentially, the therapist sets up the patient through asking questions, leading the client to an admission and new understanding which in turn leads to better behavior.

Frequency of Sessions

Adlerians probably do not differ from other therapists regarding frequency of sessions. This is generally a function of a cooperative decision reached with the client and can vary from once a day to once a month for ongoing clients to the usual regimen of once a week.

Related to this is length of therapy: How many visits will a client make to an Adlerian therapist? Speaking only for ourselves, a fair proportion of clients, perhaps as many as 10 percent, come once and are not seen again. The reasons for not beginning or no longer continuing therapy can vary from the therapist refusing to take the patient, to the patient not liking the therapist, to the therapist giving the client in that one session whatever information or help was sought. We have seen some clients for extended periods, several for well over 10 years with, however, long breaks between a series of, or single, sessions. One of us sees a client annually who was initially seen for 10 sessions. The client phones in and asks for his "annual checkup." However, we would estimate that the average number of sessions for successful therapy runs about 12 to 30 hours, considerably fewer than those reported for the "depth" systems such as Freudian or Jungian analysis, and somewhat more than reported by some systems such as Ellis' RET or Glasser's Reality Therapy.

GOALS OF THERAPY

While in a global sense the goals of Adlerian therapy are probably no different from those of most other types of therapy, we nevertheless couch our terms differently and perhaps have different expectations. Operationally the goal of therapy may be defined as making the therapist superfluous.

The question of goals in therapy is more complex than it may seem at times. For example, there can simultaneously be three sets of goals for one patient:

1. The patient may want freedom (as being permitted to do whatever he wants).
2. Members of the patient's family (including whoever is paying for the therapy if the patient is not paying for it) may want other goals, such as "a sense of responsibility."
3. The therapist may have other goals for the patient, such as the capacity to tell the truth without fear of consequences.

The three goals may not really be incompatible. The apparent conflict may have to do with priority, which goal should be sought first. But what if the goals are not compatible?

What can result if the therapist's and the patient's convictions conflict? Say that a patient is determined to wreak revenge. Should the therapist "go along" with revenge desires? If the therapist is being nondirective does this apparently condone what the therapist does not believe in? The same issue occurs in counseling. Mother wants her teenage daughter to come in by 10 P.M. The daughter strenuously resists this domination. The therapist may be on either the mother's or the daughter's side. Should the therapist remain neutral or interject an opinion?

Therapy has another commonly met problem: the difference between stated and unstated goals. Frequently, what the client says at the beginning of therapy is not the major concern, although the initial statement may be related to the general problem. Therefore, it behooves the careful therapist not to rush to a solution of the stated problem because doing so may mask the more important problem. Even when the patient finally gets to the more important problem this may still not be the fundamental problem! Something else more basic still may be troubling the person.

To illustrate, in reference to the case history at the end of the book, if the client came in because he felt he was not doing as well in school as he should have, and wanted to change fields—this would be the stated problem. Underneath he might consider that the real problem had to do with improper relationships with professors. And yet, the true problem which may emerge only after many sessions might be his relationships with authority figures, a sense of diminished self in relation to powerful others.

Another way of looking at therapy rests on the view of persons as a combination of three heuristically divisible factors: thoughts, feelings, and actions. As Adlerians we see the individual as an indivisible entity. Nevertheless we recognize that people can be thought of as divided into parts for various reasons. Just as a doctor will take a grain of sand from a patient's eye if that is the present problem, so too, a psychotherapist will deal with a patient's sexual problem, but that problem is likely to have three components: cognitive (thinking), affective (emotional), and conative (behavioral).

In view of this, the therapist can take the position that the total person is to be simultaneously treated intellectually, emotionally, and behaviorally. But this is very difficult to do. Perhaps the sole method that works on these three levels simultaneously is psychodrama. Consequently the therapist ordinarily concentrates on one of the three levels. Adlerians generally tend to focus on cognition as the basis for the other two levels—the individual is discouraged (emotions), is ineffectual (behavioral) because of incorrect ideas (cognition). Consequently, to make one feel better (a good goal), and to make one behave better (another good goal) the best way is to make one think better (the basic goal). An Adlerian therapist wants to know how a person is thinking, to discover what is wrong with the cognition, and then change that person's thinking. This in turn will affect that person's actions, and then the change in actions will change feelings.

We can look at goals of psychotherapy in many ways. We have just discussed greater understanding. That is what Adlerian therapy is all about: learning for understanding. It is an educational process. The process consists of learning about one's self, about others, and about life. Also, but as a consequence of understanding, Adlerian therapy is directed to goals of changing behavior (What would be the value of greater insights if they didn't lead to better behavior?), which finally, and possibly most importantly for the individual, leads to new and better feelings, like feeling at one in the world, feelings of belongingness, feelings of accomplishment, feelings of being accepted. Lastly, the therapist's ultimate goal is for the patient to no longer need the therapist, to be able to go into the world confidently and competently, feeling safe, secure, comfortable.

INDIVIDUAL RESPONSIBILITY

"Alles kann anders sein," said Alfred Adler, "Everything can be something else." Essentially, no matter what the situation, it could be something else—

you can change it in thought or action. Thus, a tense person could be relaxed; a depressed person could be cheerful. Life is not something predetermined either from the point of view of infinity or by events in one's life. Rather, life can be modified by the individual in terms of that person's perceptions, decision, viewpoints, judgments: the individual is responsible—to some greater extent.

"Soft determinism," discussed earlier, bears on individual responsibility. We are responsible for our own lives, and we can make decisions to change. Are you overweight? Don't blame it on heredity, unless you happen to have a rare disease or physical condition. Most people who are overweight are in this condition simply because millions of times in their lives they have bent their elbows too often—that is to say, they stuffed themselves. Did your mother worry over your weight? Did your father insist that you eat more? Did you develop bad eating habits? All that is in the past. What will you do at your next meal . . . and your next meal? It is your responsibility.

You do have a choice. You do have control. You don't have to go along with what your parents said or did, you don't have to continue your present way of life, you do have responsibility for your life.

Of course, you cannot control your moods directly. If you feel anxious or guilty or fearful and continue to think of yourself as ineffective, inefficient, or inadequte, you cannot change that just by willing or wishing. But you do have it in your power to make *some* changes in your behavior. You can start an exercise program, you can start going to school, you can stop nagging, you can go into therapy, you can seek a job, you can start a reducing program, you can start seeking for friends, you can stop drinking. Each of us can do something about our lives to make them better, to become more effective and more efficient, to change ourselves.

Why don't we? The basic answer for most of us, using our own terms, is that we are discouraged, and so we are lazy, we don't believe that things will work, we are not sure that others will permit us, and other excuses of that sort. In Individual Psychology we lump all these negative thoughts and feelings under the heading of discouragement. This is what Adlerian psychotherapy is about: changing discouraged people into courageous and responsible people.

If Social Interest is so important, and if children and adults want positive attention, why is there so much maladjustment and misbehavior? What motivates children to misbehave or adults to act neurotic and self-defeating?

Adlerians do not see people as being psychologically sick, but discouraged. The process of psychotherapy is not seen by Adlerians as "curing" anything, but as a process of encouragement.

To be able to get others to be encouraged is extremely difficult. The child who feels that he cannot succeed, who is operating on the basis of goal four, has given up, feels helpless. To change this pervasive point of view is really most difficult. The adult who accepts failure philosophically and who believes that she cannot change is also discouraged. The good parent and the good therapist both have the same job: to help a person believe in him or herself. How this can be done cannot be easily explained, but the Adlerian literature on family counseling and psychotherapy centers on this important point.

The basic fault of most self-help books is that they tell you what you already know—you are responsible—and then they make you feel more discouraged by telling you of others who have pulled themselves up by their bootstraps. We are concerned here that whatever you are is a function of three factors— *heredity* (about which you can do nothing), *past environment* (about which you can do nothing), and your *present behavior* (about which you can do something).

Some people who go into therapy know full well what they should do, but instead of doing what they should do, they "go into therapy" and in that way put the responsibility for their inaction—inadequacy—on the therapist, on others as usual. A good example would again be the woman who is overweight. She goes to a doctor who says to eat less and to exercise more. Now this person already knew this but nevertheless keeps overeating. Instead of making up her mind to do what is necessary, she now seeks "professional help" and may go to a hypnotist, a psychologist, a nurse practitioner, a dietician, or a psychiatrist, to "get motivated" to do what she knows she should do. Sometimes this is just an escape.

The position taken in this section is simple: individuals are responsible for their behavior. One has considerable control over one's life. Even if you are in a mental institution or a prison or in bed in a hospital with polio, you do have some control over your behavior. We are not the playthings of the gods. We are not the victims of our heredity. We are not the puppets of our parents. We do have control and we are self-responsible.

This point is crucial to the theory of Individual Psychology as well as to its practice. We are speaking about the character and strategies of psychotherapy. We have, and will, stress its educational characteristics, the need for cooperation between equals in the relationship between therapist and client, and the strong, directive nature of the Adlerian therapist's interactions with the client as the therapist attempts to elicit self-understanding, and encourage thought and behavior in the social interest.

People are much stronger than they are credited with being by many schools of psychology. How do we know this? One very obvious way is through looking at the tremendous ingenuity and effort so many people go through to maintain their life styles, even when this means displaying absurd symptoms, going through great intrapersonal agony, and messing up their lives with others. They suffer and suffer and suffer on their own recognizance because of the way they have decided to live—because of the life style and goals they created. A strong demand to face up to their ill-logic, having their nose rubbed in their own non-sense, not supporting their crazy symptoms and outlandish goals may prove uncomfortable for some people for some time. But we believe that most people can take it.

As Adlerian therapists, we will not take responsibility for supporting, maintaining, or facilitating faulty life styles and useless behavior. Direct, "hardheaded," "rough" talk from Adlerian therapists is, almost always, part of an attempt to make the client accept responsibility. In effect, in one way or another, we say to the client, "Change and understanding are up to you. We will help you in that direction but will not be party to your staying the way you have been. We care too much, we respect you too much, we value you and what you can be too much to join you in your pursuit of self-defeat."

This is our aim even if we get to the point where we have to say, as one of us once heard Dr. Dreikurs say to a patient, "You know your life style. You know what you are about, what you are after. And you keep doing it and coming here feeling sorry for yourself. And you want me to feel sorry for you. I am sorry that you do not want to change, but I don't feel sorry for you when you keep doing what you know will only keep you a mess. I'm leaving. If you want to talk to me again you have to want to change. As long as you want to be the way you are I can't help you." When he came out and was asked about what had just happened, he told us he was just saying the truth about the patient and the way he felt. If she would not take responsibility for herself and for changing, it was a waste of his time and of her time and money. She could do it if she would. Shortly afterward, she came and asked for him, said she understood and would show him. To which he said, "Don't show me, show you."

ADLERIAN COUNSELING

In this chapter our concentration has been on counseling/therapy, stating that the two are really similar, differing only quantitatively. However, we have been, for the most part, stressing psychotherapy, patients and techniques, and to remedy this imbalance we will now concentrate on straight counseling.

The word counseling implies advice. You go to an attorney—a counselor-at-law—for advice. You go to a family counselor for advice about your family. You are in a quandary; you don't know how to handle a particular problem and you go for advice just as you might go to a mechanic or a physician for informed opinions.

Parenting Counseling

A most advice-filled book in the Adlerian literature is *The Practical Parent* (Corsini & Painter, 1975), where highly specific advice is offered for 24 problems that parents are likely to have with children. To take some examples of problems and the essence of the advice given:

Getting up in the morning problems. Get the child an alarm clock and if the child does not set the clock, and is late, let the child accept the consequences of the tardiness.

Child who does not do assigned chores. Set up some logical consequences, such as that she is not to eat until her pet has been fed, as per an agreement reached earlier. Only after the dog or cat is fed can she then eat.

Children who fight in the family. In this book three suggestions are made to be considered in this sequence: *(a)* do nothing, enjoy watching the fighting but keep out of it; *(b)* leave the area and go somewhere else where you will not be the spectator of the struggle; or *(c)* expel all fighters from the house with instructions to come back only when the fight is over.

Bedwetting problems. If the child is old enough, the advice goes as follows: *(a)* get a covered pail large enough to hold wet garments, sheets, and so on; *(b)* inform the child that from now on if he should wet again, then the soiled materials are to be put in this pail; *(c)* the child will be shown where the new materials—sheets and pillowcases—are to be found; and *(d)* the child will be told that it is up to him whether to change sheets and clean up, if he wets again.

Under no circumstances is the parent to check rooms, or to make comments, or to praise the child or in any way to mention bedwetting again. If the child persists in the bedwetting, and only then—not before—should the physician be informed of the problem, since in practically 100 percent of such bedwetting cases the cause is psychological, not physiological.

From whence come these various specific advices? They come first from an overview of the relationships between adults and children as visualized from Adlerian theory. Thus, if we really believe in mutual respect, and if we really believe that children are and should be responsible, and if we believe that pampering is harmful to children, and if we believe in mutual cooperation, then every one of these pieces of advice makes sense. If, on the other hand, we see children as helpless, as needing "love" and "petting," and that requiring them to do for themselves is unfair, then the advice given above will seem harsh and cruel. The various kinds of advice that one will find in parenting books written by people of various persuasions and orientations will differ considerably in terms of the individuals' theories.

We now come to the issue of self-correcting of the counselor through experience. All ethical professional counselors are interested in results, and they will follow up on clients. This is precisely what Adlerians will do; and in our estimation and our experience, Adlerian advice, when followed by parents, works always—or almost always.

However, so will other advice. People who have a different theoretical/philosophical orientation also report good results. How to explain this? For example, one counselor suggests that parents punish severely upon infractions and that after the punishment they should demonstrate how much they love the child in every way.

We now come to two other important considerations in comparing various systems of counseling: the first has to do with the long-term versus the short-term goals; and the second has to do with what is known as the "elegance" of the counseling. Let us consider both of these.

If a child has a habit of nose picking, thumb sucking, or nail biting, one way to stop it would be to put the child's arms in cylinders so that the elbows cannot be bent. Plastic tubes could be purchased or fashioned that would extend from the shoulder to the middle of the forearms. Certainly this procedure would stop indulgence in these habits, but we can imagine the consequences to the child as well as to the tranquility of the family if the typical five-year-old were to be so treated. Also, the child might in later years develop all sorts of symptoms of maladjustment as a result of the treatment, as well as a negative perception of the people who so treated him. Yes, one can punish a child so severely that he will no longer do something because of sheer terror, but the long-term consequences may be very harmful. We advise: *Always* treat the child with dignity. *Always* ask the child to discuss the problem, the solution and to accept the consequences. The parent is not to proceed unless the procedure makes good sense in terms of logical and natural consequences.

The second part of counseling variations has to do with elegance: logic, expediency, appropriateness, common sense, and economy. Let us say that there are two approaches to problem X, and that approach A takes 100 hours, calls for a lot of expense, generates a lot of conflict; and that approach B takes 10 hours, costs little, and works smoothly. The latter form of counseling procedure would be the more elegant. Take, for example, the advice given to parents about sibling fights: *(a)* bear it (stay and look on); *(b)* beat it (go somewhere else, where you won't be bothered); and *(c)* boot 'em (get all fighters out of the house). This has a certain elegance and simplicity. Other suggestions—such as interfering through trying to find out who started the fight, sending the kids to their rooms separately, or punishing one or all in the fights—tend to take longer and generate conflicts. They are not as clean and as simple.

Marriage Counseling

The same general philosophy of looking for theoretical coherence in dealing with marital disputes or difficulties is found when Adlerians give marital advice. We always consider the importance of equality between the sexes in counseling. We believe in fairness, logic, freedom, self- and other respect, and consequently in giving advice to marriage partners, which after all is a function of counseling. We tend to be at the same time logical and psychological—we use our good sense and we also consider any advice in terms of our general theory.

For example, a wife complains that when she and her husband go to parties, the husband flirts outrageously. Her solution has been to look on in anger, and when the couple comes home they get into a fight. She asks the counselor for advice, hoping the counselor will criticize the husband for his behavior. But the counselor does not do so. "Next time that happens, leave the party and go home," the counselor advises. The wife is shocked. How can she do this? It would be an embarrassment. Who does such things? Adlerians do. The wife is told to inform her husband that if he flirts to such a degree that she feels uncomfortable, she will either take the car (if she has the keys) or take a cab home; and then—and we advise this strongly—she will say absolutely nothing to the husband about the incident, and she must be prepared to continue to act in exactly the same manner in similar circumstances. Again, we have the question of self-respect to consider, as well as the fair and respectful way of dealing with the husband and letting him know in advance exactly what she intends to do.

Adlerian Logic of Counseling

Notice that in all the abbreviated descriptions given, the general process goes as follows:

1. The counselor tries to understand the problem.
2. When the counselor feels relatively certain of the nature of the problem (which comes from theory and from experience), the counselor explains the client's options and gives specific advice.
3. The client then gets to understand both the theory behind the advice and exactly what to do. Consequently, the counselee now has cognitive data. We have reached the counselee's mind, and we are dealing with reason, as well as with logic. To finish this step may take a few minutes or many hours.
4. Now the counselee is ready to put into action what has been discussed —and generally the advice works out well. In an amusing article by Corsini (1979), the "betting technique" originally developed by Rudolf Dreikurs is explained. In this technique, the counselor actually will make a money bet that if the advice is followed, good results will ensue. So, if the client succeeds, he or she loses the bet!
5. The counselee now tries out the suggested procedures and then reports back.

One of the authors who has done public counseling for over 20 years under Adlerian auspices, and who has trained approximately 100 other counselors, has not yet heard of a single instance in which, when Adlerian advice was followed in parent/child relationships, the advice did not work out. In the Adlerian literature there are dozens of reports of such counseling which should be read for more specific information (cf. Allred, 1974; Beecher & Beecher, 1966; Brind, 1942; Deutsch, 1956, 1967).

Perhaps the most evident example of the correctness of Adlerian theory comes from counseling: no other system is as elegant in its counseling—handling a wide variety of problems simply, easily, logically, respectfully, and economically. On top of that, results are almost always considered to be successful when the advice is properly followed. Well over a million people have read the primary book on family counseling by Dreikurs and Soltz (1964), and the popularity of the approach continues to grow, because it works.

Chapter 11

Psychotherapeutic Approach and Initial Interview

Adlerian therapists for the most part assume an attitude of friendly equality with their clients. The Adlerian therapist tries to be authentic, respectful, concerned, interested, seeing the client as an individual in distress, desiring help, even if unknowingly planning on sabotaging the treatment. The Adlerian therapist has a flexible attitude directed to the job at hand, and does not want to be a guru or leader but, rather, an educator and a facilitator. The ideal therapeutic relationship is seen as natural, unforced, of two mutually respectful adults examining one person's problem in a partnership.

THE THERAPIST AS MODEL

All forms of psychotherapy work to various degrees and all therapists are successful to various extents. What is common to all therapies? The main element appears to be simply good relationship with another person whom one trusts. Usually, a good deal of the therapy has already taken place before the formal psychotherapy actually starts: a voluntary decision to come for therapy is an important change factor. A further general factor in successful therapy may be the client's modeling of the therapist, who becomes a kind of role model. The client observes the therapist as carefully as the therapist observes the clients, as George A. Kelly (1964) noted.

How the therapist talks, thinks, and acts hopefully provides clients with a view of a person worthy of being imitated. The therapist unwittingly teaches the patient by example. We see this in such charismatic people as (to mention some therapists we have known personally) Rudolf Dreikurs, Carl Rogers, Albert Ellis, George Bach, Arthur Lerner, Fritz Perls, and Will Schutz, whose clients imitate them often in style of dress, manner of delivery, thinking processes and the like.

Adlerian therapists, in part because of selection factors, in part because of their predisposition and in part from experience, try to, and may, become "like" the theory. An ideal Adlerian therapist acts as a whole person in the social interest, encouraging confidently with feeling and sensitivity and with social purpose. One hopes to live the theory, in and out of therapy, and thereby model the theory—in and out of the psychotherapeutic setting.

THE THERAPIST AND THERAPY

Whether therapy is more a function of the person of the therapist than the theory or the procedure is not clear. The Fiedler (1950) study indicates that the experience of the therapist was the single most important reason for therapeutic ability, which suggests that if you have a choice of therapists, all factors considered, select the one with the greater experience. After all, one should learn something as one goes along.

Why would a person choose to become an Adlerian? It is easier to get training in psychoanalysis, nondirective therapy, or behavior therapy. Training is more readily available in Gestalt therapy and Transactional Analysis. We hypothesize there is a relationship between one's personality and the personality theory one selects. For example, Freud's psychoanalysis is highly cognitive and operates on a long-term basis and is quite suitable for people with long-term attention spans. Jung's analytical psychology has a strong introverted and mystical aspect. Moreno's psychodrama calls for highly extroverted creative people. Rogers' person-centered therapy is low-keyed and self-effacing. The terms used to describe these personality theories are about the same that could be used to describe these theorists!

Freud . . . . highly cognitive
Jung . . . . introverted, mystical
Moreno . . . . extroverted, driven
Rogers . . . . low-keyed, self-effacing

Psychotherapists tend to select a theory compatible with their own personality. Thus, a Jungian-type might be more attracted to Jung's theory and an Ellis-type will be attracted to Ellis' theory and, of course, one with a personality represented by Adler's theory will be attracted to his theory.

Adler was a friendly, jovial, concerned person, filled with common sense, an ideal "uncle." And while Adlerians range widely in their personalities, nevertheless their manifest "Adlerian" personalities may tend to distinguish them from other psychotherapists.

The personalities of members of any particular group become more rather than less the same. If you keep saying on reading this book "That's right," or "Yes, that is the way things go," you are finding confirmation of your own ideas, and you will be likely to seek out others who think in the same way, to affiliate with Adlerian theory in thought and its adherents in action. Adlerian therapists generally take a somewhat different view about therapeutic relationships in comparison to some other professionals. We view counseling and therapy as learning processes, and see ourselves as facilitators, more or less like tutors: educators and encouragers. The relationship within therapy or counseling or outside of the office need not be formal. Thus, the therapist may take a relaxed attitude, stretch out, be casually dressed, and need not have a desk between him/herself and the client, may use identical chairs of equal height as did Adler.

Some Adlerians may do counseling and therapy with friends. Adlerians do not care to hear confessions—terrible things that one has done. While confession may relieve the individual, the main issue, as they see it, is learning, and one *can* learn from anyone.

While most people doing counseling or therapy tend to avoid social relationships with clients, some Adlerians will, selectively, meet with those they are working with, if the circumstances seem to warrant. They do not necessarily, exclusively maintain a "professional" distance outside of the office or consulting room. Their position is that we can have multiple, always ethical, friendly or collegial relationships with people, including clients.

Ideally the Adlerian therapist intelligently carries out the proper procedures of psychotherapy in formal psychotherapeutic settings, *but* most important is a warm human in keeping with the positive aspects of Adlerian theory. The therapist is authentic in dealing with patients as equals, operating with respect, and caring and acting as a model while doing therapy.

ASSESSMENT

There are two general positions about the value of formal assessment in psychotherapy. One is that the entire therapeutic encounter is a constant process of assessment. From the first interview to the last, the therapist is studying the patient. The second position is that a formal assessment should be carried out at the beginning of therapy. There are supporters of both of these positions as well as other points of view among Adlerians as well as non-Adlerians. Since we have been trained in the Adlerian tradition of Dr. Rudolf Dreikurs, we both rather consistently do formal life style evaluations at the beginning of psychotherapy.

Some Adlerians, and we fall into this group ourselves, will use projective instruments such as the Rorschach and the Thematic Appreception Tests, even though our interpretations may not be the usual ones since both of these tests were originally developed in terms of Freudian/Jungian rather than Adlerian conceptions. The most general methods Adlerians employ in assessment are the initial interview; the Life Style interview, which includes family constellation and early recollections; observations of clients; reports and documents; and unstructured interviews.

The Initial Interview

Adlerians probably come to tentative conclusions about patients more quickly than do devotees of other schools. Also, Adlerians probably relate their notions about a patient to the patient sooner than do other therapists. We believe that Adlerian theory allows us to understand a person quickly. We are respectful of and see ourselves as equal to clients; therefore we believe in sharing our understanding as it comes. In the initial interview, we usually attempt to:

1. Come to first hypotheses about the person by:
   a. Observing the patient's initial behavior.
   b. Asking questions to get at the person's purposes and goals.
   c. Interpreting the person's behavior and responses in the session.
2. Share our hypotheses about the person, making educated "guesses" in order to:
   a. Get confirmation from the person of the validity of our hypotheses.
   b. Illustrate our interest and attention.
   c. Show our willingness to risk failure, as we present hypotheses which the patient may say are wrong, in the common cause of helping the patient.
3. Explain the nature of our therapy, and come to a tentative plan for the therapy, that is, explain reasons for the life style interview and interpretations, number of sessions expected, frequency, and so forth. Some questions that an Adlerian therapist might ask are as follows:

Why are you here? What are your symptoms or problems?

Have you had counseling before? With whom? How long? What did you learn? (Notice the emphasis on the cognitive aspect: *learning.*)

What are your expectations? What could be successful counseling/ therapy in your opinion?

Also the therapist would be most interested in such matters as:

The client's attitude. Is he optimistic or pessimistic? Cooperative or negative?

The referral. Did the client come in voluntarily or under pressure from someone else?

Are the patient's expectations reasonable?

Relationship with therapist. Does the therapist feel comfortable with the client and vice versa?

Guessing. Right from the beginning, watching the patient's behavior, the facial expressions, the tone of voice—everything—leads the therapist to some sort of "hunch" about the client's purposes, goals, the meaning of symptoms. This is the so-called stochastic concept of psychotherapy—a series of guesses, narrowing down the possibilities as one goes along. Sometimes the "answer" seems evident. The therapist "knows" immediately what the client is about. The technical problem now is one of technique. Should one say, "I know just what is wrong with you . . ." in five minutes?

Indeed some Adlerian therapists might do so. Others will be more cautious, hesitating to make any judgments as long as possible. Adlerians would take a conservative attitude in that opinions, not judgments, are expressed, but a liberal stance is shown immediately. Opinions might be stated something like, "I'd like to tell you right now the impression I get from you. It may be incorrect, but if I get this impression, others may have it also. . . ." Or the statement might go as follows: "I have tried to be neutral and perceptive, and it seems to me that on an overt level of behavior you act in. . . ."

Most usually Adlerians will "guess"—they will present their working hypothesis. They will do this so the client knows it is an hypothesis, and that it thereby deserves confirmation or negation from the client. And they will do so in a way to involve the client in the shared process of coming to an understanding of the purposes of the client's symptoms, behavior, life style. The therapist might involve the client by saying, "Would you like to hear what I think at this point?" or "I've got an idea. I want to see what you think about it." When the client agrees to hear the therapist's hypothesis, the therapist may still qualify it so the client does not get the impression that the therapist is presenting him with "the answer." The therapist may preface the hypothesis with "Perhaps you are . . ." or "Maybe you want . . ." And then the therapist will wait for the client's response. It may be, "You are absolutely right," which allows quick movement.

However, the client may respond, "That seems sort of right," in which case the therapist would want the client to join in the effort by saying something like, "How can you improve it?" or "What would be right?" Amazingly often the client will then tell you exactly what he or she is about, saying, for example, "I always want to be right" or "I am deathly afraid of failure."

The therapist's early hypothesis may be wrong. There is value in the therapeutic relationship in your being wrong. You prove to the client that you are fallible, and that you do not mind. You are willing to risk being wrong, a small failure indeed. You prove your humanity. Sometimes, from the client's viewpoint this is the first time an authority is seen as admitting error, failure, or faults. One of us had this pointed out to us, in a somewhat different context. A borderline psychotic patient came for a session one wintry day while we were practicing in Chicago. At the door he fumbled and nearly fell over trying to remove his overshoes. I said, "Gosh, I hate taking those darn things off. It's so clumsy and awkward. You get hot and sweaty if you haven't taken off your overcoat." In the middle of the session, he mentioned this seemingly trivial incident and laughed saying, "I didn't know you could think about things like that. When you said that I almost fell over."

"Bread and Butter" Issues.   Toward the end of an initial interview the therapist should have come to a tentative diagnosis and prognosis as well as a decision about suitability and need for psychotherapy. Likewise, the client should have come to a judgment about the therapist and whether to continue. If either does not want to go on, the session should, if possible, conclude on a positive note, with the client benefiting in some way from the session. If the therapist and client agree that they see some value in continuing, it is worthwhile to have an understanding of the process. The therapist might say:

> Before we go on I'd like to tell you a little bit about the kind of therapy I do and how I would like to proceed. You may already have an idea of how I will be as a therapist. I want to work with you in an open and frank way. If I have something to say I'll certainly say it, and I expect that you will do the same.
>
> We have already come to a bit of a consensus about your problems. We have agreed that it might hinge on your needing to be good (or whatever other goals are implicated and agreed on in the session). As an Adlerian therapist I have a procedure and interview questionnaire I like to go through in order to get as good a handle as we can on what we call your life style. When we do this we will, I hope, be able to have a good idea of what you are after, of your goals, and how these are causing your problem.
>
> Usually it takes about three sessions to collect this information, to do this questionnaire. While we were doing it we can still talk about anything that is bothering you. When it is finished I will interpret for you, boil it down to a few basic issues. If we can both see that these are the heart of what is troubling you we can then go on.

There is no standard way of doing the above, and many Adlerians do not do systematic life style interviews. This is just an example. In essence we are trying to give the client some idea of what is going to happen.

With some clients the therapist cannot estimate the length of therapy, whereas with others this can be done. One of us always enters therapy as if it were time limited, and most Adlerians, most of the time, do relatively short, if not time-limited, therapy. So this therapist would continue:

> When we finish the life style interpretation session we may want to modify this plan, but right now I think we will probably want to see each other for eight (or four or six or whatever) sessions after we finish the life style, if that sounds OK to you. You can stop at any time. I would, though, appreciate it if you call to tell me so. Therapy has to be worthwhile to you for you to continue.
>
> I will see you through the eight visits after we complete the life style, unless we both conclude that you do not need to continue that long. At the eighth session we can see how we are doing. If at that time we both think we should have some additional sessions, I have the option of continuing or not. If I do not think progress is being made, you are not changing and/or working on it, I can quit. I want to help and will not continue if I am not helping. You are going to have to work in order for change to occur, for things to get better. If either I do not think I am helping, or I think you are not working I will quit at the end of the eighth session.

Experience has shown us that clients see this as a fair position. Clients who want to change will set to work vigorously within this time-limited system, and clients who are ambivalent about change, but who want to continue therapy, will work strenuously before the therapist's option runs out. In either case the time-limited proviso provides incentive for the client to make good effort in relation to the therapy.

Also at this first meeting, frequency of sessions should be set, and other ground rules, such as telephone calls, emergency visits, and no show. The manner of payment, in a private practice setting, is also important to arrange. If it is not arranged suitably and amicably, it can become quite an irritant. One of the authors has developed a system for making even this part of therapy therapeutic.

At the end of the initial interview, when amount of compensation had been settled according to what the client can afford, I say something like:

> I prefer people to pay each time they come. If that is not possible we can make other arrangements, but I prefer this way for two reasons, First, if you pay each time I am never in to you and you are never in to me. I do not want you coming with the feeling that you owe me, and I do not want to feel that way. Sometimes people might keep seeing a therapist because they do not feel they can afford to stop; they would have to pay up. This way we are always even. Second, therapy is work. I hope we will enjoy the process but that is not the aim. Every time you visit it will cost you. By paying each time I hope you will consider each time whether it is worth it. Have we made progress?

A SECOND WAY OF OPERATING

The preceding material of this chapter was written by one of us, and this section was written by another. We both share practically identical ideas about Adlerian philosophy and theory, but as therapists we operate somewhat differently. To disabuse the reader from thinking that the above is the only way Adlerians operate, or even the way we recommend that Adlerian therapists should operate, following is another general way of operating. The reader will see that while there are some differences due to individual experiences, these have nothing to do with the important element of Adlerian thinking, but merely different styles of operating.

The Initial Interview—A Second View

I am most interested in getting an immediate "feeling" of my client, and when the client enters I attempt to become neutral, saying little, presenting myself as a kind of living Rorschach card, as it were, interested in seeing how the client acts. So, from the beginning moments I am analyzing his or her behavior, trying to act exactly the same with all clients. I don't offer to shake hands, I don't give my name, I don't smile, but after they enter, I sit down and, with a neutral look, I wait to see what will happen.

Client 1 may smile, thrust out his hand, announce his name, look around the office and take a chair and then wait for me to begin.

Client 2 may come in, look helpless and, when I seat myself, keep standing, looking hopeless and helpless, and we may engage in a kind of struggle, each waiting for the other to begin. I will not keep such a person waiting too long, and with a gesture I will point to a chair.

Client 3 comes in, doesn't even look at me, and begins with a long story of why she has come in.

And so on. In other words, I know that new clients are probably anxious and nervous, and are likely to operate in ways that may give me clues to their unique personalities.

Having been myself trained, before becoming an Adlerian, as a nondirective therapist, I try to wait for the client to start things off. I know that the client generally feels that I am in charge, but I want to assume the attitude that now we are equal, even though it is my territory. If the client does not start, I may give my name and say something like, "Well, we are here together, and I am most interested in knowing what brings you here, and I hope I can be of some help to you. Please tell everything." Having said that, I again wait to see what reactions will take place, and they vary considerably, from those who play helpless and expect me to ask questions to those who will take the floor and talk without interruption for almost the entire hour.

Usually, somewhere along the middle, my own strategy goes somewhat as follows: I now ask the client if I may have the floor. I then will generally do the following, more or less in this order: *(a)* I will respond to the client's statements up to that point, saying perhaps something like, "In my experience, marital problems eventually come down to two stubborn people, each wanting their own way, and each unwilling to cooperate. My belief is that the secret of a good marriage is to learn how to give in to your mate." In other words, I will try to make some general statement, to give some indication of my general position—and frequently this statement is a surprise, since the client does not expect such a reaction. A second thing *(b)* that I frequently do is something that almost no one ever experiences in life. I say something like this: "I am going to tell you my first reaction to you, my immediate reaction to you. You may have noted that when you came in I was quiet and didn't say much. I have been watching you, trying to develop an impression about you. I may be completely wrong, but this is how I see you. . . ." And then I give an analysis. Since only today I saw a woman client for the first time, I can more or less repeat my statement to her.

> I was tremendously impressed how "busy" you were all the time, dropping your umbrella, fixing your coat, moving the chair about, searching over and over again for your glasses, generating the impression of almost desperate movement. Also, I noticed the fixed smile on your face like that of a frightened child. When I would look away from you and then look back, your face changed and you looked tired and sick, but then you put on your smiling mask again. I am just so impressed that you, a woman of 50, acts just like a frightened child brought to the principal's office.

This type of reaction on my part may generate all kinds of reactions, but generally I find that the client is impressed by my forthrightness and they get the courage to respond in kind. In other words, I am most concerned to get away from the usual behavior that people engage in when they first meet, and I want the other to know just what he or she will find.

Then *(c)* my next step ordinarily is to ask the person to respond to me, and I ask, generally, something like this: "I know you are in a new situation, and I know that I am more experienced and I am fairly sure I may have overwhelmed you, but now I want to know just how you react to me. I am sure you are watching me and studying me just as I am studying you. What do you think of me?" And the reply, whether it be a safe, noncommittal response, an angry response, a reasonable one, or an aggressive one, gives me further clues about the kind of person with whom I am dealing.

Then I ask what I think is the important question:

> Now, I think selecting a therapist is one of the most important decisions that one makes in life. Have you formed an opinion about me, whether I am the therapist

for you? I really want you to get the best therapist, so you can tell me now whether you want to work with me; if not, then that's OK. I'll refer you to someone else if you want. Or, if you want to, you can think it over, and not make another appointment. Or, if you do, and you change your mind and think it over, and decide you want not to see me, that's fine, and you can cancel the appointment.

I avoid any pressure on the client to come to any decisions about future visits, and I will not set up a specific number of sessions.

Regarding payments, I say the following: "My fee is this and it is the same as what other people of my experience charge. My secretary will bill you monthly. Pay what you owe me if you can; if you can't, pay what you can; and if you can't pay at all, that is all right with me too. I don't want you to think that I will not see you if you can't afford to pay me."

This attitude incidentally has paid off in the sense that most of my clients do pay me in full. If they want to, we can negotiate on fees, and I am always careful to ask them whether they think they can afford what they agree to pay. My secretary has strict instructions to bill a person twice, and the third time to say that whether the client (or ex-client) will pay will be up to him or her, but there will no longer be any billing. I have had people send me money sometimes years after I last saw them, and overall I think I get as much percentagewise as my colleagues who are more businesswise than I am.

We then set a schedule, and the client is always made aware that he or she is the purchaser and I am the supplier, and that I am that person's employee, to be hired to do the best job possible.

The final step is this: I explain to the client that I am an Adlerian, and that I represent a particular point of view about personality theory and psychotherapy, and I may give the client the names of some books to examine if he or she wishes. I then explain that I ordinarily spend some time taking a life style examination, and explain what it is, and ask the client whether he or she would want to start on it immediately on the next session, or whether we should have some exploratory talks. For some clients, I get to the life style on the next session, for some I wait several sessions, for some I may have it after several months, and for some I never do a life style analysis. Only recently I saw a young man whose sister was in therapy with me, and he fully expected a life style to be done. I told him that I didn't think he needed one, and that we should immediately get to work on his big problem, his excessive shyness. I began to do some role playing with him since I got the impression that this was what he needed. Indeed, he caught on, enjoyed the session, came back the next week feeling most fulfilled because he had been more socially aggressive, eager for more role playing, and during that session he said to me that he had dreaded going through all that life style business with the early memories.

What he doesn't know is that if I think that this will be called for, at the right time, I will ask him to submit to such an evaluation.

A great deal can be accomplished in an initial interview. We have attempted to outline some of the aims and procedures that might be part of Adlerian initial interviews. In the next sections we will discuss in depth the Adlerian life style procedure, its application and meanings.

Chapter 12

Life Style Assessment

The particular assessment procedure we shall discuss in this chapter, emanating from Adler, was developed by Rudolf Dreikurs (1954, 1967). It has been modified by a number of other individuals and is probably further modified by each therapist to some degree. We shall differentiate between Life Style (with capital letters), to refer to the assessment procedure, and life style (with lower-case letters), to refer to an individual's style of life, personality. So, we take a Life Style to discover a person's life style.

ASSESSING GOALS-PURPOSES

The procedure we shall explicate is not the sole way Adlerians determine life style. Some simply interview their clients with the idea that over time meaningful knowledge of the patient or client will come with greater experience, the same way eclectic counselors and therapists operate.

In marriage and family counseling, life styles are not usually obtained. In child counseling, Adlerians determine children's goals with relative dispatch by analyzing the manner in which they attempt to find their place in the class, with friends, and in the family. Alfred Adler used to amaze professionals by correctly predicting the onstage behavior of children he had never seen before (Seidler, 1936).

Adlerians view people as being strong, self-creative, and responsible. By and large individuals get what they are after—the effect they have on others is what they want to achieve. This notion may seem outlandish to a newcomer to Adlerian psychology. If a person is consistently pathetic, inept, clumsy, and stupid in everything he tackles, so that he is never asked by anyone to do anything, Adlerians conclude that *this is precisely the goal of that person.* If a person is so good as to be taken advantage of, demeaned, and used by all in sundry ways, we say *that is exactly that person's purpose.* If a person never can make a decision, never seems to come to a conclusion, always seems to be struggling with problems, but never comes to an answer, *that is completely that person's goal.*

"Why does George always seem to do the wrong thing?" one might ask. An Adlerian answers the question by saying that George intends to be what he is! It is his goal to make mistakes, to be inept, stupid, and clumsy. If you do not accept this Adlerian view, how would *you* explain George, who is generally cloddish, clumsy, and always goofing up? Such a person receives benign neglect from most people, accompanied by a watchfulness—we know he is there and we want to know what he is doing, preferring that he be doing nothing, or at least nothing that has to do with us. We cooperate with his goal—"to be let alone to do my own thing and keep people off my back." By looking for general patterns of behavior and how people react, we are able to determine the goal of a person such as George with relative ease.

Working backward from the behavior of George to the underlying beliefs that make up his life style syllogism requires a subtle understanding. People may come to the same general kinds of behavior and consequences from a wide variety of premises—their life style syllogisms. Two possibilities for George's basic beliefs come to mind. He may be convinced of his inferiority: *(a)* I am absolutely incapable, *(b)* the world is populated by competents, therefore *(c)* I have to act so that they let me alone. Or this syllogism may underlie George's behavior: *(a)* I am a misunderstood genius, *(b)* the world is bent on making me conform to plebian norms, therefore *(c)* I have to see to it that they let me alone to do my own thing *and ultimately* to show them my genius.

Teasing out basic beliefs by using the Life Style procedure is relatively easy once the process is mastered. An early key to finding the beliefs that make up the client's life style is to evaluate your own reactions to the client. In the case of George you may feel manipulated by his "forcing" you to have certain attitudes toward him and, in a sense, that is just what is happening. Since everyone operates in terms of his biased apperceptions and life style, everyone attempts to reach private goals and manipulates others so that they will react to them in coherence with these goals. In that sense, all behavior is manipulative. However, we do not have to degrade this fact. Rather, we use it to understand people's goals and life styles.

We attempt in a Life Style assessment to identify those most comprehensive units of the individual's personality or life style which are broad intentional dispositions, future-oriented, that we call goals. We attempt to identify the unique quality of the goals of each person by analyzing the pattern and direction of elementary units and by illustrating how goals attract, guide, and inhibit them.

The Life Style assessment procedure attempts to ascertain relatively few cardinal characteristics. As diagnosticians we can identify and understand, and as therapists we can help the client change, the relatively few cardinal characteristics which attract, guide, and inhibit behavior and signify that we are each unique.

Adler referred to the "three entrance gates to the mental life": (a) family constellation, (b) early recollections, and (c) dreams. We have discussed family constellation as an important situational variable in the development of personality in Chapter 7. Early recollections and dreams function to remind us of and reinforce our basic notions, our goals and views of self and the world, and guide us in pursuit of our goals.

LIFE STYLE PROCEDURE

The Life Style procedure is a structured interview to obtain information about the family constellation, early recollections, and dreams of a client. Answers given provide information for the therapist to tentatively interpret the client's life style. There are a number of formal formats for the Life Style Questionnaire (Eckstein et al., 1975; Morris, 1978; Mosak, Schneider & Mosak, 1980; Mosak & Shulman, 1971). Any therapist may develop a derivation of any of these questionnaires, stressing questions thought to be valuable. Even with minimal exposure to the theory and practice of Individual Psychology, some people are able to make insightful and potentially valuable interpretations. A well-trained, experienced therapist can collect and interpret life style material with a clarity, finesse, and sophistication which yields statements which precisely describe the client's uniqueness.

We will now describe the general Dreikurs procedure for collecting and interpreting life styles, explaining it in enough detail that the reader can understand in general what we do and why we do it. Our intention is not to "teach" the reader how to do Life Styles. One cannot learn to do Life Styles by reading alone. Training by modeling and observation under direct supervision are necessary to reach a professional level of proficiency in Life Style interpretation.

Family Constellation

The basic notion underlying the family constellation concept is that individuals want to belong, to fit in with others, to have a place in the primary human group—their family of origin. The first and most important exposure to a group is one's original family. The way in which we perceive ourselves as adults is dictated to some degree by the way in which we perceived ourselves in relation to others in our family of origin. Later social perceptions are dictated by earlier perceptions. However, no aspect of the family constellation and its component parts—birth order, parent characteristics, family modes, or myths—*necessarily* dictates the child's or adult's social notions. The child's perceptions, however, of these aspects strongly influence the adult's perceptions. Truly, the child is father of the man.

Birth Order. Generally, information relating to birth order is gathered by asking questions of three types: *(a)* descriptions of each sibling as remembered by the client, *(b)* specific information on the social groupings of the siblings, and *(c)* comparative ratings of the client and siblings on selected characteristics. Dreikurs' method asks for older brothers' and sisters' names, with how many years they are older or younger than the client. This gives an indication of possible birth order position as opposed to ordinal position. For example, a client may have had two older siblings—a brother 4 years older and a sister 2 years older, and 2 younger siblings—a sister 8 years younger and a sister 10 years younger. Although the client is a third child—that is, the client's ordinal position is third, his birth order designation may more likely be the youngest of three, with the two girls who came along 8 and 10 years later constituting a separate grouping.

Descriptions of the siblings and self as children give additional important information. From these descriptions we begin to get some notions of the client's values and the family's values as seen by the client. In this questioning we try to get an insight about the role the client developed in the family as well as the view the client had of various members of the family. Everything in our search is intended to find cardinal characteristics.

Suppose that a client says, "My older brother was very handsome. My older sister was very pretty. My next sister was nice looking, and my youngest sister was cute. I was plain." These sentences provide a clear clue to a major life theme. Themes may, however, be complex. For example, a client might describe an older brother as being strong, masculine, and bright, an older sister as being feminine and social. The client describes himself as a child as being nice, but has no clear memory of the younger two siblings. From this we might hypothesize that the younger two were not relevant to the client's search for a place in the family and we might further guess that the older brother and sister had already staked claim to rather special important territories—achievement and excellence—and the only option left to the client to find his role in the family was to be "nice."

From the descriptions of the siblings, as well as the ages, sexes, and spacings, we begin to get ideas of the family's values, the groupings, and the client's strategy for fitting into the family. Clients often describe themselves as children in a way almost identical to how one would describe them as adults.

Some therapists, in collecting life style data, will proceed through the protocol without interpreting. This uninterrupted process, they believe, provides a greater unity to the Life Style summary phase and adds coherence and drama when the Life Style data is interpreted to the client. This is especially the case in multiple therapy (Dreikurs, 1952a, 1952b), when the senior therapist interprets the information given by the associate therapist with the client present.

However, there is value at times in interpreting bits of information and making tentative hypotheses as one moves through the data collection. Collecting Life Style data may take as long as three to four hours and another hour for interpretation and summary. This may mean four or five sessions from the beginning of the data collection until the summary. During this time, a client may need some buoying up, some information, some belief that the therapist is beginning to understand him or her, and that the client is getting something out of the process. Therefore, one may periodically point out the possible significance of the client's answer to a certain question. In instances where a client's description as a child is essentially identical to a present description, pointing this out may allow the client to see value in the Life Style procedure, to open up, and to really get involved. Usually there is little difficulty in getting people involved and getting them to answer personal inquiries which are generally seen as interesting and benign.

Another important question bearing on family constellation has to do with the relationships between the siblings and the subgroupings of siblings. Questions which ask who played together and who fought most, who is most like and most unlike the client, give evidence of the nature of the client's relationship with siblings. Another question often asked is: Which sibling, if any, had a serious illness or injury? The relevance of this question comes from the sense of inferiority that might arise from seeing oneself as "the sick one." However, "a" sick one in the family may have implications for the entire family system, whether this be a legitimately ill or injured child or one labeled "sick" by its deviant behavior.

Usually in Life Style questionnaires, the client rates self and the other relevant siblings on a series of descriptors. By "relevant" we mean the siblings the client was involved with as a child in finding a place within the family. In the example of the five-child family given above, the client was probably the third of the group of three who played and fought, competed, and cooperated. This was the relevant group for the client, and the two sisters who came later were probably not very important for our purpose of learning about the client's life style.

The data collection process demands that the therapist make decisions throughout. The therapist has to decide which siblings should be included in the ratings. With small families of two or three siblings closely spaced, all are included. However, in larger families and where there are large age spaces between siblings, the relevant group must be determined. Usually the therapist would make a tentative decision and check it out with the client. The therapist might say, "It looks like you and your two older siblings formed one group and your two younger sisters formed another. Is that right?" If the answer is "yes," then the therapist might say "Let's just refer to you and the older two as you rate the three of you from most to least on each of the following characteristics. However, if you think that any of the younger sisters is important on some of the characteristics, please include her."

The words used in these ratings vary on different lists. They may be grouped as Morris (1978) has done. He has grouped attributes such as intelligence, grades, and standards of achievement to determine the client's relative ranking on achievement—athletic, feminine-masculine, and so on. Such groupings point out commonalities—how the various descriptors relate to each other.

Any descriptors may be put together in a variety of ways according to how the client rates herself in relation to the others or, if the client is an only child, how she rates herself on some sort of personal standard from high to low. In interpreting these ratings, the therapist is not looking for absolute truths but, rather, for dominant self themes and ways in which the client fit into the family.

The night before writing this section, one of the authors began to collect Life Style data from a young man who came in because he was feeling uncomfortable in a number of aspects of his life. He was the third of three sons, with a sister born some years later. It was concluded that the three sons should be the group for comparative rating. This group of questions was interpreted with him and since he accepted the interpretation and we have some confirmation of the validity of the interpretation, we will use his ratings as an example.

Doug thought he, of the three brothers, had the highest school grades, was the most helpful at home, complained most often, was most mischievous, was most openly rebellious, felt most sorry for himself, was most considerate, used charm most, was most sensitive, had the best looks, and had the highest standards of accomplishment. He said he was the lowest on industriousness, conforming, pleasing, criticalness, sense of humor, and strength. When asked about his role in peer groups, he said he was either the victim or a co-leader.

What can one make of these responses? In a sense Doug does not stand out completely on any one grouping. He got the highest grades and had the highest standards of accomplishment of the three brothers, yet he felt he was not the most intelligent and that he was the least industrious. He was most helpful at home and charming, but made mischief and was rebellious. He was between his two brothers on consideration, selfishness, temper, getting his own way, idealism, materialism, standards of right and wrong, and femininity-masculinity. He asked about midway through the list if his answers were OK; could I make any sense of them? This prompted an interpretation at the completion of the list. His question itself seemed to be interpretable within the context of the rating interpretation.

So at the end of collecting the ratings I said, "This looks like the pattern of a little boy—lost and confused—searching for acceptance. It looks like he would be willing to be the way others wanted if he thought it gave him a chance for acceptance. He's on the search for acceptance." To which Doug said, "That's right but it's not a search for acceptance, it's a fight for acceptance."

I then commented that this was like his asking me in the middle of the ratings if he was answering correctly. Then I asked, "What kind of client would you have to be for me to accept you?" He said he didn't know and I said, "I don't know either. I guess I'll just have to accept you as a person. You won't be able to find out the way I want you to be so you can be the way you must be to be accepted," and he laughed. Such laughs are like the "aha" response in insightful learning related to the recognition reflex and are evidence that the therapist has hit home.

The basic purpose of the life style questions is to understand a particular client and a particular family and to determine the unique way the client figured out for finding a place in the family. The strategy for making interpretations is therefore clinical judgment.

Parents. Among other information forthcoming from the life style questionnaire is an understanding of a general tone of the family—its basic values, mottoes, and myths. This information is directly sought in the questions about family relationships. Clients are asked to describe separately their father and mother as remembered, as well as who was each parent's favorite child, parental ambitions for the children, and the child most similar to each parent. These questions, along with a description of the parents' relationship and the influence of any other adults who lived with or who strongly influenced the family, allow a number of general conclusions to be drawn about the effect adults had on the client's life style.

Some of the conclusions come from family tradition, such as the mother being seen as pushy, the father always working, parental ambitions for the children to be financially successful, parents' relationships described as seemingly friendly but each one doing his or her own thing, and so on. Patterns of dominance may come through—"Dad dominated Mom, Mom dominated older brother, older brother dominated me, I dominated the dog." Longings, wishes, goals of the client may emerge—"My parents never showed affection to each other or to us; I don't know which of us was the favorite; I am not sure if they really liked any of us."

There can be complicated derivations when parents have been divorced, remarried, and so on. Whom the child identified with, if anyone; whether there was a possibility of having a place in the family—all can become issues. The integration of all of the material from the entire questionnaire is the fodder the therapist must ingest to come up with a meaningful, unified interpretation.

Summary of Family Constellation Material. The life style summary includes independent, separate summaries of *(a)* family constellation; *(b)* early recollections and other projective type material, such as dreams; and then *(c)* integration of these into *basic mistakes.* An advantage of separate treatment is that the *family constellation* and *early recollection* summaries may give somewhat different views but, importantly, they should complement each other. By interpreting them separately, the therapist performs a reliability check on the validity of the final interpretation.

In summarizing the family constellation material, the therapist conveys the "facts" of the client's family life and his or her place in it—the "facts" being the client's perspective. We call this perspective "fact" because it is the basic belief—the self-created truth of how life appears for the client and on the basis of which the client operates. It has been "truth" for the client throughout life, without the client knowing it. The therapist's conclusions regarding these facts are communicated in the simplest, clearest, and most appropriate language.

The therapist summarizes the meaning of birth order and the dynamics of the sibling group with the strengths and weaknesses of special meaning to the client. Although some Adlerians prefer long, detailed summaries, in our opinion they do not have the value or the force of a short summary. The life style summary is intended to communicate "cardinal characteristics." These are generally few. They are best understood and modified by the client when short, simple and easily comprehended. Brevity is at the heart of a good family constellation summary. Following are some examples of family constellation summaries written in the first person.

A 38-year-old woman who came for counseling when her husband of 17 years announced he wanted a divorce:

> I was a second child in a fairly tenuous family. My sister wasn't much and stayed out of my way. My parents conformed and played the parent and spouse roles but didn't care—or didn't care enough. I didn't look much like a girl so I could make it partly as a boy—but I could also be a charming girl—but I could also be a bitch. My motto was: Give to Caesar that which is Caesar's—be all things to all men—but however you do it, get what you want.

Ben in his late 20s who had not finished school, was unmarried and had no long-term relationships, and had never held a job for over a few months:

> I was the baby boy with an older sister and an idealized older brother, in a highly fractionated family, with little affection. Everyone had a role but me. Everyone had a strength, a role, a place—but I was overlooked. Therefore I could enjoy myself, have fun, be a real pretty boy, and make mischief when I wanted to be noticed.

A female college junior who wanted to live on a kibbutz in Israel after graduation was having terrible battles with her parents, who had other career goals for her:

I am the youngest of four children; the youngest of three girls with an eldest brother at a distant, unknowable, unattainable pinnacle. In my family the ideals, the code, was to achieve, be good, and get along. I found my place by being the achieving, good, cooperating baby.

The purpose of the family constellation is to lead a highly complex individual to see him or herself in an accurate but simple way. We are each, at bottom, very simple fundamentally but very complex in details. We may appear to ourselves and others as confused, contradictory, and complex, but it is the therapist's job to find the underlying simple structure of our life style.

Early Recollections

The theory behind early recollections is implicit in the positive, optimistic attitude of Individual Psychology. Most of us carry, as "useless baggage," ideas and memories which seem to lack value. Adlerians see these mental sideshows, encumbrances, detours, as being purposeful creations.

What are the purposes of memories? Why do we remember some things and not others? Why would two grownup siblings remember such different events from their early life? Why should one remember some things of so long ago so clearly, when they seem to be of such minor importance? Are early memories meaningless?

Early memories are capsule summaries of one's *present* life philosophy. For example, suppose that you ask a pair of adult identical twins (as one of us has done) for early memories. Twin A remembers mostly friendly, happy memories, while twin B remembers mostly sad or traumatic memories. What they are showing is that A is *now* an optimist while B is *now* a pessimist. These memories maintain one's view of one's self and of the world. They are like the keel of a boat: they preserve stability and give direction.

Adler took the view that persons remember certain incidents in their early lives to reinforce their view of themselves, the world and their place therein. They remember particular events from childhood because the situations or events as construed reinforce their basic views of life. Adler (1932/1962) wrote:

> Among all psychic expressions, some of the most revealing are the individual's memories. His memories are the reminders he carries with him of his own limits and of the meaning of circumstances. There are no "chance memories." Out of the incalculable number of impressions which meet an individual, he chooses to remember only those which he feels, however darkly, to have a bearing on his situation. Thus his memories represent his "Story of My Life"; a story he repeats to himself to warm him or comfort him, to keep him concentrated on his goal, to prepare him, by means of past experience, to meet the future with an already tested style of action. (p. 57)

Procedure. Essentially, the procedure for obtaining early recollections is simple: the client is asked to give his earliest memories. Such memories fall into two groups: *recollections* and *reports.* A recollection is a specific memory, such as "Once my father picked me up and put me on his shoulders so that I could see the parade." A report, on the other hand, is a general memory, such as "Every summer we used to go to the beach," or "My folks always told me that when I was three I curled my hair." The specific memory—*not the report*—is what the Adlerian therapist wants. Below we shall summarize some major diagnostic aspects of early recollections. (See Olson, 1979, for a full presentation of early recollections.)

Of all procedures in a therapist's armamentarium, none is simpler than early recollections. The therapist can simply say "Tell me your earliest memories. I would like to start with your earliest specific, concrete, single memory—something that happened once that you can remember, not something that was told to you." If this still does not elicit recollections, the therapist may say something like "My own first memory is . . ." or "Close your eyes and think back to when . . . What do you see?" When the patient produces a memory, the therapist ordinarily writes it down word for word and may probe to assure that he or she has understood exactly *(a)* what is clearest in this memory—what stands out—and *(b)* what feeling (emotion) is involved in this memory. A person reveals a good deal about herself through recounting an early memory. For example, take this early memory. What do you make of this person?

> I was walking with my mother in a strange neighborhood. I was about three. She went into a store and left me outside. A strange boy came over to me and without reason hit me. When my mother came out I was crying. She yelled at me because she felt that I had provoked the boy who hit me.

The above person was one with whom one of the authors had close dealings for many years. Few people could get along with him, but the writer of these lines was able to do so easily, since he "understood" the meaning of the memory. We suggest that the reader re-read this memory carefully. What does it tell you about this person? Here is our reconstruction:

1. You can't even trust your own mother. She leaves you where you can be hurt.
2. You can't trust strangers. They will attack you without provocation.
3. Even your mother won't believe in you or stick up for you; the world is a hostile jungle.

This individual was characterized by deep suspicion of all people, constantly on guard, always looking for the possibilities of others harming him. He had developed a very charming personality but it included a deep fear and suspicion of others. He would cheat others and excuse himself because he was sure that others were trying to do him in. His aggressive behavior, in his mind, was simply a defense against others' hostility.

An early memory has deep meaning for the person since it has been carried for years. It is a statement of how life is viewed, and it gives us an inkling into a person's private logic. It is truly an X-ray into the human mind. In the opinion of many (see Olson, 1979), it is the most superior of all projective techniques.

Not only is the procedure for collecting early recollections simple, but the process generally seems innocuous to the client. In almost all cases people will freely give the therapist as many recollections as the therapist wants. Although some therapists ask for as many as 10 recollections as part of the life style assessment, usually about 6 are asked for.

Infrequently people are not easily able to give early recollections. One may have to give help, like asking a client to remember where he lived, any significant events that can be recalled to take off from, or even suggest specifics: holidays, beginning school, or a new baby. This almost always helps. Rarely will a client be unable to remember anything. In these rare cases the therapist should just go on with the interview. Some therapists suggest that the client who can remember nothing should "make up" some early memories. That the client cannot remember incidents may be quite relevant clinically. In most cases persons who do not have early recollections do not have guiding fictions; that is to say, these people did not develop usual specific basic beliefs and have therefore muddled through life not really knowing what they, or life, is all about. They need not necessarily be anxious, or confused but, rather, are lost, aimless, and may well have been referred for therapeutic help, have come compliantly, but not have known why. There may be other hypotheses for the absence of memories, but this absence is in itself worth investigating.

For example, we had a client once—a woman in her 40s, who was deeply depressed, who later committed suicide—whose first memory was at age 18. The memory had to do with a discussion she overheard her parents having about their not having enough money to buy a bicycle for her younger brother. The precipitating cause of her depression, incidentally, was that after a lifetime of poverty, her husband made a great deal of money—and she was totally unable to adjust to this unexpected prosperity.

Interpretation and Summary.   The key in the early recollection summary is similar to that in the family constellation summary—brevity, accuracy, and understandability. The therapist reviews all the client's recollections, looking for themes and consistencies, searching for the individual's private logic. Particularly, the therapist looks for themes about the client, other people, and life. Sometimes there are single themes and sometimes more than that for each aspect of the self, the world, life, or the future. The therapist then integrates these themes into statements in the form of the syllogism of the life style. Following are some examples of early recollections from two clients and the summary syllogism.

Ben, a man in his late 20s, who had no wife, no job, nor any direction in life, gave these early recollections:

Age 5: I remember throwing a rock at a car, and the guy stopped. Mother pulled me to the door where this guy was and she let the guy holler and scream at me. I felt really bad 'cause I'd tried concealing my identity.

Age 6: I was sitting in front of our house watching a guy swinging on a bar. He fell off and cracked his head open. I was horrified.

Age 7: My cousin got in a fight with the school bully and I stole the bully's cap. One of the teachers made a big deal about it but I denied it. With about 10 or 12 kids around she gave me a heavy lecture. I felt justified but bad. But I didn't admit it.

Early recollection (ER) summary: "(1) I am a little watcher and an ineffective doer in (2) a world that is punishing and cruel. Therefore, (3) I must try to keep safe and still do what I want—avoid, run, be wary, lie, fight being controlled or manipulated."

Christopher, a man in his late 40s, gave the following early recollections:

Age 5: My mother bought me skates. I couldn't skate well. Mother made me skate around the block once a day. One day she caught me cheating. She made me put on my skates and took a switch and started hitting me with it. I'd fall and get up and got hit all the way home. I was pissed; thought it was unfair; and I was disappointed.

Age 5: I was told not to go ice skating on Sunday. I got my skates and went and fell and split the skin on my head. I came home and Mom and Dad were there. Mother took me into the bathroom to wash the cut. She started yelling, and I said . . . she said . . . I said. She popped me in back of the head and it hit the towel rack and put another goose egg right where the other one was. I was upset; there was no cause.

Age 5: The roomer who lived downstairs spent a lot of time with me. He built me a good-size model sailing boat and I helped him with it. He talked to me. We finished the boat and I wanted to take it up to show Mom. He said he didn't want to until he built the stand and finished it. I felt upset, disappointed and hurt.

Age 7: The people I stayed with when Mom was sick weren't home when I got back one afternoon from playing. The house was locked. I spent the night on the front porch. I thought it was fun alone. They finally came back and said "Come in." I wanted to stay on the porch. There was a big damn fight and I ended up going into the house and spent the night in my room. I felt lost, and resentment.

ER summary: "(1) I am a little screw-up. (2) The world has precise, but not understandable, expectations for my behavior. (3) No matter what I try, no matter how I assert myself, positively or negatively, I stay alone, sort of enjoy it, but then I'm alone and maybe lost."

As the reader may see, we look across the early recollections of clients to see how they see self, world, and future outcome. Sometimes the same theme runs across all recollections, but possibly not. When integrated, if the therapist is correct, the client will sometimes agree, and maybe light up with a "recollection reflex." Usually, if the therapist has illustrated to the client that therapy and the Life Style assessment are cooperative ventures, the client will help by changing words or phrases or emphases to get the summary just right.

One of the insights we obtain from early recollections has to do with the structure of the personality. Notice that the memories of Ben—the "little watcher"—are typically short and simple, while Christopher's memories are long and complex. Usually, intelligent and complex clients tell long and involved memories. People oriented to a here-and-now attitude toward life tend to have short and simple memories. If all memories were the same theme— such as a client of ours in which every memory was of an animal or a plant, but no humans—we can be certain such a person tends to be simple and deeply set. If the memories "contradict" each other, we tend to have a complex and contradictory person. A person who invests a lot of feeling in memories tends to be emotional and sensitive. One who does not is likely to be phlegmatic and objective. The "feel" of early recollections due to their structure contributes also to an understanding of the client.

Early Recollections as Vocational Indicators.   Say a client's early recollections are filled with color and form—for example, "I remember a music box my grandmother gave me for my fifth birthday. It was beautifully shaped and was of a white color with pink and blue tracings. I just so enjoyed looking and listening to it." That this person has an artistic temperament seems an obvious conclusion.

Frequently, people have no idea that what they are doing vocationally is not what they really should be doing, or they have certain potentials or interests of which they are not aware. To give a simple example, after hearing an early recollection, the diagnostician may "see" the scene clearly. Somehow, the narrator has been able to communicate very well. Such people tend to have potentials in the fields that involve communication skills, such as lawyers or teachers or writers. Or, let us say that a person's early recollections are filled with items of machinery—a boat, a motor, a car. Such a person may have a tendency toward engineering or mechanics. This general topic (Holmes & Watson, 1965; Manaster & Perryman, 1974) has not been explored as thoroughly as might be desired. Keeping in mind that one of Adler's three tasks is *occupation,* more research in this area would be quite worthwhile.

The opposite conclusion regarding occupations is probably even more important: that is to say, using early recollections to get indications of what fields an individual should avoid. Say that a person who had no people at all in his early memories is employed as a salesman. It would seem evident that there is a discrepancy between his inner nature and work. This discrepancy, unknown to the individual, may be the reason why the person is maladjusted vocationally.

A couple came for marriage counseling. They had been married upon his graduation from college. The woman's parents gave the young couple a furniture store as a wedding gift. In this position the man had to deal with salespeople and with clients. On the surface, he was quite happy with his work. However, his behavior belied this, since he had great trouble waking up mornings. Sometimes the wife would open the store while he was still sleeping. An analysis of this man's early recollections showed a concern with chance-taking and with dealing with risks. He had taken a business course, but what had really turned him on was the whole topic of speculation. It seemed evident that he was essentially a gambler. In discussing various occupations, he expressed an interest in finance. Further discussions indicated that he really wanted to be a stockbroker. He was encouraged to pursue this line of work, and after discussions with his wife and in-laws, he sold the store and went into the investment business, in which he was very happy and in which he did quite well.

Dreams

Adlerian therapists may ask for dreams and will analyze and interpret them throughout the process of therapy. In the Life Style assessment it is usual to ask for any remembered childhood dreams, as well as recurrent and current dreams. In keeping with Adlerian theory, dreams are seen as purposeful—reminders of what the person is about and what the person expects and is planning to do. Dreams are prodromic rehearsals for future behavior.

The value of dreams in terms of the unity and consistency of the individual is well illustrated by the recurring childhood dream of Christopher, whose Life Style material we have examined on page 187–188. His "place" as seen by the family constellation material was "to be left alone to create my world and to stay peripheral." In the early recollection summary the therapist's conclusion was that he wanted to "stay alone, sort of enjoy it, but then I'm alone and maybe lost" (p. 187–188). When asked to tell of a childhood dream, he said that the following dream recurred from the time he was seven or eight until his early teens:

> I was alone, ended up alone. It was like a picture puzzle, pieces like cloud shapes, individual pieces. Whatever I wanted, as I was going to it, the clouds came in front of me. I was alone and lost.

Although dreams may be collected as part of the assessment procedure, they are usually used as a first confirmation of the summaries of the other two main parts—family constellation and early recollections.

BASIC MISTAKES

In the two examples of early recollections and family constellation summaries from Ben and Christopher, notice the considerable overlap within each man's reports, which are signs of reliability. We look at what is common in the two summaries of each person, then in the dreams we try to find which elements about self, world, and mode of operating are particularly stressed. Such stressed elements usually indicate what Adler called "overdriven attitudes." They are exaggerations, absolutes, unwarranted conclusions, rigid "directions" for the person's behavior which cannot bring the person happiness or belonging. These "basic mistakes" justify the person's behavior and set the tone for all the person sees. The therapist's task is to present basic mistakes concisely to the client so they are understood and can be illustrated in present and past behavior. They can be used to examine behavior that the client is contemplating, so that the client can "catch himself" in future actions and thoughts.

The last sentence you have just read implies a most important concept in Adlerian psychotherapy. What it says, in its fullest implications, is:

1. People are basically good and want to live righteous lives.
2. They generally operate useless lives, acting in unhealthy ways through ignorance.
3. Through psychotherapy they are made aware of their basic mistakes.
4. As a result of psychotherapy they are in a position to monitor themselves and behave rationally and normally through "catching" themselves in the act of acting incorrectly.

Consequently, that sentence represents a climax of Adlerian psychotherapy. Ben, the "baby boy" in his late 20s, agreed to the following basic mistakes:

I exaggerate the dangers of life.

I must be safe.

If anything bad can happen it will.

I am a victim.

It is better to be outside and safe than inside and trounced.

I am a nice mischief-maker.

The basic mistakes related to Christopher, the man who is lost and peripheral, were:

I have to do it myself.

It's lousy, but I'm better off by myself.

The world would have to be my way for things to be OK.

I can't do as well as others.

I don't understand what I should do—if I try to do what I think I should, it will get screwed up.

Basic mistakes represent exaggerated apperceptions and useless goals. It is ofttimes difficult for people to see how a mode of operating such as "having to do it myself" can portend a goal of superiority. In effect it is the individual's view that she can beat the system, in this case by being alone and doing her own thing, without recognition that the "system" is her own mistaken perceptions of it. What she is doing is building a mistaken view of herself and the world and then fighting for a goal that, in a sense, conquers the injustices, inequities, or other mistakes she has envisioned and created.

ASSETS

The therapist may become so involved in the assessment technique that the client becomes temporarily lost in the shuffle! Most of what is found in Life Style summaries usually is, and is construed by the client to be, negative. Within the right kind of therapeutic relationship the client will not fret over negative information, but will see it as something to understand and change. Because the Life Style procedure is usually done early in the relationship between the counselor and counselee—possibly before good relationships are developed—the conclusions reached about the client's life style can be discouraging—the opposite of what psychotherapy is all about.

Since encouragement is a basic part of Adlerian therapy, an important part of the Life Style assessment consists of pointing out the client's assets, strengths, and talents, as well as deficits and mistakes. Some assets are readily noticeable and should be stressed. The therapist should also search and point out those positive qualities which may not be so apparent and that often the client will not acknowledge. Often clients do not want to discuss or even acknowledge their assets. They would rather focus on faults, mistakes, problems, errors, so that they can correct them. Just as when they go to a physician they might disregard comments about healthy organs so, too, in therapy they want to concentrate on what is wrong, not on what is right. The therapist should give due attention to a person's assets and report them routinely in the Life Style summary.

People often develop strengths in conjunction with their mistakes, goals, or biased apperceptions. A patient may be depressed—morose—and see herself as a failure. Her basic mistake may be wanting to be number one—ahead of everyone else. The patient may feel that she is a failure as a vice president, since she is not president; or a failure as the parent of three brilliant kids and one nice, social kid, rather than having four geniuses. Without being dishonest, or falsely encouraging, the therapist should note the client's assets, so both therapist and client can make maximum use of these strengths in trying new thoughts and behaviors in the process of change.

Ben, the young man characterized as a "little watcher," was informed that he was a fine-looking fellow with a great love of life and fun which made him well liked and an enjoyable companion. These assets, however, effectively kept him successful at avoiding work and responsibility. The therapeutic task became to have him use these assets, which he had employed for useless goals, toward useful purposes.

Christopher, the loner artist/craftsman, had artistic creativity which had brought him considerable acclaim. His sensitivity to human suffering, as well as his protests against injustices, had brought him great respect. These assets, which he had seen only as indicative of his isolation, eventually became the core of his new self-respect after therapy.

SUMMARY

All Adlerian psychotherapists share the same theory, have the same general attitudes of helping the client to self-understanding, to change useless to useful behavior, and to encourage the client to make worthwhile changes. Nevertheless, everyone develops a unique style of operating. Even psychotherapists will tend to follow their teacher's style differently. Since both of us were trained originally by Rudolf Dreikurs, we have accepted (as have many other Adlerians) Dreikurs' general procedures even though, naturally, we differ ourselves in our therapeutic operations.

We come to an interesting difference between Adlerians and Freudians: Freudians tend to differ considerably among themselves with respect to theory, but they tend to operate rather similarly, generally using the couch and free association as well as interpretation of dreams. Adlerians, on the other hand, do not have major differences among themselves with respect to theory, but they will differ considerably in how they conduct therapy.

We have covered in this chapter a variety of ways of operating in therapy. Some Adlerians never do a formal Life Style analysis, but continually feed back new understanding to their clients as they go along. We ourselves are eclectics and will use a variety of techniques when we feel they are called for—but we try always to be consistent relative to the theory of the therapy and its underlying philosophy.

Chapter 13

The Process of Counseling and Psychotherapy

Adlerian psychotherapy is seen as a teaching/learning process rather than as a treating/curing methodology. At times the therapist is teaching the client, sometimes the therapist is learning, and at times both are learning or both are teaching. For Adlerians, mental illness is a myth since even seriously disturbed people are not sick in the conventional sense of being the victims of "something" outside or inside of themselves—something foreign, harmful—"attacking" them. In a sense, they are willing victims of themselves, having the responsibility for having taken on certain ideas and roles even though usually without awareness.

Over time the competent therapist develops expertise with a series of techniques. Some therapists use only one or perhaps two techniques, such as listening and questioning; some others use dozens; below are some techniques Adlerians employ. No technique is unique to Adlerians, most are used by therapists of differing orientations; but Adlerians tend to avoid some techniques. We shall go through some common techniques alphabetically.

ADVICE

Adlerians will not hesitate to give advice if they feel that the client is ready to accept it. Sometimes, the therapist will heighten the drama before advice-giving as follows:

Client: What should I do?
Therapist: I know exactly.
Client: What?

Therapist: Don't you think you should figure it out for yourself?

Client: I can't.

Therapist: Maybe if I tell you then you will say that it won't work.

Client: Well, tell me.

Therapist: Only if you tell me in advance that you will do it.

Client: You want a blank check?

Therapist: Yes. Are you bankrupt?

Client: I am. I'll do just what you tell me.

Therapist: Okay. Now this is what to do.

The trick for therapists is not to give advice unless they are fairly certain that the advice is likely to be followed.

ANECDOTES

These must be used with care, since they can easily backfire. A client can become discouraged upon hearing success stories. Generally, the therapist will tell the patient a story of another patient with exactly the same problem and how that patient overcame that problem. Or the therapist may tell about personal experiences and what they meant. The major purpose is to make the client feel part of humanity, and to realize that others with the same difficulties have succeeded, even the therapist.

ARGUMENTS

Most therapists avoid arguments, defined as repetition of the same notions. Albert Ellis (1962) is an exception. Ellis introduces disputations or arguments in his therapeutic process. Whether to argue with a client has to be very carefully evaluated. Generally, arguments about philosophical, religious, political, or social issues are avoided, since in these areas the therapist is not an expert. Arguments, in therapy, should be about psychology, common sense, or social living, and should be used to make clients more aware, to illustrate life style in the battle, and to encourage the client to do in therapy what otherwise would not be done, that is, take a stand, get excited, and so forth.

BEHAVIOR MODIFICATION

The term *behavior modification* has one meaning if spelled with small letters and another if capitalized. Capitalized as Behavior Modification, it means a form of changing behavior by the use of rewards and punishments. At the present time there is considerable literature on Behavior Modification. This mode of treatment is rejected by Adlerians on philosophical/theoretical grounds, since rewards and punishments are seen as autocratic, with people of superior strength (in the general sense) having the power to reward and punish inferiors. We see Behavior Modification as being useful for training animals, in dealing with young children who are not able to reason (Sajwaj, Libet, & Aguas, 1974), with psychotics (Atthowe & Krasner, 1968), and with mental retardates, but not with normal children and adults, except perhaps in very persistent behavioral situations such as when bedwetting has become a well-established habit (Mowrer, 1938).

When spelled with small letters, Adlerian therapists and counselors are behavior modifiers generally through cognitive means, helping individuals to understand their errors, changing the thinking of clients, and thus changing their behavior. Behavior Modification, however, changes the environment and works from the "outside in" rather than from the "inside out." We do behavior modification work from the inside out.

CLARIFICATION

This process involves achieving a common understanding by therapist and client, usually through interpretation, definition, and explanation. Adlerians may employ Carl Rogers' (1951) system of having X repeat what Y said until Y agrees that X truly understands.

CONFRONTATION

This is a variation of an argument, a kind of "rubbing one's nose into the matter." An example illustrates the technique of confrontation:

Therapist: You think your husband is wrong in what he does—leaving the house?

Client: Yes, he should not run out.

Therapist: What do you do when he gets angry?

Client: I run out.

Therapist: So he runs out when you are angry, and you run out when he is angry. What's the difference?

Client: He might hit me, that's why I run out; that's the difference.

Therapist: You don't like to be hit.

Client: Of course not.

Therapist: But he doesn't like to be nagged. You leave when he does something you don't like, and he leaves when you do something he doesn't like. Can it be that your nagging is just as unpleasant for him as his hitting you?

Client: They are not the same.

Therapist: But you said you hated it when your mother nagged you. What did you want to do then?

Client: Run away.

Therapist: Aren't you doing what your mother did, and isn't your husband doing what you wanted to do? Run from nagging?

Client: Maybe. I guess you're right.

EMOTIONAL SUPPORT

This means that the therapist shows concern for, sympathy for, understanding of, and appreciation of the patient. The therapist should be a warm, caring, loving human being, truly interested in people, and able to express genuine attitudes. The key word here is *genuine.*

Therapist: I can really appreciate your feelings of despair.

Client: I sometimes feel so alone: no one really cares.

Therapist: I know how it is. There are times when I have felt alone, also. It's a terrible feeling.

All "techniques" must be used naturally and honestly. To say to a client who bores you, "I am really interested in what you are saying," would be completely antitherapeutic in that one would be generating confusion in the client. Such behavior would be an example of "mixed messages," considered by some theorists to lead to schizophrenia. A client is supported by the therapist's genuine caring, which will certainly not express itself by approving the unapprovable, accepting the unacceptable, or valuing the detestable. Support must be given to the whole person, caring for the whole person, and not to behaviors or beliefs about which you do not truly care.

GIVING UP

This unusual technique is quite powerful when properly employed, and like every powerful technique, should be used infrequently. There are two approaches. In one the therapist gives up (as a technique), and in the second the therapist advises a patient to give up. We can show it best by examples. Say that a husband and a wife have come to an Adlerian therapist for counseling and we are at this point.

Therapist: Well, that is my advice. What do you think?

Husband: To me your advice is a lot of bullshit.

Therapist: Everything?

Husband: Everything. None of it makes any sense to me.

Wife: We have to give it a chance. Dr. _____ has a lot more experience than we do. He's the expert.

Husband: Well, he asked my opinion, and I think it just is wrong advice.

Therapist: Well, I'll tell you what I think. You should go to a counselor you have confidence in. Why don't you go to a better one? I can suggest some names of some good people who have different ideas than mine.

In this kind of "giving in," the following may result:

Husband: Well, I don't mean you don't know your business.

Therapist (still using the same technique): Thank you, but it seems to me that you did listen carefully to what I said, and that you are fairly certain that what I said is wrong . . .

Husband: I don't mean wrong, I mean it won't work.

Therapist: Well, if it won't work, it is wrong. After all, you are paying good money to get good advice. If the advice doesn't seem good to you, you won't follow it, and it is a waste of your time and money. My suggestion is that you find a counselor whose ideas agree with yours.

Husband: Now, what I meant was that what you said would not work with my child. I know Rick.

Therapist: And I say that what I suggest may work with Rick—but only if you do it exactly the way I say to do it.

Husband (backing down): I don't know.

Therapist (coming in for the kill): I do.

Wife: Don't you think we ought to try it?

Husband: I still don't like it.

Therapist: It's your decision.

Husband: Okay, I'll try it.

Therapist: Good. Now, let's go over it again.

This "giving in" technique is a kind of aikido or judo process—of apparently giving up, stepping back—and really is a kind of redirection. The therapist is basically saying, "If you are so smart and know better than I do, why don't you solve your own problems?" but, of course, saying it in a tactful manner. Another example further illustrates this technique.

Wife: My husband is always trying to kiss me.

Therapist: This is a problem for you?

Wife: Well, he does it at inappropriate times, such as when we have guests, when we stop at a red light, in a restaurant, that sort of thing . . . when I want to read, even when I am sleeping.

Therapist: Do you like kissing?

Wife: Yes, of course, but when it is appropriate, but not indiscriminate kissing.

Therapist: Do you have any idea why he keeps doing it?

Wife: I think he does it to embarrass and annoy me.

Therapist: You think he enjoys discomforting you?

Wife: I am pretty sure he does.

Therapist: And you have been telling him not to do it, but it does no good. Is that right? (Wife nods.) What better way might there be to handle it?

Wife: Kick him in the belly—you know what I mean?

Therapist: The lower belly?

Wife (laughing): That's what I mean.

Therapist (realizing that the kissing is a means of low-grade violence between angry people): Can you think of a better way to have him stop annoying you?

Wife: No.

Therapist: Look, if he does it to annoy you, and if he won't stop when you ask him to, what could you do?

Wife: I don't know.

Therapist: Do you remember what the turtle did to the fox in Uncle Remus' story?*

Wife: No.

Therapist: When the fox threatened to drown the turtle, the turtle made out she was afraid. So the fox threw the turtle into the river to drown, but the turtle simply escaped by walking along the bottom of the river stream.

---

*Possibly some of the very best "Adlerian" books were written by a person who no doubt never even heard of Adler—Joel Chandler Harris (1848–1908), who wrote *The Tar Baby* and *Uncle Remus and Br'er Rabbit.*

Wife: I don't understand.

Therapist: What I mean is make believe to your husband that you like kissing; give in and let him kiss you and pretend to enjoy it.

Wife: Oh! Then, if he thinks I am enjoying it, he'll stop it.

Therapist: Yes, if his intention is to bother you ...

Wife: Makes sense; just give in and enjoy it. What an idea! It makes a crazy kind of sense.

HOMEWORK

Another technique that Adlerians use is homework. For "homework" the therapist asks the client to do something fairly specific between visits. Examples might include onetime behaviors, such as:

Visit the grave of a relative.
Tell the truth to your husband about your infidelity.
Buy a surprise present for your wife.

Other examples are changing a behavior pattern for the time between sessions, such as:

Stop complaining about finances.
Stop hitting your child.
Become more cooperative in the family; make your own bed.
Be pleasant to your employees.

Or what Behavior Modification calls, monitoring can be advised, such as keeping track of specific behaviors, possibly in relation to feelings or situations, such as:

Every time you feel anxious, make a note of the situation and what you do.
When you think you have been really "smart," look at the reactions of those around you.
Make a list of everything you are "afraid" of.

The degree of specificity, the nature and amount of homework will vary, of course, from person to person and, naturally, must be very carefully "assigned." One must not take over a client's life. It would be a mistake to require something that the client cannot or will not do. Homework usually calls for some degree of reality testing in the face of something the patient has not been willing to do or recognize.

A somewhat unique situation occurred with us once. Max—a client—stated that he had a terrible secret that he could not tell to the therapist. We asked what it was. He could not tell since if we knew, then we, too, could be implicated, and we might be harmed. Puzzled by what this could mean, we let it pass. Max brought it up again at the next session, and finally reluctantly said something to the effect that he had broken a federal law and could go to prison. He stated that if we knew, we would be obligated to tell the authorities or we, too, could go to prison for knowing and not telling. Again, we let this go. We wondered if he had stolen some atomic secrets and sold them to a foreign power. However, when he brought up his secret again, we pressured him to tell us what it was. Finally he told his secret—he had not filed his income tax report for the prior year!

Now came the process of trying to get him to report it. We went over and over this matter, but he stubbornly refused. Finally, we had enough of this, and after a session we walked with him to the income tax bureau and practically pushed him to the desk of a revenue agent. After the interview, the client felt much relieved that he had gotten his "crime" off his chest.

The end of this incident? He got an income tax refund! He had paid the government more in withholding taxes than he was legally required to do! Sometimes homework requires a tutor!

HUMOR

A powerful technique is humor—to help the client see the funny side of life. Humor, of course, can be cruel or kind. There are many ways of dealing with human problems, and one of them is to attempt to find what is comic. Here is an example:

Husband: My wife thinks I am too staid and too proper.

Therapist: What do you think?

Husband: I am normal.

Therapist: Why is this a problem?

Husband: She just keeps nagging me that we don't have fun, that we are stick-in-the-muds, and things like that. I just don't know what she wants.

Therapist: She may want some excitement. Can you think of anything that she would not ever believe you capable of doing?

Husband: Something ridiculous?

Therapist: Yes.

Husband: How about my suggesting that we go to a nudist colony for a weekend?

Therapist: How would she react to that?

Husband: She'd think I was out of my mind (starts to laugh). I just can see her reacting to that.

Therapist: A really extreme thing for you to suggest . . .

Husband: You bet!

Therapist: What do you plan to do?

Husband: No, I won't suggest that. Maybe I'll buy some funny clothes.

Therapist: Such as?

Husband: Something in the vogue, something I'd never wear. Just show up some day with a turtleneck sweater or something (starts laughing).

Therapist: You'd get a great kick out of surprising her . . .

Husband: You bet.

The therapist who puts the idea of doing something outrageous into the patient's head does this from the sense of doing something comic as an antidote to a rather staid personality.

If a person can learn to laugh at herself, it is a sign of normality. To have a cosmic and comic view of life, to see how foolish we are, to realize the nonsense we see and do, is a sign of health. The wise therapist helps the client to laugh at herself and to appreciate the foolishness of her behavior (O'Connell, 1975).

Telling appropriate jokes frequently makes a point clear. Leading the person to see the silliness of someone else's behavior gives instruction in a pleasant manner. Telling about mistakes we have ourselves made can relieve tensions. Adlerians use humor as frequently as appropriate (and as frequently as they have a good story to tell). Here is a classic joke we frequently tell, made famous by the humorist Danny Thomas:

A man was driving a new car on a Sunday morning testing it, dressed in old clothes, when he suddenly had a tire blowout. Angry, he stopped the car and examined the burst tire, then opened the trunk of the car and took out the spare tire and the tire tool, but he found there was no jack in the car! He searched the trunk carefully, then the inside of the car—no jack! He then remembered that he had passed a gas station about a mile back and started to walk to the station. As he walked he began to think:

"When I get to the station the attendant will be alone and when I ask him if he will come to my car, he will tell me he is alone and that he doesn't want to close up the station. Then, I will ask him if he will lend me a jack. He will look me over and ask me what kind of car I have. I'll tell him I have a Cadillac, and he will ask me what year it is. Then, when I tell him it is brand new he won't believe me, and when he asks me why I didn't use the jack in the car and I tell him there was no jack, he won't believe me. So, I'll ask him for the loan of a jack.

He will tell me that I have to give him a deposit. I will tell him that I didn't take
any money with me, and he will refuse to lend me the jack . . ."

At this point the man came to the gas station and the attendant said, pleas-
antly, "Good morning."

"Go to hell and keep your damn jack."

This is the so-called Charlie Walsh phenomenon—so named after a client
(name changed) who would imagine all sorts of unpleasant consequences and
then act as though they were real. The example of the man who thought he
would go to prison for income tax evasion was pure Charlie Walsh! Such jokes
sometimes illustrate well to clients the comic stupidities of human nature—
but as usual we recommend that humor be used intelligently. Jokes can
backfire!

INTERPRETATIONS

Formal interpretations of family constellations, early memories, and dreams
are very much a part of Adlerian therapy. Of course, the therapist interprets
behavior and its purpose in the life style throughout the course of therapy. As
the patient learns, changes of behavior should be interpreted for fuller self-
understanding. Dreams and early recollections will change along with behavior and should be periodically reinterpreted to emphasize change and to
demonstrate the unity of the person.

NONDIRECTIVE INTERVIEWING

This form of interviewing, popularized by Carl Rogers (1951), calls for the
therapist to listen carefully and to respond with feeling and understanding so
that the client will feel understood and accepted, thus preparing the client to
go ahead. "From what you are saying, Barbara, it sounds to me as though you
really have strong feelings about Donald and that you would really want to
marry him," the therapist says, repeating the essential idea, but also acknowl-
edging the feelings of Barbara.

QUESTIONS

A common technique in therapy is to ask questions. There are dangers, as we
have been pointing out in every technique, including asking or answering
questions. The situation may not become what therapy is for an Adlerian—
a meeting between equals. The situation may become a superior-inferior relationship, since a question demands an answer! The clever therapist knows what
questions to ask. Usually, short, open-ended questions are best:

"What do you want?"

"Why did you do that?"

"How do you feel?"

But one should be wary of getting into an exclusive question-and-answer type situation with the client. This kind of relationship is not therapeutic, although it may be educational and useful in some counseling. A valuable mode of questioning is the Socratic method. The therapist knows what she wants to attain and continues a line of questions to elicit from the client the answer the therapist has in mind but which she wants the client to work out.

"The Question"

"The Question" is a special technique probably only used by Adlerians which illustrates Adlerian thinking very well. Say a client comes in with some somatic complaint and the issue is whether the complaint is really physical or psychological. The therapist asks "The Question": "If you did not have this symptom, what would you do?" If the answer goes something like "Well, then I could look for a job," then the symptom is probably functional—that is, imaginary, made up by the person to prevent "looking for a job." If, however, the answer were "I wouldn't be suffering so much," then most probably the symptom is "genuine"—that is to say, it is physiologically based. A fuller exposition is found in Dreikurs' (1962) article, "Can You Be Sure the Disease Is Functional?"

REASONING

Reasoning is somewhat like argument and confrontation, but now the therapist genuinely does not know the right answer and works out the problem on an equal basis with the client. "Could it be . . ." the therapist asks, or "How about . . ." The two of them more-or-less brainstorm or reason out the particular problem. They try to come to a solution that pleases both of them.

REASSURANCE

This kind of emotional support indicates the therapist's feeling about the patient. We have to be very, very careful not to assure success, since if the client should try something and fail, this may shake the client's confidence in the therapist. The reassurance has to do with the client having the courage to try something new. It is the trying rather than the success or the failure that counts.

RECOGNITION REFLEX

In doing counseling with young children, sometimes it is important to know *why* a child does what she does. *What is her motivation? What is her secret goal?* We know that the child does not know. She has no idea what makes her act the way she does. She has no insight.

However, if she is told exactly the reason for her misbehavior, the evident "shock" of recognition is the *recognition reflex.* The procedure is extremely difficult to do well. Having the child's complete attention, if the correct reason is advanced, the child has a startled reaction—eyes open wide, mouth opens and stays open, or she may suddenly freeze. The technique cannot be well described—and it is very difficult to learn. Examples might be:

"Is it possible, Jessie, that you cry a lot to get mother's attention?"
"Could it be, Jimmie, that you hit your brother to show your parents that you can do just what you want—nobody can tell *you* what to do?"

The recognition reflex, usually in the form of a smile, may be seen in adults, also. The reflex is useful for both the therapist and the client. It is a clear sign that the therapist's statement and interpretation hit the mark. By pointing the reflex reaction out to clients, the therapist can illustrate how deeply understood this fact is for the patient. The crucial element in presenting the statement that brings a recognition reflex is the accuracy of the idea as well as the wording. Both must be just right for the client. This is why it takes experience and sensitivity to produce this effect.

SHOCK TECHNIQUES

"Suppose that you opened the closet door and found both your daughter and your wife hanging by their necks?" the therapist asked. The client replied, "I'd be happy my wife is dead, but I would be unhappy about my daughter." Then he added, "I have fantasized my wife dead—I guess I would like her dead. I guess I'd even be willing to have my daughter dead if it were necessary." He then put his head between his hands—hid his face. "I never thought I'd confess this. God—as you said it, I could practically see it. I guess that's what I really want."

"Aren't you killing her, bit by bit, right now?" the therapist went on. "Are you not conducting yourself to drive her to insanity and perhaps suicide?" This second shock question made the client look at the therapist. "I guess I am a coward and want her to kill herself. I am afraid to do it directly. I am unwilling to have a divorce."

And the conversation went on from there until the therapist pressed the client by pointing out his alternatives: (*a*) change his ways and make his wife happy, (*b*) get a divorce and give her a chance to start a new life, or (*c*) continue as he was doing and kill her slowly, meanwhile ruining his daughter's life.

This kind of shock technique, of course, should only be used with the most extreme caution. With an understanding of the purposes of a person's behavior, and their personal goals, valid predictions of consequences, even if dire, are possible.

SUGGESTIONS

Keeping in mind the tendency of the client to look up to the therapist and to put the therapist on a throne, and the natural tendency of any therapist to appreciate this adulation, the client tends to want suggestions—even orders, but when the suggestions are given, they tend to be rejected for any of 40,000 reasons. Consequently, the art of using suggestion is to try to make the client think that he thought of them himself because of the logic and common sense of the suggestion. This calls for cautious questioning, the use of "could it be . . ." or "have you ever thought about . . ." and so on, in a gentle manner, leading the client by easy stages to a suggestion.

SILENCE

An important technique, and indeed the hallmark of a good therapist, is to be silent. The patient asks a question, and the inexperienced therapist rushes in with an answer. The more experienced therapist leans back, smiles, looks the patient in the eye, but does not reply.

> *Client:* "So you won't tell me?" (Silence.)
> *Client:* "Can't you answer?" (The therapist keeps looking at the client and says nothing.)
> *Client:* "Well, I suppose you just won't answer, and I suppose you think I know the answer myself." (The therapist nods and smiles broadly.)
> *Client:* "I guess you're right . . ."

It will be noted that in a number of Adlerian techniques the injunction to the trainer (be it parent or teacher) is to be silent. Actions speak louder than words, and are much more effective. *Act, don't talk* is frequently the advice given in training.

WAGERING

One of the authors saw Dr. Rudolf Dreikurs in a double session (that is, with two therapists) say to the patient, "Want to bet $2?" The patient accepted the bet to the effect that if she did something exactly as Dr. Dreikurs had said, the consequences would be just as he said they would be. Surprised at this, I informed Dr. Dreikurs that I, too, had on several occasions bet with my clients if they doubted that something would happen as I said it would (Corsini, 1979). This process should be known as the Dreikurs Betting Technique and in his honor, if anyone should ever use this procedure, always bet no more and no less than $2. Also, always win! Always bet on a sure thing!

Wagering, as a technique, must be used, as is true for anything in therapy, with judgment. This book or any kind of training—personal or impersonal—can only provide broad outlines. However, here are some guidelines:

1. Use this technique rarely.
2. Use it when you face an impasse.
3. Use it when you are sure you will win if the client will follow directions exactly.
4. Make the terms of the bet very clear. Possibly write them down, and give the client a carbon.
5. Set the date for the decision and the payment.
6. Always bet no more and no less than $2.
7. Call it the Dreikurs Betting Technique.

As is the case with any of these techniques, as superficial as some may seem, philosophy and theory are involved. For example, if one comes to a "yes/no" situation, where you say "yes" and the client says "no," your willingness to put up money shows your concern and your assurance. The client knows that you really want the client to do what you suggest; that you are not just betting to win $2. You put the person on his honor to do what the bet is all about. The person is honor bound to report truthfully. This technique shows a kind of equality—you are willing to put your reputation on the line. Betting is ordinarily done between equals.

I have used this technique perhaps 25 times in as many years, so it is not used indiscriminately. Also, I have never lost. I have always taken the money —to do otherwise would demean the client. The clients were always glad to pay the $2.

Betting may be seen as a kind of "trick" to get the client to do something that would not ordinarily be done. In a sense it is an experiment, forced on the client, who would ordinarily not do something due to fear or to lack of confidence in self. You as the therapist/counselor are saying, "Do it! You'll succeed! If you should not, then I'll pay off the bet!"

THE LIFE TASKS IN THERAPY

Since, according to Adler, we all have three main tasks in life—love, occupation, and society—it is useful to "test" people who come for counseling and for therapy in these tasks. Formally it may be done as follows:

> According to Adlerian philosophy, each of us has three tasks in life: First, to get along with our family—with husbands or wives or children; second, to be satisfied with our work; and third, to have friends, community—to be part of society. I would like to ask you to estimate on a percentage basis how happy you are in each task. If you are moderately happy—about average—in your marriage, then that would be 50 percent. If you are extremely happy, then that might be 95 or 99 percent; and if you are extremely unhappy, then that would be 5 percent, or even 1 percent.

The client usually catches the idea quickly, or perhaps after a bit of urging will give estimates, so that we may get something like this.

	Percent
Family	35%
Job	95
Friends	85

This person gets along OK with job and with society but has home problems. Later, when the professional relationship is to end, we then again check. If the ratings are

	Percent
Family	85%
Job	80
Friends	75

then it is obvious that a decided change has occurred in the family.

This rating can be useful in another way. Sometimes clients come in and they don't seem to know what to say. By this technique, attention is drawn to more specific life problems and in some cases we may find that the person is unsuccessful in all three areas. We have had clients who claimed to be at or below the 5 percent level of happiness/success in all three areas of life. Such devastated people need extreme care. It is a great pleasure to the therapist, upon checking later in the therapeutic process, to find upward movement in all three areas.

In a less formal way, the life task notion is a useful guide throughout therapy. We have found that people will come for therapy with a problem in one life task while evidently successful and satisfied in the others. Ofttimes upon investigation we find that these are relatively healthy people with a particular misconception in that one life task area or a lack of knowledge in that area. In these cases counseling/education in that area is usually sufficient to bring the person to a satisfactory place in that life task also. However, sometimes when someone comes in complaining of a problem in a life task the discussion goes as follows:

> *Therapist:* You say that the difficulty you are having has to do with your getting into arguments with fellow employees and bosses at work. Do you have that problem at home?
>
> *Client:* No, never. The wife and kids don't argue with me.
>
> *Therapist:* What about with friends? Do you have many arguments with your friends?
>
> *Client:* I used to, but I have stopped all that. I couldn't take the stupidity of the PTA and the church group so I don't go anymore. We don't have other friends. We're a home-loving family.

In this example one can see that by checking across the life task areas, essentially by having a framework for looking at all facets of life, the therapist can determine the extent of the problem. In this example, our first hypothesis would be that this fellow is a dictator who has to be right and it is affecting all of his relationships and all facets of his life.

Throughout the course of therapy, as difficulties are expressed by the client, or problem behaviors are noted, it is worthwhile to use the life tasks as a sort of checklist. Not only is it informative for the therapist, but the client can begin to see that in some instances the same behavior is differently received in different situations and in other instances the client has been blind to the extent of the problem.

If one has not used a holistic approach before, it might be surprising to find how frequently people are consistently misbehaving, pursuing the same useless line of movement—of behavior—throughout their life, and do not know it. The unity and consistency of the life style predicts this, and the life task notion is a good tool for checking it out.

A MAP OF HUMAN RELATIONS

Frequently it is valuable to be able to demonstrate various psychological dynamics by illustrations. We have mentioned how Adler used to indicate upward movement, from minus to plus, by drawing a line going upward, and then showing how one can go to the useless side or the useful side at choice points in life as found in Figure 9–1. Another illustration of value in counseling is a life space drawing seen in Figure 13–1, which comes from an article by Kefir and Corsini (1974). The triangle represents a map. Any person's interaction with either another person or with several people at any time can be pinpointed on this map. Thus, let us examine extremes to make the situation clear.

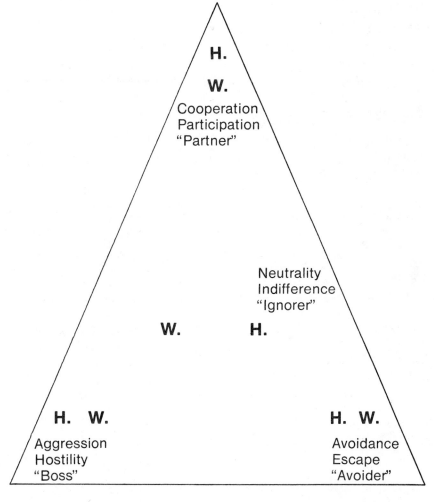

FIGURE 13–1. *A map of human relations. If "H" stands for "husband" and "W" stands for "wife," imagine these four marriages. Plot on this map a number of marriages you know.*

1. The exact middle. This means "absolutely no interaction." Thus, two people seated side by side on a train—absolute strangers who do not acknowledge each other in any way—are not interacting. Or, to make it even more clear, Lin Pang in Peking and Harold Smith in Peoria, who don't know of each other's existence, are at the exact middle of this triangle—no relationship whatever, no interaction, a perfect zero.

2. The top corner. This means complete and absolute cooperation. An example might be a man and a woman involved in a dance. Each is cooperating with the music and each is responsive to the other. Another example would be two people pulling on a rope to lift a heavy object, with each person cooperating as much as possible.

3. Bottom left corner. This is complete aggressive, hostile interaction between people, such as occurs when a parent in a rage is whipping a child. Another example would be someone deliberately spreading gossip about another person with the intention of hurting the person.

4. Bottom right corner. This would mean escape, moving away from a person. The classic example would be running away from home. Another example occurs when a husband or a wife abandons the other, wanting a divorce.

This map can be used clinically in many ways. An example follows, referring to the map. A counselor meets with a husband and wife and draws the map on the blackboard, and asks the couple some questions, and has them put marks on the blackboard.

Counselor: I have explained this map to you. Do you understand it?

Husband and wife: Yes.

Counselor: Fine. Now, Harold, would you indicate on this triangle where you want to be in relation to your wife. Just make an X on the blackboard. (Harold puts an X near the top corner.) Now, Wanda, would you do the same. Where do you want to be; where do you want to be in relation to Howard? (She puts her X near his.) Fine. Both of you say you want to be cooperative with each other. Now, Howard, would you put a circle to show us where you think your wife actually is.

Harold (making circle near bottom left corner): Right here, because she is bossy, always telling me and the kids what to do.

Counselor: Now, Wanda, would you make a circle where you see Howard; how he operates in the family. (Wanda draws a circle near the lower right-hand corner.)

Wanda: That's where he is. He has no consideration for us; doesn't really care for us. Simply does what he wants. Won't go with us to church; just out with his beer-drinking friends; looks at TV football games all day Saturday and Sunday.

Counselor: OK, now can we agree? Each of you wants a cooperative relationship. Harold sees Wanda down at the lower left—bossy; and Wanda sees Harold at the lower right—escaping. Now, would you both please write your first initial where you think you are. (Harold places it near the middle but near lower right, and Wanda near middle near lower left.) Well, we now have three sets of marks (Figure 13–1). Xs show where you both want to be, up near the top—cooperative; Os to show where you think the other is—Wanda bossy and Harold escaping; and your initials to show where you see yourself—both near the middle, but Harold does see himself escaping somewhat, but not as much as Wanda sees him, and Wanda does see herself bossy, but not as bossy as Howard sees her.

Wanda: Sure I'm bossy, but I have to be. He won't do anything.

Harold: Sure I escape, but I have to. She's so bossy, like her mother.

Counselor: The thing is, do you two really want to improve?

Harold and Wanda: Yes, of course. Sure thing.

Counselor: Now here's how it can be done. We are going to examine specific situations and we will try to agree among the three of us where it belongs on this map. Now let us take a specific situation. Wanda, want to mention one?

Wanda: Yes. On Sundays I would like the family to go to church together. Harold agrees, but instead he watches TV and never gets ready.

Counselor: Is it true, Harold?

Harold: I guess so.

Counselor: Let's put a dot on the triangle. Harold, where would you fit on the triangle if this is so—that you are not ready to go to church as you promised, but instead watch TV?

Harold: Well, you know, she nags me . . .

Counselor: I am sure, but just indicate your behavior . . .

Harold: About here . . . (points to lower right-hand corner).

Counselor: And when he doesn't do what he promised, what do you do, Wanda?

Harold: Her behavior is nag, nag, nag.

Counselor: Is that true? (Wanda nods) Well, then where does that fit on the triangle?

And so on. After this is over, it is evident to both husband and wife that they do in fact operate in the bossy and the escape corners. With the map they can "see" where they fit—where they are; and from then on it is easy to redirect their behavior—to find the route to where they want to be.

PSYCHOTHERAPY WITH MORE THAN TWO

Multiple Therapy

Rudolf Dreikurs (1952a) developed the procedure of multiple therapy and used it in his private office for many years. Anyone who is interested in understanding Adlerian psychotherapy should know what it is and how it is employed. Multiple therapy illustrates well much of the flavor of Adlerian therapy. Multiple therapy goes usually as follows:

1. A client makes a first appointment with a senior therapist, during which time the client is informed that two one-hour diagnostic interviews with an associate therapist are to be scheduled.
2. At the second interview the client meets with the associate therapist, who briefly reviews the client's reasons for coming and begins to take a Life Style interview (p. 187).
3. A third hour with the associate therapist is held and more Life Style data is obtained. The Life Style data collection is completed.
4. A fourth session is scheduled with both therapists. The associate therapist reports Life Style interview findings to the senior therapist. The senior therapist might ask questions of both the client and the associate therapist. Finally, the senior therapist dictates the Life Style summary to the associate therapist. There then follows a three-way conference concerning this summary to try to reach a consensus on the client's life style.
5. The client and the associate therapist begin a series of interviews to "work on" the implications of the Life Style summary. Usually the client and the associate therapist have three sessions and then a fourth session with both the associate therapist and the senior therapist. This pattern of three and then one is maintained until the therapy is terminated.

Dreikurs (1952b) stated that there were several advantages to multiple therapy:

1. The therapy is shorter, and consequently more effective and efficient.
2. This system is an example of "two heads are better than one" in that the associate therapist has the opportunity to consult with the senior therapist.

3. This system prevents excessive dependency on one therapist and shows the client that therapists can disagree and be found wrong.
4. An associate therapist who might be going along the wrong road might be able to see errors and go in a different direction.

In using the terms *senior* and *associate,* it should be understood that therapists in one office might play the different roles with different patients. Thus, Harold Mosak might be the senior therapist with client A while Bina Rosenberg is the associate therapist; with client B it might be Dr. Rosenberg who is the senior therapist and Dr. Mosak the associate.

What makes this system particularly "Adlerian" is the concept of sharing/ equality and the absence of "secrecy." This is compatible with the concept of public family counseling which Adler developed in Vienna. One of his intentions was to train professionals who were observers in his thinking (Seidler, 1936; Spiel, 1956).

With this, the psychiatric interview came out of the closet, from the secrecy that doctors' interviews traditionally had. This "democratic" conceptualization is still not accepted in many quarters, and it is still difficult for some people to go along with it. Nevertheless, Adlerian family education centers with open discussions do exist and they are philosophically related to multiple therapy.

A more advanced form of multiple therapy might occur in a marriage treatment. Imagine a couple first going to a senior therapist. Then imagine the husband and the wife each seeing a different associate counselor. Then imagine a meeting of the two therapists and the two clients meeting with the same senior therapist. This conceptualization might even be compounded with four or more therapists meeting with four or more members of a battling family. The important notion, however, is a movement from a one-to-one situation to a sharing, open discussion between all therapists and all clients in group sessions.

Group Therapy

One of the pioneers of group therapy was Alfred Adler. In 1922 in front of groups he began to advise parents and teachers how to treat problem children. Subsequent to the presentations there would be discussions and people who participated often found that they benefited directly and personally. However, Adler never attempted formal group therapy. The great Adlerian exponent of group therapy was Rudolf Dreikurs. Terner and Pew (1978) give this account:

> Once due to an overcrowded schedule he [Dreikurs] suggested that three of his patients come for a joint interview. The two men and the one woman were all at a state in their therapy where Dreikurs wanted to give them some theoretical insights. He also felt that in this way he could save considerable time.

When the group session ended, all three agreed that they had benefited more from the group discussion than from individual interviews and proposed to Dreikurs that they continue to work together. (p. 79)

Group therapy is a natural form for Adlerians. Adler himself was a highly gregarious person, and in this respect he was different from Freud. To the extent that a personality system is essentially a reflection of the personality of the founder of that system, the procedures and processes will be affected by the essential nature of the individuals involved.

Hospital therapeutic groups are a unique Adlerian invention. Developed by an English Adlerian—Joshua Bierer (1951, Bierer & Evans, 1969)—the therapeutic groups have been employed at the Alfred Adler Mental Health Clinic in New York (Mohr & Garlock, 1959) and also at the St. Joseph's Hospital in Chicago (Shulman & Hoover, 1964). The essential concept is that the therapists should do no more for patients than is absolutely necessary. To develop responsibility in the patients is the major concern, and is achieved through permitting patients in these institutions to meet democratically to decide how to organize and run themselves and their affairs. One can readily see the analogy with education. In Adlerian education one of the aims is to get children to develop self-responsibility and this is achieved by giving children a considerable amount of freedom and self-direction. In mental hospitals, learning to become responsible for self is the concern. The book and movie, *One Flew over the Cuckoo's Nest*, illustrates exactly the opposite sort of philosophy: subjugating patients to administrative convenience. This Adlerian philosophy is an example of a hopeful, optimistic view of humankind rather than the pessimistic view found in most schools and hospitals.

Adlerians use group therapy flexibly. Thus, one patient may start in individual therapy and progress to group therapy. Others may be in both simultaneously. The general notion is that therapy has to be individualized, with the client having a decisive vote in what to do.

The Adlerian group therapist attempts to make the group a representation of society. The group begins to develop its own norms and its own culture. Adler's words in another connection are quite appropriate for the goals of group therapy: "As soon as the patient can connect himself with his fellow men on an equal and cooperative footing, he is cured" (Adler, 1956, p. 347). We see here another example of Adlerian Individual Psychology as a social psychology, the very opposite of what its name—at first glance—implies.

Adlerian group therapy methods are based on the Adlerian therapist's optimistic belief in the capacity of people to improve themselves and a belief in the value of encouragement and democracy. Within the group the same techniques are used as in individual therapy, individuals' goals and the purposes of their behavior are illustrated in action and interaction among group members. Many Adlerians conduct Life Style assessments of individuals before they enter groups, giving them and the therapist the tool of understanding the individual's goals to build on in the group. Adlerian therapists are, in groups as well as in individual therapy, directive and highly goal-oriented; that is, they have the aim of efficiently moving the client into useful endeavors in the social interest.

Group Life Style.   It is possible in a group for all members to share their life style summaries so that every member gets an understanding of all the others, and so that every member can contribute to the process. Frank Walton (1975) has developed a set of procedures with six phases, not all of which need to be used, for this purpose.

1.   Each person has a set number of minutes, usually 10, to tell the rest of the group everything about themselves, sticking to the present tense if possible, and dealing with the three life task issues: (*a*) social/friends, (*b*) occupation, and (*c*) family/love life.
2.   The group members, after hearing the statement, are asked to reply or comment and are asked to react to (*a*) the total presentation, (*b*) commonalities with what were heard, (*c*) feelings toward that person, and (*d*) attitudes and intentions.
3.   A number of suggestions are made for understanding the person's family constellation and family life.
4.   The family constellation and the meaning of early family life on present personality for each person may discussed.
5.   Each person shares several early memories with the rest of the group.
6.   Interrelations are made and discussions are held about the meaning of these early memories.

Chapter 14

Family and Group Counseling and Therapy

When people refer to counseling and therapy we usually assume they are talking about the procedure in which a single patient and therapist participate. They could just as well be referring to situations in which more than a single patient is the object of treatment because all applications are targeted at individuals, in the sense that each participant will hopefully develop from the process, but the major aim of the group treatment is to help large numbers of persons at the same time.

CONCEPTS IN COUNSELING CHILDREN AND FAMILIES

A basic issue which underlies interventions with children is: Are children inherently good or bad? Some philosophers believed that children were naturally evil, and indeed in traditional Christian thought children were born in sin and needed baptism to cleanse them. Some philosophers, notably Jean Jacques Rousseau, believed that children were inherently good and should be allowed to develop in terms of their essential nature. Among personality theorists, the outstanding proponent of children's built-in evil was Sigmund Freud, who stated, in effect, that children wanted sexual relations with the parent of the opposite sex and wanted to kill the same-sexed parent.

Alfred Adler disagreed. His view was more like that of John B. Watson, the behaviorist, that children were "neutral" and could be influenced to go into any direction. In an article from a "lost" newspaper article originally printed in 1930, discovered by Janet Terner of the Library of Congress, Adler stated, "Man is not born good or evil, but can be trained in either direction."

The child, Adler stated, is like an immigrant coming to a new land, knowing neither the language nor the customs of the inhabitants, and is ready to take on the values, the attitudes, the notions, and the language of those among whom he finds himself. The child thus is neither good nor bad: he just is— and is ready to learn and to be formed. Adler's common sense and courage were such that he refused to go toward either of the polarities of goodness or badness.

Unconscious Intentionality

"But," the agitated mother said, "he *really* cannot put his shorts on right. He *always* puts them on with the opening in the back. When he discovers this, he has a fit. He is so angry."

"Mother," the counselor said, "do you think it is possible that he does this on purpose?"

"No! No!" she cried out angrily. "I know you psychologists. You think everyone does everything on purpose. Not in the case of Eddie. You should see him. How upset he gets when he finds he didn't succeed! If you only saw him, you'd know I am right. He just can't do them right."

The counselor smiled. "Do you think I can convince you that he knows how to put them on right?"

"Never! I know what I know. I know what I see."

"May I ask a couple of questions?"

"Of course," the mother replied, holding herself firm and straight, not trusting the counselor, whom she suspected had some crazy theory and was going to try to change her mind.

"Let me ask you this first question. Suppose that your child were really unable to know, say he was blind, and say that the pants were half black and half white. Say that the right way would be for the white to be in front, the black in back. How often would he have the black in front?"

"I guess half the time."

"Now, how many times have you seen Eddie put on his shorts?"

"Lots of times."

"Has he ever put them on right?"

"Never."

"What do you think about that?"

The mother pondered. "Well, if he really doesn't know, he should get them right some of the time."

"That's right. By pure chance he should get them on right 25 out of 50 times. But you help him. You give him attention and service. You reward him for doing it wrong by giving him attention, and if he did it right, you'd pay no attention." Mother's mouth was open in surprise. Her chin dropped. The logic was overwhelming.

This incident, often cited by Dr. Harold Mosak, illustrates unconscious intentionality. Eddie did not consciously intend (most probably) to put his shorts on backward. His anger was probably genuine. Nevertheless, doing it wrong 100 percent of the time when he would have done it wrong only 50 percent of the time if he didn't really know tells us that he intended to put them on backward, whether he was aware of his attention or not.

Children's behavior is purposeful, just as is adult behavior. Within Adlerian theory we see people's behavior always as movement toward goals. Children's goals naturally are developed within the context of their family and immediate environment. Their creativity may allow them to create unrealistic notions of their world, but there is a logic to their construing of their world. If the mother in the above example attends to her child's nonsensical behavior, it is perfectly logical for the child to conclude that he should do ridiculously incompetent things to get service and attention.

The development of more possible goals coincides with the expansion of the individual's environment. "The mistaken goals of attention, power, revenge, and display of inadequacy are found in children. In adolescence, in addition to these four goals, you find others such as excitement, entertainment, and fun. In adults you find additional mistaken goals, such as money and power." (Dreikurs, 1971, p. 10).

Adlerian treatment of children is intended to bring children to realistic assumptions, which make them realize that they have to carry their own weight as an equal member of their family and eventually of society. One of the techniques geared toward this aim has to do with consequences.

Consequences, Natural and Logical

Instead of rewarding children when they do what we like or what they are "supposed" to do, and punishing them when they do what we do not like or what they are not "supposed" to do, Adlerians stress using natural and logical consequences in training children. We shall now attempt to define consequences and to distinguish them from reward and punishment. Robert B. Ingersoll presaged the Adlerian position by saying, "In nature there are neither rewards nor punishments; there are only consequences."

Natural consequences are the easiest to understand. What the procedure amounts to is *doing nothing*. The parent, employer, trainer, or supervisor, essentially *(a)* gives information about the consequences of the behavior or nonbehavior to the person to be trained (only if this seems necessary), *(b)* looks on while the person acts or does not act properly, and *(c)* permits the person to receive the natural consequences of the behavior.

"Keep the nose of the airplane above the horizon," the instructor says to the student pilot, "or you will lose altitude." Sure enough, as they fly at their intended level of 4,000 feet, the student pilot lets the nose dip below the horizon and soon notices that he is at 3,500 feet. The instructor, seeing everything, does nothing, says nothing, knowing that the "natural consequences" will soon be obvious to the student pilot, and that as a result of the experience, the student pilot will be more careful in the future.

"The toaster is hot," mother says to the tot who climbs up on a chair and wants to touch the toaster, which has just popped up a piece of toast, "and if you touch it, you'll get burned." The tot pays no attention. Mother looks on, says nothing, and waits. Were the toaster red hot so that the child would get a severe burn, she would intervene and take the child away. But satisfied that the consequences will be painful but not harmful, she watches. Let us say the child does touch the toaster. He gets a minor burn and starts to cry. Mother now puts the child's hand in cold water, but she is very careful not to criticize (a form of verbal punishment). The results of this kind of behavior are the following:

1. The child learns to trust mother.
2. The child learns that mother cares for him.
3. And, primarily, the child learns directly the result of his behavior.

Should mother have stopped him from touching the toaster, he might well have felt that she was unfair to him, preventing him from doing what he wanted. He would not have learned a lesson. If mother had spanked him for keeping on in the act of touching it, or if she had spanked him after he touched the toaster, he would have additional evidence that people are cruel to him.

Natural consequences, therefore, involve learning from experience. A parent, an employer, a trainer, or a friend has the obligation to give information, as well as the obligation of preventing the person from doing what might be harmful or fatal. Thus, we don't permit a child to poke his finger into an electric fan to "find out for himself" at the risk of the child losing a finger, even though we might permit such a child to touch a warm toaster. The school of hard knocks is the best teacher.

Natural consequences is one of the most important training tools of parents and teachers. Too often, we do not permit children to fail. One of us, imbued with the feeling of intellectual superiority and the belief that he could not fail any course, and that last-minute boning up would be of help, "fooled around" the whole semester in Chemistry 1. When the final examination came, he failed! This was such a shock that it still reverberates to this day—a natural consequence par excellence.

A logical consequence, on the other hand, is something *you do or you do not do* if someone else does something or does not do something in terms of a contract, expressed or implied. Please read the prior sentence again, carefully, to get the full meaning.

Both you and the recipient of the consequence should agree that the consequence is logical. This should be implicit in the logic of the event. The consequence, then, whether favorable or unfavorable, is seen by both persons as fair. Some examples:

Jim agrees to rake Mr. Brown's front yard, and Mr. Brown agrees to pay Jim $5 for this. Jim does not do this. The logical consequence—Mr. Brown does not pay Jim.

Jim—a constant forgetter—agrees to take out the garbage before going to bed, and agrees that if he forgets, father or mother can wake him up to remind him. He forgets and is awakened from a sound sleep by one of his parents, who reminds him as per their agreement to take out the garbage. As a result of two or three such reminders, he no longer forgets.

There is a reasonable order in coping with others and the world, what Adler called "the common sense of social living." If one understands this order, many potential problems are eliminated. If one does not recognize the logical order in dealing with others and the natural order in dealing with objects and events, problems are inevitable. Persons responsible for others—such as parents and supervisors—frequently shield their charges from the consequences of this order. By allowing the consequences of events to occur (natural consequences) or arranging for the consequences to occur (logical consequences), the onus of negative consequences falls on the order of life, the recipient of the consequences learns the order and benefits from this knowledge, unable to blame others.

The natural and logical order in living is not absolute. Touching a toaster will not always lead to a burned hand—the toaster may be cold. Talking back to a parent may not always bring a reprimand—the parent may be otherwise involved and not notice, or may find if funny. The effort in educating parents and in helping families with difficulties is in establishing the parameters for all persons, particularly the children, for understanding and behaving in conjunction with the order of life. Parents' behavior sets the stage for children's understanding.

Parental Inconsistencies

Of the many possible errors that parents make, a common devastating one is inconsistency. "No," says the mother upon being asked something, and then later relents and says "yes." The child does something and father smiles; later, the child does the same thing and the father scolds. Naturally, people cannot always be consistent, and maybe they should not be, otherwise they would be only machines. However, to help children learn good habits, good attitudes, and the natural and logical order, parents should have a fairly consistent way of dealing with them, so that the children can predict their parents and generally predict others.

Consistency is most important in parent-child relationships during that period when the parents are changing their style of operating with their children. A good deal of theoretical-experimental research done by psychologists shows the following: when the "teacher/trainer"—in this case the parent—tries to change ways of behaving toward the child, in an attempt to get the child to change ways of operating, the child will attempt to get the parent to continue in the old ways. A power contest may occur as a result. If the parent is 100 percent consistent despite efforts of the child to break the parent, then after a short period of stiff resistance, the child will change and make a new adjustment. However, if the parent even once gives in and goes back to the old ways of operating, the child will persist for a much longer time, calculating that perhaps the parent will give in.

Here is an example: a child whines for money to buy candy. Father first says "no" but always gives in if the child continues. Say that now father has been counseled, and decides no longer to give in. Let us say that father from now on absolutely never gives in to whining. The total time that the child may continue whining may be five hours, perhaps distributed over two weeks in 40 whining periods. But, let father, in the third hour of this whining, give in and let the child have money for candy, and this one bit of inconsistency may mean that the child, instead of whining for a total of 5 hours distributed over two weeks, may now continue for a total of 15 hours of whining distributed over four weeks.

In doing family counseling, the counselor should make a strong point of the importance of not starting any new mode of dealing with children unless the parents are both convinced of what they will do and will stick to it.

Mr. and Mrs. Smith were terribly worried about the fighting between Sam and Jon, their twin sons. Mrs. Smith was especially fearful that Sam would hurt Jon because he was so aggressive, and she induced her husband to supervise them closely, to break up their fights, lecture to them, send them to separate rooms, and otherwise give them lots of attention. The parents were counseled to keep out of the fights and to use the three Bs (bear it, beat it, boot them out) in dealing with fights. That is to say, to stay in the room and say nothing if the twins were fighting; and if the particular parent could not bear to hear the noise, to get up and "beat it" out of the room, going somewhere else; and then if this was not advisable to "boot them out of the house," telling them not to come back until they had settled their quarrel. This procedure seemed sensible to the father, but not to the mother, who insisted that she would use this method dependent on the degree of force that the children were displaying—in short, if the kids were very aggressive, she would separate them. The counselor strongly advised her not to interfere. Mother stated that Sam was terribly aggressive and she just could not stand by to see Jon beaten so viciously. Father said that he would agree to use the suggested procedure regardless of how much fighting was going on. The counselor then gave father permission to use the new method. The following week, after the father had refused to break up fights, the mother agreed to do the same, and to be completely consistent.

Two weeks later when the parents were reinterviewed, they reported three things: *(a)* for a while the fighting had gotten worse, *(b)* that now there was very little fighting, and *(c)* the aggressor now was Jon—not Sam!

A month later there was practically no fighting. Mother even stated that once she sent the twins out of the house to continue their fighting, suggesting that they take sticks and hit one another—an example of antisuggestion. The kids were so flabbergasted by the suggestion that they stopped their fighting immediately.

In a sense, the normal person is one with a consistent character—one who is predictable. We must not confuse constancy, consistency, predictability with something that is quite abnormal: rigidity. The normal personality moves constantly in one direction. But the rigid personality will not deviate at all. In common parlance we call such people stubborn, narrow-minded, rigid. That is not the desired outcome in suggesting parental consistency.

Bedwetting

A good example of Adlerian ways of dealing with problems of children is how bedwetting is handled. Bedwetting is usually psychological in origin, not physiological. The question we ask is this: *What goal is the child achieving through bedwetting?* We do not think that he cannot stop it. We assume that there is some goal to be gained. We would like to know what the goal is and refuse to give in to unreasonable demands so that the child will no longer attempt to achieve that goal.

Greg, age four, would show up at his parents' bed, his pajamas wet, and ask to get in bed with his parents. The father grumbled, not liking to have his wet child in bed with him. But mother couldn't stand him being wet, and didn't want to have the child go back to a wet bed, so she would let Greg into the bed. The parents consulted an Adlerian counselor. "Tell Greg he can get into bed with you only if he is dry." The advice made good sense to the father, and the mother acquiesced. They informed Greg of the new rules. The next morning he showed up, but he was wet. "Sorry," he was told by both, and he went reluctantly back to his room. The morning after he showed up, but this time he was dry. "Come in," he was told. In a week he was dry every morning. There was no need for him to wet or, for that matter, to wake up to go to his parents' bed.

Adlerian thinking is well exemplified by the usual advice we give to parents who have bedwetters. It goes generally as follows:

1. Tell the child that from now on bedwetting is her problem.
2. Tell the child that if the bed is wet, she is to put the wet things in a special separate container if they are to be washed.
3. Inform the child that it is up to her to make the bed from now on, or not to make it.
4. The parents are absolutely and completely to keep out of the bedwetting situation from now on. Show no interest. Do not check the room. Make only perfunctory comments such as "too bad" or "that's good" if the child reports wetting the bed or not wetting the bed.
5. This method, if properly employed, with parents showing no interest in the bedwetting, should lead to a satisfactory solution within a month.
6. If the bedwetting keeps on for an extended period of time explore with the child the electronic wake up system (Mowrer, 1938), or we suggest that the child be taken to a physician, preferably a psychiatric pediatrician.
7. No comments, no complaining, no complimenting. The parent is to act as though the bedwetting problem is the child's problem and and not the adult's.

This system of dealing with enuresis which evolved from Adlerian concepts of equality and respect, as well as mistaken goals of children, has been employed for over 50 years and has been used with a very high degree of success on thousands of cases. The philosophy and theory of Individual Psychology is inherent in the first four steps of this method of handling bedwetting.

While O. H. Mowrer's system of behavior modification, using a gadget which will sound an alarm when the child wets the bed, thus waking him, can be successful for stopping bedwetting, it seems to us that a method which *(a)* does not depend on mechanical contrivances, and *(b)* which puts the burden on the child and which leads the child to feel that he or she did it on his or her own is superior to a mechanical device.

Our system is intended to achieve three things: *(a)* to stop the bedwetting, *(b)* to teach parents that they can trust their children to solve their problems, and *(c)* to help children learn that they have the ability to meet life's difficulties on their own—to build up their self-esteem by doing things for themselves.

Family Therapy

There is a decided difference between family counseling and family therapy. The first, pioneered by Adler in 1922 when he counseled parents and teachers, and extended by Rudolf Dreikurs in the United States, calls for the counselor to give direct advice to parents for relief of immediate problems and to teach parents how to handle difficulties at home. Family therapy is quite a different matter. It is the treatment of the whole family, generally families in considerable trouble with aggressive or withdrawn adolescents.

Among the Adlerian and neo-Adlerian writings on family therapy are articles and books by such people as J. E. Bell (1961), Danica Deutsch (1967), J. Franco et al. (1962), C. F. Midelfort (1957), and Vincent D. Foley (1974).

The important concept in family therapy is that the identified problem person, patient (such as the black sheep of the family or the "crazy one"), may actually have taken this role out of necessity in order to have some place in the family, or to keep the family together. The identified patient may be no "sicker" than anyone else in the family—it is just that this person plays a role needed in the family. The person may be the family scapegoat.

There are a variety of opinions on how to conduct family therapy. We shall not attempt to summarize them, as summaries are available elsewhere (Foley, 1974), but shall consider family therapy from the Adlerian point of view.

Family disturbances are often due to the attempts of parents to prevent children from having their own way. The children's "way" may be "useful" or "useless," may be quite normal and usual and abnormal and unusual, or they may be legal or illegal. In any case, major conflicts often exist between parents and one or more children. However, other patterns exist. Father may be alone while mother and the children may be together. Or mother may be excluded, with father and the children in a solid group. It may be that some of the children are on mother's side and some on father's side. It may be that the entire family is united except for one child, who is on his or her own.

To give an example: a couple came to see one of the authors because they were worried about one of their children. They had four boys. Father and mother were athletic, liked to hike and sail, and this was true of three of the four boys. The second oldest son did not like athletics, liked to be in his room and to draw pictures and write poems. The other five members were in constant turmoil against Peter, wanting him to come along with them to the beach, or wanting him to come view some sporting event, with him constantly saying that he didn't want to.

The parents told their story of how they wanted to keep the family together, how they tried to get Peter to experience what the other members liked, how they supported his efforts to write poetry and draw pictures, but that they were worried about his isolation from the family.

When Peter was interviewed, he seemed a normal, intelligent, sociable, friendly person, who stated he just didn't like such athletic activities. He showed his poems and drawings, and they seemed to be of good quality for a boy of 13. He stated he had some friends, was doing well in school—about as well as his brothers—and generally seemed quite well adjusted.

A conference was then held with the parents and the children at which time all opinions were listened to, with the counselor controlling the interaction to make sure that father and oldest son, who were the most verbal, did not dominate the meeting. Eventually, the consensus was reached that Peter had the right to run his own life, that he was old enough to be left home alone, and that the majority had no right to dominate his interests. Father finally reluctantly agreed to stop putting pressure on Peter.

Subsequent interviews with the parents indicated that father was somewhat concerned that Peter might turn out to be a homosexual. These fears were dispelled through giving father basic information about homosexuality. Mother had supported father's attitude mostly through fear of gaining his displeasure, but was quite happy that Peter would be left to his own devices.

As a result of this family therapy, relationships improved, and not too surprisingly, after a while, Peter voluntarily started attending various sports events and participating in some strenuous family activities without any pressure being put on him. A new balance was struck, and as a result, the father and other brothers began to admire Peter's work rather than, as before, derogating it.

Essentially, the "cause" of family disharmony of this type is a lack of respect, with someone or some "ones" trying to dominate, or to make another do what they want and not what the other person or group wants. Sometimes it is the group against one person as in the above example. Sometimes it is one person against the group. Such was the case in the following family.

Carl was the only son, the second child, with one older sister and two younger sisters. Father was not successful. He had quit a job of many years standing to go into business for himself and had lost the family savings, and then had to go back to his hated job. Mother was more successful. She had started as a salesperson in a store. She brought in about two thirds of the family income. As a result of both parents working so hard, the children did not have as much parental attention as most children would have.

Carl became a bully and beat his sisters if they did not do what he wanted. He was his father's favorite. The parents fought and bickered constantly about Carl's misbehavior and bullying. On top of this, Carl began coming home late at night, stealing, lying. He was highly unreliable. The family was inundated by complaints from neighbors of all sorts of misbehaviors, including loud profane "dirty" langauge, "taking" things that did not belong to him, sexual precocities, and the like. Additionally, teachers in the school kept sending the parents "love notes," as Rudolf Dreikurs termed them—complaints about Carl.

We were called in to help this family. The facts were soon evident. The son was the "black sheep" and his role in the family was to make all the others unite against him. Were he to stop his misbehavior, then his parents would separate since father's relative failure and mother's relative success would split them. Also, his sisters needed him to have someone to feel superior about.

The solution in this particular case was probably not ideal, but it was finally decided by all, including the son, for the son to move out of the family situation and to move in with a relative. This done, peace descended on the family, and the youth made a good adjustment with his relatives. A year later, upon graduating from high school, he rejoined the family and the adjustment was relatively good from then on.

The basic concept in family theory is that the members thereof operate in relation to one another, and that the so-called identified patient may not be any sicker or maladjusted than anyone else, but is only carrying the family burden.

The techniques of family therapy are essentially the entire battery of techniques available to the individual and group therapist and child therapist or counselor. At least this is the case in Adlerian family therapy. In attempting to remediate a family problem, any combination of techniques and members of the family may be used.

Private Family Counseling

The flexibility needed to adequately and efficiently counsel disturbed families may be illustrated in the following. We have had couples come in to explain their home situation and their "problem" child. After we described the dynamics of the family system as we saw them and suggested some approaches for correcting the "problem," they believed they had all the help they needed and were never seen again. Most phone within two to three weeks to say how things have improved. Sometimes after seeing the parent(s) alone, we have followed up with full family sessions. Ofttimes after a telephone description of the trouble from a parent, we see the entire family together for the first time. This may be followed by more full family sessions, or sessions with just the parents, or just the children, one parent or both parents in individual meetings, and, of course, possibly sessions with the "problem" child alone, depending on our judgment.

We have found it a nice touch, and sometimes necessary, to finish with a family by seeing them all together at least once. It sometimes helps to bring some things out in the open and, in effect, put it all together so they start out "on their own," without whatever dependencies on the therapist which may have developed. But even this "nice touch" is at the discretion of the therapist. The notion is to do only as much as is needed. With sufficient understanding, most families will work things out on their own. And, of course, the door is open, the phone handy, and we are always available.

Public Family Counseling

The process of public family counseling is basically the same as private family counseling. The primary difference, outside of the audience and public setting, is in the counselors' discussions with the audience. However, even this difference is not too great inasmuch as the counselor would carry on a similar discussion with the family members. However, by themselves a family may not have the range of ideas that an audience group would have and, most importantly, they would not have the support of a larger group for the commonness of their problems and ideas for their solution.

Adler's original open family counseling sessions have become a part of the American scene. In the United States there are more than 50 centers employing these procedures (Dreikurs, Corsini, Lowe and Sonstegaard, 1959). The process generally goes as follows.

1. A set of parents visits a center for the first time. There they observe a set of parents being interviewed by a counselor. Then the children of the parents are interviewed, a playroom worker reports on the behavior of the children while the parents were being interviewed, and following a discussion with the group, the counselor gives the parents advice. Following this, a second set of parents will be interviewed. These were originally counseled some time before, so this is a follow-up meeting.

2. Let us assume that the visiting parents like what they see and that they desire to be counseled. They will then be interviewed by an intake worker, who will decide whether public family counseling is appropriate. If so, an appointment is made, usually two or three weeks from the time of the interview, so that these parents will get an opportunity to see at least three sets of parents being counseled. During the times that the parents are in the counseling room, the children are in a playroom under supervision and observation.

3. At the public family counseling session the parents are interviewed by the counselor, who ordinarily asks them such things as *(a)* the names and ages of their children, *(b)* how many counseling sessions the parents have attended, *(c)* what, if anything, they have learned from attending so far, *(d)* what their concerns are about their various children, and *(e)* what the parents have done so far to solve their family problems. After this information is obtained, ordinarily the parents are asked to describe a typical day. Or, the parents may be asked to evaluate family problems using a form, such as the Family Relationship Index (Corsini, 1980).

The counselor attempts to locate several major problems of concern to the parents. There are 24 problems ordinarily handled by these counselors (Corsini & Painter, 1975), since not all problems are suitable for open family counseling. The usual problems may start with difficulties about children getting up in the morning and going to bed at night, and feature such major and common problems as fighting between siblings, eating problems, neatness, and school maladjustment.

4. The parents are now told that their child or children are to be interviewed, and that the parents have the right to stay or to go during these interviews. Most parents prefer not to be present during the interviews, feeling that their presence will disturb the children or not permit them to be open in their replies. In some cases, while the parents are present, the counselor asks for the playroom worker to come in to report all observations about the children. In other cases, the playroom worker will report following the interview with the children.

5. The children are brought in and interviewed by the counselor. In 9 out of 10 cases, the children like the interview and cooperate well. In 1 case out of 10, children will be uncooperative, will exhibit fear, and will not respond, will scream, or will show opposition in some other way. In most of these cases, an experienced counselor can still get some information or is able to kindly bring the child to some degree of cooperation. One general aim of the counselor is to uncover the hidden reasons for the child's misbehavior through questions designed to uncover the major goal of the four goals that presumably are behind the misbehavior.

6. The parents now come back, and the counselor zeroes in on the selected problem. There can be a discussion with the audience relative to effective and ineffective methods of handling the particular problems, as well as a directed discussion with the parents.

7. The last part of the counseling session is direct advice to the parents on handling the problem. They are given specific instructions. After they have heard the advice, they are routinely asked to repeat instructions, and asked whether they intend to follow the advice. Following this, an appointment is made for two weeks later, although in some cases the next appointment may be the next week or several weeks later.

An extremely high percentage of parents who come for this sort of help get satisfaction. In practically every case, if the parents follow the advice, they get favorable results. This is in part due to the screening which usually results in parents being accepted only if they are "normal" and the problems are "normal" and the children are "normal." Since the advice given is "canned," as indicated in Corsini and Painter (1975), that is, generalized for any of the major 24 problems, and since tens of thousands of parents have been given the same kind of advice for the same kinds of problems, it is highly likely that any set of parents, if they do as they are counseled, will have success.

These demonstrations tend to be quite dramatic and exciting and generate a considerable amount of interest on the part of the parents and educators. Many parents go on from this point to attend parent study groups and/or to become active in the various family education centers in which they originally got some counseling help.

Walton and Powers (1974) nicely sum up the mistaken approaches to dealing with children which are the meat of what must be changed in family counseling. The issue, as always, is in the maintenance of a superiority-inferiority relationship. They say that "Basically there are two mistaken approaches that parents and teachers use in dealing with children. One of these is the pampering or overprotective approach. The other is the suppressive-autocratic approach" (p. 14). Within superior-inferior relationships the children's responses to these approaches make sense: "The pampered child takes satisfaction in putting us into his service, and the suppressed child takes satisfaction in showing us that we cannot control him" (p. 15). The counselor must see to it, directly with the child and indirectly by showing the parent and teacher, that the child is given responsibility. Two means which have been proven effective in altering family systems and getting the primary points of equality, democracy, and responsibility across are the family council and parent study groups.

The Family Council

While the family council concept certainly antedates Adlerian psychology, no other psychological school of thought has accepted so enthusiastically this notion of a family meeting in a formal manner, operating completely democratically. Found in summary form in practically all Adlerian family counseling books (Corsini & Painter, 1975; Dreikurs et al., 1959; Dreikurs & Soltz, 1964), it is also the subject of some independent publications (Corsini & Rigney, 1970; Dreikurs, Gould, & Corsini, 1974).

We shall discuss briefly the purposes and the ideal practices of the family council. There are several important purposes:

1. To allow free communication among family members.
2. To avoid emotional showdowns and violence in the family.
3. To teach children and parents democratic means of settling differences.
4. To operate an orderly and peaceful home.

The ideal family council has the following elements:

1. It is formal: it does not just happen to occur. When the family council is going on, nothing else is going on. In short, a family does not have a family council while eating or while on a driving trip.

2. Attendance is voluntary. Anyone can enter or leave a meeting.
3. Decisions are always temporary: until the next meeting.
4. Meetings are scheduled in advance according to some schedule.
5. Chairmanship rotates among all those capable of being chairman.
6. There are agreed on roles of the meeting.
7. No one can be thrown out of the meeting. No one can interrupt anyone who has the floor. Parents cannot assert any authority.

In the family council a member of methodological-procedural problems exist and some of them are as follows:

1. Usually parents, especially fathers, tend to dominate the early meetings. Parents must be very careful not to speak more than their exact mathematical share of the time.
2. The first sessions tend to be nonproductive and parents must be careful not to be discouraged.
3. Parents are highly likely to violate democratic procedures, such as when the father, as a member of the group, suddenly asserts his authority and tells another member to "shut up."
4. Parents should be careful to live up to the spirit and the word of decisions made by the group.
5. Parents should be careful to avoid making any decisions that really should be made by the total group: this means any decision that can affect others.

The Value of the Family Council. By its proper use, depending only on the intelligence, goodwill and common sense of the entire family, any family can raise itself by its own bootstraps and "cure" many of its ills through this democratic way of communicating and settling issues. The anger and violence that is a natural concomitant of an undemocratic family, the sneaking about and lying so common in many families, the distrust and bad feelings that are inherent in many families and, above all, the constant bickering found in every undemocratic family can be replaced by order, good humor and good relationships simply by using the family council properly.

Parent Study Groups

Another form of parent education consists of parent study groups. Ordinarily, these groups function more or less like a Great Books course, with the leader being a parent who organizes the group, which includes from a half dozen to a dozen people. The instructor is the textbook used. The three most popular books appear to be Dreikurs and Soltz's *Children: The Challenge,* Dinkmeyer and McKay's *Raising a Responsible Child* and Corsini and Painter's *The Practical Parent.*

The usual way of operating is to have the contents of the book divided into sections, and every week a different chapter or set of chapters is discussed. The leader is not seen as an expert, and all questions are referred back to the text.

There is no way of estimating how many such self-help groups exist in this country, but at any one time during the school season, there are probably well over 1,000 such groups of people learning about parenting on their own.

The parent study group itself is a democratic undertaking. Certainly, its value comes from the knowledge and techniques learned in the texts. Yet there is additional value from the give-and-take of ideas about the text, and the finding of common problems with other parents and the working out of solutions with them.

Whether through improved parenting through study, family counseling or family therapy, the underlying assumption of intervention to remediate child or adolescent problems is well stated by Willard and Marguerite Beecher (1955/1966): "We operate on the policy that the mistaken over-all family relationship, that misled the child in the first place, has to be restructured if the child is to be put on a more constructive path. If the child has not been brought into line with social demands for self-reliance and cooperation, there is a mistake in the *whole family gestalt*" (p. 176).

Marriage Counseling

There are a number of ways for couples to come into marriage counseling. They may, one or both, feel that there is something wrong with their marriage and come for help. Very frequently, they come for help with a "problem" child and in the course of treatment the problem is seen as lying within the family system and particularly within the interactions between, and relationship of, the parents. Sometimes an individual comes for help and the marriage partner is brought in, either because the partner's assistance is needed in changing the situation for the good of the client, or because change in the partner is what is called for—the client is relatively OK.

What is marriage counseling—therapy, counseling, or education? It may be any and all. Therefore, the full range of techniques applicable to other counseling and therapy situations is useful in marriage counseling. Sometimes marriage counseling is carried out with both partners present, sometimes with each alone, and back and forth. The therapist must ascertain, as far as possible, what the intention of each of the partners is. Certainly the obvious reason for coming for marriage counseling—to improve the marriage—may be uppermost in the minds of both partners. Quite often, however, other goals or intents are primary. One or both partners may want to "prove," in front of the other, how right one is and the other isn't. One may want to show that the other's values or habits are wrong and destroying the marriage. This desire may be primary; only secondarily is the future of the marriage considered. The therapist must consider the life styles of the partners and the interaction of the life styles. If the "accuser" has a goal of being right, the accusations may be false and the marriage problem may be more pathological. If the "accused" has a view of the world which says he or she has no place and the hostile world pushes one around, the accusations may be demanded by the life style. There is the full range of combinations of life styles in marriages and the Adlerian family counselor must work with each partner on changing life style and on understanding the spouses' life style to make a better match.

One of the elements thought to be important in predicting the viability of marriages is the family constellations, especially birth order, of each of the two partners. Toman's theory which predicts "better" and "worse" matches makes some sense on a probabilistic basis within Adlerian theory. "Toman (1959) proposed that *(a)* people tend to select marital partners from sibling positions that are complementary to their own in both seniority/juniority and sex; and *(b)* those marriages which are based upon complementarity have a greater chance of success than do others" (Birtchnell & Mayhew, 1977, p. 18). The research support for Toman's theory is at best mixed, but the notions are worth keeping in mind. That is exactly what an Adlerian marriage counselor would do. The counselor would be making idiographic analyses of each partner's life style, including family constellation, and investigating and exploring the extent of the basic mistakes for pathology and the clash of goals for the potential of marital harmony.

It is probable that any two people, with any two life styles, could live together and maintain their marriage. The question is whether they would want to, and whether the effort, which may be immense, is worth it to either or both. "To quote Adler, 'It is not a question of whether one or the other is right or wrong but whether they want peace.' Therefore it is very helpful for the counseling process to ascertain whether the partners basically want to maintain their marriage" (Deutsch, 1956, p. 78).

The partners may not know whether they want to keep their marriage going. Their movement within their marriage may be so much a function of their life style, goals, and mistaken beliefs that they have no view of what a desirable outcome would be for them. Harper (1960) lists some irrational beliefs common to, he says nearly universal to, marriage and family problems. These irrational beliefs would cohere with the individual's life style and would necessitate an educational process within the therapeutic process. Two examples of these irrational beliefs are:

Irrational Belief No. 1. It is absolutely essential for my mate to love and respect me, no matter how stupidly, boringly, or annoyingly I behave, and, if he (or she) does not, then we do not have real and true and deep and lasting love in our marriage and things are positively calamitous. . . .
Irrational Belief No. 2. If my spouse and I loved each other truly at the time of marriage, then the love would be everlasting and our relationship positively wonderful. Conversely, if serious problems arise and persist, then we did not love

each other enough, obviously, or things like this would never have happened. (Harper, 1960, p. 203)

Deutsch (1956) well sums up the Adlerian view of marriage counseling:

The purpose of marriage counseling . . . is to demonstrate that apparently irreconcilable differences are symptoms of personality disorders in one or both partners, and can be overcome by an indeterministic approach. . . . It is our task to de-dramatize situations and thus help a client to bring more objectivity towards the role he is playing in this 'human comedy.' Alleviating thus his guilt feelings, we can activate positive attitudes and courage for shared responsibility. Although this type of counseling has a definite therapeutic effect, it may often serve only to detect underlying causes and to prepare for further psychotherapy, especially in cases where the disturbance stems from a deepseated neurosis or psychosis. (p. 83)

Marriage counseling holds the potential for improving individual lives in or out of the existing marriage and getting people what they want—to be in or out of the existing marriage.

Marriage Conferences

Corsini (1970b) has suggested a method for couples' communication, a technique which can be of help with couples who are in a power contest. Essentially, the system goes in the following steps:

1. The couples agree to read instructions about the conference.
2. They then agree to follow the instructions strictly with no deviations.
3. Then they settle on four one-hour conferences at a time mutually convenient, when likely not to be interrupted, and when both are reasonably fresh.
4. Both meet at the appointed place at the proper time, and then on the minute the woman begins first by talking (if she wants to) for exactly 30 minutes.
5. Meantime, the husband must sit still, no moving or smoking, or interrupting—nothing, just listening, for a half hour, at which time (a clock is in view of both) she stops.
6. The man now has a half-hour for himself and now the woman must listen to him for a half-hour.
7. Neither can leave the room for the hour even if neither said anything during the whole period.
8. Following the first and second and third sessions, neither husband or wife is to refer to anything mentioned, during the sessions, between

sessions. (This is probably the most difficult and most important part of this system.)

9. The next scheduled session takes place with the husband leading off.
10. The third and fourth sessions are like the first and second.
11. Following the fourth session, the couple usually returns to the marriage counselor who suggested this artificial communication system in the first place and reports results. They may go through another round, and this time they are permitted to vary the procedures, say, having less than a half-hour.

In reporting on this method of self-improvement, a number of couples have reported gaining greater understanding of their mates and learning how to respect the other. This forced listening, and having someone who will pay attention to you for a full half-hour, is unusual for some couples.

Choice of Mate

Research in marriage plus experience of marriage counselors shows some rather interesting "facts" about marriage, happy and unhappy. One of these has to do with mate selection, which is probably the single most important life decision ever made by any person. A most fascinating apparent conflict seems to exist. On the one hand, all the solid research on marriage comes to one conclusion: the happiest marriages are between people who are basically alike. These are the findings of Burgess and others (Burgess & Cottrell, 1939: Kelley, 1941; Terman, 1938) in terms of social factors, historical factors, and personality factors. On the other hand, "love"—that is, romantic love, seems to be a function of the meeting of needs. Thus, for example, if a young man has a need for someone to listen to him and if a young woman has a need for looking up to someone, the two are likely to fall in love.

Technically, the first of the two "findings" is known as homogamy and the second heterogamy. So, what we have is the scientific fact that similars get along best and the romantic fact that you want to marry the one you are in love with.

Ideally, the solution might seem to be that we ought to marry only those who are similar to us in such matters as age, religious ideas, socioeconomic backgrounds, cultural factors, political/economic values, hobbies, interests, and the like *and* with whom one is in love. The unfortunate fact seems to be that the very reasons one marries a person are the very reasons one divorces that person. To give an example: Tim married Helen because she was *(a)* thrifty, *(b)* quiet, and *(c)* a good housekeeper. He divorced her after some years of marriage because she was *(a)* a miser, *(b)* had no conversation, and *(c)* had no interests outside the home.

About the most we can say as Adlerians about the choice of a mate is nothing but common sense:

1. Do not marry in haste. A long acquaintanceship and a long engagement is desirable. Get to know the person in depth.
2. If you marry, you are likely to not only marry the person but also your intended's family and friends. If you don't like either, keep away.
3. The single most important part of marriage is conversation. The time spent talking with one another will be considerably more than that spent on anything else. So, if before marriage you do not have good solid conversations, watch out. If either is much brighter or more verbal than the other, this can be a cause for discontent.
4. Attempt to get opinions of family and friends about the other person. They can often see what you cannot.
5. Try to get away with the other person for as long a period as possible, in a kind of pre-honeymoon, say on a camping trip, or other situation of a group type or even alone, to see how the two of you can stand each other for long periods of time.
6. Try to be with each other in a wide variety of situations, not always in the same environment, that is, on the job, at each others' homes and at a restaurant, but also in parks, on beaches, and on trips.
7. Remember that each of you is on your best behavior and that unconsciously each of you is trying to impress the other. This is why dropping in at unexpected times, being together for long periods, and so forth, can be of great value in making judgments.
8. Keep in mind that marriage counselors frequently find that the very thing that you like most about a person before you marry is the very thing that you may dislike most after you are married, and try to imagine having too much attention, or affection, or anything else.

Growing in Groups

As must be clear at this point, Adlerian psychology always stresses the social nature of persons' thoughts, behavior, and feelings. Moreover, Adlerian psychology has emphasized the ways in which the environment, from the microscopic level of family to the macroscopic level of society and civilization, affects the individual in the creation of his or her life style and the healthfulness of goals. Adler's (1964a) *Social Interest* and Dreikurs' (1971) *Social Equality: The Challenge of Today* strongly indicate the potential thrust of Adlerian thinking into the realm of societal restructuring, toward more democratic, egalitarian, cooperative modes. Adlerian psychology has not, as yet, substantially altered society. However, in psychiatric milieus, in groups, and as will be seen in Chapter 15, "Education," in classrooms and schools, Adlerian psychology has attempted to provide and structure environments in keeping with mental health principles as defined by social interest and responsible, useful behavior.

Encounter Groups

The essential difference between an encounter group and a therapy group has to do with the status of the people in the two groups. According to Shapiro (1978), "the focus in encounter groups is generally interpersonal, whereas the focus in a therapy group is generally more intrapsychic" (p. 12).

It is evident that Adlerians would be attracted to groups that are focused on interpersonal as well as intrapsychic aspects. However, there has been relatively little mention of encounter groups in the Adlerian literature. Corsini (1970) indicates that many such groups are nothing more than disguised orgies. O'Connell (1971) also decries some of the mistaken practices of people in the encounter group movement.

Both Corsini and O'Connell have run encounter groups on an experimental basis. Corsini calls his process "Awareness Training Institutes" and O'Connell calls his "Encouragement Labs." However, to date, there has been no great effort on or acceptance of encounter procedures by Adlerians. This is probably true because of a general conservative aspect of Adlerians. They are usually willing to try anything that makes sense. However, they tend not to become committed to anything that appears "faddish" or useless and therefore they wait until sufficient evidence has been achieved to indicate the process is really worthwhile.

Adlerians could be said to still be struggling with the techniques, aims and implications of the entire encounter group and self-awareness movement. In a review of Schur's (1975) *The Awareness Trap: Self-absorption instead of Social Change,* Manaster (1977) points out how bothered Adlerians must be by Schur's conclusion that "current awareness thinking ignores social context (especially social class), blunts social purpose, and threatens to obliterate the last vestiges of social responsibility."

Chapter 15

Education

There is probably no better illustration of Adler's sense of purpose, his lofty aims, and his social interest than his efforts in education. As Adler developed his personality theory, it became increasingly evident that the creation of the life style was affected by environment, especially the family. To whatever degree the interactions within the family and greater environment of the child were faulty, on the useless side of life, there was an increased tendency for the child to develop faulty values and goals. However effective therapy and counseling might be, Adler believed that there was no way to cure everyone after the damage had been done. Although the effort was worthwhile, it was unlikely that all parents could be reached and sufficiently well taught so that all children would have the opportunity of developing their life styles in a faultless environment. The best opportunity for remediating faulty life styles of children therefore is through the schools.

Adler attacked the issue on all fronts. He initiated the process and his followers continue to treat individuals in groups, and to educate children and parents. He attacked the problem of mental health through education in the broadest sense and began "teaching the teachers." This approach took two directions simultaneously: to teach the teachers to deal with individual children to prevent and correct basic mistakes, and to teach teachers to run classrooms by methods which held maximum promise for promoting social interest and thereby mental health.

Adler worked with Otto Spiel (1956, 1962) and Ferdinand Birnbaum (1935a, 1935b) in developing Individual Psychological experimental schools in Vienna. They put their understandings of Individual Psychology into practice in the classroom. That work has continued in other settings and countries since that day.

The primary proponent of Individual Psychology applied to classrooms was Rudolf Dreikurs (1968, 1971) who, with a large group of followers, trained hundreds of teachers and further developed the techniques of Adlerian psychology in the classroom. The most recent development in this area has to do with application of Adlerian principles on a schoolwide basis. This system is called Individual Education.

ADLER'S EDUCATION OF CHILDREN

The following two quotations from Adler's (1930a), *The Education of Children,* encapsulate his position regarding education:

> When a child is robbed of his faith in the future, the result is that he withdraws from reality and builds up a compensatory striving on the useless side of life. An educator's most important task—one might almost say his holy duty—is to see to it that no child is discouraged at school, and that a child who enters school already discouraged regains his confidence in himself through his school and his teacher. This goes hand in hand with the vocation of the educator, for no education is possible except with children who look hopefully and joyfully upon the future. (p. 84)

* * * * *

> In the rearing of children there are some things which the parent or teacher must never allow to discourage him. He must never grow hopeless because his efforts do not meet with immediate success; he must not anticipate defeat because the child is lethargic or apathetic or extremely passive; he must not permit himself to be influenced by the superstition that there are gifted or ungifted children. (p. 227)

Two crucial points in Adlerian child-rearing methods and philosophy and Adlerian education are underscored here. The first has to do with heredity—limitations and possibilities imposed on individuals by innate capacity. Adler did not deny individual differences. Rather, he said, "In Individual Psychology we have insisted that the mind experiences the degree of ability possessed by the organ and has to reckon with it. Sometimes the mind reckons too much with it—in that it gets frightened by some organic disability, and the fright lasts long after the organic cause is removed" (Adler, 1970, p. 176).

In this statement he recognizes that limits on ability are physiologically imposed. But, most importantly, he says that dwelling on limits produces the effect of keeping the notion of limited ability operating beyond what is necessary. He ingeniously points out after the above statement that if we look only at parents, any individual has 64 ancestors in the prior 5 generations and 4,096 ancestors in the prior 10 generations. If we wished, each of us could find hereditary bases for our strengths and weaknesses.

His point dealing with heredity is that dwelling on physiological limits will only intensify the weakness. Dwelling on strengths and potentials allows parents, teachers, and children to look for, find, and build on strengths and potentials.

His second crucial point is that "next to the idea of heredity the problem that causes the greatest difficulties for the child is the punishment for bad school reports" (1970, p. 177). He saw that "punishment is regarded by the child as confirmatory of his feeling that he does not belong in school" (p. 56). There is no way that punishment can be encouraging. If an optimistic child comes to school and is punished, he loses his optimism. If a negative, pessimistic child comes to school and is punished, he is reinforced in his pessimism.

To encourage and not discourage the child is the aim of the educational process. Ansbacher and Ansbacher in Adler (1956) list the functions of the teacher with regard to the individual child as systematized by Spiel (1956). The teacher must look at the child's behavior in all its forms and interpret it, making contact with the child and showing understanding of the child without punishing him. The teacher must convey these understandings to the child so that the child with personal insight may be reeducated. "The teacher's overall function is that of a stage-director or producer who must carefully arrange situations so that they become educationally valuable" (Adler, 1956, p. 404).

In this regard Adler stressed the organization of the class as a unit to establish social interest and cooperation through a sort of benevolent guidance in an egalitarian, openly discussed, democratic, self-governing problem-solving mode. Much of what we now think of as new educational methods were used by Adler and his followers in their experimental schools, including such developments as sociometric methods, group dynamics, discussion and counseling, student-centered teaching, and peer teaching.

Adler really did not differentiate greatly between lay people and professionals in the knowledge and understandings he saw as necessary for effectively dealing with children. Certainly there were differences in the sophistication of techniques used by parents, teachers, and therapists, but the essential understandings of the child were the same. His basic philosophy for running a respectful, egalitarian, cooperative family was not really different from the philosophy for running a classroom or, for that matter, for the proper operation of society. It has fallen on his followers to amplify his philosophy into more specific techniques for practice with children for parents and teachers.

DREIKURS' PSYCHOLOGY IN THE CLASSROOM

Rudolf Dreikurs' contribution to the theory and practice of Individual Psychology in classroom management was immense. In the field of education and child rearing he predicted the "war between the generations," a systematic exposition of the basic principles in raising children, a listing of the common mistakes in raising children, a systematization of the efficient methods of training children and resolution of the power conflict, and formulations on principles and methods of encouragement (Shulman & Dreikurs, 1978).

Dreikurs saw the most common mistakes in child training including spoiling the child, lovelessness, excessive affection, withdrawal of affection, frightening the child, excessive supervision and talking, nagging and faultfinding, neglect, and physical punishment (Dreikurs, 1948).

The most efficient methods of training children and the principles for improving relationships form a technical and philosophical unity on which parents, teachers, and counselors may act. The methods include maintaining order, avoiding conflict, and encouraging the child.

Maintaining order is built on the principles of natural and logical consequences, taking time for training, consistency, and avoiding the fallacy of the efficacy of first impulses, stimulating independence, disregarding the influence of other adults, setting the stage, and having fun together.

Avoiding conflict demands adherence to the principles of using actions instead of words, using firmness without domination, the efficacy of withdrawal, understanding the child's goals, withdrawing from provocation but not from the child, and noninterference in children's fighting.

Encouraging as a method is also a general principle and calls for the inducing of compliance *and* respect, minimizing mistakes—their significance and specialness—recognizing the danger of eliciting pity for and/or self-pity in the child; instilling mutual confidence through mutual endeavors; and disclosures and family organization principally through the Family Council.

All of these methods and principles lead to the conclusive generalized approach to dealing with children which Dreikurs referred to as "effective democratic methods" (Dreikurs, Grunwald, & Pepper, 1971). Of particular note in these methods is their continuation of the tradition of Adler with stress on the deleterious effects of punishment in the classroom.

NATURAL AND LOGICAL CONSEQUENCES:
A SUBSTITUTE FOR REWARD AND PUNISHMENT

"Punishment is always ineffective; it can do nothing but confirm the opinion, 'Others are against me' " (Adler, 1956, p. 370).

Dreikurs (1942), speaking about the "Four Freedoms," eloquently explains the negative function of punishment in education.

> Fear is very often not caused by real dangers; even death loses its terror for those who have developed courage . . . Courage [the], confidence in one's own strength, is the only antidote for fear. . . . Persecution and oppression are consequences of fear as well as causes. Only frightened people suppress others. Worse than famine

and disease is the fear of losing social status, of being less than the next fellow. This fear engulfs children competing with [siblings] and rebelling against parents who either pamper or oppress them. Bringing up children without fear might prove to be more important even than teaching them to read or write. . . . How far from developing freedom from fear are educators who deliberately use fear as an educational method, who are convinced that only fear of punishment, fear of humiliation, fear of the consequences can prevent children from misbehaving? . . . [Such a teacher] wears only the title of educator without being one. (Terner & Pew, 1978, p. 201)

The idea of natural and logical consequences builds on the common sense folk wisdom of letting someone "suffer the consequences" of their actions. The use of natural and logical consequences is as appropriate for teachers as it is for parents. The definitions and principles are the same. As natural consequences are let to occur, logical consequences result from actions of others within a predefined context. Bullard (1973) presents some principles of logical consequences:

1. The consequences must be *logical.* . . .
2. The severity of the consequences must be appropriate to the violation. . . .
3. The rule being violated must have general and reasonably long-time acceptance, especially in the eyes of the one experiencing the consequences.
4. The rules must apply equally to all.
5. The rules must relate to and stem from the social order and not from the capricious whims of adults (p. 173).

Bullard further makes an essential point about the use of natural and logical consequences, which is very much in keeping with the spirit of applied Adlerian psychology—the parent or teacher must be sincere and empathetic, feeling that the outcomes are necessary but sorry that the child has brought the consequences on himself. Bullard also points out that it is not necessary for the child to differentiate between logical and natural consequences. Therefore, the teacher should probably not make this distinction but, rather, refer solely to "consequences" in class councils and class discussions.

THE CLASSROOM AS A GROUP

Group methods in counseling and therapy, and now in classrooms, are widely used by professionals of all theoretical persuasions. Since Adlerian psychology has such a broad personality theory, which integrates and explains the individual and society and their interrelationships, the use of group methods makes particular sense and is very effective.

Dreikurs, Grunwald, and Pepper (1971) begin their discussion of the group as an effective democratic method of working with children by placing groups and group membership squarely within the context of Adlerian theory, saying: "One of the characteristics common to all human beings is the need to feel that he belongs—that is, the need and capacity for association with other persons" (p. 90). The need to belong as a felt need of all individuals is one aspect of the utility of group methods in the classroom. There is a need for all members of any group to belong to the group in order for the group to exist and function well—the other aspect of the use of group methods in education. The individual needs to belong to the group and the group needs each and all individuals to belong.

Integration of the needs of the individual and of the group is evident in all of Bernice Grunwald's presentations. She stresses group discussion effectiveness in integrating all children into one class for a common purpose. The focus is on the problem in relation to everyone, and not just on the problem and one child. The purpose is common to all; the task is bigger than any one person can manage; the group needs the individual and the individual needs the group. The classroom becomes a microcosm of society. As the family has been a microcosm of society for the child until the child came to school, the classroom becomes his or her outlet to and knowledge base for the greater society. A teacher who understands the need to belong and associate with others can assist the child within the group and into the group.

"The skilled teacher, sensitive to the group atmosphere, will sense the type of atmosphere her new class has and plan a constructive program through which she can gradually change the children's attitudes. The climate of the classroom reflects the personal characteristics of all and influences in turn the development of each child emotionally, academically, and socially" (Dreikurs et al. 1971, pp. 93–94).

As Sonstegaard (1958) pointed out, the educational process involves teaching groups, a number of individuals at the same time. A teacher must be able to utilize the group not only for the good of the individual children within the classroom and to promote the class as a group, but also for her own good. Dreikurs and Soltz (1964) point out that the "frequent inability" of most teachers "to integrate all children in a cohesive classroom group is the more deplorable since . . . hostile interests of goals make for a high degree of cohesiveness. Consequently, children who oppose the educational process and are defiant and antagonistic have a superior ability to create group cohesiveness, which then is naturally directed against the teacher, particularly if [the teacher] does not exert leadership and cannot establish a favorable teaching climate" (p. 193).

Grunwald and Dreikurs are both saying that not only are group procedures in the classroom positive for education and development of the child, but that without their proper use, classroom education can be seriously impeded.

Group discussions are really quite natural in most situations. They have not seemed natural in the classroom primarily because of the authoritarian stance of many teachers. As teachers come to see themselves as leaders of a group of which they are a part, discussions make more sense and come more easily. Teachers who shy away from group discussions usually make one or both of two kinds of mistakes. They may feel unable to properly lead the group and therefore revert to a "traditional" teaching style of lecturing and preaching. They may, on the other hand, bend over backward not to be the boss of the group and just let the discussion go wild. Without leadership and the focus, ground rules and guidance that a leader will give, classroom group discussions can get out of hand. When this happens, the teacher will feel compelled to once again take control. Either extreme, over-or underleading, thwarts the aim and process of group discussions.

Some teachers avoid group discussions because they do not believe that children have the ability to understand each other and the dynamics of the group. Experience with group discussions and experience with children treated as capable shows clearly that this is not the case.

Group discussions may be fit into almost any learning situation or subject area in the class, although specific subject areas such as personal problems and the class council may best be held at set times. Dreikurs et al. (1971) state that "sometimes it is valuable to stop everything and have a discussion concerning a particular child's actions or to share a particular event or happening" (p. 105). The examples they use of events or happenings are Kennedy's assassination or election results. Clearly, dramatic, unusual events have a place in class discussion, and this format could be most useful for diminishing tension when the event has the potential for fomenting exceptional excitement or distress.

However, we believe that stopping a class for a discussion over minor events and happenings, particularly those which occur in class, is not useful. First, stopping work on a task to discuss a particular person's behavior is contrary to the common sense of communal living. It is not a natural or logical consequence, in the Adlerian sense, for progress to be stopped because of unruly or emotional behavior. It appears to us that there is very real potential for abuse of group discussion if it is used to correct individuals' disruptive behavior. In fact, by ceasing other work to deal with a child's action, by definition, we are making that child's actions disruptive. Issues of this sort should be dealt with according to the rules and consequences known within the class. Discussion of these behaviors should occur at the set time for such discussions.

Another method Adlerian-trained teachers use to assist children in understanding behavior is to use fictional stories as the meat of group discussions of behavior and misbehavior.

Role playing is also used by Adlerian-trained teachers for a number of purposes, all of which have the ultimate goal of solving relationship problems through greater understanding of behavior. Teachers may use role playing as a way of reporting, thereby illustrating the way in which problems developed in the class. Role playing is often used as a means of problem solving (Grunwald, 1969). Children can learn, among other things, that problems usually have more than one solution, that different solutions are equally appropriate, and that some solutions are better for some people and other solutions better for others. The teacher can, through close observation, learn many things about each child. There are a great variety of other techniques which may be used in role playing.

Techniques have been developed by Dreikurs (1968) and his followers for teachers to utilize all of these group methods. These techniques could certainly help the teacher who is a novice in this area. However, it is not absolutely necessary to learn the techniques prior to trying to run class discussions. An understanding of children's behavior, social interest, and a general ability to get along with kids should be sufficient. A respectful teacher attempting to lead a group discussion for the general good will probably be picked up by her or his students if she stumbles. On the other hand, role playing requires training. Role playing can be useful and can be fun. It can also be a quite powerful and intense experience. Without training a teacher could find herself with a situation she does not feel able to handle.

INDIVIDUAL EDUCATION

Until recently the major thrust of Adlerian psychology in the schools has been on training the teachers and the organization of the *classroom* as a working group, an experience group, a discussion group, and a help group. The class community, democratically organized, fostering social interest, involved in education in the broadest sense, was the focus of the Individual Psychological Experimental School in Vienna and the noted Gordon School of Tel Aviv (Dreikurs, 1974).

A recent development in the Adlerian approach to education involves *the entire school.* The principles of Adlerian psychology and education are implemented in Individual Education in the organization of the whole school, and the classroom is no longer the central focus as in the past. The most complete basic readings on Individual Education are found in a special issue of the *Journal of Individual Psychology* (1977); a training manual called *Individual Education: An Introduction,* by Edward Ignas (1978); and a chapter in *Alternative Educational Systems* (1979), edited by Ignas and Corsini. We will attempt to outline the operation of an Individual Education school, giving the theoretical rationale for the procedures, and relating them to Adlerian theory and philosophy.

Theory

Royce Van Norman, of Towson State University, wrote:

> It is not ironical that in a planned society of controlled workers given compulsory assignments, where religious expression is suppressed, the press controlled, and all media of communication censored, where great attention is given to efficiency and character reports, and attendance at cultural assemblies is compulsory, where it is avowed that all will be administered to each according to abilities, and where those who flee are tracked down, returned, and punished for trying to escape—in short in the milieu of the typical large American secondary school —we attempt to teach "the democratic system."

We thoroughly agree that this situation is ironical: that in a democratic country the educational system is authoritarian and autocratic. This is probably the fundamental reason why there is so much dissatisfaction with traditional education.

A school principal asked whether a complete educational system based on the Adlerian model could be developed. After a period of three years of planning, the system, called Individual Education, was perfected and instituted in 1972 at Our Lady of Sorrows School in Wahiawa, a small town in Hawaii.

The goal of Individual Education is to achieve the normal aims of traditional schools; achievement of the fundamentals of communication and computation and a basic knowledge of science, social science, and the humanities; as well as the development of a healthy self and a cooperative social attitude. While the traditional school may accomplish academic goals, it does neglect social and psychological aspects of the total individual. The full goals of Individual Education are the Four Rs—Responsibility, Respect, Resourcefulness, and Responsiveness.

Responsibility. On the assumptions that behavior is self-determined, and that children do learn for themselves and make their own sense out of the world within the context of their knowledge of their environment, Adlerian parents, as we have seen, allow children to experience the consequences of their actions and bear that responsibility. Responsibility in the same manner is achieved in the Individual Education system by giving children responsibility for their own education—children have to make the decision explicitly to attend the school, to follow the rules and decide what and if they will learn.

In traditional American education children are legally bound to attend an assigned school and must follow imposed rules. In the Individual Education system children are given information about the school and its rules and operation and must show an understanding and decide whether they want to attend and whether they agree to follow the rules. If they do not understand or are hesitant or ambivalent about attendance or the rules, the children will not be allowed to attend an Individual Education school.

Children cannot learn what they are unable to learn and will become bored —turned off—if they are taught what they already know; they will not learn what they do not want to learn. In Individual Education the child is given guidance through testing and feedback, but the child decides which classes he or she wants to take, at what level, when, and if. This may be an unnerving notion for parents and teachers. Adults so often feel that it is their responsibility to see that the child learns and what the child learns. The theory herein is that learning is the child's area of responsibility and that through accepting this responsibility the child will not only learn more in an academic sense, but will also learn that achievements and failures belong to the individual; they are not someone else's fault.

Respect.   In a healthy functioning democratic society, according to Individual Psychology, equality is the basic principle. We can acknowledge individual differences, strengths and weaknesses, expertise and areas of ignorance, and still base our interactions and interpersonal evaluations on equal value for all individuals as a right of existence. In Individual Education there are simple rules of discipline and organization, no rewards for achievement, no reports to parents except with the child's permission, no competition. The child is given frequent guidance and feedback about performance and encouragement to proceed according to his or her own best interests and judgment. The child is treated with respect and all members of the Individual Education partnership—other students, teachers, parents, and administrators—are due equal respect.

Resourcefulness.   As seen in Adler's typology of active/passive, useful/useless (constructive/destructive), the healthiest type or style is the active-useful. This means making maximum use of one's potential and the potential of the environment in all of the life tasks. In the traditional school, the child is assigned prescribed academic materials to learn, given specific homework, and made to take particular extracurricular courses in keeping with parents' values, such as violin, piano, or the current "in" sports, such as gymnastics and diving. An Individual Education school is designed to allow children to choose classes they wish to learn, at the level where they feel comfortable, both in traditional academic subjects and in a full range of creative subjects which are offered by the school or which the children request. Individual Education is designed to foster the child's resourcefulness by providing a full learning environment in creative subjects the child would like to learn.

Responsiveness.   This goal refers directly to the Adlerian concept of social interest, and means being responsive to the needs of others. Although responsibility, respect, and resourcefulness are all conducive to social interest, in the concept of responsiveness the totality of social interest emerges. Responsiveness in an Individual Education school comes out of the spirit of noncompetitiveness, the cooperative attitude of all, the sum of individuals—students-teachers-parents-principals—working to put together the "best" school they can, the school which provides for all, the school that takes care of the common good of all and the good of each. Responsiveness is the sum of carings—caring for the school, caring for each other. In the homeroom when children meet in small groups with the teacher to discuss problems of individual children, the problems become the group's problems and each cares to help and cares for each other. In developing creative classes, students who want to have a particular course taught want to share their enthusiasm as well as to assure that the class is taught to a sufficient number of children. The entire atmosphere of a school should exude this spirit of caring, with all persons feeling that they belong because they have chosen to belong and are working to improve the school to which they are associated, and to get the most out of it. "Every single feature of Individual Education should contribute to all four goals—no feature should in any way impede any of these four goals" (Corsini, 1979, p. 211). The three major aspects of an Individual Education school are its academic program, its creative program, and its socialization activities—each of which attends to the four goals—the Four Rs.

The Academic Program

The academic curriculum is the same as at other schools. Subjects are taught in weekly units. Each unit has a unit curriculum explanation sheet which students can use to learn what is taught in the unit, and at the end of the week each child is tested to see whether that unit has been learned.

Entering students are given standard scholastic achievement tests. These are interpreted and discussed with them by their counselor. The student then decides which subjects to take and at what level.

The students may decide that although they tested at expected normal grade level (that is average for their age) in all academic areas, they may feel very confident in language arts and social science so they begin to attend units which are further along academically in these subjects. The child may feel less confident in mathematics and science and can begin these at a lower level.

Each unit ends with a test which is clearly in line with the stated objectives on the unit curriculum sheet. Units vary in length from one period that week to five periods. Children taking all possible academic subjects will usually take about four unit tests weekly.

When a unit test is passed, this is marked on the student's progress chart. The student and counselor have copies of the progress chart. The progress chart, by illustrating only success—that is, those units which the student has successfully completed—becomes a noncompetitive and positive report for the student and the student's parents, if the student wishes to share the progress report with them. Students are encouraged, but not required, to show these progress charts to the parents.

Students attend classes at their own discretion—since they have chosen to take the unit. They only take the unit test at their request. Thus, the teachers are faced with a group of students whose stated intent is to learn the subject. The teacher's task is to teach the subject. As will be seen in the discussions of socialization and discipline, the teacher, when teaching academics, only teaches academics. There is no breaking for discussions of class problems or dealing with unruliness.

The academic program consumes about one third of the day, and yet findings on Individual Education show that children learn as much or more in approximately two hours of this unadulterated academic program as they do in the six hours supposedly devoted to teaching in the traditional school.

The Creative Program

Theoretically, the array of classes in the creative program may include anything. The choice of what is taught depends on the interests of the teachers and students, the availability of persons in the geographic area interested in and able to teach the class, and the approval of the principal. Students may express an interest in learning about anything—aviation, driving, astronomy, cooking, chess, macrame, and so on. Teachers may put up sign-up sheets for classes they wish to teach—or learn while teaching. The principal will attempt to match what students want to learn and what teachers want to teach. Possibly students, and also teachers, want to learn something about which they are all ignorant. The principal may find a parent who knows about a particular subject and who is willing to conduct the class. Former students, now in high school or college, sometimes come back to conduct creative classes at an Individual Education school which they formerly attended. The creative program may include learning about and in the community—visiting institutions, agencies, facilities in the area, possibly working or helping out in nearby companies, farms, or offices. Parents might drive the children to these places. Also, the creative program may include special tutoring or advanced labs in academic subjects for students who are especially excited by these subjects.

Corsini (1977) points out some of the values of the creative program:

> (1) it engenders love of learning; (2) it introduces people to life-long vocational and avocational activities; (3) it keeps people happily busy at constructive activities; (4) it generates feelings of competency and self-regard; (5) it enhances the importance of academic information (for example, to cook from a cookbook one

must be able to read); (6) it helps to develop warm interpersonal relations (as when teachers and children work and learn together on an equal basis, . . .); and (7) it represents a happy time which generates the feeling of school spirit. (pp. 312–313)

The Socialization Activities

The entire organization of the Individual Education school is aimed at encouragement and socialization. The importance of these aspects of education is so great that one third of the school day is demarcated for them.

The "homeroom" is the heart of the socialization activities. Each child chooses a faculty member as a homeroom teacher, called the "teacher/adviser" (TA), who acts as the *school parent*. The homeroom is run entirely democratically, with the TA having the equal obligation of using his or her persuasive powers and wisdom for guidance as well as protection of the children from danger or harm. The homeroom period is the first of the day and its activities are greatly the result of the decisions of the group, for it is learning to live democratically and cooperatively which is the reason for its existence. To facilitate the democratic activities of the homeroom, periodic class councils are held, with full parliamentary order.

The teacher/adviser has all information about the child's progress in the academic program and, generally, becomes the child's friend at school. At least once monthly the counselor schedules a one-to-one counseling session with each child. Although the primary purpose of this session is to discuss academic progress, the child or the teacher/adviser can bring up any personal problems for discussion. If these problems are truly difficult and beyond the skill of the teacher/adviser, the TA can request of the principal that a "consultant," a school counselor or other professional be brought in to assist.

On a once-a-week basis, small group discussions are held in the homeroom. The children establish who is to be in each group, with the counselor assisting the children in looking out for the good of everyone and including everyone. These small group discussions follow the same format and logic that group discussions in the classroom do for Adlerians in the traditional classroom.

Representatives from the homeroom attend the School Council, which may consist of half students and half adults or equal thirds of students, parents, and teachers. The council discusses all pertinent issues and presents reports and majority and minority opinions to the principal and school board.

Parents in Individual Education

For a child to attend an Individual Education school, the parents must agree to attend a parent study group run by the school. In this way parents come to understand the principles of sound parenting and of Individual Education.

The intent is to promote a harmony and consistency between home and school —similar adherence to democratic principles and similar understanding of the child.

In Individual Education there is no assigned homework and there are no report cards. The parents cannot take the responsibility for the child's education from the child. Parents can meet with their child's TA with the child in attendance. Children generally show their parents their progress reports and their parents see their enthusiasm over some aspect of their learning—academic or creative. The atmosphere of the home may improve considerably as the parents learn to understand the child and as the child has a respected place in his own life and in the family.

Parents may also be involved in the PTA, run for positions in the School Council, and volunteer to help in creative teaching, monitoring, and driving to special events and community creative activities, and other work around the school.

Discipline—Rules and Consequences

The essence of the rules and consequences of Individual Education is simplicity and clarity. There are three basic school rules:

1. Do nothing that could be dangerous to yourself or others, or which could be harmful to property.
2. During school hours, be under supervision, that is, during "class" time be in a "class" or en route from one supervised place to another (children are allowed to move freely throughout the day).
3. In class, if a teacher points her finger at you and then at the door, leave the room silently and immediately.

The first two of these rules seem self-evident—they constitute the minimum responsibility of the student and the school, to be safe and to be taken care of. The third seems more difficult for many people new to Individual Education to understand. We think its simplicity is misleading, but understood within the system, it makes good sense.

The children are in class at their own choice. They presumably are there to learn. They do not have to be there. They could be anywhere else in the school —in any other class, in the library, the study hall, the gym. The purpose of the class is to learn. The teacher's task is to teach. If a child behaves in a way that in the teacher's opinion interferes with the teaching or learning process, the teacher merely points the child out of the classroom. The child silently leaves and can immediately return, unless the teacher points again at the child who is returning, in which case the child must remain out of the classroom (going to some other supervised area) for the remainder of the session.

What occurs in this situation? The child has done something wrong or incorrect in the teacher's view. The child will almost certainly know what the offense was, and if not, the teacher can explain it later. The teacher ends the offensive behavior by the pointing of her finger. Consequently, the disruption to the teaching process is at an absolute minimum. The child is not castigated, ostracized, or criticized. The child is merely pointed out because his or her behavior was disrespectful, interfering with learning or teaching. If the child follows the rule and silently leaves, no rule has been violated and there are no consequences of violating that teacher's concept of order. The child can decide whether or not to return to the class, to this teacher, to this subject. There is no penalty; there has been no violation.

The child only violates this rule by not leaving when pointed out or by not leaving silently and immediately. Violations of rules are additive and the consequences are clear:

> If you break our rules, you will receive various consequences. Essentially, they are four in number: (1) a conference with your counselor and the principal after a third violation; (2) a conference with the principal, your counselor, and your parents after a sixth violation; (3) suspension for the ninth to the twelfth violations; and (4) consideration for expulsion if there are twelve or more violations. (Corsini, 1977, p. 323)

The discipline procedures are more elaborate than can be presented here, although they are equally clear. Their essence is simplicity and clarity. They are perfectly fair, not only in logic, but also in that they have been presented, understood, and agreed to prior to attendance at the school by every child.

Conclusion

There is student, teacher, administrator and parent satisfaction with student performance in Individual Education. The uniformity of the positive findings is extremely heartening. Although, as stated at the beginning of this section, there may be modifications and improvements in the system, Individual Education, relying on the theory of Individual Psychology, appears to hold great hope for remodeling education with democratic principles, social interest and personal achievement.

Based on six schools' experiences and twenty-five school years, the following six findings appear to be true of Individual Education schools:

1. Children learn more academically in less time.
2. Children like this kind of school.
3. Schools are orderly and disciplined; friendly places.
4. Children get a better education for life.

5. Teachers prefer teaching in IE schools.
6. Parents prefer IE to traditional schools (Ignas, 1978)

We optimistically believe that the growth of use of Individual Education will be logarithmic. As more people learn about it, there will be greater use and enjoyment of this Adlerian-oriented total school system—and this will be one of the major ways of making this a more Adlerian world.

Chapter 16

Individual Psychology: Our Personal Views

RAYMOND J. CORSINI

We have now finished the book. Several people have read the manuscript at various stages and generally we have been getting good reviews. Apparently the book will meet with satisfaction from the people for whom we wrote it.

Nevertheless, I am somewhat dissatisfied with what we did and so is Guy Manaster. We have kept to our plans, and during the five years of this project we have worked well together, had few disagreements and a minimum of hurt feelings (something that almost always occurs in collaboration when X says to Y that he didn't like something that Y thinks is excellent). But why are we dissatisfied now that we are writing this chapter and identifying ourselves? We each have our own specific reasons, and our own personal enthusiasms, and we want to convey them to our readers.

Even though this is, I believe, an accurate and complete (or fairly so) text on Adlerian Psychology, it still is missing something. The book has plenty of intellectual material, and a lot of action material—cognition and behavior— but little emotion. It is too dry. This, I suppose, is what the publisher, college professors, and reviewers expect of a textbook; but it is for this reason that the book is incomplete. I intend now to attempt to fill this gap, at least for myself, with a personal odyssey relative to Individual Psychology—a highly personal statement.

I suppose that one of my enduring but not endearing qualities has been a passionate search for the truth. In my early 20s, after a very, very difficult search, I gave up on the traditional religion that I had been indoctrinated with by a most ferociously devoted mother, finding that I simply could no longer believe in the pantheon of Gods and saints thrust on me. I searched for a personal philosophy in science, and found that it was accurate but vacant.

I felt the need for a means of understanding people, of making sense out of life; this need continues. Through inadvertence, I began to read the work of Trigant Burrow, a most incomprehensible writer. His theoretical position went somewhat as follows: just as every cell of the body is part of the entire body, so, too, the individual human is part of total humanity. Burrow's system, called Phyloanalysis, died, most probably because of his terrible style of writing. But the reading of several of Burrow's books did nothing for me. After this I met a psychologist, Dr. Martin Staiman, who directed me to Alfred Adler, and I read Adler's book, *Study of Organ Inferiority and Its Psychical Compensation* (1917), and recoiled from it. It was so poorly written and the thesis that inferior organs determined personality so offended me with its illogic that I decided to keep away from Adler. Then on to Freud, and at last I found someone who made sense and who wrote interestingly. But as I kept on reading, his writings began to make less and less sense, and finally I gave up in disgust. It seemed to me that Freud himself was sexually maladjusted and hung up on sex. Finally, I latched onto Carl Rogers. He also wrote well, and I found in my practice that his system worked well, even though it was very hard for me to use since I am not at all a nondirective type of person. Rogers' system seemed correct—but incomplete.

Eventually I discovered psychodrama, and indeed I've written three books on the subject of therapeutic role playing but, once again, I found Moreno's theory to be empty, even though his psychodrama seemed quite reasonable and was quite effective. The same with my friend Albert Ellis. I found his disputatious procedure and his general theory to be quite sensible, but there was still, for me, a feeling that his personality theory was partial, not all together. I kept searching for a system of psychology that was entire—that would be not only theory but philosophy, that would not be just an empty process, but that would be a complete system to explain human nature. Behavior modification, for example, was, as such, correct. There could be no argument that it worked, but what was missing was any humanistic orientation. This, it appeared, had to come from outside the system—and so I felt that every psychological system was empty—wrong or missing something important.

What was missing, of course, was the equivalent of religion. I had studied various religions, and I was repelled by their dogmatism as well as the fanaticism of some of their proponents. Something in me rebelled against the basic concepts even though some religions, such as Unitarianism, Judaism, and the Bahai faith, seemed compatible to me as such. What I wanted was something that incorporated science and philosophy, that was sensible, meaningful, entire, and complete.

In 1935, I attended a lecture given by Alfred Adler and I was impressed by his simplicity and self-control. I have reported on the incident of this meeting

(Manaster, Painter, Deutsch, & Overholt, 1977). In 1944 I started a long friendship with Regina Seidler, a former teacher who had worked with Adler in Austria. And finally, in 1953, I first met Rudolf Dreikurs. So—at nine-year intervals I had three contacts with Adler, as it were: in 1935, hearing him and reading his book; in 1944, in sessions with Regina (Mady) Seidler; and, finally, in 1953, with Dr. Dreikurs, who became the single most important influence in my life as a psychologist.

I soon discovered that Individual Psychology filled a void, giving me an understanding of human nature which was superior to that of all other systems, and which gave me in addition a philosophy of life, through the concept of *Gemeinschaftsgefühl,* a concept which Guy and I have presented rather fully in this book.

I began to realize that while Trigant Burrow and Carl Rogers, J. L. Moreno, and Albert Ellis, and many others such as George Kelly, Abraham Maslow, Fritz Perls, Eric Berne, and William Glasser were essentially correct in their assertions, they all were missing the extra ingredient that I had been looking for—a philosophy of life consistent with my own values. Finally, I realized that I now had the key to an understanding of people through Adlerian Psychology. Sure, Freud had discovered important elements, such as the importance of the unconscious—or if he had not discovered it, he had emphasized it; and sure, Jung had gone deeply into the unconscious also, and so forth and so on, but in practically all systems that I had studied there were either evident errors (as in the case of Freud) or there was no system of values as in the case of everyone else, or theirs was a system of values which I did not share, as in the various religiously based psychological systems such as Yoga, but only in Individual Psychology was there both scientific accuracy and a wholesome philosophy built on the same concepts of all mature religions—the concept of complementarity. Christianity had it; Judaism had it; Confucianism had it; but no other personality theory had it, to my knowledge, as an integral component except Individual Psychology, and so I became an Adlerian, a scientist with a value system as part of the personality theory I espoused.

GUY J. MANASTER

Collaborating with Ray Corsini has been many things, but never dull. We have, in writing this book, differed on a number of points of style, content, and interpretation. Our discussions on these points were carried out in person, by phone, in letters, and in the margins and backs of pages on the manuscript. In many instances we taught, or convinced, the other of the correctness of a particular position. In many instances we compromised, we accepted the other's position, because we could see the other's point of view even though we did not totally agree, or we altered a position until it was acceptable to us both.

As we finish the book, I look back on our collaboration and see that it has been a healthy human experience in itself. It has been a commonsensical, normal working relationship. And, it seems to me, it represents Adlerian theory and philosophy operating in everyday life.

At times I was good and angry at Ray, and clearly he was, at times, with me. Sometimes we were really thrilled with a section or example that seemed just right. When I kept Ray waiting for a piece of the manuscript I thought he should understand that I had other things to do. When he kept me waiting I reckoned that our book, or I, was just not that important to him. And I think he felt the same. But we figured it out, worked together, and got along. We did not expect perfection in ourselves or each other; we did not expect to work on a project of this magnitude without hassles; but we did expect that working cooperatively, as equals, we would get the job done relatively happily, and we did.

Walter (Buzz) O'Connell recently sent me a package with a label on the back that read "Unhappiness is not a disease." We never expected to be always happy in this project, or in life. I hope that anyone having read this book recognizes that Adlerians *know* that life is filled with problems, it is in a sense a series of problems and tasks that must be met and accomplished. Problems may be met as natural challenges and attacked with vigor, but not necessarily with joy; and resolved efficiently and effectively, but not necessarily without frustration and unhappiness.

At one level it was this commonsense, realistic aspect of Adlerian theory and philosophy which drew me to it. At another level the idea of Adlerian theory, a society—a world—imbued with social interest, where issues of personal superiority and inferiority were not fomented and augmented by the social structure and social values, was and remains for me very compelling. Attempting to operate within both the Adlerian theory, which allows greater understanding of self and others, and the Adlerian philosophy, which allows striving for perfection in the sense of doing good for a better world, has improved my life considerably—an illustration of which is the collaboration on this book.

In Dr. Corsini's preceding statement he stressed the values implicit and explicit in Individual Psychology as most important to him. I agree completely.

Most other "brands" of psychology are valueless—without values. Most are purposely so. The theorist in an effort to be a "scientist" eliminates values as unscientific or improper, that is, feeling it is wrong to put your values on others. I recognized vaguely in the middle of this century, when I came to Adlerian Psychology—and see clearly as the century draws on—that a set of values—a metaphysic—is necessary to understand others and to live an unconstricted life. It appears to me that the chore of the next decades will be to establish for the Western world humane and substantial values which promote human health and happiness. Adlerian Psychology presents the essence of such a system.

Why, if all we have said is true, has Adlerian Psychology not made greater inroads to this point in time? We have peppered the text with reasons having to do with the nature of Adler's writing, the type of work that Adlerians have traditionally done, and so on. My conclusion is that Adlerian Psychology has been too honest. The two most successful schools of psychology in this century have either damned man, and thereby provided an almost universal cop-out for people, or belittled man while holding out the promise that mechanical adjustments could improve his lot. Adlerian Psychology has put the burden of proof, of success, of progress and fulfillment on the individual. It has said, in effect, life is not a bowl of cherries; you are not and won't be perfect but might be better—it is up to you. In an age of advertising promises, when people feel that man can conquer the universe and simultaneously feel conquered by the universe—nature—the immensity of it all, an honest and realistic promise of improvement but not perfection does not sell as well as impossible dreams. I hope the reader has gotten from this book some feel and understanding for the realistic hopes that stem from Adlerian Psychology.

Chapter 17

Case History

There is no such thing as a typical case history for Adlerian psychotherapy, in part because every Adlerian therapist is eclectic in approach, although having the same theory in common. Thus, some Adlerians are soft and gentle in their approach, some are rough and ready. Some may begin with diagnostic tests, social interviews, and some start without any preliminaries.

In the field of Adlerian psychotherapy, there is a general procedure developed originally by Dr. Rudolf Dreikurs, which a number of his students, including the authors of this book, generally employ. This "system" consists of five parts:

1. A first interview of about one hour.
2. A social and family history from a questionnaire of about one hour.
3. A projective test, *Early Recollections,* which usually takes one hour.
4. The development from the above of a Life Style, a tentative diagnostic summary, which also takes about one hour.
5. The therapy proper, seen generally as helping the patient to gain more self-confidence and to gain courage through working through Basic Mistakes. This can take several months, and even years, but ordinarily Adlerian therapy lasts about 20 to 30 hours, being much faster than, for example, either Jungian or Freudian psychoanalysis.

The following case is presented more to explain technique than to serve as a human document, but should give the reader some impression of what Adlerian psychotherapy is like.

In this presentation the five steps are illustrated. However, it is purposely unbalanced, with greater concentration on the preliminary diagnostic aspect of the treatment itself.

Ronald is a fiction—a reconstruction, as is true of most case histories—but based on fact. The only veridical case histories are those that are presented verbatim, such as Alfred Adler's *The Case of Mrs. A,* which is only a fragment, showing Adler's creative genius in evaluating a case.

RONALD

Session 1

Ronald was a 40-year-old self-referred male. Short and stocky, with a wild mane of undisciplined hair, he was an extremely intense person, a man in a hurry, with no time for nonsense. He came into the first session, sat on the edge of the chair, spoke rapidly, replied quickly and pertinently, and gave the impression of great eagerness to get things done. He explained that he had already had some psychotherapy with a Rogerian therapist and from that he had gained a good deal, but he felt that he needed some more directive psychotherapy since he had a great many problems, did not feel he was effective in his life, had few friends, was not getting along with his wife, and needed some direction. He was in the field of the social sciences, had read a considerable amount in the field of personality theory and psychotherapy, and believed that Adlerian psychology was the best system for him. "Less bullshit in it" is the way he put it.

Some minor probing brought forth a good deal of material in the first interview. Below are some of the statements summarized:

"I think I could really be an important person if I weren't my own worst enemy."

"I have two contradictory goals: one to have peace and tranquility and one to have excitement and accomplishment."

"I see myself as contradictory. I keep saying to myself, 'I want this—but on the other hand . . .'."

"Like I have two personalities. I am a pretty good husband. I am a hard worker, a good provider. And yet I have a mistress. Worse—sometimes I cheat on her too."

"I want lots of money and also lots of fame, but as I see it, getting one prevents me from getting the other."

"I feel like I don't belong anywhere. I gave up my religion, and I don't have any now. I don't like people of my own nationality and have nothing to do with them. I feel close to my family, but I have moved away from them and rarely see them. I am a communist at heart but I don't want to let anyone know it. I look down on most people. I think I am really smarter than they. I am a snob. Yet, I help people a lot. I am a 'nebbish chaser' (one who seeks out the unfortunate and befriends them) and I suppose it is because I want them to know of my superiority, but I don't really believe that."

"I really don't know who I am, where I am going, what I want, and I constantly feel guilty. My wife constantly nags me to give up my mistress. Several times I have lost my temper due to her goading me and I have struck her violently. I hate my wife and yet feel sorry for her."

"I have one son, and I love him. I know the arguments between my wife and I are harming him."

"I don't know if I am a success or a failure. I suppose I can see it both ways."

"I feel I am being pulled simultaneously in a dozen ways. I know it is all my fault. Like when I was single I had six or seven girl friends simultaneously, kept this from each of them, and how I worked and went to school and kept all my dating straight I'll never know."

When asked what he wanted from therapy, following a half hour of monologue, some of the elements of which have just been indicated, he leaned back in his chair, and was silent for a minute or two.

"God, I don't know. I suppose the usual. To understand myself. To get some peace. To be more efficient. To straighten out my life. To make fewer mistakes. To have a happy family."

"Do you think I can help you?" the therapist asked.

The client again pondered. "Even a simple question like yours, I just cannot answer it simply, like 'yes' or 'no.' I want to give a long dissertation."

"Give a 15-minute one. That's how much time we have left."

For the first time, the client looked at the therapist, deep in the eyes, up and down his body, then around the room.

"Really, no, I don't think so."

"Why not?"

"Simply because I think I am smarter than you."

"Maybe so. Why not find a smarter therapist?"

"They don't exist. I don't mean smarter than you. I mean smarter than me."

"Maybe a therapist dumber than you can help you."

The client thought for a while and nodded. "You know—I know what I am saying is wrong. I am not the best in anything. So, why do I think of myself as so superior? People younger than me have happy marriages, have better jobs, more friends, are more athletic—you name it, they are better than me. Yet, I can't get over the idea that absolutely no one is as smart as me. I know I am wrong, but I just feel that way."

"Can you cooperate with me," the therapist asked, "even if you may feel that you are smarter than me?"

"Certainly, I am very cooperative, with everyone. I just want you to know my mental reservations. I speak out my mind all the time. Maybe that is why I have no friends. Everyone says I have no tact."

"OK. Now, let me explain our procedures. This first interview is to get a general picture of who you are, what you want, whether we can work together. I get the impression that you are an interesting person, and one with whom I'd enjoy working and I hope that you would get something out of it. I believe we are now ready for step 2 in the process of Adlerian psychotherapy. I was trained by Dr. Rudolf Dreikurs and I follow his method of working. Step 2 will be a structured interview. Step 3 would be a kind of projective technique, and I'll explain it when we get to it."

"Like the Rorschach."

"Yes, like it, but much more powerful in eliciting your life style."

"Does that mean personality profile?"

"Pretty much. Each of us has a style of life, how we operate, our personality. And this interview, the structured interview of the next session, the projective test, all of them add up to information that will allow me to define your life style. This session, the next and the one after that will lead to my summarizing your life style, and this means that I will formally attempt to tell you who you are, what your thinking is, what is your private logic, what are your basic mistakes and what are your strengths as I see them. Later, if you want to continue, we will work on your basic mistakes in the therapy proper.

"Very much so. I feel you are competent, and I really am looking forward to the next session."

"OK, see you next week, same time, same place."

Session 2

(Note: Dr. Rudolf Dreikurs published "The Psychological Interview in Medicine" (1954) and near the end occurs "Guide for Initial Interview Establishing the Life Style." In italics will be found the questions the therapist asked in this second session, coming mostly from this structured interview.)

Will you tell me the structure of the family you grew up in, including dead children?

"My parents first had a pair of twins who died in infancy. They were named Robert and Albert. They were premature. I was the second child and my mother decided that I was to take their place and my name comes from the combination of their names—'Ro' from Robert and 'Al' from Albert. Then I came, born about a year later. Then I had a brother Albert who died in infancy. Then another brother Albert who also died in infancy. Then, my brother Albert who is five years younger than me."

"That's one of the more remarkable family constellations I ever heard of. You had two dead brothers before you and two dead brothers after you. And when the final brother came, well, you had been the king of that family for five years. How you must have reacted to being dethroned!"

"My mother tells many stories about me. One of the things that bothers me is my guilt that maybe I was responsible for the death of my brother, the one before my living brother."

"What happened?"

"I used to take his milk away from him. My mother caught me once sucking on his bottle."

"Do you remember the incident?"

"No. My mother mentions it, but I don't remember it."

"Humm. Well, let me go on."

In what way were you different from your brother?

"Well, we were quite different. He was always neat. He was a private person and I was flamboyant. I was loud and he was quiet. You always knew what I was thinking, but you never knew what he was thinking. I was an easy-going person, but he was very, very stubborn. I was physically strong and aggressive but he was not. And yet I did a lot of reading, probably more than he and he is a big reader."

How were you alike?

"Not too much. For example, I spoke my parents' language with them, but he spoke in English. I liked a lot of things he didn't. Like sports. I liked to play ball, and he didn't. He was more of a sissy compared to me. I was more aggressive, more flamboyant, more often in trouble. He was a nice good kid. My mother said that she didn't have to do anything to bring him up, he was no trouble, but me—oh, my!"

What kind of kid were you?

"Active, very active, always on the go, full of projects. Always in trouble, never anything delinquent, but active. I liked to climb things, do dangerous things, very adventurous."

What kind of kid was your brother?

"Good kid. Quiet. Kind of gentle. Low keyed. I gave him a hard time. Picked on him a lot. I was much stronger than him, and five years older. I really gave him a rough time, and right now I am still guilty about it."

I'd like you to rate yourself and your brother on some qualities. How would you rate yourself and Albert on intelligence?

"Well, we are both very intelligent. Both creative. He is an artist, and very successful. He did better than me in school, but I went further than him academically. I think we are about equal, but me more intelligent in some ways and him more in others."

Hardest worker?

"We were both hard workers, but I think I possibly am the harder worker. It is a toss up."

Best grades?

"He did better. My grades were always very low. I got tested when I was a kid at a settlement house when I was about nine years old. I got into a research project and I was tested and re-tested on the Binet Test. I got an IQ over 160. The director of the settlement house made a big fuss over me. But I graduated from elementary school just in the middle of my class. And yet when the whole school took a Regents' test, I had a score of 97 and the next highest was 92. The same in high school and college. I got an overall grade of 76 in high school and yet got 94 on the High School Regents. When I entered college I was in the top one tenth of 1 percent of students who entered on entrance tests. The dean called me in to tell me that. And yet I got only two As in my whole college career and not a single A for my master's. Matter of fact, I got more Cs than Bs. And yet, when I took a civil service exam I, who was absolutely last in terms of my grades, came out number 1, not only over my fellow students but some 200 others who took the same test."
"So, you do well on tests but get poor grades from teachers."
"That's been the story of my life."
"Well, hopefully, we can explain this paradox."
"Explain that and all this therapy would be worthwhile. How the hell is it that I am so smart—and the tests always say that—and I am so stupid—all the teachers agreed on that."

How about helping around the house?

"Me. I did most of the work. My mother became a widow when I was six, and I became the man of the house. My brother was a goldbricker, knew how to get out of things. My mother picked on me, and I had much more to do than him. Every Saturday I had to polish all the furniture to her liking."

Who was the more conforming?

"Now, that's hard to say, You would think Albert, but it was really me. He did his own thing. Somehow, my mother picked on me all the time. I have always been conforming. He was smoother than me, got his own way."

Who was the more rebellious?

"Me. That's funny. I was more conforming and more rebellious. Like, I would stand up and say, 'That's not fair' or I'd say, 'No.' So I rebelled openly. Albert, however, would simply say 'Yes' and then do what he wanted."

Who tried most to please?

"Me. I tried real hard to please my mother. When I would earn money I'd give it to her. Albert, if he made money, bought candy and ate it."

Who was more critical of others?

"I don't know. I think I was pretty critical, but I don't know about Albert. He didn't say much. You didn't know what he thought."

Who was more considerate?

"I think I was. He was selfish, how I see it. I was more sensitive about others."

Who was more selfish?

"I think he was. Hard to say . . . My uncle tells how he bought me and my cousin two identical cars, just different in colors. I was willing to let my cousin play with my car, but he wouldn't let me play with his—and he wanted to play with mine. Anyway, I never was a selfish type."

Who had his own way more?

"Albert. Like I said, he did what he wanted. Very stubborn. I tried to have my own way, but I was stopped by my mother."

Who was more sensitive—easily hurt?

"Hard to say. I was always very sensitive, and maybe he was too. It was hard to tell. He kept his own counsel."

Temper tantrums?

"Me! I really would have them. Periodically. Still do. If I am crossed or teased or injured or something I practically go out of my mind. I have a violent streak in me. Scares me. I could kill when I lose my temper. Once, we were waiting to play tennis. The court rules say people have to give up the court in one hour. My friend and I waited an hour. This couple of guys wouldn't give up the court. I asked them. They said 'go to hell.' I wanted to go after them with my racket. My buddy held me off. I really think I would have killed one. Anything that is unfair just burns me up. I really go out of my mind. Like crazy. Scares me. I am very violent."

Sense of humor?

"Hard to tell. I think I was more of a funny one. But I have a cruel sense of humor."
"How's that?"
"Well, I like to tease people, make fun of them, say outrageous things."
"Does that give you any idea why you did so poorly in school?"
"Not really. What's the connection?"
"Well, we'll see. But keep this in mind."

Who was more idealistic?

"I think I was. I doubt my brother really has any idealism. He is too practical."

Who was more materialistic?

"I think both of us. Maybe him. Hard to tell."

Who was more athletic?

"Me. He didn't go for athletics. But I was never good in sports."

Who was more spoiled?

"Hard to say. I don't think either of us. Maybe Albert since my mother let him get away with more things, like I had to do more things."

Who was more punished?

"Me! I got 1,000 times more punishment than Albert. Practically every day from the time I was 7 to about 12 or so, my mother would beat me with a line rope. I'd run under the bed. She'd make me come out telling me the longer I stayed there the more whipping I'd get. She was very strong, and she hurt me terribly. One day I made out I fainted and she went on and on and I didn't respond. She got scared. Thought I had fainted. She started to kiss me, hugged me. And then—this is how she tells it—I started to go 'ha—ha'—like I fooled her—and then she beat me more. It was important for me to tease her."

"Wow. You were really something!"

"That's why I am here."

What were you punished for?

"I never did any delinquent act, never. Just dangerous things. Or being caustic. Making fun of people. Things like that. I can't remember but I think that literally I got whipped by my mother 300 days a year. Once I had a new suit. She told me not to get dirty. I climbed a tree and tore the suit or something. I really got it that day. But the worst time was at a family party I said that I thought that some of the chicken's gizzard had gotten into the soup. My mother said nothing then. When the people left, many hours later, she went into a tirade that went on, literally, for hours. I can still remember how I felt."

"How?"

"Just like the worst shit in the world. And yet, I felt she was unfair. I only made a remark about some sand in the chicken soup."

Who had the more friends, you or your brother?

"Me, I think. I had more. I changed them frequently. He had a few close friends."

Who was the leader in your group?

"I don't think I ever was a leader. I don't think we had a leader. I tended to have one close friend—Johnny Davis—and a lot of acquaintances. My brother tended to be with a small close group."

Did you take care of your brother?

"Yes, when he was little. I'd take him to the nursery. I used to set up his fights too."

"What does that mean?"

"Well, in our neighborhood what counted was the pecking order. This was established by fights. I was pretty high, although in earlier years I was scared. My brother was a kind of sissy, like I said. So, to get him to be a regular fellow, I'd set up some fights for him, and then I'd train him, and he won all his fights, and he got a good reputation that way."

Did you and your brother fight a lot?

"I can't remember. I know I mistreated him. He was always so much smaller than me that he didn't dare fight back. I think he did what I told him. But I never broke his spirit. I used to make him put his head under the chair, otherwise I'd beat him. I was cruel to him. But I suppose I wasn't really to blame."

Who was father's favorite?

"My father died when I was six and my brother was not quite two, and so I can't answer that. But my mother used to tell me that my father used to say that he could talk to me like to an adult even when I was very young. He was a violent man too, by the way."

Who was mother's favorite?

"I think I was. She loved us both. She was a very good mother. But I think she loved me most. Maybe because I gave her the most trouble. Like she told me recently that she had never heard of another child as difficult as me."

"Does that tell you anything about how you did in school?"

"I don't know. There must be some connection."

"In Adlerian theory, everything is connected."

How old was father when you were born?

"He was about 25 and so was my mother."

What kind of man was he?

"Violent. Explosive. I can remember how he once threw a plate of food at me. After he was buried, my brother still had bruises from the whipping my father had given him, and my brother wasn't quite two years old. My father was very volatile, very emotional. I remember my mother saying, and I am translating this: 'I am sure he (my father) would have killed you, so I am happy that he is dead.' He was a hard worker, friendly person, people liked him, my mother adored him, but she was afraid of his emotionalism and violence."

What kind of person is mother?

"She is shrewd, peasant shrewd. A fighter. Very popular. People just love her. She is a great story teller. She is very, very religious. Very devoted mother. Most proud of her kids. She still carries a card that says that I was in the top one tenth of the first percent of the kids that entered that college I went to. Anytime my brother or I do anything outstanding, like getting in the paper, everyone knows about it. She lived for us. Never dated another man after my father died. A real saint."

Who is more like father?

"Me. I have his violence and emotionalism. My brother is more like my mother, softer and more controlled."

What was the relationship between your parents?

"Hard for me to say. I think they loved each other. I never heard them quarrel."

Who was dominant?

"I suppose my mother. She was a powerful person, very shrewd, very clever."

Did they agree on bringing up the children?

"I don't know, but I suppose that his violence scared her. She used to tell me that she punished me a lot but always hit me on the legs, behind, and back. My father punched you right in the face. Did it to me twice and knocked me out. I can remember both times. So, I imagine that she didn't like his emotional outbursts."

Did they quarrel openly?

"I never remember, but you know my father died when I was about six. I think if they did, they did it out of my hearing."

Who was more ambitious for the children? In which way?

"Well, I don't know about my father, but my mother was very ambitious. She wanted us not to be laborers like my father and the rest of our relatives. She wanted us to work with a pen, as she put it. And that's what happened. I am a writer, as you know, I make a living mostly out of writing fiction."

Did any other person live with the family?

"No, but after my father died, my mother, my brother and I went to live first with my father's brother and his family—and then we had to leave—the story is that I was impossible, my aunt didn't want me; and then we went to live with my mother's brother—and the same thing happened. We had to go live on our own, because of me."

"Do you think that has anything to do with your poor academic record?"

"No, I can't see the connection, but apparently you do. I suppose you want to tell me your thinking."

"Eventually."

"OK, you're the boss."

"Fine. We have finished our hour. See you next week for the projective test."

Session 3

Today, we shall have the projective test I talked with you about. Essentially it will be an analysis of your early memories. Let me explain what is an early memory or an early recollection. It is a specific—and I want to emphasize that —a single, clear-cut memory of a specific event. For example, were you to say: 'I remember we used to . . .' then I would stop you. That is because you would remember several combined events, like going to the beach. However, were you to say, 'Once, when we went to the beach I remember digging the sand and I found a ring . . .' then, that would be an early recollection. Is that clear?"

"Yes. A single specific event."

"OK, will you tell me your earliest memory?"

"Yes. It occurred when I was about three I believe. My mother and father and I were on a train. I was seated between them. Like they were watching me, making sure I didn't leave them. I was terribly bored. I could see nothing but trees and telephone poles passing by the window. I wanted to get away. I began sliding down the seat, very slowly so that they shouldn't know what I was doing. I finally got on the floor of the train. I remember it was dusty and dirty. I began to crawl forward under the seats. I remember being intrigued by all the legs of people I could see. I kept on crawling forward. I think I went as far as I could go, maybe four or five seats and then there was a wall blocking my way. I saw an oilcan—I can still remember its color, it was brass colored. I picked it up. I can still feel it, cold and greasy. I turned it upside down and some oil flowed out. Then I aimed the can for some man's shoes and began to pour oil on his shoes. Suddenly, he yelled, reached down for me, and pulled me out. I was screaming in a panic. Then the conductor came and grabbed me. He lifted me in the air asking to whom I belonged. My father came and got me. He was furious and began to spank me. That's it."

"Thanks. Now, what stands out most clearly?"

"All of it,"

"Suppose you were to draw a picture of the incident, what would you draw?"

"Maybe—me crawling, exploring under the seats."

"What feeling is involved in this incident?"

"Several—boredom, desire to escape, taking a chance in getting away, my courage in crawling, my delight in seeing the feet and the can, my experimenting with the can, my pouring oil on the shoe of the man, knowing that it was wrong to do so, my fear on getting caught, my getting punished—all of that."

"A remarkable memory. I can see why you are a writer of fiction."

"Thank you."

"Your earliest memory in terms of its details and feelings indicates you are really a writer. Well, can we have a second memory?"

E.R.2—"I am not sure of the sequence, but this next one I remember goes as follows. I am up on the roof of an apartment house with my mother and a number of other women, and they are looking down the street below for their husbands. I can hear my mother say, "I think that is my Joe, and I see he has a package with him. I hope it is ice cream.' "

"Anything more?"

"I think that what impressed me most was that she could identify him from the top of the building, when I couldn't see him. I didn't know it then but I have very poor vision. I am nearsighted. I now have glasses, and I suppose I needed them even then. But that she could see him and the package impressed me."

"What is the clearest thing about the memory?"

"I don't know. Just being there with these women, I suppose."

"Any feelings?"

"Like I said, surprise at my mother's ability to identify my father when I couldn't."

"Thank you, have you a third incident?"

E.R.3—"Yes. I am with my mother. We are walking in a park. I think I was about five. There was some discussion that I was going to go to school. She sat on a bench and told me to go and play, which I did. I ran to the swings. Then, she called me back. I sat down and she said, 'I have a surprise for you' —and she opened her purse and inside was a small pie. She divided it in half. It was an apple pie. And we ate it."

"Anything stand out?"

"My surprise at seeing the pie. First, I had never seen one that small. I think it was perhaps six inches across. Second, where had she gotten it?"

"Any feelings?"

"My surprise, and pleasure of being with her."

"Thank you, have you a fourth recollection?"

E.R.4—"Yes. I was about five. I had a kite. I had a ball of string. I wanted to wrap the string around a stick. Somehow or other I thought I had to unravel the whole string to get to the other end, and so I unwrapped the string and I got it all over the room. Then I heard my father come in. I knew I had done something stupid. He came in and asked me. I told him what I was doing. 'Stupid!' he yelled. Next thing I saw his fist coming at me—and I went blank. He knocked me out."

"What stands out in this memory?"

"My terror of his finding me with all this string hopelessly mixed up."

"What feelings exist in this memory?"

"Like there is nothing I can do right."

"OK, can I have another memory?"

E.R.5—"It has to do with my father. He was a laborer. He had told me that he had tamed a couple of mice and that they pulled a little wagon he had made. He promised to bring them to me. I remember my asking him, time after time, when he would bring them. He would always say, 'Tomorrow' or 'Gee, I forgot.' "

"Can you remember one specific time?"

"Yes, what I told you was one specific time, but he and I had this conversation a number of times."

"What feeling is involved?"

"Like distrust, and hope, and uncertainty. Did he really have those trained mice?"

"How old were you?"

"I think about five."

"Any other memories?"

E.R.6—"Yes. We were living in a tenement, up on the top floor. A woman came to the house. It seems her gas had been turned off or something. Anyway, she wanted to heat some water on our stove. My mother said it was OK. Then, when the water was boiling she took the pot back. But the door of our apartment was closed We had a long narrow dark hall. I shouted, 'I know how to open the door' and I ran down the hallway. I hit the pot, knocked over the water, and scalded my leg. See—I still have the scar on my leg. I remember my father putting ink on my leg."

"What is clearest?"

"Me running down the hallway to open the door."

"What feelings?"

"Not too clear. Just that I shouldn't be so impulsive."

"Thank you. Do you have a seventh memory?"

E. R.7—"I don't know, Let me think. Yes. With my parents I was on a shoot-the-chutes in Coney Island. The scenic railway. My hat blew off. And we never found it. I remember my father being angry with me. It seems this was the second time I had lost my hat this way."

"Anything special stand out in this memory?"

"Well, I remember looking, seeing the hat fly away, and my fear of my father and my hope we'd find the hat. But we never did. And his anger with me."

"Feelings?"

"Scared. I blew it again. I did something wrong. My fear of punishment."

"Do you have an eighth memory?"

E. R.8—"Yes. My father was in his bedroom. He had pneumonia. There were doctors around. Suddenly he appeared. In a white nightgown. Like he didn't know anything. He was out of his mind. Fell against things. In a high fever. Somebody took him back, had to wrestle him back."

"What is clearest?"

"His look of fear—bewilderment—he was dissociated—in a fog—helpless—dying."

"And your feeling?"

"Terrified. He was so strong, but now was so helpless that someone was able to make him do what he didn't want to. My knowledge of death."

"Do you have a ninth memory?"

E.R.9—"Yes. My father was dead. He was in a coffin in the house. I went to look at him. I saw a part of his body had turned green. Like rotting meat. He had been in the coffin in the house two-three days."

"What stands out clearest?"

"The dark stain, the rotting meat."

"What feelings did you have?"

(The patient started to cry. Tears roll down his face. He covers his face with his hands and begins to call out, "Papa, papa . . . papa." The therapist waits. Finally, the tears are over.)

"I think this is the first time I have ever cried over his death. I didn't know I felt this way. I have some happy memories of him too. Like he was dancing with a broom once, the broom was supposed to be a guitar, and he was telling my mother the story of an opera he had seen or something. And once I remember going clamming with him. I was supposed to watch when a clam would spout water and we would run and dig it up."

"So, all your memories of your father are not bad."

"No, not all of them."

"Any special feeling about this one you told me seeing him in his coffin?"

"Sort of like an awed feeling that a living person would turn rotten, putrefy, that this would eventually happen to me. Like my first understanding of death."

"How old were you?"

"About six. A little older, maybe six and a half."

"OK, now let us have your tenth memory. That will be the last."

E.R.10—"I was in the first grade. I had trouble getting along. I was in the same seat with another boy. His name was Oscar Habile. I remember putting my arm around him. It was a good feeling, like I had made a friend. Then, someone came into the class. The teacher called me out. It seems my father had died. That was the last time I went to that class."

"What stands out?"

"My good feeling of friendship—and then it ends."

"Yes, that is your feeling, but what in the memory stands out?"

"My putting my arm around Oscar—and then being separated."

"Thank you very much. Now, I would like to begin my analysis of your early memories. Each little story represents your private logic. I will write down the various themes I find in them, putting them as 'I' statements. Your memories represent your conclusions about life. So, let us start with the first one and let us examine it with great care."

Memory 1. (To the reader: we suggest you reread the early memories one at a time and try to figure out what they mean before you read these conclusions.)

I am a nomad.

"That's true. I am a kind of gypsy. How on earth did you figure that one out?"

"Easy. Your first memory is on a train. You are on the go."

I get bored easily.

"True. I do get bored very easily."

I can't stand restrictions.

"Absolutely true. I am a free soul."

I am tricky or clever or creative.

"Yes. I do feel that way. Where does that come from?"

"You manage to escape from your parents even though they are both seated on either side of you."

I am adventurous.

"Sure, I can see that, crawling, being scared, but doing it anyway."

I am reckless.

"Does that come from experimenting with the oilcan?"
"Yes."

I am hostile.

"Wait a moment. Where does that come from?"
"Your pouring oil on the feet of some man. I think there is more to that than simple experimenting. Didn't you know it was wrong to do that?"
"Yes."
"This is a very important part of the memory. Possibly the second most important."
"What's more important?"

I get caught when I misbehave.

"Ah!" (Patient had a moment of insight.)

Punishment is inevitable. I never get away with my misbehaviors. Nevertheless I do things to get punished even though I always get caught.

"Wow! All that from that one memory?"

Memory 2. "According to Adlerian theory, the individual is unified, and your first memory tells the whole story about your personality. But let us go on to the second one, the one of the roof. I'll just pick one or two elements." *Women are superior to me.*
"Because my mother could see when I couldn't?"
"Yes."
"Maybe it means adults—or others are superior to me."

Memory 3. "Possibly. But the third incident with you in the park with mother producing the pie reinforces that. On top of that your father never did anything that you admired in any of your memories." *Women are important to me.*
"How do you get that?"
"All your memories of mother are of her being supportive, loving, caring. *Women are good but men are bad.* Or, perhaps, *Women are caring, men are dangerous.*"
"Makes sense."

Memories 4, 5, and 6. "The fourth memory with the kite string is another important one. I pick up several items of your private logic. *I am stupid. Father is dangerous. I do things wrong. Punishment is inevitable.* The fifth one with the mice says: *I can't trust men.* The sixth one with the hot water: *I am impetuous. Life is dangerous. Be careful.* Here, incidentally, your father applied ink to your burn. Anything about that?"

"Well, as you saw I have a pretty terrible scar on my leg and I used to think it was because he put ink on it, like he didn't know the right thing to do."

Memory 7. "Well, that reinforces the whole concept you have about men being dangerous, stupid, evil, weak, and so on. The seventh incident about the hat really summarizes a lot about you. *I cannot control myself. I do everything wrong. Punishment is inevitable. I just am helpless.*

"How do you get all that out of that incident?"

"Well, it is the second hat. Your feeling of helplessness watching it sail away. Your pessimism is shown by your not finding the hat. Your father's anger with you."

Memory 8. "The eighth incident with your father in a high fever and out of his mind in a nightgown says something like this: *Life is uncertain.* No, I think there is a profounder meaning in this incident, *Punishment is inevitable.* Or, maybe . . . I am not too sure . . . what do you think?"

"I remember my first feeling. It was funny. To suddenly see him in the middle of the day, in a daze, not knowing where he was, stumbling into the living room, in his nightgown. That first feeling of incongruity, of my father who was so strong changed immediately to fear. Maybe he was coming to kill me. Then, it changed to puzzlement that he allowed others to return him. It was the last time I saw him alive."

(Client stops talking, closes his eyes, and some sort of internal struggle seems to be going on. Therapist waits, thinking perhaps client will cry again, but he does not.)

"Wow. This is heavy stuff. Well, what do you get out of my next memory?"

Memory 9. "The putrefaction probably says something like this: *We all die. Everything ends.* I think it is a powerful existential statement. Does death have a special meaning to you?"

"I am terrified about death. Every once in a while, especially when I am in bed at night about to go to sleep I think, 'Can it be possible that I, too, will be dead some day, a stinking putrefying corpse? Is it really true that I will die? The thought of not being any more, well, it is really awesome. Like what is the meaning of life? What's the purpose of anything? We all come to the grave eventually."

Memory 10. "Well, now let us go on to the last memory. Time is running out. That too has profound implications. *Nothing good lasts. I can never have a friend. Nothing really remains good for me.* Just as you started a good relationship with Oscar, it was terminated."

"This is heavy stuff."

"Yes. Well, I'll see you for the fourth session next week, same time. I'll try to put this together, assembling your life style, which will give us a kind of tentative plan to begin your therapy."

Session 4

"Good morning. How do you feel?"

"Pretty good. I have been thinking about the early memories and your interpretations. They seem simplistic."

"Possibly. Adlerian psychotherapy operates on a commonsense basis. A lot of people want complications. People are paradoxical, simple and complex at the same time. But let us try to avoid any judgments about Adlerian theory now. Did you have any other thoughts?"

"I cried again about my father. He has been dead now for over 35 years. I hardly knew him. I have had some more memories. Some violent and some not, but always emotional. Then I thought of how my mother always beat me in reality and yet I didn't recall any violent or punitive scenes with her. I am all mixed up. My whole life was one of violence. As a kid I was always being beaten up by my teachers, the kids in the street, and my mother."

"Well, let me complete my life style analysis of you, and then we can begin to try to straighten things out. I have gone over your materials, and this is my summary. But please keep in mind that everything is tentative. Ready?"

* * * * *

Ronald is the older of two living children out of a total of six boys. He was expected to replace his parents' first two dead twins, Robert and Albert, since his name combined both their names. After him, two additional boys died, so that his parents had five children and only one—Ronald—lived. Mother treated him like a prince. He could do no wrong. He became a monster and no one else could control him. Two relatives gave up on him. He wanted his own way at any cost and he became a terror. His father, who had a short fuse and a violent temper, reacted strongly against this child who possibly had competed successfully for the mother's attention. Mother in effect said that she was glad that father had died. Ronald became a tyrant against his brother and kept him down. Later on, his mother possibly had enough of him, and possibly felt that he was somehow implicated in the father's death and became excessively punitive. However, Ronald fought everyone and was punished by mother, by the school authorities and by the children in the street. The world was against him. He had no friends.

He developed a strong and inconsistent attitude toward women: He respected and feared them. His attitude toward men was fearful but also disrespectful, every man was his enemy.

Overconcerned with power, he unnecessarily struggled, making enemies on all sides, and has sabotaged his good potentials.

Private Logic (from the Early Recollections)

I don't know where I belong, and I am not sure anyone wants me. I do what I want, but people are against me, catch me and punish me. I never get away with anything. I feel everyone is holding me back and I have to get things on my own. I respect women and see them as superior and I am afraid of men who are brutal. There is little use in struggling since everything ends in failure.

Basic Mistakes

1. He is essentially a pessimist, and does not believe in his success.
2. He is excessively fearful of men and shows them hostility unnecessarily.
3. He is excessively dependent on women and fearful of them.
4. He operates to generate hostility in others.
5. He has little insight into his behavior, sees others, but not himself.

Assets

1. He is very bright and creative.
2. He seems to be open to understanding.
3. He has a strong feeling for people.

"Well, Ronald, this is more or less the way I see you. This is your life style. Please remember it is a tentative diagnosis. What did you get out of it?"

"It seems like the mountain labored and brought forth a mouse. Nothing seems new or wonderful. Also, I can't agree with much of it. And I can't see where you got all your conclusions."

"Which ones?"

"Well, the first basic mistake, about my pessimism. I see myself as an optimist. I take chances. I do things, I don't hold back. I am always a gambler."

"Yes, I agree with that, but your credo is, 'Don't worry; everything is absolutely certain to go wrong.' As a matter of fact the one thing I am absolutely certain about you is that you are a pessimist, you are certain everyone is against you, that you cannot have friends, that people will take

advantage of you, that professors will not like you. You are absolutely convinced of the hostility of the world against you."

"But it's true!"

"Of course it's true. But can I make a very simple point? It is true because
you have made it true, and you make it true. For example, take your relationship with me. How did you treat me?"

"I gave you my honest opinions. I spoke frankly."

"Yes, but what did you say?"

"Like I wasn't sure of you. I still am not!"

"You insulted me. You told me I wasn't very bright. You expressed openly
—honestly—your contempt. As your therapist, this didn't bother me, but as
a human being, it hurt. You said in effect you were superior to me. As a
therapist, I knew that it was a façade; you possibly feel inferior. You don't
believe that I or anyone can really like you—or that we won't punish you—
but you don't realize your pessimism about being accepted that makes you
strike out at others. When they retaliate you start everything."

"Let me get what you are saying. You claim that I hit out first?"

"You start hostilities with your so-called honesty and your teasing. Then,
people react to your hostility with their hostility. But you don't realize what
you do. You only see what others do to you. But your hostility comes out of
your pessimism. You think they are going to get you so you want them to know
first that they'd better be careful of you."

"Christ! You seem to be saying that I set people up. I expect them to attack
me, so I get the first blow in. That's quite a bundle you are handing me. I am
to blame about everything. I can't buy it. How do you explain my bad grades
in school when I am so smart? Why was I only average in high school and yet
when I took entrance tests in college I was in the top one tenth of 1 percent?
Why did I get a master's degree with not a single grade of A—and yet when
I took a civil service test on the subject I got the highest grade? How come
everyone is against me?"

"Any hypotheses?"

"None."

"Could it be that you do something to antagonize people?"

"Not on purpose."

"I repeat my question."

"I must. But I don't see how. After all, I took 15 courses for my master's.
I studied hard. I knew my subject. The civil service tests proved it. How could
I be at the very bottom of my class in terms of grades and at the very top in
terms of tests? And this has happened many times in my life. Like I really
know my stuff but no one believes it . . . or maybe something else . . ."

"Like what?"

"Maybe they know I know it and dislike me for knowing it . . ."

"Like teachers are jealous of you because you are so smart ..."

"It could be ..."

"Fifteen of them, all insecure about you, all of them giving you poor grades, because of your superiority?"

"It could be. Maybe I threaten them somehow. Maybe I am a genius, they know it, they resent it, they then give me poor grades. One teacher had to miss a class session. He asked me to teach that session. I took over for him. But do you know what grade he gave me?—B! Does that make sense? Or, in this course I took recently. The professor gave a midterm examination. I got the highest mark. I was sure of an A. But again, I got a B at the end."

"I think you have established solidly one point: you really are smart. You really know your stuff. And yet your professors almost uniformly give you poor grades. Good knowledge—poor grades. What you don't see is how it is that this discrepancy comes about. Your hypothesis is that it is jealousy. These professors see you as bright and knowledgeable so they then punish you by giving you poor grades. What other hypothesis can you establish?"

"According to you I do something to antagonize them! I can't see that."

"But don't we both agree that you do something—whether it be making them feel inferior to you because of your brilliance or whether it is something else—to explain the discrepancy between your good knowledge and your poor grades?"

"Yes, but I don't know what it could be."

"Neither do I, but in view of your life style, it seems to me very probably that you antagonize them, whether it be because of your brilliance or because of your attacks on them ..."

"Attacks? How do I attack them?"

"I don't know. But they misjudge you, they give you poor grades, and even if objective tests show you know your stuff they still give you poor grades ..."

(We have gone into one session in quite some depth to give a feeling of what the verbal interaction between the therapist and the client might be. Essentially, the therapist now has gained some insight into his client. He "sees" the client as pessimistic, fearful, not sure of his place in society, wanting to be accepted, but hostile, contact shy, and so on. He attempts to get the client to begin to see himself objectively. The client, however, responds with excuses, explanations, defenses, and avoids "owning" the problem. This is resistance, found in all therapies. Below is reported part of a later session which "broke the case" as it were.)

Session 10

"Look, you keep telling me how I antagonize people, I upset people. I deny that. I really try to get along. I try to help people. I go out of my way. I want to give you a good example. Sunday night, my wife and I were invited to a party, given by two friends of ours, Stan and Evelyn. They had invited two other couples. Stan had to talk to someone on the telephone. Evelyn was in the kitchen, coming back and forth. My wife and I were talking to one another. The other two couples were talking to each other. It was an awkward situation. So, I tried to make the evening successful. I got everyone's attention by saying 'Do you know the game called *Napoleon in the Icebox?*' The other two couples said they didn't. 'It's a lot of fun,' I told them, and I started to explain it. Well, they were interested, and just as I was about to finish the explanation how to play the game, Evelyn comes in and announces, 'Coffee is ready.' Then, she yells at Stan to get off the phone. He comes in, and starts to tell everyone about the phone call. Then, Evelyn goes after the coffee. So, I start to finish telling about the game, when the husband of one of the couples got up to go to the bathroom. So, I gave up. That's how *that* went. Screw them!"

"Is this an example of how unfair people are to you? You try to help out, make a party lively, and it all turns out poorly."

"That's right. That's exactly how it went, and how it goes for me."

"That is not my interpretation of what went on."

"What possible alternative explanation would you have?"

"First, you are a guest in these people's house. Second, you decide that things are not going the way you think they should. People are talking to their mates, but that is not the way you think it should be. So, you take the initiative. You decide you want to play and explain the game. When the hosts do whatever they want to do, like feed their guests, you feel they are unfair to you. As I see it, you were rude, bossy, and tried to run the show, and when you didn't succeed, you sulked."

(The client was speechless. For more than five minutes, therapist and client looked at each other, with not a word said. The therapist waited, excited, since the client, who was usually very voluble, now was thinking, reflecting.)

"If you are right, then everything is explained. My poor grades, why I don't have friends, why I have gotten fired . . ."

"What do you think?"

"I meant well, like to help the party get going."

"I am sure of that."

"I think those people I tried to help didn't like me. The couple that started talking avoided me. I supposed I showed my displeasure."

"Probably."

"My friends probably thought I was intruding on their prerogative. After all, it was their home."

"Well, what do you think?"

"Maybe that is the way it is. Maybe I want to be the boss. Just like when

I was a kid. I didn't sit on the seat between my parents, but decided to slide off and explore. Like I want my own way . . ."

"Does this have anything to do with school?"

"Well, I would never study the assigned textbook. I'd study a different textbook."

"What do you mean?"

"Like in biology. We have one text, but I would study another."

"Did you think the other texts were better?"

"I didn't want to study the same text everyone else did."

"Why?"

"I don't know. But maybe it has to do with not wanting to be controlled, to do my own thing, like I wanted to learn but didn't want to submit to their discipline. Like I didn't trust them. I wanted to compete with them, or something. I guess I didn't trust them. Wanted to do things my own way."

"Can you put it together? All of it?"

"It is starting to come together. I am afraid of people, especially men. They can harm me. I must not let them direct me. So, in an attempt to be free of them, I do stupid things, like when I slid off the seat on the train, and I get them mad the way I got my father mad when I didn't wind up the string the right way. It's all crazy."

Session 15

(This was a particularly heavy session in which the client did practically all the talking.)

". . . well, you know how guys tend to have a kind of fetishistic attitude toward women sexually, in my case it was breasts. I'd look at women as they walked and I looked at their breasts, and if they weren't wearing a bra and I could see the outlines of the nipples I'd get a sexual feeling, something of the sort, but not really erotic. Anyway, I was a tit man, and still am. Maybe it is because of something my mother told me. When I was a kid maybe three or four months old, and we were living up in the mountains of Colorado, my father was a stonecutter there, and she got some sort of fright, my father told her someone was going to kill us. Anyway, she told me that her milk ran dry, and I began to lose weight. I was 10 pounds at birth and at three months I had dropped down to 7 pounds because she had no milk in her to feed me and she couldn't find something else that I would take. They had no doctors there. Anyway, finally, they found that condensed milk was OK, I was able to swallow it, so maybe . . ."

(At this point the client stopped his monologue and stared ahead, gasping for air, making choking noises. The therapist waited, a bit frightened, as the client kept gasping, his face in a rictus of agony. Finally, tears began to fall, finally he struggled to say something, and the words were disjointed.)

"... father ... died ... my fault ... I was bad ... my mother let him die ... so I should live ... he would not be dead if it weren't that I was ... so bad ... I killed him ... my being bad ..."

(A long period of silence, tears were running down the client's face, finally he controlled himself.)

"I understand it all now. I can put it all together. It is all so simple. I see it all. My parents wanted children, especially my mother. She lost her first two. Then I came. I was very precious to her. And then came another, and he died. So she was very protective of me, against my father. It was him or me, and she went for me. He must have been jealous of me. Then, she had another child. He too died, and so her concern and possessiveness was even greater, five children and only one living—me. I must have been spoiled rotten. Probably my father hated me, was jealous of me, and he and my mother fought over me. I didn't know this, of course. On top of that I was overactive, I have always been filled with high energy. So, I suppose his violence was due to his jealousy of me, or his fear that my mother loved me more than him. And I was spoiled as a young kid. When my father was dead my mother changed. She decided that I had to be disciplined, and now she began beating me. Maybe she too felt I was guilty of my father's death, maybe her sexual repressions were expressed sadistically, I don't know. Anyway, here I had had a mother who gave me everything, and my father who had been my enemy was dead. I felt —that is why I was crying—that mother decided that he should die and I should live—the reason my mother decided to let him die was because I was bad—like my crawling under the seat of the train or losing my hat or getting the kite cord all mixed up—so she decided I would live and he would die. So, I had guilt that my father died because I was bad and she had anger that he died on account of me. Anyway, I faced a world I didn't understand. Father beating me, and now that he was gone, my mother beating me. She told me later she did it because she was afraid that because we lived in a delinquent neighborhood I might become a delinquent and the only way she knew of controlling me was to whip me. I don't know. I found every hand against me. In my school, the teachers whipped us, and I got more than my share. In the street, I was a minority member and the kids were after me and beat me. So, I saw all the world as dangerous. I was good at nothing. Because of my bad eyes, I couldn't see the blackboard so I did poorly in the elementary school. I couldn't play anything well because of my eyes. I was strong but not fast. I had no success anywhere. My cousin had things better—his parents both worked and they had lots of money compared to us. Anyway, everything led me to consider that the world was a hostile place, and my only recourse was to get in the first punch, let everyone know not to fool around with me. So, I assumed an aggressive stance toward life. People were my enemy. Yes, teachers were my enemies, the kids in the block, my mother, everyone. To survive meant to be strong, to be smart, to get the first punch in, to scare them.

"Now, I think I can see how they all saw me, they saw me as aggressive to them. When I pass in front of a house and a dog comes running at me, yipping and yapping, I see him as aggressive, but he sees me as aggressive. He is defending his territory from me, but I think I am only minding my own business. We each misinterpret each other."

Session 30

(This was the last session, and the reconstruction is meant to indicate how an Adlerian therapy might end.)

"How do you feel?"

"Pretty good. I think we're ready to call it quits."

"Feel you got what you came for?"

"Not completely, but I don't want to get dependent on you."

"I can understand that."

"Things are going better. I have gained a lot of insight into myself, and can see myself more objectively, and I feel better about myself. I am not cured by a longshot, and I don't know whether I want to be like everyone else, or even liked by everyone, but I feel stronger now, more capable of getting along. I really have come a long way. I feel much more comfortable with people."

"How do you show it?"

"Well, I listen more to others. I don't talk about myself so much. I am more humble, or more reasonable. I give others more space. I don't feel as fearful of others. Things of that sort."

"Good. Should we go over your basic mistakes? Remember any of them?"

"Yes, we have gone over them all lots of times, so I should remember them. The first one was that you thought I was pessimistic, and I couldn't see it. I see it now. I thought I was being realistic, every man is my enemy. I thought no one could really like me. You had to give me things, otherwise you were not my friend. Like women, they had to give me themselves sexually otherwise they didn't like me. I didn't really share myself with anyone. I operated secretly. I didn't trust people. And I fooled myself to think it was the opposite. I really was fearful. I tried a lot of things, but I usually messed them up because of my pessimism, like I couldn't really succeed. I was a kind of adventurous, not-giving-in pessimist, like you said, 'Don't worry, everything will go wrong.' That was me, all right."

"Now, the second basic mistake I made was that I was unnecessarily fearful and so I was hostile. I had my boxing gloves on and whoever came near me got a punch. The third mistake had to do with my attitude toward women. I was overdependent on them and also overfearful. I needed their goodwill and would do anything to get them to like me, and if they showed any disinterest,

I almost died. Now, I have a bit better attitude towards them, but not completely.

"What was the fourth one?"

"Generating hostility . . ."

"Well, they are all more or less variants. I was scared of people and expected the worst from them—that was my pessimism—so I would attack others. It was a pattern, to come on strong, to show my muscle. I really am watching this, and succeeding. I am much less blatant and flamboyant. I could shrivel up when I think of how I came into this office, full of bull and critical of you."

"So you are a nicer guy?"

"Well, I suppose so. Different anyway."

"Remember your final mistake?"

"Yes, I was a poor interpreter but a good observer, or something like that. I saw others clearly but not myself."

"Did you get out of therapy what you wanted?"

"Yes, I am satisfied. I know I have a long way to go yet, and I suppose that my life will be a bit different, but I feel I am more courageous now, see myself in a better light, and get along better. My life going better in a lot of ways. When I think back on my life with all the handicaps, the only survivor out of five brothers, ignorant immigrant parents, a brutal father, a powerful mother, living in a ghetto, developing such a fearful and hostile attitude, feeling unacceptable to others, never having a girl friend, having had intercourse before I ever kissed a girl, never having any money, never dating, my crazy sexual history, my poor visual capacity, and all that sort of thing, it is hard to believe I managed to survive and to be successful. Reminds me of what Nietzsche said, *'What doesn't kill me, makes me stronger.'* So I got stronger, but in a crazy way. I used my strength to defeat myself. You know what, I have my own theory of what's wrong with people. Maybe it is different from the Adlerian view."

"What's that?"

"I think everything wrong with people is fear. I had guilt—that's fear. I had anxiety—that's fear. I had hostility—that's fear. I was afraid of not being accepted. I was afraid of strangers. Everything was a kind of phobia. I was like in the song afraid of living and afraid of dying. But not now, I am not so scared any more."

"Good, I am glad of that. I am sure that personality theories can be interpreted in a variety of ways. From my point of view, you were discouraged, didn't think you could succeed and so were pessimistic about being accepted, about being loved, about everything. As a result, instead of moving along in a steady useful direction, you went in a zigzag fashion, inconsistent, kind sometimes, and cruel sometimes. We call it operating in useful versus useless fashions. This means instead of going in a straight upward line, you spent a lot of energy going in opposite directions, taking a lot of time getting to your destination. Can you see that?"

"Very clearly. I wanted to move upward, and did, but like I ran first northeast then northwest, then northeast and so on, instead of going directly north."

"Well put. Well, I guess our therapy is over. I wish you good luck."

"Thanks, and I want to tell you that I think you are pretty smart."

"I agree. Thanks."

Appendix

Research Abstracts

Adlerian literature amounts to well over 10,000 articles, tests, books, and book reviews, as listed by Mosak and Mosak (1975). Of these, perhaps only about 250 may fall into the area of nomothetic empirical research studies. We have selected a number of representative research studies from the *Journal of Individual Psychology* which have been abstracted with the help of Brenda Williams. The reader may wish to read the originals of these investigations to get a more complete representation of research in Individual Psychology.

Allen, T. W. Willingness to accept limitations scale: Further cross-validation and item analysis. *Journal of Individual Psychology,* 1969, *25,* 52–55.
　　The "Willingness to Accept Limitations" scale was given to college freshmen to determine whether the degree to which a person accepts limitations and yet makes an effort to succeed nonetheless (as measured by the WAL) is related to college success.
　　Results indicated that students scoring above the median on the WAL also had significantly higher grade point averages at the end of their first year.

Angeli, D. Immediate elder sibling as a factor in task performance. *Journal of Individual Psychology,* 1973, *29,* 167–172.
　　Two positions regarding sibling factors in performance have been advanced by Adler and by Schachter. Adler stated that second borns are always "under steam" to catch up with their elder siblings, while Schachter concluded that firstborns are under pressure because they have been dethroned and, therefore, tend to seek security, and thus both elder siblings and second borns should conceivably perform better in given situations than do other children. Two hypotheses were tested: *(a)* subjects with an immediate elder sibling (IES)

would exhibit a higher level of task performance than would those with no immediate elder sibling (NIES); and *(b)* the NIES group would perform better when given a simple task with "ego-involving" instructions but the IES group would perform better on a complex task. Ninety-six male undergraduates were subjects. The tasks involved simple and complex card sorting.

Results showed that the IES group performed faster on all tasks regardless of complexity or instructions. However, this group also made more errors and reported a higher anxiety level than did the NIES group.

Attarian, P. J. Early recollections: Predictors of vocational choice. *Journal of Individual Psychology,* 1978, *34,* 56–62.

This research investigated the relationship between early recollections and students' choice of college major. Three trained Adlerians tried to guess 31 students' majors after reading five recollections from each subject. Holland's Self-Directed Search (SDS), a "vocational counseling tool" based on the notion that occupational choice was an expression of one's personality, was also used to predict the students' academic majors.

Results, although not entirely consistent due to one judge's difficulty with the task, indicated some efficacy of using early recollections for vocational and educational guidance. However, the SDS scores did not predict college majors significantly.

Berrett, R. D. Adlerian mother study groups: An evaluation. *Journal of Individual Psychology,* 1975, *31,* 179–182.

To test the hypothesis that mothers' attitudes and behavior as well as children's behavior will improve in accordance with Adlerian principles after a parenting course based on *Children: The Challenge,* three experimental study groups met for 10 weeks, two of the groups receiving both pre- and posttests and one receiving only the posttests. Instruments used were the *Attitude toward the Freedom of Children-II,* assessing liberal or authoritarian attitudes in parents; the *Child Rearing Practices Scale,* to assess mothers' child-rearing practices; and the *Child Behavior Checklist,* to evaluate children's behavior.

Results from all three groups indicated a positive change on all measures, though not all changes were significant. The evidence supports a democratic approach to child rearing which "emphasizes individual responsibility."

Bliss, W. D. Birth order of creative writers. *Journal of Individual Psychology,* 1970, *26,* 200–202.

Are creative writers (of both prose and poetry) similar to scientists in birth order position? Results indicated that a far greater percentage of scientists than writers were firstborn or only children.

An Adlerian explanation is that firstborns may be more conservative and therefore "less original and artistically creative" than later borns.

Crandall, J. E. A scale for social interest. *Journal of Individual Psychology,* 1975, *31,* 187–195.

Noting the crucial role of social interest in Adlerian theory, Crandall reported initial attempts to validate a Social Interest Scale (SIS) by comparing its scores with measures of overt behavior, values, personality characteristics, beliefs about other people, perceived meaningfulness of life, social desirability, and birth order. Subjects were volunteers from college and high school psychology classes. Social interest was defined using Ansbacher's criterion of "interest in the interest of mankind." The scale was developed by choosing traits relevant to social interest from a standard list of personality traits. A panel of psychology faculty and graduate students served as judges, and paired equally desirable traits having and not having to do with social interest. Subjects were required to select one of each pair as being their preference.

Results indicate a significant positive relationship between social interest scores and peer ratings of behavior; valuing equality, peace, and family security, perceived altruism and trustworthiness of others, and scores on the Purpose in Life test. Negative correlations were obtained between SIS scores and valuing excitement and pleasure, hostility and depression. Finally, middleborn women scored significantly higher on the SIS than did firstborn or laterborn women, although no differences for birth order were found for men.

Crandall, J. E. The effects of stress on social interest and vice versa. *Journal of Individual Psychology,* 1978, *34,* 40–47.

Questions have arisen over the stability of social interest as opposed to its variability in stressful situations. To determine the effect of "physical stressors," rather than the more typically studied threats to self-esteem, 21 males and 27 females were administered anagram puzzles while subjected to a tape recording of various human and industrial noises for approximately 30 minutes. Two different forms of a scale combining the *Mood Adjective Check List* (which measures elation, surgency, anxiety, and sadness) and the *State Social Interest Scale* were given as pre- and postmeasures, as well as the *Controlled Repression-Sensitization Scale* (HCRSS) to control for defensiveness.

The following results were obtained: *(a)* noise was perceived as a stressor, as determined by significant differences on the pre- and postmeasures; *(b)* both "repressors" and "sensitizers" (according to a median split of the HCRSS scores) showed less "sadness" and more "surgency" than did the low social interest group on the MACL scales. Thus physical stressors affect mood and social interest, and the ability of social interest to provide "courage and psychological strength" in the face of a stressful situation was noted.

Croake, J. W., & Haydn, D. J. Trait oppositeness in siblings: Test of an Adlerian tenet. *Journal of Individual Psychology,* 1975, *31,* 175–178.

Some Adlerians have postulated an "extreme difference in personality development" between the first and second siblings, a proposition which the present study tested for two-sibling families by use of the *Sixteen Personality Factor Questionnaire*. Subjects were divided into brother-brother, brother-sister, sister-sister, and sister-brother pairs, and also compared specifically on the basis of their greater and lesser age differences: those who were zero to five years apart (90 pairs), and those who were two to three years apart (57 pairs). Trait oppositeness was defined as a score differing more than 33 centiles of the population at large.

Results indicated that, for the brother-brother pairs from zero to five years apart, a difference was found only on one dimension—ego weakness versus ego strength. Limited additional differences appeared when the age span was two to three years apart for all but the sister-sister pairs, thus failing to substantiate an "extreme difference" in sibling personality traits. However, it was emphasized that the smaller age differences do apparently increase trait oppositeness to an extent.

Dailey, C. A. The experimental study of clinical guessing. *Journal of Individual Psychology*, 1966, *22*, 65–79.

Built upon Adler's statement that his students should be trained "in the art of guessing," the present study was designed to test whether, in fact, persons can guess correctly the events in a given person's life on the basis of what is already known. Cases were drawn from biographies and clinical histories with each case divided into 15 episodes. Initially, subjects were told only the occupation of the person to be described.

Results from both business people and college students supported the notion that prediction is possible.

Eckstein, D. G. Early recollection changes after counseling: A case study. *Journal of Individual Psychology*, 1976, *32*, 212–223.

Noting Adler's crucial formulation that early recollections (ERs) are "chosen" by the individual because of their meaning for one's current life situation, Eckstein pointed out that ERs are believed to change during the course of successful therapy, either in content or in emphasis. The present report detailed one client's ER changes before and after nine months of therapy. The *Early Recollections Rating Scale* was employed to analyze each ER separately and also to compare the pre-and posttherapy ERs. Eight experienced Adlerian psychologists served as raters.

A significant improvement was found on six of nine scales divided into "behavior" and "affect" variables as well as on total "affect" and "behavior." The results support the holistic view of the individual which Adler stressed, as well as the value of ER data to assess therapeutic change.

Freeman, C. W. Adlerian mother study groups: Effects on attitudes and behavior. *Journal of Individual Psychology,* 1975, *31,* 37–50.

The current study measured the impact of Traditional Mothers' Discussion Groups as compared to Adlerian Mothers' Study Groups. Traditional groups are open-ended, focusing on individuals' concerns as they are raised, while Adlerian groups are based on the theory of Individual Psychology. Subjects were 36 mothers divided into the two treatment groups which met for 10 weeks each, and a control group was employed. Measures used were the Scale II of the *Attitude toward the Freedom of Children* to indicate authoritarianism or liberalism, and the *Child Rearing Practices Scale,* which was filled out by a third-party observer of family interactions, and the *Child Behavior Checklist,* measuring specific misbehaviors as well as those bothersome to the mother. All scales were filled out at the end of the 10-week period for all three groups.

Results indicated significantly less authoritarian attitudes by "Adlerian mothers" than by the other two groups. Their children also had significantly fewer bothersome behaviors than did those of the control groups. Both treatment groups were seen as being more effective than the no treatment group.

Frick, W. B. Healthy interpersonal relationships: An exploratory study. *Journal of Individual Psychology,* 1967, *23,* 58–66.

To understand "the characteristics of the healthy, growth-promoting interpersonal experience" (p. 59), Frick asked students in English and psychology courses to anonymously describe such relationships.

Based on responses from 69 female students, this type of relationship was seen to have the following characteristics: *(a)* viewed as a learning and growth experience, *(b)* free self-disclosure, *(c)* based on mutuality, *(d)* the learning and growth transferred to other relationships, *(e)* façades and pretenses were gone, and *(f)* self-centeredness was diminishing. In line with the thinking of Adler, self-development and the development of social interest are seen as being interdependent, and as being two expressions "of the same growth process."

Hammer, M. Preference for a male child: Cultural factor. *Journal of Individual Psychology,* 1970, 26, 54–56.

To validate the Adlerian notion that the disadvantage of women is due to cultural-attitudinal factors, subjects from various subcultures were asked to state whether they would prefer to have a male or a female child if they knew they could only have one child.

Results indicated that both married and unmarried college men and women preferred to have a boy rather than a girl. Married noncollege men also preferred a male child, but women in this category preferred to have a female child.

Herrell, J. H. Birth order and the military: A review from an Adlerian perspective. *Journal of Individual Psychology,* 1972, *28,* 38–44.

Distinguishing among types of power in the military (reward, coercive, expert, referent, and legitimate), the author hypothesized on the basis of Adler's statements regarding personality variables of persons in different birth order positions that "first-borns should be overrepresented among military leaders; that they would, in general, be more successful in military service; that they would be more prone to neurotic disturbances and less to character disorders than later-borns; and that first-borns would commit fewer violent crimes than later-borns in the military" (p. 43). Previously published studies reviewed gave general support to all these hypotheses.

Hjelle, L. A. Relationship of social interest to internal-external locus of control and self-actualization in young women. *Journal of Individual Psychology,* 1975, *31,* 171–174.

Based on a review of the locus of control literature, the hypothesis was that internally controlled people would exhibit higher social interest than would those who were externally controlled. This was measured by the *Internal-External Scale* and the *Social Interest Index.* Persons high in social interest were also presumed to be more self-actualized, in Maslow's terminology, with the latter being assessed using the *Personal Orientation Inventory.*

Results obtained for all relationships supported "Adler's criterion for psychological maturity; that is, a cooperative empathic attitude toward others."

Kal, E. F. Survey of contemporary Adlerian clinical practice. *Journal of Individual Psychology,* 1972, *28,* 261–266.

Kal conducted a survey of Adlerian therapists to determine the extent to which they follow an Adlerian mode of treatment.

Results indicate that *(a)* mental health was considered to be "social participation"; *(b)* symptoms were expressed in terms of "mistakes"; *(c)* the individual's response to the family constellation was of critical value; *(d)* early recollections were used to assess themes in living; and *(e)* insight occurred when goals and purposes were recognized, but emphasis was also placed on practicing insights outside of therapy. Length and mode of treatment, diagnosis and role of religion did not differ substantially from other theoretical applications of therapy.

Kaplan, H. B. The relationship of social interest to cooperative behavior. *Journal of Individual Psychology,* 1978, *34,* 36–39.

Cooperative behavior is assumed to be the "most effective means for succeeding in the life tasks," which are, in turn, the evidence of a person's level of social interest. To test this hypothesized relationship, 290 high school students were administered the *Social Interest Index* and the *Prisoner's*

Dilemma Game, a payoff matrix game which depends on cooperation for
mutual benefit in a pair. Two categories of high social interest and low social
interest were formed, with 35 pairs in each group, each pair playing 20 trials
of the *Prisoner's Dilemma Game.*

Results showed that the two groups differed significantly in the amount of
cooperation exhibited both on the initial trial and over the entire 20 trials,
supporting the relationship between social interest and cooperation.

Lemay, M. L. Birth order and college misconduct. *Journal of Individual
      Psychology,* 1968, *24,* 167–169.

Examining the issue of birth order when considering antisocial characteristics, Lemay notes that Adler as well as other theorists see the firstborn as being
more conforming and dependent, while laterborns are thought to be more
rebellious. Thus, it was hypothesized that firstborns would be underrepresented among college females receiving disciplinary action, while secondborns
would be overrepresented. Subjects were female university students who had
been referred for either campus or civil violations over a four-year period.

Findings supported both hypotheses.

Levi, A. M., Buskila, M., & Gerzi, S. Benign neglect: Reducing fights among
      siblings. *Journal of Individual Psychology,* 1977, *33,* 240–245.

On the basis of Dreikurs' technique of noninterference by parents into
sibling fights, the authors designed and installed a program in which six sets
of parents were exposed only once either to "an explanation of Dreikurs'
principles and methods" or to a role-playing situation as well as educational
techniques. Both groups kept diaries of sibling fights for one week before the
treatment session, prior to implementation of the technique, and again for one
week following both the instruction and a session one week later to check up
on difficulties. After eight months, parents were asked to keep a log of sibling
conflicts for one week as a follow-up measure.

Results indicated a significant reduction of fights occurred on both the
posttest and the follow-up measure for both treatment groups.

Levinger, G., & Sonnheim, M. Complementarity in marital adjustment: Re-
      considering Toman's family constellation hypothesis. *Journal of Individual
      Psychology,* 1965, *21,* 137–145.

The present study tested Toman's assumptions that persons whose sibling
configurations are duplicated in marriage will show good adjustment, and will
consider their marriages to be satisfactory. Couples in "normal" and "disturbed" marriages (decided on the basis of their participation in counseling)
were given a conflict disposition score based on Toman's predictions.

Neither birth order and rank order divisions distinguished between normal
and disturbed couples as predicted, nor were results significant on the "satisfaction" indices. Because of these negative results, couples were then asked to

rate their need for dominance, the influence of each spouse and desired influence of each. Again, "results . . . do not support the idea that birth order is associated with either actual or desired social influence or with the need for dominance."

Manaster, G. J., Cleland, C. C., & Brooks, J. Emotions as movement in relation to others. *Journal of Individual Psychology,* 1978, *34,* 244–253.

Some personality theorists such as Karen Horney have conceptualized emotion in terms of movement toward, away from, or staying the same in relationship to others. To determine whether "lay people" understood terms representing emotions in this same way, 149 students in a college of education were presented with a list of such words, ranked on a scale from 1 (movement toward) to 5 (movement away from).

Factor analyses confirmed that these words did pertain to movement, either positive, negative, or neutral in nature. The 20 words with the lowest means were more variable in content than were the 20 words with the highest means, which came primarily from a factor identified as "satisfied and glad." Although this study was not intended to examine the purpose of emotions, the authors point out that if the *outcome* of emotions can be equated with their *purpose,* then an understanding of why people act in a given way becomes apparent.

Manaster, G. J., & Perryman, T. B. Early recollections and occupational choice. *Journal of Individual Psychology,* 1974, *30,* 232–237.

Using past literature on early recollections (ERs), the authors devised a scoring procedure for rating ERs according to the presence or absence of variables in seven categories: *characters, themes, concern with detail, setting, active-passive, internal-external control,* and *affect.* This procedure was then used to score three ERs each from 81 college students, with the hypothesis that their ERs would vary in content in ways consistent with their chosen occupations.

Significant differences existed between groups on the variables "mother," "nonfamily members," "number of character types," and "neutral affect." Results were consistent with the hypothesis in that they could be explained on the basis of the differences between the skills required and tasks performed by those in these various occupational groupings. For example, both nursing students and counseling students scored higher on the "mother" variable, suggesting a helping, supportive orientation, while teaching students scored higher on "nonfamily members."

Nelson, M. O., & Haberer, M. H. Effectiveness of Adlerian counseling with low-achieving students. *Journal of Individual Psychology,* 1966, *22*(2), 222–227.

Students who had been low achievers in high school were divided into groups receiving Adlerian and those receiving "causal-diagnostic" counseling. Both groups were enrolled in remedial course work. Their grades in the remedial program as well as course grades during the following year were compared.

Results indicated that although the group receiving Adlerian counseling had significantly better grades during the summer program, this difference began to fade as the academic year progressed, and disappeared completely by the end of the spring term. It was suggested that since the Adlerian method was more effective in producing good short-term grades than was the other method, more research would be desirable in the area of longer-term Adlerian counseling.

O'Connell, W. E., & Hanson, P. G. Patients' cognitive changes in human relations training. *Journal of Individual Psychology,* 1970, *26,* 57–63.

To compare the belief changes of subjects who actively participated in Adlerian psychodrama treatment ("protagonists") to those who observed but were inactive ("nonprotagonists"), scores were obtained for both groups on the Personal Beliefs Inventory both prior to and following treatment.

Combined results for both groups indicated a significant change on total PBI scores following treatment, with the most change reflected on items pertaining to "self-hatred, ideas of perfection, and fear of others" (p. 59). When the protagonists' and nonprotagonists' scores were compared, item differences generally reflected an internal as opposed to an external locus of control, respectively.

O'Phelan, M. L. Statistical evaluation of attributes in Adlerian life style forms. *Journal of Individual Psychology,* 1977, *33,* 203–212.

Life style inventories, formulated to provide therapists with an understanding of clients' goals, intentions, and behavior patterns, may have various formats but yield basically similar data. The hypothesis that the attributes can be placed in six categories—achievement, social proprieties, gender, interpersonal mechanics, right-wrong, and posture—was tested in the present study to determine if the above categories were consistent with a factor analytic interpretation.

Using the first two pages of the Minnesota Form of the Life Style Inventory, in which subjects compare themselves with their siblings on 37 attributes, results indicated that such categories are statistically valid. Data were gathered from a clinician's files, using 144 subjects. Other hypotheses dealing with differences between males and females, birth order groups, and victims as compared to other typologies were partially supported; however, significant differences between males and females were in the opposite direction from expectation.

Platt, J. L., Moskalski, D. D., & Eisenman, R. Sex and birth order and future expectations of occupational status and salary. *Journal of Individual Psychology*, 1968, *24*, 170–173.

The present study considered sex of the subject as well as birth order position in terms of future expectations of salary and status.

Results for undergraduate education majors showed that among males, firstborns had highest expectations for status, followed by only children and later borns, in accordance with Adler's observation of the firstborns' concern with status. Differences regarding salary expectations were nonsignificant. For females, status expectations were not significantly different among birth order groups, but firstborns expected higher salaries, followed by later borns and, finally, only children. Trends for males were more in line with theoretical predictions regarding birth order differences than were findings for females, suggesting the importance of considering both sex and birth order variables, as the authors suggested.

Reimanis, G. Anomie, crime, childhood memories, and development of social interest. *Journal of Individual Psychology*, 1974, *30*, 53–58.

Noting the inverse relationship between anomie and crime, Reimanis tested the hypothesis that male youths convicted of crime would have more childhood memories than would "normal" groups in the following areas: *(a)* high family mobility, *(b)* general household disorganization, *(c)* cold or rejecting parents, and *(d)* father with whom they did not identify. (Childhood memories are presumed to be accurate indications of one's social interest, in that the phenomenon of "selective attention" may be operating.) Subjects were 103 convicted males awaiting determination of their sentencing, with two comparison groups—college males in introductory psychology classes, and high school males. Differences were assessed using an adaptation of Srole's (1956) anomie scale and childhood experience memories scale developed earlier by Reimanis. A significant difference was found between normal and deviant groups on both the anomie scale and 21 of the 74 items on the memories scale, with other items differing in the expected direction, although not significantly. Results on the memories scale indicated that "offenders remembered more experiences that would be opposed to the development of social interest," especially remembrances of a cold but overprotective mother and a rejecting or absent father.

Rogers, G. W. Early recollections and college achievement. *Journal of Individual Psychology*, 1977, *33*, 233–239.

The relationship between early recollections (ERs) and an individual's view of the world and self in the world was examined, using college grade point average as an indicator of achievement. Ninety-seven students in introductory psychology classes were instructed to write five ERs, which were then scored using the *Manaster-Perryman Early Recollection Scoring Manual.* Twenty-six of the possible 42 variables accounted for 75 percent of the variance in GPA, and 4 of them, Active, Travel—Setting, Outside in Neighborhood—Setting, and Auditory Detail—Content, accounted for 50 percent of the variance. Using these four variables in the prediction equation, the error was still $\pm$ .82; therefore, the equation is not of much practical utility. However, of most interest is the fact that the variable "Active" accounts for over one third of the variance alone, suggesting a "tendency" to act rather than "be acted upon" for high achievers. High achievers tend to "feel responsible for (their) destiny," and view circumstances as under their own influence rather than subject to chance or to others' influence.

Smith, W. D. Changing preference for a female child. *Journal of Individual Psychology,* 1976, *32,* 106–107.

The current study replicated a previous one by Hammer (1970) in which students were asked to state their preference for sex of a child if they could have only one child. Subjects were 293 undergraduates—108 male and 185 female.

Results indicated a significant difference in preferences by sex, with only 17 percent of men and 47 percent of women preferring a female child. When compared to the 1970 study, a significant difference was found in the responses of women, as only 23 percent preferred a female child at that time. It can be concluded that women's disadvantages may be cultural, as Adler proposed, and, further, that disadvantages are decreasing, although significantly so only as seen by women.

Teichman, M., & Foa, U. G. Depreciation and accusation tendencies: Empirical support. *Journal of Individual Psychology,* 1972, *28,* 45–50.

It was hypothesized on the basis of Adler's statements concerning the attitudes of neurotics that such persons depreciate and accuse their parents more than would "normal" individuals. Two studies tested this hypothesis: in the first, American students were asked to rate parents and other significant figures on 15 bipolar constructs. Results were analyzed by comparing descriptions applied to parents and others. Neurotic subjects rated parents, particularly the mother, consistently more negatively than did normals. In the second study, Indian mental patients were compared with normals on a scale which required subjects to rate parents on "giving" and "taking away" behavior. Patients described their parents, particularly their fathers, more negatively than did well-adjusted subjects. Thus both studies give support to the hypothesis.

Verger, D. Birth order and sibling differences in interest. *Journal of Individual Psychology,* 1968, *24*(1), 56–59.

The present study tried to determine whether interest differences among siblings were related either to birth order positions or to interests of parents.

It was hypothesized (1) that first- and third-born children would be more similar in interests than firstborns and second borns; (2) that the distinction between the above two pairs is related to differences between the parents; (3) that the difference between first and second children is positively related to parental differences; and (4) that the differences between first and third children are negatively related to parental differences. Subjects were 70 families with three children, all of the same sex and all above the sixth-grade level. Children of parents in the lowest and highest quartiles of interest differences were compared.

Results for all hypotheses were in the expected direction, although the most striking conclusions were drawn for the second hypothesis. Thus, in families in which the parents had quite different interests, first and second children were also different but first and third children were similar. In families having great parental differences, fathers had much higher scores on the "masculine pursuits" scale, suggesting that perhaps father's masculinity furthers competition between siblings.

Wagner, M. E., & Schubert, H. J. P. Sibship variables and United States presidents. *Journal of Individual Psychology,* 1977, *33,* 78–85.

Noting various studies which indicate relationships between sibship variables on the one hand and social prominence and success, intellectual, creative and academic achievements, and personality characteristics on the other hand, the authors examined the factors of ordinal position, family size, and sex of siblings for the 38 presidents of the United States.

A chi-square analysis indicated a significant overrepresentation of eldest children, while youngests, onlies, and middles were underrepresented, with onlies significantly so. Furthermore, presidents' siblings were predominantly male or mostly male, and only 55 percent of their families were "intact to age 16." It was hypothesized that such positions in families are critical in that individuals may "become very strong or very weak" in response to such rather extreme situations.

Wark, D. M., Swanson, E. O., & Mack, J. K. More on birth order: Intelligence and college plans. *Journal of Individual Psychology,* 1974, *30,* 221–226.

After citing several studies which generally indicate a positive relationship between earlier birth order position and higher verbal intelligence, the authors outline the current study, in which the relationship of (1) verbal intelligence, and (2) post-high school plans is examined in relation to birth order position.

Data based on standardized tests given to 11th graders indicated that a very strong relationship existed, as expected, between early birth order position and verbal intelligence as measured on the Minnesota Scholastic Aptitude Test. Concerning post-high school plans, firstborns were more likely than later borns to attend college, whereas later borns were more likely to plan to attend vocational school or to plan for no more schooling. The authors deny that these effects are the result of socioeconomic factors by pointing to a study which held this variable constant and found similar results.

West, J. D., & Bubenzer, D. L. A factor analytic consideration of life style data. *Journal of Individual Psychology,* 1978, *34,* 48–55.

Common patterns and characteristics have been observed in life styles of individuals, by Adler and his followers. To gain empirical support for some of these postulated similarities, a new scale, the Self-Administering Life Style Inventory, was developed according to categories taken from the Life Style Inventory. The 173-item scale was administered to 200 males and 200 females. A section called for subjects to describe three early memories which were scored by trained judges.

Factor analysis revealed seven factors which accounted for significant variance, including the parental relationship, three factors having to do with the subjects' establishing themselves in social groups, maternal influence on gender, and the impact of the father. These results are seen as initial attempts adding to the "needed statistical confirmation of theoretical assumptions."

White, P. H. Personality and interpersonal attraction: Basic assumptions. *Journal of Individual Psychology,* 1965, *21,* 127–136.

Noting previous research on interpersonal attraction as well as relevant contributions from the Adlerian concept of social interest, White hypothesized that a possible area of study not previously examined would be that of the attractiveness of certain basic personality characteristics, rather than complementarity of similar traits between two individuals. In this study, the personality characteristics of "intimacy" and "formality" were assessed, the assumption being that persons rated high on intimacy and low on formality would be seen as more attractive overall, regardless of the characteristics of the person rating them. Thirty high school counselors rated each other on the above dimensions and also chose three persons in the group with whom they would most at least like to maintain relationships. Results confirmed the hypotheses; regardless of the similarity of the rater to the person rated, those seen as more intimate and less formal were also seen as more attractive. It was suggested that other characteristics could also be studied in this manner.

References

Ackerknecht, L. Roleplaying of embarrassing situations. *Group Psychotherapy,* 1967, *20,* 39–42

Adams, B. N. Birth order: A critical review. *Sociometry,* 1972, *35,* 411–439.

Adler, A. Das Zartlichkeitsbedürfinis des Kindes. *Monatschr. Padag. Schulpol.,* 1908, *1,* 7–9.

Adler, A. *Über den neurosen Charakter.* Weisbaden, Ger.: Bergman, 1912.

Adler, A. *Study of organ inferiority and its psychical compensation.* New York: Nervous & Mental Diseases Publishing Co., 1917. (Originally published in German, 1907.)

Adler, A. A doctor remakes education. *Survey,* 1927, 490–495. (a)

Adler, A. *The practice and theory of Individual Psychology.* New York: Greenberg, 1927. (b)

Adler, A. *Problems of neurosis.* London: Kegan Paul, 1929.

Adler, A. *The science of living.* London: Allen & Unwin, 1930.

Adler, A. The structure of neurosis. *Lancet,* 1931, *220,* 136–137.

Adler, A. Über den Ursprung des Strebens nach Uberlegenheit und des Gemeinschaffsgefühles. (On the origins of the striving for superiority and of social interest.) *International Journal of Individual Psychology,* 1933, *11,* 257–263. (Also in Adler, 1964, 29–40.)

Adler, A. The fundamental views of Individual Psychology. *International Journal of Individual Psychology,* 1935, *1*(1), 5–8. (a)

Adler, A. Prevention of neurosis. *International Journal of Individual Psychology,* 1935, *1*(4), 3–12. (b)

Adler, A.   *The Individual Psychology of Alfred Adler.* (H. L. Ansbacher & R. R. Ansbacher, Eds.). New York: Basic Books, 1956.

Adler, A.   *Understanding human nature.* (W. B. Wolfe, trans.). Greenwich, Conn.: Premier Books, 1957. (Originally published, 1918.)

Adler, A.   *What life should mean to you.* London: George Allen & Unwin, 1962. (Originally published, 1932.)

Adler, A.   *Social interest.* New York: Capricorn Books, 1964. (a)

Adler, A.   *Superiority and social interest.* (H. L. Ansbacher & R. R. Ansbacher, Eds.). Evanston, Ill.: Northwestern University Press, 1964. (b)

Adler, A.   *The science of living.* New York: Doubleday, 1969. (Originally published, 1929.)

Adler, A.   *The education of children.* Chicago: Henry Regnery, 1970. (Originally published 1930.)

Adler, A.   *Cooperation between the sexes.* (H. L. Ansbacher & R. R. Ansbacher, Eds.). Garden City, N.Y.: Anchor, 1978.

Adler, K.   An Adlerian view of the development of treatment of schizophrenia. *Journal of Individual Psychology,* 1979, *35,* 144–161.

Allee, W. C.   *Animal aggregations.* Chicago: University of Chicago Press, 1931.

Allen, T. W.   The Individual Psychology of Alfred Adler: An item of history and a promise of a revolution. *The Counseling Psychologist,* 1971, *3,* 3–24.

Allred, G. H.   *On the level with self, family, society.* Provo, Utah: Brigham Young University, 1974.

Altus, W. D.   Birth order and its sequelae. *Science,* 1966, *151,* 44–49.

American Medical Association Committee on Human Sexuality. *Human Sexuality.* Chicago: American Medical Association, 1972.

Ansbacher, H. L.   On the origin of holism. *Journal of Individual Psychology,* 1961, *17,* 142–148.

Ansbacher, H. L.   Individual Psychology. In R. J. Corsini (Ed.), *Current personality theories.* Itasca, Ill.: F. E. Peacock, 1977.

Ansbacher, H. L.   Adler's sex theories. In A. Adler, *Cooperation between the sexes.* (H. L. Ansbacher & R. R. Ansbacher, Eds.). New York: Anchor Books, 1978. (a)

Ansbacher, H. L.   The development of Adler's concept of social interest: A critical study. *Journal of Individual Psychology,* 1978, *34,* 118–152. (b)

Arlow, J.   Psychoanalysis. In R. J. Corsini (Ed.), *Current psychotherapies.* Itasca, Ill.: F. E. Peacock, 1979.

Asch, S.   Opinions and social pressure. *Scientific American,* 1955, *193,* 31–35.

Atthowe, J., & Krasner, L.   Preliminary report on the application of contingency reinforcement procedures. *Journal of Abnormal Psychology,* 1968, *73,* 37–43.

Becker, S. W., Lerner, M. J., & Carroll, J.   Conformity as a function of birth order, payoff, and type of group pressure. *Journal of Abnormal and Social Psychology,* 1964, *69,* 318–323.

Beecher, W.   Guilt feelings. *Individual Psychology Bulletin,* 1950, *8,* 22–31.

Beecher, W., & Beecher, M.   *Parents on the run.* New York: Agora Books, 1966. (Originally published, 1955.)

Bell, J. E.   *Family group therapy.* (Public Health Monograph No. 64.) Washington, D.C.: U.S. Government Printing Office, 1961.

Berne, E.   *Transactional analysis in psychotherapy.* New York: Grove Press, 1961.

Bickhard, M. H., & Ford, B. L.   Adler's concept of social interest: A critical explication. *Journal of Individual Psychology,* 1976, *32,* 27–49.

Bieliauskas, V. J.   A new look at "masculine protest." *Journal of Individual Psychology,* 1974, *30,* 92–97.

Bierer, J.   *The day hospital, an experiment in social psychiatry and synthoanalytic psychotherapy.* London: M. Lewis, 1951.

Bierer, J.   The day hospital. *Social Welfare,* 1955, *9,* 173–180.

Bierer, J., & Browne, I.   An experiment with a psychiatric night hospital. *Proceedings of the Royal Society of Medicine,* 1960, *53,* 930–932.

Bierer, J., & Buckman, J.   Marlborough Night Hospital. Treatment with L.S.D. and group therapy. *Nursing Times,* 1961, *57,* 594–596; 637–639.

Bierer, J., & Evans, R. I.   *Innovations in social psychiatry.* London: Avenue Publishing Company, 1969.

Birnbaum, F.   The Individual Psychological Experimental School in Vienna. *International Journal of Individual Psychology,* 1935, *1,* 118–124. (a)

Birnbaum, F.   Applying Individual Psychology in school. *International Journal of Individual Psychology,* 1935, *1,* 109–119. (b)

Birtchnell, J., & Mayhew, J.   Toman's theory: Tested for mate selection and friendship formation. *Journal of Individual Psychology,* 1977, *31,* 18–36.

Block, J. M.   Conception of sex roles. *American Psychologist,* 1973, *28,* 512–526.

Bolles, R. C.   Whatever happened to motivation? *Educational Psychologist,* 1978, *13,* 1–13.

Bottome, P.   *Alfred Adler: A portrait from life.* New York: Vanguard Press, 1957.

Brind, B.   Child guidance as a community service. *Individual Psychology Bulletin,* 1942, *2,* 52.

Brown, J. F.   *Practical applications of the personality priorities.* Clinton, Md.: B. and F. Associates, 1976.

Bruck, A.   Do we need the concept of "guilt" feelings? *Individual Psychology Bulletin,* 1950, *8,* 44–48.

Bullard, M. L.   Logical and natural consequences. In H. H. Mosak (Ed.), *Alfred Adler: His influence on psychology today.* Park Ridge, N.J.: Noyes Press, 1973.

Burgess, E. W., & Cottrell, L. S.   *Predicting success or failure in marriage.* New York: Prentice-Hall, 1939.

Clark, K. B.   *Dark ghetto.* (Forward by G. Myrdal.) New York: Harper Torchbooks, 1967. (Originally published, 1965.)

Collard, R.   Social and play responses of first born and later born infants in an unfamiliar situation. *Child Development,* 1968, *39,* 325–334.

Corsini, R. J.   Counseling and psychotherapy. In E. Borgatta & W. Lambert (Eds.), *Handbook of personality theory.* Chicago: Rand McNally, 1968.

Corsini, R. J.   Issues in encounter groups: Comments on Coulson's article. *Counseling Psychologist,* 1970, *2,* 28–34. (a)

Corsini, R. J.   The marriage conference. *Marriage Counseling Quarterly,* 1970, *5,* 21–29. (b)

Corsini, R. J.   Individual education. *Journal of Individual Psychology,* 1977, *33*(2a), 295–349.

Corsini, R. J.   Individual education. In E. Ignas & R. J. Corsini (Eds.), *Alternative educational systems.* Itasca, Ill.: F. E. Peacock, 1979.

Corsini, R. J.   *The family relationship index.* Columbia, Mo.: Parenting Publications, 1980.

Corsini, R. J. (Ed.).   *Handbook of innovative psychotherapies.* New York: Wiley, 1981.

Corsini, R. J., & Painter, G.   *The practical parent.* New York: Harper & Row, 1975.

Corsini, R. J., & Rigney, K.   *The family council.* Chicago: Rudolf Dreikurs Unit of Family Education Association, 1970.

Corsini, R. J., & Rosenberg, B.   Mechanisms of group psychotherapy. *Journal of Abnormal and Social Psychology,* 1955, *51,* 406–411.

Dana, R. H.   Psychopathology: A developmental interpretation. *Journal of Individual Psychology,* 1965, *21,* 58–65.

Deutsch, D.   A step toward successful marriage. *Journal of Individual Psychology,* 1956, *12,* 78–83.

Deutsch, D.   Group therapy with married couples: The birth pangs of a new family life style in marriage. *Individual Psychologist,* 1967, *4,* 56–62.

Dewey, J.   The reflex arc concept in psychology. *Psychological Review,* 1896, *3,* 253–270.

Dinkmeyer, D., & Dreikurs, R.   *Encouraging children to learn: The encouragement process.* Englewood Cliffs, N.J.: Prentice-Hall, 1963.

Dinkmeyer, D., & McKay, G.   *Raising a responsible child.* New York: Simon & Schuster, 1973.

Dreikurs, R.   *Seelische impotenz.* Leipzig: Hirzel, 1933.

Dreikurs, R.   The educational implications of the "four freedoms." *Individual Psychology Bulletin,* 1942, *2,* 68–71.

Dreikurs, R.   The four goals of the maladjusted child. *Nervous Child,* 1947, *6,* 321–328.

Dreikurs, R.   *The challenge of parenthood.* New York: Meredith, 1948.

Dreikurs, R.   Patient-therapist relationship in multiple therapy. Its advantage to the therapist. *Psychiatry Quarterly,* 1952, *26,* 219–227. (a)

Dreikurs, R.   Patient therapist relationship in multiple therapy. Its advantage for the patient. *Psychiatry Quarterly,* 1952, *26,* 590–596. (b)

Dreikurs, R.   *Fundamentals of Adlerian psychology.* Chicago: Alfred Adler Institute, 1953.

Dreikurs, R.   The psychological interview in medicine. *American Journal of Individual Psychology,* 1954, *10,* 99–122.

Dreikurs, R.   Can you be sure the disease is functional? *Consultant,* Smith Kline and French Laboratories, 1962.

Dreikurs, R.   *Psychodynamics, psychotherapy, and counseling: Collected papers.* Chicago: Alfred Adler Institute, 1967.

Dreikurs, R.   *Psychology in the classroom* (2d ed.). New York: Harper & Row, 1968.

Dreikurs, R.   *Social equality: The challenge of today.* Chicago: Henry Regnery, 1971.

Dreikurs, R., Corsini, R., Lowe, R., & Sonstegaard, M. (Eds.).   *Adlerian family counseling.* Eugene, Ore.: University of Oregon Press, 1959.

Dreikurs, R., Gould, S., & Corsini, R. J.   *Family council.* Chicago: Henry Regnery, 1974.

Dreikurs, R., Grunwald, B. B., & Pepper, F. C.   *Maintaining sanity in the classroom: Illustrated teaching techniques.* New York: Harper & Row, 1971.

Dreikurs, R., & Mosak, H. H.   The tasks of life. I. Adler's three tasks. *The Individual Psychologist,* 1966, *4,* 18–22.

Dreikurs, R., & Mosak, H. H.   The tasks of life. II. The fourth life task. *The Individual Psychologist,* 1967, *4,* 51–55.

Dreikurs, R., & Soltz, V.   *Children: The challenge.* New York: Duell, Sloan and Pearce, 1964.

Eckstein, D., et al.   *Life style: What it is and how to do it.* Hendersonville, N.C.: Mother Earth News, 1975.

Ellenberger, H. F.   *The discovery of the unconscious.* New York: Basic Books, 1970.

Ellis, A.   *Reason and emotion in psychotherapy.* New York: Lyle Stuart, 1962.

Falbo, T.   The only child: A review. *Journal of Individual Psychology,* 1977, *33,* 47–61.

Fiedler, F. E.   A comparison of therapeutic relationships in psychoanalytic, nondirective, and Adlerian therapy. *Journal of Consulting Psychology,* 1950, *14,* 436–445.

Foley, V.   *An introduction to family therapy.* New York: Grune and Stratton, 1974.

Forer, L. K.   The use of birth order information in psychotherapy. *Journal of Individual Psychology,* 1977, *33,* 105–113.

Franco, J., Hildreth, H., Boszormenyi-Nagy, I., Midelfort, C., & Friedman, A.   Family treatment of schizophrenia: A symposium. *Family Process,* 1962, *1,* 101–140.

Freud, S.   *The origins of psychoanalysis.* New York: Basic Books, 1964.

Furtmuller, C.   Alfred Adler: A biographical sketch. In A. Adler, *Superiority and social interest.* (H. L. Ansbacher & R. R. Ansbacher, Eds.). Evanston, Ill.: Northwestern University Press, 1964.

Giovacchini, P. Psychoanalysis. In R. J. Corsini (Ed.), *Current personality theories.* Itasca, Ill.: F. E. Peacock, 1977, 15–44.

Goldstein, K. *The organism: A holistic approach to biology derived from pathological data.* New York: American Book Co., 1939.

Gordon, T. *Parent effectiveness training.* New York: Peter Wyden, 1970.

Grunwald, B. Role playing as a classroom group procedure. *Individual Psychologist,* 1969, *6*(2), 34–38.

Harper, R. A. Marriage counseling as rational process-oriented psychotherapy. *Journal of Individual Psychology,* 1960, *12,* 197–207.

Harris, I. *The promised seed: A comparative study of eminent first and later sons.* New York: Free Press of Glencoe, 1964.

Holmes, D. S., & Watson, R. I. Early recollections and vocational choice. *Journal of Consulting Psychology,* 1965, *29,* 486–488.

Horney, K. *Neurosis and human growth.* New York: Norton, 1950.

Huber, R. J., Lomax, S. S., Robinson, S., & Huber, P. P. Evolution: Struggle or synergy. *Journal of Individual Psychology,* 1978, *34,* 210–220.

Hunt, J. McV. *Intelligence and experience.* New York: Ronald, 1961.

Ignas, E. *Individual education: An introduction.* Chicago: Industrial Relations Center, The University of Chicago, 1978.

Ignas, E. Y., & Corsini, R. J. (Eds.). *Alternative educational systems.* Itasca, Ill.: F. E. Peacock, 1979.

Jahn, E., & Adler, A. *Religion und individual psychologie: Eine prinzipelle auseinandersetzung über menschenfuhrung.* Vienna: Rolf Passer, 1933.

Kazan, S. Adler's Gemeinschaftgefühl and Meyeroff's caring. *Journal of Individual Psychology,* 1978, *34,* 3–10.

Kefir, N., & Corsini, R. J. Dispositional sets: A contribution to typology. *Journal of Individual Psychology,* 1974, *30,* 163–178.

Kelley, E. L. Marital compatibility as related to the personality traits of husband and wives as rated by self and spouse. *Journal of Social Psychology,* 1941, *13,* 193–198.

Kelley, E. L. Consistency of the adult personality. *American Psychologist,* 1955, *10,* 659–681.

Kelly, G. A. *The psychology of personal constructs,* Vols. 1, 2. New York: Norton, 1955.

Kelly, G. A. The language of the hypothesis. *Journal of Individual Psychology,* 1964, *20,* 137–152.

Krausz, E. O. The commonest neurosis. In K. A. Adler & D. Deutsch (Eds.), *Essays in Individual Psychology.* New York: Grove, 1959.

Lazarsfeld, S. Sexual cases in child guidance clinics. In A. Adler & Associates, *Guiding the child.* London: Allen & Unwin, 1949. (Originally published, 1930.)

Lecky, P. Self-consistency: A theory of personality. New York: Island Press, 1945.

Manaster, G. J. *Adolescent development and the life tasks.* Boston: Allyn and Bacon, 1977. (a)

Manaster, G. J.   Birth order: An overview. *Journal of Individual Psychology,* 1977, *33,* 3–8. (b)

Manaster, G. J.   Review of E. Schur, *The awareness trap, Journal of Individual Psychology,* 1977, *3,* 162–163. (c)

Manaster, G. J., Cleland, C. C., & Brooks, J.   Emotions as movement in relation to others. *Journal of Individual Psychology,* 1978, *34,* 244–253.

Manaster, G. J., Painter, G., Deutsch, J., & Overholt, B.   *Alfred Adler: As we remember him.* Chicago: North American Society of Adlerian Psychology, 1977.

Manaster, G. J., & Perryman, T. B.   Early recollections and occupational choice. *Journal of Individual Psychology,* 1974, *30,* 232–237.

Maslow, A. H.   *Motivation and personality.* New York: Harper, 1954.

Masters, W. H., & Johnson, V. E.   *Human sexual inadequacy.* Boston: Little Brown, 1970.

Meyeroff, M.   *On caring.* New York: Harper & Row, 1971.

Midelfort, C. F.   *The family in psychotherapy.* New York: McGraw-Hill, 1957.

Mohr, E., & Garlock, R.   The social club as an adjunct to therapy. In K. A. Adler & D. Deutsch (Eds.), *Essays in Individual Psychology: Contemporary application of Alfred Adler's theories.* New York: Grove Press, 1959.

Montagu, A.   *The natural superiority of women.* New York: Macmillan, 1954.

Moreno, J. L. (Ed.).   *Handbook of group therapy.* New York: Philosophical Library, 1966.

Morris, P. L.   *LSA: Life style assessment process.* Arnold, Md.: Adlerian Counseling Services, 1978.

Mosak, H. H.   Lifestyle. In A. Nikelly (Ed.), *Techniques for behavior change.* Springfield, Ill.: Charles C Thomas, 1971, 77–81.

Mosak, H. H.   Adlerian psychotherapy. In R. J. Corsini (Ed.), *Current psychotherapies.* Itasca, Ill.: F. E. Peacock, 1979.

Mosak, H. H., & Lefevre, C.   The resolution of "Interpersonal conflict." *Journal of Individual Psychology,* 1976, *32,* 19–26.

Mosak, H. H., & Mosak, B.   *A bibliography for Adlerian psychology.* Washington, D.C.: Hemisphere, 1975.

Mosak, H. H., & Schneider, S.   Masculine protest, penis envy, women's liberation and sexual equality. *Journal of Individual Psychology,* 1977, *33,* 193–202.

Mosak, H. H., Schneider, S., & Mosak, L. E.   *Life style: A workbook.* Alfred Adler Institute of Chicago, 1980.

Mosak, H. H., & Shulman, B. H.   *The life style inventory.* 1971.

Mowrer, O. H.,   Enuresis—A method for its study and treatment. *American Journal of Orthopsychiatry,* 1938, *8,* 432–459.

Murphy, L.   The widening world of childhood. New York: Basic Books, 1962.

Nikelly, A. G.   Developing social feeling in therapy. In A. G. Nikelly (Ed.), *Techniques for behavior change.* Springfield, Ill.: Charles C Thomas, 1971.

Nystul, M. S.   Identification and movement within three levels of social interest. *Journal of Individual Psychology,* 1976, *32,* 55–61.

O'Connell, W. E.   Ward psychotherapy with schizophrenics through concerted encouragement. *Journal of Individual Psychology,* 1961, *17,* 193–204.

O'Connell, W. E.   Adlerian psychodrama with chronic schizophrenics. *Journal of Individual Psychology,* 1963, *19,* 69–76.

O'Connell, W. E.   Equality in encounter groups. *Individual Psychologist.* 1971, *8*(1), 1–6.

O'Connell, W. E.   *Action therapy and Adlerian theory.* Chicago: Alfred Adler Institute, 1975.

Olson, H. O. (Ed.).   *Early recollections: Their use in diagnosis and psychotherapy.* Springfield, Ill.: Charles C Thomas, 1979.

Orgler, H.   *Alfred Adler: The man and his work, triumph over the inferiority complex* (4th ed.). London: Sidgwick & Jackson, 1973.

Papageorgis, D.   Repression and the unconscious: A social-psychological reformulation. *Journal of Individual Psychology* 1965, *21,* 18–31.

Patterson, G. G.   Physique and intellect. New York: Appleton-Century, 1930.

Perls, F.   *Gestalt therapy verbatim.* Moab, Utah: Real People Press, 1969.

Piaget, J.   The stages of the intellectual development of the child. Lecture to the Menninger School of Psychiatry, March 6, 1961.

Rank O.   *Will therapy.* New York: Knopf, 1936.

Rogers, C.   *Client-centered therapy.* Boston: Houghton Mifflin, 1951.

Rom, P.   Salome and Oscar Wilde.   Unpublished paper, 1977.   ,

Sajwaj, T., Libet, J., & Aguas, S.   Lemon juice therapy: The control of life-threatening rumination in a six-month-old infant. *Journal of Applied Behavioral Analysis,* 1974, *1,* 557–563.

Schachtel, E. G.   On memory and childhood amnesia. *Psychiatry,* 1947, 10.

Schur, E.   *The awareness trap: Self-absorption instead of social change.* New York: Quadrangle/The New York Times Co., 1975.

Seidler, R.   School guidance clinics in Vienna. *International Journal of Individual Psychology,* 1936, *2,* 75–78.

Shapiro, J. L.   *Methods of group psychotherapy and encounter.* Itasca, Ill.: F. E. Peacock, 1978.

Sheldon, W. H., Hartl, E. M., & McDermott, E.   *Varieties of delinquent youth.* Darien, Conn.: Hafner, 1970.

Shoobs, N. E.   The application of Individual Psychology through psychodramatics. *Individual Psychology Bulletin,* 1946, *5,* 3–21.

Shulman, B. H.   *Contributions to Individual Psychology.* Chicago: Alfred Adler Institute, 1973.

Shulman, B. H., & Dreikurs, S. G.   The contributions of Rudolf Dreikurs to the theory and practice of Individual Psychology. *Journal of Individual Psychology,* 1978, 34, 153–169.

Shulman, B. H., & Hoover, K. K.   Therapeutic democracy: Some changes in staff-patient relationships. *International Journal of Social Psychiatry,* 1964, *3* (Special Edition), 16–23).

Shulman, B. H., & Mosak, H. H.   Various purposes of symptoms. *Journal of Individual Psychology,* 1967, *23,* 79–87.

Shulman, B. H., & Mosak, H. H.   Birth order and ordinal position: Two Adlerian views. *Journal of Individual Psychology,* 1977, *33,* 114–121.

Skinner, B. F.   *The behavior of organisms.* New York: Appleton-Century-Crofts, 1938.

Smuts, J. C.   *Holism and evolution.* New York: Viking, 1961.

Sonstegaard, M. A.   Interaction process and the personality growth of children. *Group Psychotherapy,* 1958, *11,* 1.

Sperber, M.   *Masks of loneliness: Alfred Adler in perspective.* New York: Macmillan, 1974.

Spiel, O.   The Individual Psychological Experimental School in Vienna. *American Journal of Individual Psychology,* 1956, *12,* 1–11.

Spiel, O.   *Discipline without punishment.* L. Way (Ed.). (E. Fitzgerald, trans.). London: Faber & Faber, 1962.

Starr, A.   *Rehearsal for living.* Chicago: Nelson-Hall, 1977.

Stotland, E., Sherman, S. E., & Shaver, K. G.   *Empathy and birth order: Some experimental explorations.* Lincoln: University of Nebraska Press, 1971.

Szasz, T. S.   *The myth of mental illness: Foundations of a theory of personal conduct.* New York: Hoeber, 1961.

Terman, L. M.   *Psychological factors in marital happiness.* New York: McGraw-Hill, 1938.

Terner, J., & Pew, W. L.   *The courage to be imperfect: The life and work of Rudolf Dreikurs.* New York: Hawthorn, 1978.

Tharp, R. G., & Wetzel, R.   *Behavior modification in the natural environment.* Chatsworth, Calif.: Academy Press, 1969.

Toman, W.   *Family constellation: Its effects on personality and social behavior.* New York: Springer, 1959.

Walton, F.   Group workshop with adolescents. *The Individual Psychologist,* 1975, *12,* 26–28.

Walton, F. X., & Powers, R. L.   *Winning children over: A manual for teachers, counselors, principals and parents.* Chicago: Practical Psychology Associates, 1974.

Way, L.   *Adler's place in psychology: An exposition of Individual Psychology.* New York: Collier, 1962.

White, R. W.   Motivation reconsidered: The concept of competence. *Psychological Review,* 1959, *66,* 297–333.

Wolfe, W. B.   *How to be happy though human.* London: Routledge & Kegan Paul, 1932.

Wolpe, J.   The systematic desensitization of neuroses. *Journal of Nervous and Mental Diseases,* 1961, *131,* 35–39.

Zeigarnik, B. V.   The tasks of psychopathology. In *Problems of experimental pathopsychology.* Moscow: Gos. Nauch Issled, Institute Psikhiatric, 1965.

Index

311

Individual Psychology composition was by Datagraphics of Phoenix. Manufacturing was performed by Kingsport Press of Kingsport, Tenn. Internal design was by the F. E. Peacock Publishers, Inc., art department and Jane Rae Brown designed the cover. The type face is Times Roman.